FORCES IN MOTION

FORCES IN MOTION
The Music and Thoughts of Anthony Braxton

GRAHAM LOCK

PHOTOGRAPHS BY NICK WHITE

FOREWORD BY ANTHONY BRAXTON

A DA CAPO PAPERBACK

Library of Congress Cataloging in Publication Data

Lock, Graham.
  Forces in motion.

  (A Da Capo paperback)
  Reprint. Originally published: London: Quartet Books, 1988.
  1. Braxton, Anthony. 2. Jazz musicians—United States—
Biography. 3. Composers—United States—Biography. I. Title.
ML419.B735L6 1989   785.42′092′4   88-33474
ISBN 0-306-80342-9

Published by Da Capo Press, Inc.
A Subsidiary of Plenum Publishing Corporation
233 Spring Street, New York, N.Y. 10013

The doors of the horizon are thrown back; its bolts are unbolted
— Egyptian Pyramid Text

To my parents,
to Susie,
and to synthesis, the great dream

Anthony Braxton and Graham Lock would like to add
a special dedication to Warne Marsh,
who died on the bandstand in December 1987

CONTENTS

Metaroad

Road

Metaroad

Road

Metaroad

Road

Quartet

Road

Metaroad

Road

Postscript 1

Postscript 2

Postscript 3

Catalogue of Works, 1966–86

Discography

Bibliography

Index

ACKNOWLEDGEMENTS

I would like to thank Annette Moreau and Rachel Sinfield of the Contemporary Music Network and John Cumming and John Ellson of Serious Productions for making it possible for me to go on the Braxton Quartet tour, and Tony Cresswell from Serious for making sure we all survived it; Nick White for taking the photographs; Val Wilmer and Katy Zeserson for reading, and suggesting improvements to, the manuscript; Barry Jones and Judith Cook for their help with the astrological information; and Jill Purce for suggesting several useful lines of investigation into the spiritual and mystical dimensions of music.

I would also like to thank all the creative musicians who, over the last few years, have taken the time to answer my questions and whose perspectives – though neither they nor I realized it at the time – have helped to shape this book: they include Lester Bowie, Betty Carter, Ornette Coleman, Josefina Cupido, Malachi Favors, Charlie Haden, Abdullah Ibrahim, Laka Koc, Steve Lacy, Chris McGregor, Roscoe Mitchell, Sun Ra, Sam Rivers, Max Roach, Archie Shepp, Irene Schweitzer, Cecil Taylor, Mal Waldron, Mike Westbrook, Randy Weston and many more. I would particularly like to thank Mal Waldron and Eric Dolphy for their LP *The Quest*, which first turned my head to the beauty of creative music.

I'm very grateful to the many people who have supplied me with information, support, advice and other kinds of help along the way: they include Derek Bailey, Richard Cook, Michael Cuscuna, Jan Diakow, Malcolm Green, Jan Kopinski, George Lewis, Phil McNeil, Misha Mengelberg and Anthony Wood; Andy Isham produced many of the illustrations in the book; I'm especially grateful to Chris Parker of Quartet Books for thinking this book was a good idea in the first place, and for his continuing help and support.

I'd like to say a big thank you to my housemates – Teri Connolly, Nicole Dalle, Nick White and Nigel Wright – for the pens, the typewriter, the encouragement and the innumerable cups of tea they lavished on me, even while producing various books and children themselves; thanks too to Hackney Council for Clissold Park, its ducks, deer and trees – a haven of green.

Last, and most of all, I'm deeply indebted to Anthony Braxton, in particular, and also to Marilyn Crispell, Mark Dresser and Gerry Hemingway for the patience and good humour with which they have answered all my questions, both during the tour and since; for their kindness in sending me various scores, documents, magazines, books, records, tapes, etc; and for their help in clarifying sections of the manuscript. My two weeks on the road with them were a pleasure and a privilege for me; I learned so much then and I am still learning from them now. I hope this book will serve as a celebration of their musics; to them all I give my most heartfelt thanks.

Graham Lock, September 1987

FOREWORD

What a time cycle we live in. The stock market has gone crazy, farmers are not able to sustain themselves (and in many cases are starving) – materialism has returned and as a people we are more separate from each other than ever. A new conservative mood now stretches over the land and the political climate of this time period has only underlined the complexity and beauty of physical universe plane existence. In this context the concept of existence is as real as the act of thinking (for all practical purposes) – and the challenge of the next time cycle will call for a re-examination of our experiences 'in this realm' – this must be so if we care about the children or the future. Slowly but surely we will find ourselves going back to study the 'ancients' – to be healed and purified (so that we can rededicate ourselves to fight against ignorance and oppression – whatever form). A new century is coming! A new century is coming!

If the subject is 'fulfilment through sound' and if the purpose is to understand this time period, it will then be important for our species to re-examine the vibrational and concrete variables that have set the stage for present-day creative music perception dynamics (GRATIFICATION – EVOLUTION – CORRESPONDENCE – DIFFERENTIATION). This is so because creativity does not exist in a vacuum – we all live in a world of thoughts, feelings and hopes. For that reason I thank the masters from the World War One and Two time era for the beautiful bounty of work we have inherited. *THERE WAS MUSIC ALL OVER THE HOUSE (MAN!)* You know these people, and it does one no good to ignore their 'specialties' (if I can write it that way). Were it not for their efforts I would have been lost in a 'sea of fire and ice'. I thank the heavens for music – the heavens!

I would also like to take this opportunity to thank Graham Lock for his vision and dedication (power) – I am profoundly indebted to this man. He has approached me and my life's work with real respect, and I could not have hoped for a better document. It was always clear to me that only a creative person can write with insight about creativity – and I was right! Read the book and like or hate me if you will – but I wouldn't have had a chance with an average writer. I respect Graham Lock's efforts because he respects his profession – Lock has technique but he is not a technocrat.

xv

My hope is that this book will serve as a call to arms for creative music journalism. The restructural musics from the post-Ayler/Cage continuums have not been documented correctly and this 'MIS-AWARENESS' must be addressed.

Thank you for your work, sir.

Anthony Braxton, Mills College, 2 November 1987

Road

And yet, who knows very much of what jazz is really about? Or how shall we ever know until we are willing to confront anything and everything which it sweeps across our path?

— *Ralph Ellison*

Metaroad

They teach you there's a boundary line to music. But, man, there's no boundary line to art

— *Charlie Parker*

Oh time, strength, cash and patience!

— *Herman Melville*

INTRODUCTION

If somebody uses tradition as a way of limiting your choices, in a way that's as racist as saying you have to sit at the back of the bus.

— Anthony Davis

A wet afternoon in Leicester. I'm interviewing Anthony Braxton in a gloomy hotel room when the subject of the Ganelin Trio comes up. On one of their first LPs to be released in the West, the Russian group had included a track called *Who's Afraid of Anthony Braxton?*

'Yeah, I heard about that,' Braxton says, with a typically quizzical raise of the eyebrows. 'I hope they were joking. I mean, who's Anthony Braxton? He's just a guy who could use some coins.'

What he hasn't heard about is the interview in which the trio's saxophonist, Vladimir Chekasin, is quoted as saying: 'When I am playing I could get under a table, but Braxton never could . . . he is too serious about what he is doing.'

As I read it out, his face tightens in anger.

'I'm not interested in responding to that. If that's what he thinks, great. Next question.'

'You don't want to say anything?' My turn to raise a quizzical eyebrow.

'What is there to gain?' Braxton sighs bitterly. 'This is consistent with how Europeans have dealt with people like me for the last 3,000 years. Invariably, the Europeans will say: "What I do is better than what you do." My position has always been that the concept of saying: "My art is better than your art" is not only invalid, it's irrelevant.

'The thrust implications of trans-African functionalism have nothing to do with how this man feels about what I do or whether I get under a table – I'm not interested in that, it's not my purpose. I

1

determine my own variables and my own value systems, based on the route of my life; they're not about matching up to someone else's expectations.'

The route of Anthony Braxton's life, and his refusal to match expectations, have made him one of the most controversial figures in creative music. His AACM colleague Leo Smith, writing in 1977, remarked that his music 'has too often been criticized unjustly and praised for the wrong reasons'; while another musical associate, guitarist Derek Bailey, writing in 1980 in reference to what he called 'jazz's retreat into academicism', noted that:

> Braxton, a favourite target for the propagandists, has been attacked for: betraying his race (as was Louis Armstrong), being an intellectual (as was Charlie Parker) and diluting the musical purity of his tradition (as was John Coltrane). In short, he stands accused of just about all those things which have previously served to enrich and strengthen jazz. Braxton [is] recognized by the musicians who work with him as an outstanding musical figure . . . if jazz no longer values the sort of qualities he represents then it has a pretty arid future.*

Braxton's refusal to heed boundaries (musical, intellectual, political) has drawn flak from the most diverse quarters: both white racists *and* black nationalists, for instance, appear to resent his interest in so-called 'European' forms and have criticized him for not sticking to 'jazz' – an irony which might be farcical had not the common narrowness at its core played a part in prolonging the times of poverty and frustration with which he has had to contend. A second irony is that Braxton's entire musical philosophy is steeped in an *African* mystical lineage that reaches back to ancient Egypt and, he maintains, has shaped the very essence of the African-American creative music tradition. The final irony is that those critics who fuss about his supposedly 'European' influences have not only misunderstood *his* work, but also distort the nature of creative music itself in their failure to recognize the ritual and 'vibrational' factors, the 'meta-reality implications', which derive from the music's spiritual origins.

Braxton talks later about his musical beliefs and his profound disagreements with both current 'jazz' journalism and, on a higher level, the Western materialist philosophy which constricts our notions of the real and the possible. But, for now, perhaps this is an appropriate moment to introduce a little information about the

*Bailey, 1980, p. 75 (fn)

route of his life and about the music which, from East and West, black and white, has excited the outrage of those who have (to borrow A.B. Spellman's description of sixties critics) appointed themselves the guardians of last year's blues.

Anthony Braxton was born in Chicago in 1945 and grew up, 'a dreamer', in one of the city's poorer districts on the black South Side. In 1965 he abandoned an initial plan to teach philosophy and chose to dedicate his life to music; the following year he joined Chicago's newly-formed Association for the Advancement of Creative Musicians (AACM) and was immediately involved in the rhythmic, textural and structural experimentation that characterized the new Chicago music. After releasing two LPs, including the epochal *For Alto*, a double album of solo saxophone music, he moved to Paris in 1969 with violinist Leroy Jenkins and trumpeter Leo Smith; but their group, the Creative Construction Company (CCC), broke up and Braxton returned to America where, for several months, he made his living as a chess player, hustling matches on the New York chess circuit.

A CCC reunion concert in May 1970 enticed him back to music and he joined Chick Corea, Dave Holland and Barry Altschul in the group Circle; a year later, when Circle too broke up, Braxton returned to Paris and wrote a lot of his early piano music there. In 1974, a long-term recording contract with Arista Records brought him back to the States, accompanied by his wife-to-be Nickie, and they settled in Woodstock. Over the next six years, regular LP releases on Arista (together with a smattering of European releases) began to reveal the extraordinary scope of Braxton's music; but wranglings with Arista, particularly over his *Composition 82* – a 303-page score for four orchestras – ensured that his contract was not renewed. Braxton remained on the East Coast, living in New Haven, Connecticut with Nickie and their three children, until 1985 when, after several years of extreme poverty, he was appointed to a professorship at Mills College in Oakland, California.

Those briefly are the biographical facts and Braxton talks of them in greater detail later. The music is something else again; the range

---

*Braxton's compositions actually have diagrammatic/pictorial titles; for reasons of space, compositions are referred to by their opus number throughout the text, but the full titles are all depicted in the 'Catalogue of Works', below

and profusion of his musical activities have been truly astonishing.
Though his first instrument is alto saxophone – on which he stands
at the forefront of a modern lineage that runs through Charlie
Parker, Eric Dolphy, Ornette Coleman – he is also a multi-
instrumentalist, a virtuoso on most members of the saxophone,
clarinet and flute families (with a particular interest in instruments
at the extremes of register), and competent too on piano and
percussion. He is an improviser, a composer, an interpreter, a
conductor. His recordings include several LPs of solo saxophone
music; notated pieces for string quartet, tuba ensemble, two
pianos, and four soprano saxophones; free improvisations with the
Company groups; the multi-orchestral *Composition 82*; avant-garde
big-band music (which Braxton calls creative orchestra music); four
'traditional' LPs of bebop standards; duos with musicians as
diverse as Muhal Richard Abrams, Giorgio Gaslini, George Lewis,
Max Roach, Gyorgy Szabados and Richard Teitelbaum; and a
series of quartet records which explore, in brilliant variety, the
multiple interlacings of composed and improvised musics. The
records encompass marches, ballads, blues; frenetically fast bebop
lines and experiments with 'spatial' music and 'modular notation';
there is the ferocity of *For John Cage* (*Composition 8F*), the serenity
of *Nickie*, the graceful charm of *Maple Leaf Rag*, the snorting
humour of *Ornithology* on a contrabass clarinet. Then too there is
the 'ritual & ceremonial' music of *Composition 95*, the dramatic
'image' music of *Composition 113*, and the startling heterophony of
recent quartet concerts, all linked to the increasingly metaphysical
direction of Braxton's work. In the light of such a dazzling
spectrum of invention, it is no wonder that Leo Smith can claim:
'When listening to Braxton's music, one can easily hear the
unfolding of his select cultural heritage along with the collective
heritage of all humankind.'*

Yet it is only a small exaggeration to say that Braxton's recorded
output – he's made over forty LPs under his own name and
appeared on fifty more or so by other artists – represents merely a
handful of leaves from the forest of his total *oeuvre*, which stands to
date at nearly 350 compositions. Many of his notated pieces, for
example, remain unrecorded (thanks to what he once referred to as
the 'what makes you think you can play classical music, nigger?'
syndrome), as does the bulk of his marvellous creative orchestra

*Leo Smith, 1977

music and almost all of his other works for large and/or unusual ensembles, from a 1971 piece for 100 tubas (*Composition 19*) which has never been performed, to a new work for two dancers, six mobile soloists, organ and two chamber orchestras (*Composition 132*) which received its first and only performance thus far at San Francisco's Grace Cathedral in October 1986.

Braxton's latest large-scale project is *Trillium*, a series of twelve operas comprising thirty-six interchangeable acts or 'dialogues', of which two acts have so far been written and one performed. Meanwhile, he continues to work at his multi-orchestral scores – a Series A which will include pieces for six orchestras, ten orchestras, and 100 orchestras 'in four different cities connected by satellite and TV systems'; and a Series B of pieces that will link orchestras on three planets, five planets, in different star systems, and in different galaxies!* (One begins to see why a man for whom not even the sky is the limit might resent being told to play 'under a table' or in 'the little box' which, he says, the critics have currently made of jazz.)

To return to earth, in Leo Smith's view: 'It is clear that Braxton's contribution to creative music has been to open up a field of new rhythmic elements, and, through his particular solo work on the alto saxophone, to establish the single-line instrument . . . as a major solo tool, bringing the family of instruments to its truest harmonious relationship.'† It is certainly the case that Braxton was the first person to develop, on record, a complete and specific language for solo saxophone, and he explains elsewhere how and why he came to do this. As for new rhythmic elements, the pulse track structures, also discussed in detail later, are his most recent and arguably most radical contribution to the field; but on a more general level, one could perhaps point to his early statement that 'tempo is a limited use of time – I think of time as all time' and, within that, cite his uses of *extreme* time. I'm thinking of those accelerated, bebop-inspired lines where the combination of manic

*Relating his interest in multi-orchestralism to an early love of parade musics, where several bands would march along all playing different tunes, Braxton has written: 'It is as if the whole of the universe were swallowed up – leaving us in a sea of music and colour' (notes to *Composition 82*). Series B is perhaps an attempt to *swallow the universe*: not as an act of ego or destruction, but as a form of synthesis in which everything, even being itself, will be transformed (for the duration of the concert) into a sea of music and colour. The ideal of synthesis, of cosmic and global harmony, is certainly a vital aspect of Braxton's musical philosophy
†Leo Smith, 1977

speed and complex phrasing is so daring that it sometimes verges on
hilarity – provoking what Arnold Wesker called 'the laughter of
pleasurable incredulity', that such a thing was even possible – and
which to play must be akin to skiing down Everest. (As Marilyn
Crispell later says of one piece, 'It was jump or die.') I'm thinking
too of a piece like *Composition 76* (*For Trio*), which Braxton
describes as 'a static sound space', where there is no forward linear
movement at all and the music is like a necklace of moments caught
at the point of coming-into-being; this is a non-Western concept of
time, more like the timelessness of meditation. Like meditation, it
may not be immediately accessible or effective: you have to learn
the discipline of attunement, of finding how to listen, how to be in
that moment and that time; the practice of humility. (I think this is
true of listening to all musics, from Webern to James Brown to
Javanese gamelan.)

Other aspects of Braxton's compositional methodology will be
discussed later; just as important, though, is his influence in a
wider context, as a catalyst for new ways of thinking and playing.
Here is the great percussionist Max Roach (whose bebop creden-
tials are second to no one's) explaining why he chose to record two
duo LPs with Braxton in the late 1970s:

> To me, Anthony Braxton, from a creative point of view, is more like Charlie
> Parker than someone today who apes Charlie Parker. I think he exemplifies the
> *spirit* Charlie Parker had – the fact that he dares to do something else, to try
> another direction. So, in my search for growth as a drummer, to play with
> Anthony Braxton or with Cecil Taylor is just as exciting and challenging for me
> as it was to play with Charlie Parker or Bud Powell – they make me think of
> other things to do on the instrument.*

Braxton's interest in extreme registers, in extreme times, in solo
and multi-orchestral musics, in free improvisation and extended
composition, shows a man keen to try all the options, to break
through all the barriers; with him, anything and everything

---

*From unpublished part of interview with author. See also Lock, 8/85. This respect is
entirely mutual. Asked at one of his London lectures about performing with Max Roach,
Braxton replied, 'I can tell you Mr Roach is a very inspiring person to work with. He's a role
model for me, for all of us. From Mr Roach, as well as from the AACM, I learned how
important it is to be involved in the community, to work with young people. Playing with
him I also learned that there is really no difference in the progression cycles of the music – I
mean that he knew what I was doing and I knew what he was doing. There was no time-lag
factor at all, except for me trying to keep up with him!'

becomes possible – and not merely on a technical or structural level, but conceptually too, at the level of consciousness itself. Few musicians in any time, at any place, can have been so utterly in love as Braxton is with what he would call the *is*-ness of music, in all its varieties. It is this love which, I guess, has not only seen him through the hard times but also provides the foundation stone for his ideals and visions of world change. In his *Tri-axium Writings 2*, he writes: 'The challenge of tomorrow is directly related to whether all of the children of this planet can realize their potential – and this cannot happen unless each child is able to dream "those great dreams" that motivate dynamic participation.'* Here he leads by example: by insisting on the right to realize his own potential and to dream his own great dreams, he offers us an image of the future that celebrates and affirms humanity – no mean achievement in the era of nuclear threat, apartheid, ecological havoc, mass starvation, etc etc. His visions of global and galactic harmony may be dismissed as the impossible fantasies of a madman, but to me they feel like a liberation, an incitement to live: here is a future I'll gladly embrace, while the other possibilities just fill me with dread. William Blake wrote that '*The Imagination is not a State, it is the Human Existence Itself*'; Braxton's imagination has, I think, enriched all of our existences. Like Blake, like Tarkovsky – and like Cecil Taylor and Sun Ra too – he is a metaphysician, an alchemist, a man who opens doors you didn't know existed.

To conclude, I had better explain the circumstances of this book. I first met Anthony Braxton at London's Actual Festival in October 1984. (This was the famous occasion when Braxton *forgot* he was to play the world première of his latest solo work, *Composition 113*, and left the score behind in America! If geniuses have to be absent-minded, then, as we will see, Braxton certainly qualifies.) The day after the concert I was able to interview him briefly for an article which later appeared in *Wire*.† I'd half-expected him to be a formidable interviewee – and he was; but he also proved to be the most enthusiastic and inspiring music lover I'd ever come across. In fact, he was interested in *everything* – astrology, ecology, feminism, physics – and had a keenness to communicate that was less a breath

*T-a W2, p. 197
†Lock, 6/85

of fresh air than a minor whirlwind. I left almost walking in the sky, a thousand new thoughts and questions exploding in my head; later, when I learned he would be returning to England for a twelve-concert tour in November 1985, I knew I had to be on that tour too, even if I had to write a book to do it.

Thanks to the assistance of various people at the Arts Council's Contemporary Music Network (who set up the tour) and at Serious Productions (who took care of its day-to-day organization), and thanks also to the forbearance of the musicians and tour manager Tony Cresswell, I was able to travel with the quartet on the tour and to attend all twelve concerts, as well as the various lectures, pre-concert talks and workshops which Braxton gave around the country. During our thirteen days on the road, I interviewed him nine times (a total of fifteen hours on tape) and talked also to the other members of the quartet: Marilyn Crispell (piano), Mark Dresser (bass) and Gerry Hemingway (percussion), all of whom had known Braxton for several years, although Mark was a newcomer to the quartet music. The shorter 'Road' sections of the book are taken from my daily notes and provide what Braxton would call a 'physical universe level' view of the tour; the 'Metaroad' and 'Quartet' sections, which comprise the greater part of the book, are based on the interviews and, particularly in the case of the later Braxton interviews, sometimes venture on to more of an abstract universe level.

It will, I hope, be evident that this is not a biography nor a critical analysis in which the critic attempts to assess and judge the artist. My sole intention here has been to *learn* about Braxton's music. How is it structured? How has it evolved? What is its purpose? Who were his models? What is his philosophy of music? Of life? How do all the parts fit together? Then, rather than try to interpret or translate his ideas, many of which were unfamiliar to me, I thought the most sensible (and honest) policy was to present them in his own words – thus, the question/answer format (although I have edited and restructured the tapes to provide what I hope is a clarity of focus not possible with verbatim transcripts of any conversation).* Let me stress too that this book is very much an introductory glimpse into Braxton's musical universe, simply a

---

*The same desire for clarity prompted me occasionally to insert into the text extracts from our 1984 interview, where I considered they usefully amplified Braxton's trains of thought. However, the only extensive use of such extracts comes at the beginning of 'Sound Logic, Sound Magic 4'

sketch-map that tries to establish a few starting-points for future explorations. This is not false modesty. Braxton himself has already completed eight books – the three volumes of the philosophical *Tri-axium Writings* and five volumes of detailed *Composition Notes* – and is planning further texts which will eventually provide a comprehensive guide to his entire musical output and its *raison d'être*. (I've added a 'Postscript 2' on the *Tri-axium Writings*; publication of the *Composition Notes* has been repeatedly delayed due to lack of money and until they are available no close examination of Braxton's structural processes and intentions will be feasible – this is one reason why my notes on the concerts tend to be impressionistic rather than a study of their music-science.)

As for the world of forces, vibrations, musical mysticism and ancient Egyptian mysteries which we will later encounter, I have tried, in the opening section on Sun Ra and in 'Postscript 1', to suggest possible contexts for Braxton's often cryptic comments; but I am no expert in this field and I am not sure that either is the most appropriate point from which to approach Braxton's own mystery system beliefs. His philosophy certainly touches on very abstract and mystical levels, and if people sometimes find his terminology difficult I think it is because his whole way of looking at things goes way beyond the strictures of the Western philosophical perspectives within which many of us were brought up.* I have tried in the editing to alleviate such difficulties wherever possible, though without simplifying or distorting Braxton's ideas: his principal philosophical concepts (or at least those appertaining to music) are discussed either in the interviews or in 'Postscript 2'; the extensive contents list is intended as a guide to where specific ideas are examined, and I've also cross-referenced in footnotes wherever I thought it helpful. A certain amount of skipping to and fro in the text may be inevitable, but my hope is that, even if at the beginning of the book there are a few references which are not readily explicable, by the end the reader will have at least as much understanding as I do of the methodology and metaphysics, the

---

*Not that Kant, Marx or Wittgenstein are exactly light reading. I think there is certainly a degree of racism behind the abuse hurled at Braxton's sleevenotes, for example, even though his grammar may not always be 'correct'. As he told a *Cadence* interviewer, no one ever complained about fifty years of 'liner notes written in the most beautiful English, where the Queen herself would have approved of the structure. But . . . which didn't know what the fuck they were talking about.' Carey, 1984, p. 6

music-science and sound-wonder, which lie at the heart of Braxton's unique sonic cosmos.

Not that my understanding is complete. A fortnight proved insufficient time to ask all my questions and those I did ask were not all answered in the way I had anticipated. Anyone looking for a cut-and-dried explanation of Braxton's diagrams – that mysterious assortment of codes, chess moves, mathematical formulae, geometrical drawings and hieroglyphic images with which he titles his compositions – may feel frustrated (as I was, initially) by his refusal to match that expectation too. All I can offer is Leo Smith's comment that:

> Braxton's titles are primarily mystical, and any advanced student of mysticism or metaphysical science can readily read the code and symbolism embedded in his titles. The universal way of transmitting absolute laws of nature is through the use of symbols that are derived from and in combination with the dot, curve and straight line. Letters and numbers provide the outside meaning of this language. So to give some coherence to what seems confusing, I'll only say that Braxton has utilized the language in its complete form.*

At the risk of reintroducing confusion, I think Braxton's titles, like his music, require anagogical understanding, and I doubt that 'explication' is either possible or desirable. Imagine a very personal mystery system that draws on, say, Egyptian hieroglyphics, astrological correspondences, Druidic runes and voodoo *vèvè* and you may have some idea of the kind of areas to which (I guess) Braxton's titling systems are related. To this I can only add my intuition that, if Albert Ayler was right and music is the healing force of the universe, then Anthony Braxton, meta*physician*, is writing the prescriptions.

---

*Leo Smith, 1977

ASTRO BLACK MYTHOLOGY

i

My mouth came to me and Magic was my name.
> – *Book of Knowing the Modes of Existence of Rē*
> (Egyptian magical papyrus, *c*. 300 BC)

The day that Anthony Braxton flies into London there are heavy traffic jams in parts of the city because of a protest march against police racism. The march is in response to the police shooting of Cherry Groce in Brixton and the death, during a police house search, of Cynthia Jarrett in Tottenham: two incidents which have already provoked the most violent uprisings in recent British history. 'One law for black, one law for blue,' proclaim the protest banners. Driving through Brixton in mid-afternoon, tour manager Tony Cresswell finds the streets swarming with police.

'It looks like they're expecting trouble,' he tells me over the phone. 'I'd stay away if I were you.'

By evening, though, the streets are quiet and empty, the only sign of activity a small throng of people by the entrance to an old cinema that is now a nightclub. Something very special is about to happen here. Tonight, for one night only, Brixton will have visitors from outer space.

In the shadows of the dimly-lit stage the musicians' fez-like helmets glint and twinkle. Clambering over chairs, leafing through sheaves of music, they settle into their places: two drummers, bass, guitar, trumpets, trombones, half a dozen reeds – among them the wizened figure of altoist Marshall Allen and lugubrious tenor giant

11

John Gilmore. All are wearing the strange helmets and glittering chainmail tunics. At the front of the stage, set beside the horns, imposing, mysterious, decorated with mystical symbols, stands the huge Ancient Egyptian Infinity Drum, reputedly carved from a tree felled one night, near the band's communal home, by a solitary flash of lightning.

The horns set up an eerie wailing as singer June Tyson begins the chant: '*the Sun is coming, the Sun is on his way*'; and from the backstage depths a portly figure waddles ceremoniously into view flanked by writhing dancers. A rainbow of lights illuminates the stage and we can see that tonight he has discarded his space-age skullcap and the customary lurex cape festooned with images of suns, stars and the ringed Saturn, his home planet: instead he is clad in a large fur hat and full-length leopard-skin cloak. Tonight he is not a Space Magician, he is an African Doctor.

He flings up his arms and the band fall silent.

'I have many names,' he intones softly into the microphone. 'Some call me Mister Ra, some call me Mister Rē. You can call me Mister Mystery.'

The audience raise a ragged cheer at the familiar greeting. His arms drop and the band launch into a mêlée of frenzied sound. Sun Ra permits a sly grin to crease his ancient face, then his arms shoot skyward: silence. Down: cacophony. Up: silence.

'I am not a part of Earth history,' he tells his startled listeners. 'I belong to the Kingdom of Mythology.'

The arms fall and the band fire into a Fletcher Henderson tune, first stop in a three-hour magical Mister Rē tour of time and space; from the roots of African-American music to the farthest reaches of what he calls the Omniverse. Rampaging big-band tributes to Duke Ellington and Jelly Roll Morton jostle with free-form flurries and Ra's own acoustic piano blues or earth-shaking synthesizer solos; dancers cavort in fantastical costumes, trumpeters wrestle on the floor, still blowing, and the entire band dance circles frontstage, clapping and chanting their space songs: '*We travel the spaceways, from planet to planet*', '*On Jupiter the skies are always blue*', and, every time, '*Space is the place, yeah space is the place*'.

It's after midnight when we float, dazed and dazzled, on to Brixton Hill. Driving home across a deserted city I rue the circumstances that have brought two great visionary musicians to town at the same time only to keep them apart. Braxton had hoped to attend the Sun Ra concert, but the flight from California proved too tiring; while we travelled the spaceways, the man who composes for orchestras in different galaxies had been grounded by jet lag. The next morning he regrets it: Sun Ra, Braxton tells me, is 'more important than any of us realize, one of the real masters'. He's certainly one of the most radical forces in creative music. A pioneer of synthesizers and electronic keyboards, of modal music, of looking to Africa for inspiration (and finding chants, raps, polyrhythmic percussion), of reasserting pride in black music and black culture. His music not only anticipated the work of players like Albert Ayler and John Coltrane, it has since seeped into every nook and cranny of modern music, from Funkadelic to Stockhausen to the Art Ensemble of Chicago. His band, the Arkestra, includes celebrated artists like Marshall Allen and John Gilmore, yet is also a tightly-drilled unit: Ra's penchant for hard work – '*Saturn is the planet of discipline*' – is matched by his emphasis on group values rather than virtuosity for its own sake. Sun Ra is the patriarch who almost single-handedly has steered big-band music into the Space Age, keeping alive the tradition's spirit while expanding – seemingly limitlessly – its repertoire and potential.

Sun Ra's special significance, though, may lie in his awareness of what music *is*. Before Albert Ayler proclaimed that '*Music is the healing force of the universe*', Ra was writing titles like *Medicine for a Nightmare* and *Cosmic Tones for Mental Therapy*. The spiritual power of sound, the roots of this knowledge in African mystical traditions, and music's role as an agent of transformation are aspects of a Ra cosmology which many musicians, from John Coltrane to Anthony Braxton, have been drawn to explore for themselves. In fact, though I have little inkling of it that night in South London, I will later learn that Braxton, like Sun Ra, aligns himself (at least in part) to a black spiritual lineage that reaches back through African history to the mystery systems of ancient Egyptian civilization.

But I'm jumping ahead of myself. To begin with, because he is such a crucial influence on contemporary African-American music and because a brief look at his cosmology may later help to illuminate Braxton's own thinking, let us venture a little farther into the strange, heliocentric worlds of Sun Ra.

ii

Love and life/Interested me so/That I dared to knock/At the doors of the cosmos.

– Sun Ra, *Door of the Cosmos*

Herman 'Sonny' Blount was born in Birmingham, Alabama, between seventy and seventy-five years ago.* Like many Southern blacks he migrated during the Depression, following the blues northwards, and finally settled in Chicago where he worked as a pianist and arranger.

Big-band swing was the predominant black pop music of the time and Blount was a keen fan, particularly of the Fletcher Henderson Orchestra. He got a job with Henderson at the Club Delisa in 1946 but quit a few weeks later because the band said his arrangements were too difficult to play. Henderson persuaded him to return for a while, but Blount's musical thinking was already a little 'out': in 1948, working in a trio with Stuff Smith and Coleman Hawkins, he wrote an arrangement of *I'll Remember April* that, years later, Hawkins remembered as 'the only music I've ever seen that I couldn't play'.†

For several years Blount made his living around the Chicago clubs, playing and arranging for housebands that catered for every kind of visiting jazz and blues artist. He also began to collect musicians to play his own compositions, and on 12 July 1956 the small Transition label took Herman Blount into the studio to record his first LP as a bandleader. Except that Herman Blount no longer existed. Sun Ra from the planet Saturn had taken over his body and, in a neat reversal of the year's hit science-fiction film *Invasion of the Body Snatchers*, announced that he had come to bring new life to a somnolent world, to awaken the inner eye of the human race.

INSTRUCTION TO THE PEOPLES OF THE EARTH. You must realize that you have the right to love beauty. You must prepare to live life to the fullest extent. Of

---

*Sun Ra has denied that his surname was originally Blount; Arman and Lee seem to be other possibilities. For a fuller account of his biography, see Wilmer, 1977, pp. 74–92
†Quoted in Wilmer, 1977, p. 62

course it takes imagination, but you don't have to be an educated person to have that. Imagination can teach you the true meaning of pleasure. Listening can be one of the greatest of pleasures. You must learn to listen, because by listening you will learn to see with your mind's eye. You see, music paints pictures that only the mind's eye can see. Open your ears so that you can see with the eye of the mind.*

In mid-fifties America such declarations, together with the band's theatrical garb and song titles like *Call for All Demons* and *Lullaby for Realville*, must have marked Sun Ra as an extreme oddity, despite the obvious big-band and bebop influences still audible in his music. Then, as his musical parameters rapidly expanded, so his sleevenotes became more cryptic. 'The impossible is the watchword of the greater space age,' he wrote on the sleeve of *Rocket Number Nine Take Off for Venus*. 'The space age cannot be avoided and SPACE music is the key to understanding the meaning of the IMPOSSIBLE and every other enigma.' This fascination with the impossible is a keynote of Sun Ra's work; the 1968 French students' slogan, 'Be realistic – demand the impossible', precisely echoes Ra's own sentiments: 'The impossible attracts me,' he once remarked, 'because everything possible has been done and the world didn't change.'†

Sun Ra's entire career can be seen as an attempt to make the impossible happen, to make the world change. Music has never been the sole focus of his interests: in the 1950s he was active politically, heading a nationalist group that urged blacks to take advantage of new discoveries in science and technology; he attacked organized religion for its passivity in the face of racial oppression; he wrote poems and pamphlets on the spiritual dimensions of black culture (some of which may have influenced John Coltrane's thinking as much as Ra's music did).‡ In the early sixties, Ra was a founder-member of the Jazz Composers' Guild, a musicians' self-help organization which tried to wrest back control of their music from the reactionary establishment of club-owners, promoters and record-company executives. Though such ventures did not always bear immediate fruit, their influence can be seen in the

*From the original sleevenotes to *Sun Song*; quoted also in the sleevenotes to *Pictures of Infinity*
†Quoted in Cutler, 1985, p. 71. See also Ra's poem on 'The Potential' in Simpkins, 1975, p. 94
‡See Simpkins, 1975, pp. 94–101

remarkable flowering of African-American music and radical politics that characterized the later sixties.

On a more personal level Sun Ra's labours have brought formidable successes. He has released over 150 LPs, most of them on his own record label, Saturn, a shoestring operation set up in Chicago in the mid-fifties and one of the earliest instances of a musician-run label.* Thirty years later it's still a shoestring operation and Ra still issues his records in plain white sleeves with (if you're lucky) hand-written titles and track listings; but it still exists. There have been occasional licensing deals and one-off releases on other labels, but the bulk of Sun Ra's music remains on his own label and under his own control. One price he has paid for his independence is that many of these records are poorly recorded/edited/pressed; but while poverty has obviously been a factor here, Ra has never judged his music in terms of commercial appeal or hi-tech fetishism. Just as Leadbelly described the blues as 'the real news', so Sun Ra has said that each of his records is an issue of a cosmic newspaper.

If Saturn's survival is impressive, so is the fact that Ra has kept a big band going through three decades of relative poverty. Their home-base has shifted from Chicago to New York to Philadelphia, they have boasted a plethora of evocative names – the Myth Science Arkestra, the Intergalactic Research Arkestra, the Blue Universe Arkestra, the Cosmo Jet-Set Arkestra, the Astro-Infinity Arkestra, etc, etc – but Sun Ra's ensembles have proved a consistent testing-ground for many of the period's finest musicians: the list of illustrious alumni includes Ronnie Boykins, Marion Brown, Charles Davis, Richard Davis, Von Freeman, Craig Harris, Clifford Jarvis, Frank Lowe, Pat Patrick, Julian Priester, Pharoah Sanders, James Spaulding, Clifford Thornton and Wilbur Ware. Today the Arkestra is probably the only working band on the planet able to perform the complete spectrum of black musics, from *King Porter Stomp* to jazz-funk to free-form electronics; and Sun Ra's achievement in leading the Arkestra through an era when both economics and the vagaries of fashion militated against the survival of big-band music can hardly be overestimated. Here, at least, he has made the impossible happen.

*Sun Ra was aided considerably by a colleague, Alton Abraham, who ran the organizational side of Saturn Records for many years until he subsequently fell out with Sun Ra

iii

Behold my house of light/Is said to be a house of darkness/Because it is invisible.

– Sun Ra, 'Darkness Light'

(Extracts from an interview with Sun Ra, 10/83)

'I LIKE ALL THE SOUNDS
THAT UPSET PEOPLE'

L: Were there any particular sounds that first attracted you to the synthesizer?

R: I like all the sounds that upset people, because they's too complacent. There are some sounds that really upset 'em and I like to shock 'em out of their complacency 'cause it's a very bad world in a lot of aspects. They need to wake up to know how bad it is, then maybe they'll do somethin' about it.

L: You think music can spur people into action?

R: Of course it can. It's just . . . you have a lot of commercial folks on this planet who took the music and used it to make money, but now people have heard so much of that music they've been sated with sound. But the spirit, it gets very little food I'd say. And the spirit needs something too. It says, 'What about me? I need some beautiful music or beautiful poetry.' I think the people on this planet are starving their spiritual selves.

See, music is a spiritual language, 'n' that's what I have to offer, so I'm gonna put it out there and maybe people will do somethin' right. They may not want to, but they be *compelled* to (*chuckles*).

GOODBYE TO AMERICA

L: Could you tell me about the big-band tradition in America?

R: Oh yeah, there was some kind of deliberate campaign in America to get rid of the big bands. America was like a place of creation, a wonderful place, when the bands were created, and the people had theatres, you could go and see everybody and everybody had a chance. Then America got materialist-minded and some people who were righteous got in control and they felt music was unnecessary (*chuckles incredulously*). That happened in the black race too, the righteous people got in control and they put up churches and things. They thought they didn't need music so they didn't support art and beauty. You might as well say goodbye to America, it can't survive without art. Like the Bible says, if you're righteous overmuch you're gonna destroy yourself. Over-righteousness can always destroy nature.

Sometimes they give grants to artists, you know, but money can't do anybody any good unless people survive. You can't be in an environment of destruction and be happy, you can't really have sympathy in your heart for people and see them dead or dying, see them approaching to Armageddon – you can't be happy with that unless you so completely selfish and blind that you don't care.

COMPULSORY TUXEDOS

L: Could you tell me a little more about the bands themselves?
R: Each band had its own style, see. The arrangers were very important too, but it was a creativity thing, they weren't writing for money. Then the white groups saw that these bands were doing well, so they hired the black arrangers and then they sounded better. Then, because of the discrimination in America, they got the jobs; they still doin' it. And then the black bands no longer had people to teach 'em, so it deteriorated down to combos. Today you have a lot of white big bands, they can't play anything but traditional things and they have to wear tuxedos (*laughs*). They can't come out like the black bands did and play what they want to play. The black bands were close to the people, everybody had a good time, every dance was a party. Then something happened to the black race, they got to be very righteous and talent stopped, creation stopped, and that's the way it is today. Take us in Philadelphia. Not too many black people know about us, and when we play in America not too many black people show up.

KEEPING THE CREATORS DOWN

L: You said that after the big bands the music deteriorated, but what about the new music of the 1960s? Weren't you very involved in that?

R: I was the spearhead of that, but they was keepin' me down like, in the past, they always kept the creators down. They'd get somebody who'd imitate, somebody who'd come along and play and the world would think, 'Oh, he's great', but no, they'd just be imitating what the creators were playing. They wouldn't let the creators through 'cause then they wouldn't have anybody to feed off.

The world has got to put up musicians who care about humanity. They can no longer push up those who just turn out commercial, people who just care about themselves. It's very bad to have a limited-minded man in any position of influence on this planet with those nuclear weapons standin' there – they uncompromisin'. That's why we did the song *Nuclear War.* (*Sings*): '*If they push that button, yo' ass gotta go*' (*laughs*).

'BEAUTY IS NECESSARY
FOR SURVIVAL'

L: You said earlier that America was getting too righteous and materialistic. How about the political situation there now? Do you think things have improved for black people since, say, the Civil Rights Movement and the work of Martin Luther King?

R: Well, what Martin Luther King was talkin' about may have been correct, but the advances – the so-called advances – that the darker people have made in America, that was cut off by Reagan. So, really, what good was his death? If people would only base what they done on culture and beauty, they would immediately become part of the nation of the world who know that beauty is necessary for survival. But they don't know that.

It's like in America, when we get through playin', the white people'd be asking me, 'Why aren't you more known in America?' I say, it's because your people are backing something that's commercial rather than something that's creative. It's because you people don't have a culture (*chuckles*). They never heard talk like that before, but it's true. See, my music's not American, I'd say my music belongs to the world.

iv

Astro black American/The Universe is in my voice . . . Astro thought in mystic
sound/Astro black mythology.

– Sun Ra, 'Astro Black'

Hard work and determination played their part in Sun Ra's success,
but these attributes were firmly grounded in a lifeview which
saw beauty, discipline and the spiritual as prime values, while
commercialism, apathy and 'righteousness' were their opposites.
Nor did these values exist in a vacuum, but grew up within the
context of a black historical and cultural awareness that informs
all of Sun Ra's work, from the antiquity of *Pyramids* to the
contemporary slang of *Nuclear War.*

Though he has long been an avid science-fiction fan, it's unlikely
that the transformation of Herman Blount into Sun Ra really had
much to do with *Invasion of the Body Snatchers.* A more plausible
inspiration can be found in the history of Africans in America and
the fact that slaves were no longer identified by their original
African names but by the names of their slave-masters. Later, as
the blues developed, a tradition grew up of musicians rejecting
these 'slave' names and choosing their own, or adopting the names
given to them by the black community: thus, Muddy Waters,
Howlin' Wolf, Little Walter, Memphis Slim, Leadbelly, Son
House, Robert Nighthawk and innumerable others.* Of course,
there were also precedents for black bandleaders to mark their
eminence with names like Duke and Count; but rather than take a
title from the European aristocracy (and no doubt well aware that
the white media had already dubbed white bandleaders 'King' of
this and that), Herman Blount took his title from Rē or Ra, Sun
God of ancient Egypt, one of the first and greatest of human
civilizations, and an *African* civilization, a *black* civilization.†

*The political implications of naming have long played an important part in African-
American history; decades before the media fuss about Malcolm X and Muhammad Ali,
African-Americans had been rejecting their slave names and often adopting Islamic or
African names in their place
†Sun Ra's interest in ancient Egypt may have been influenced by the book *Stolen Legacy,*

Sun Ra researched African history, introduced African instruments into the Arkestra, and named compositions for *Nubia* and *Aethiopia*. Egypt remained a particular reference point: he studied hieroglyphics, named songs after Pharaohs and intermittently renamed his Saturn label the Thoth label, gluing pictures of the ibis-headed Egyptian Moon God on to the record sleeves.*

If the blues gave Sun Ra his black name, they may also have provided him with some of his space imagery: the migrant bluesman with *'ramblin' on my mind'* is not so different from the Arkestra and their interstellar travels – *'lookin' for work, why not try Mars?'* And in the spirituals of the black church, with their veiled references to freedom and deliverance, there is a possible precedent for Sun Ra's visionary chants of universal harmony and a tomorrow where *'there is no plane of sorrow'*.† This is not to say that Sun Ra is

---

written by the black scholar George G.M. James and first published in 1954. James claimed that not only had ancient Egypt been a black civilization but that the origins of classical Greek philosophy and science could be traced back to the Egyptian mystery teachings; in fact, he argued that many Greek thinkers had simply stolen their ideas from Egypt. James's theses contradicted two centuries of racist 'scholarship', with the result that *Stolen Legacy* was ignored by the white academic establishment, though it was much prized in black intellectual circles. Whether by chance or design, Sun Ra's cosmology carries many echoes of James's description of the Egyptian mystery teachings: for instance, the emphasis on discipline, the importance of the Sun God and the concept of a heliocentric universe, and the indissoluble links between magic, science and philosophy. Like Sun Ra, James too was working to rekindle black pride: he proposed his 'New Philosophy of African Redemption', describing it as a 'necessary escape' for black people from the false traditions of European superiority and a Christian religion which had been racially biased ever since it was first established, by the Roman emperors Theodosius and Justinian, as a means of suppressing the Egyptian mystery teachings. For more on James and the influence of ancient Egypt, see 'Postscript 1'

*Thoth is predecessor to the European gods Hermes (Greece) and Mercury (Rome); and to the African gods Esu (Yoruba) and Legba (Fon), the last of whom crossed the Atlantic in the slave ships and survives as Papa Legba in Haitian voodoo mythology and as Papa La Bas in the hoodoo mythology of the United States. Thoth is credited with the invention of magic, alchemy, writing and mathematics; as Hermes Trismegistus he played a vital role in the European Renaissance (see 'Postscript 1'); as Mercury he is astrological ruler of Gemini, birthsign of both Sun Ra and Braxton. See also Jung, 1983, pp. 193–250, for his other exploits and incarnations

†Since the blues and the spirituals represent two conflicting philosophical traditions (see Finn, 1986, especially pp. 153–83, and Jones, 1969, pp. 182–211), perhaps it would be more accurate to see Sun Ra's songs as translating the promises of the spirituals (the preserve of the 'righteous') into a more magical world where the blues meets science fiction (and fact). In particular, Ra's espousal of ancient Egypt would have grated with the righteous who, in adopting Christianity and its Bible, tended to identify with the persecuted Israelites and thus saw Egypt as the enemy

simply a Cosmic Bluesman or that Rocket Number Nine is the modernized Zion Train – the resonances of the Ra cosmology will not reduce to a single interpretation – but it seems reasonable to assume that there will be many points of contact with the black traditions of which he was obviously aware. (And, of course, speaking in codes has been a part of the African-American tradition since the slaves were forced to devise means of communication which their oppressors could not understand.)

However, looking at Sun Ra's work within the context of African-American cultural history is not without its complications; because if his celebration of ancient Egypt is part of an assertion of black pride, his views on the black race in America are more equivocal. While he has nothing but contempt for the racism of a white society which 'has never done anything for me but try to stop me, try to make my so-called life ugly like the rest of Black people',* he also has little patience with those African-Americans who accept that ugliness as their lot: 'They live lies,' he has said. His espousal of black nationalism, his critiques of black Christianity, his exaltation of ancient Egypt, can all be seen as attempts to provoke African-Americans into fighting the ugliness of poverty and racism, in part by reminding them of their heritage of 'truly natural Black beauty'† which Sun Ra felt the big bands in particular had represented.

Every aspect of Ra's work – the emphases on independence, discipline and group values – can be seen in this context, and each has its particular spiritual or political purpose. Today, he is still urging us to fight the old ugliness and warning of its new facets on recent titles like *Hiroshima* and *Nuclear War*. His goal remains to prepare people, particularly African-Americans, for future change. 'The real aim of this music,' he has said, 'is to coordinate the minds of the people into an intelligent reach for a better world, and an intelligent approach to the living future.'‡ Or again: 'In the Black race . . . Musicians weren't planning nothing for their people as far as change is concerned. I had dedicated a so-called lifetime to doin' exactly that 'cause I knew we was gonna need it.'‡

If it seems a forlorn hope that the economic and political ills of the world can be affected by music, it's clear what Sun Ra thinks

*Quoted in the sleevenotes to *Pictures of Infinity*
†Quoted in Wilmer, 1977, p. 92
‡Quoted in the sleevenotes to *Pictures of Infinity*
‡Quoted in Simpkins, 1975, p. 97

of the impossible. And magic, making the impossible happen, remains a potent force in African mystical thought: not only in Africa, where it originated with Thoth, but along the routes the slave ships took, magic persists in Haitian voodoo, Jamaican obeah, Cuban santeria, and in the hoodoo of the American South that crept northwards with the blues and re-emerged in the mystical allusions of sixties creative music.

There are people who decry Sun Ra's work as escapist or opportunist. Even within the black community he has his detractors: Betty Carter, for instance, has said, 'It's nothing but bullshit. Sun Ra has got whitey going for it.'* If spending three decades in relative poverty is opportunist, then Sun Ra is guilty. It's true too that his concerts are spectacular, entertaining and often funny; but I think it's clear that essentially Sun Ra is both serious and magical – perhaps, serious *because* he is magical. As Julio Finn points out: 'The fact is that far from being a substitute for it, magic was a *form of* blacks' political agitation; the fact is that the Afro-American has never accepted the status quo.'† And Amiri Baraka, writing as LeRoi Jones in 1966, declared, 'Sun Ra speaks of evolution of the cosmic consciousness, that is future or as old as *purusa*'.‡ So Mister Rē is not a freak, a con-man, a madman, or even a singular genius: genius he may be, but he is part of a black historical continuum that reaches back through the blues and slavery to an Egyptian civilization that began 5,000 years ago and lasted for nearly three millennia. It is this perspective, which Sun Ra personifies, that we will need to remember later, when Anthony Braxton too speaks of ancient Egypt and the mystical powers of music.

---

*Quoted in Taylor, 1983, p. 279
†Finn, 1986, p. 127. He adds: 'Why do black people believe in magic? Ask a fish why it stays in water. To the black mind, magic *is*.' Other black writers have criticized such statements as racial stereotyping of the most oppressive kind. I think it is safe to say that African-derived spiritual beliefs are often very different from European-derived spiritual beliefs
‡Jones, 1969, p. 210

ROAD

TUESDAY 12, LONDON

I meet Braxton at his hotel at 10 a.m. He's recently started a teaching job at Mills College in Oakland, California, and wants to buy John Coltrane, Ornette Coleman and Charles Mingus records for a modern-music course he'll be teaching next semester.

'There's a new Warne Marsh LP out,' I tell him as we head for the shops (I know he's a big fan). 'Volume three of the Copenhagen concerts.'

'Really!' Braxton's face lights up. He lets out an earsplitting 'whee-haw' and dances a little jig on the steps of King's Cross underground, to the alarm of passers-by.

My last vestiges of apprehension vanish. This is not the super-cold, super-brain of media report; this is a *music lover*.

Two hours later we're staggering around the West End, each clutching a large box of records. Braxton's blown nearly all his *per diems* for the tour and is looking forward to two weeks of near-starvation. 'Boy, Nickie Braxton's gonna murder me when I get home,' he mutters.

I suggest lunch. 'There's a good vegetarian place up the road.'

'OK, I'll eat,' says Braxton, 'but is there a McDonalds nearby?'

'McDonalds? You want to eat at *McDonalds*?' I put on a brave face, but I'm devastated. My idol has feet of hamburger meat?

'You're a vegetarian? So is Gerry Hemingway,' Braxton consoles. 'You guys must be secret millionaires. I have to eat cheap.'

'But hamburgers,' I remonstrate. 'They're destroying the rain forests because of hamburgers – napalming the local Indians, ruining the soil, poisoning the atmosphere . . .' I stop in mid-zeal; this may not be the most diplomatic way to begin a fortnight on the road.

'I'm sure you're right,' Braxton sighs, 'but remember, jazz musicians have to deal with the problem of *no coins*. On the road you either eat well and go home broke or you eat junk food and go home sick. Sick, but solvent. And if you have a family at home like I have, it's really no choice.'

As he tucks into his Big Mac I recall the note in Hans Wachtmeister's Braxton discography about a concert the Creative Construction Company played in Paris in 1969: 'I guess among the "instruments" should also be mentioned the fried chicken, which Braxton ate on stage during the concert. In fact, this was a regular feature during the late-1969 concerts and caused quite some consternation among the French critics.'* I can imagine. *Merde! The chicken's really cookin', but is it jazz?*

WEDNESDAY 13, LONDON

I meet Braxton at 1.30 p.m. Stephen Firth, the Contemporary Music Network's Education Co-ordinator, arrives to escort us to the Guildhall School of Music and Drama where Braxton is to lecture on his composition methods.

Stephen suggests a snack first. Luckily, there's no McDonalds nearby, but there is a Wimpy. Damn it, my second fishburger in twenty-four hours! In the cafe, Stephen tilts his trilby at a rakish angle, hitches his thumbs under his braces, and quotes Shakespeare for us.

'What is it he says in the *Merchant*? "The man that hath no music in himself is fit for treasons, strategems and spoils. The motions of his spirit are dull as night. Let no such man be trusted." I think that's it.'

'Not to like any kind of music, that's an illness,' Braxton concurs.

When we get outside again the sun has vanished and there's a chill in the air. Stephen looks at Braxton, in open-neck shirt and thin cardigan.

'Don't you have a coat?' he asks.

'No. I forgot it.'

'The hotel's only just around the corner,' I say. 'There's time to fetch it.'

'No, I forgot to bring it from California.' Braxton's customary

*Wachtmeister, 1982, p. 56

quizzical expression deepens to a puzzled frown. 'It was a nice day when I left, I kinda forgot I was going to be in England in November.'

Braxton's Guildhall lecture is the first of a series: talks at Newcastle, Sheffield and Leeds will follow, plus, the day after the tour ends, a six-hour lecture and workshop at the Royal Academy of Music. I'd imagined Braxton would be either a very redoubtable or a very charismatic speaker; unusually, he's both.

He starts at the speed of light, talking so intensely and rapidly it's almost impossible to keep track. His range is extraordinary: from the composite, spiritual nature of ancient world culture, through 'the suppression of women intellectuals as witches in the Dark Ages', to the Western media's current misdocumentation and misunderstanding of 'trans-African functionalism', that is black culture and particularly jazz. Three thousand years of world history flash by in the first twenty minutes. He pauses. 'Any questions?'

Stunned silence. The students seem shell-shocked by the rate of information and by the unfamiliar terminology. The lecture teeters on the brink of a chasmic culture gap. Then, gradually, Braxton pulls it around. He slows the pace, talks about his own music, plays records, throws in self-deprecatory asides. The students respond; shock gives way to curiosity then engagement. Questions come in a flurry. At the end, a large group stay behind to pursue personal queries or ask for an autograph. Braxton deals with them all graciously and enquires about the Guildhall's music courses. 'Are they teaching you about the master women composers and the importance of the trans-African and trans-Asian continuums?'

Nope, is the unanimous reply. 'But at least now we know they're not,' someone says.

The more specifically methodological points that Braxton raised in his lectures are covered in 'Postscript 3', but I think it will be useful here to note his comments on his initial approaches to composition. He says that in 1965 he made the decision to 'make music my life's purpose'. When he joined the Association for the Advancement of Creative Musicians in Chicago in 1966, his interest was the relation of form to movement, of music to visual formations: many of the musicians in Chicago, he says, began to develop alternative vocabularies and structures.

His own musical language grew out of the solo context. He'd been very influenced by the solo piano music of Fats Waller, Arnold Schoenberg and Karlheinz Stockhausen, and had tried to develop a piano music of his own. But he wasn't a good enough pianist and so he developed instead a language for alto saxophone. His interest in structure dated from the first solo concert he gave, in 1967. This was supposed to be an improvised concert: 'I imagined I was just going to get up there and play for one hour from pure invention, but after ten minutes I'd run through all my ideas and started to repeat myself. I felt like, "Oh my God, and there's still fifty minutes to go!" I thought, hmm, I better make sure this doesn't happen again. So the question became, How to proceed?'

The first answer was 'to section off various components, formings', and use these as the basis for new vocabularies which could then be fed into 'a modular system'. 'Now I was interested in improvisation only for its ability to generate structural dynamics and vibrational dynamics.' Generating this material became 'the science' of his music.

Braxton hands around a sheet of 'Language Types' with their visual designations. These, he explains, are just ten examples from a pool of over 100 'sound classifications' that he has built up over the years and which comprise the primary components of his musical language (see p. 28).

He says he will take one example from the sheet – 4. Staccato line formings – and show the different ways it can be used as a 'generating form'. This he does in detail, playing recorded examples of each category of generating form (see 'Postscript 3', i). Towards the end of the lecture Braxton refers to his *Composition 25*, explaining that at one point the musicians are required to rub balloons as part of 'a multiple sound/fabric environment'.

'Why balloons?' someone asks.

'Well, I didn't have enough money for the electronic equipment that could make those kinds of sounds,' he replies. 'I'm interested in the expanded reality of sound opened up by the post-Webern continuum, but I'm restricted to using cheap materials. So, you know, I was walking down the street one night and I thought, "Hey! I gotta have balloons!" '

'If you're so limited by poverty,' asks someone else, 'would you consider trying to make a popular record?'

'I don't try to make *un*popular records,' Braxton says. 'I'm not against people buying my records or me being rich. I'd love to be a billionaire shipping tycoon! But I have to do what I believe in. *I would rather I like my music and people hate it, than for them to like it and me hate it.* I'm not going to make a boogaloo or a funky record

1. Long Sound

2. Accented Long Sound

3. Trills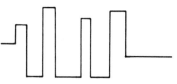

4. Staccato Line Formings

5. Intervallic Formings

6. Multiphones

7. Short Attacks

8. Angular Attacks

9. Legato Formings

10. Diatonic Formings

Language Types

tomorrow, not because I don't respect boogaloo, it's just that I don't know anything about that music. It doesn't excite me as much as, say, opera does right now. So my heart is not into doing that.'

Braxton barely has time to rush back to the hotel for a coffee before he's facing a second set of questions at a pre-concert talk chaired by Charles Fox. He explains again that it was his limitations as a pianist which had led him to develop a solo music on the alto saxophone.

'It's my dream,' he adds, 'that in eighteen, twenty years' time you'll go into a cellar-bar one night and find this dingy, smoke-filled room where a woman is leaning on the piano singing torch songs, and the pianist will be sitting there with his collar turned up, cigarette dangling from the corner of his mouth, mirror shades – that'll be me.'

He talks about his *Trillium* operas, a planned set of twelve three-act operas, the acts actually being thirty-six interchangeable 'dialogues'. *Trillium*, he says, has to do with 'the third part of the order that I'm trying to establish: 1) my music; 2) the *Tri-axium Writings*, which is a restructural philosophical system; 3) rituals'. *Trillium* is 'a platform to express my worldview' and will be part of a projected twelve-day festival of world culture. As *Tri-axium* had to do with the number three, so *Trillium* has to do with the number twelve. (*Which in numerology also reduces to three: 12 = 1+2 = 3 – GL.*)

There's a question about the relationship between composition and improvisation in his work. He replies that his work is generally structured in some way, that sometimes areas of open improvisation are written into the structure while at other times the improvisation may be defined by the language of the composition. 'For example, in the quartet music we use different languages in different pieces. It's like we have one conversation in French, say, then one in German or Italian. And there will be scored parts in which I structure what is said and open parts where people can say what they like, except they have to say it in the language of the piece. Or they don't *have* to, but that's like the agreement we make before we start the piece. Then, at other times, it's like: "OK, I'll meet you at the end of the piece." '

Q: 'What would happen if a person suddenly changed languages in mid-conversation?'

Braxton gives an exaggerated frown. 'Then they'd better have something *very* important to say. And it had better be *only* expressible in the language they've changed to. I'm really only talking about respect: respect for the family of the music. But this kind of language shift rarely happens. People who want to do that would tend not to stay in my groups.'

He adds that he has used between thirty and forty different kinds of notation to date, and six different systems of titling his compositions. But 'the real challenge of creativity is to be honest – know thyself. Music involves living, it's not just the execution of sounds in space. Some of the best musicians I've met have had nothing to do with music.'

The final question is about the relationship of chess to music. 'Well, it's the movement of forces in space. A good chess game can be translated into a musical composition, so can a physics theory.'

Three hours later, at the end of the concert, I have an inkling of what he's talking about: I feel as if a falling apple had just zonked me on the head.

LONDON CONCERT, BLOOMSBURY THEATRE

First Set (Primary Territories)
Composition 122 (+108A)
Composition 40(O)
Collage Form Structure
Composition 52
Composition 86 (+32+96)
Piano solo (from *Composition 30*)
Composition 115

Second Set (Primary Territories)
Composition 105A
Percussion solo (from *Composition 96*)
Composition 40F
Composition 121
Composition 116

First reactions – I'm elated, confused. Many beautiful moments, but I can't see how they fit together or even which are improvised, which notated. It's like wandering through a dream landscape, in which all the contours are moving at different speeds and in different directions. I get a headache trying to map what's happening according to my (erroneous) preconceptions: at times everyone seems to be playing notated material, but from different compositions. (I later learn they are: Braxton is exploring 'collage form structures' in which two, three or four people play two, three or four compositions simultaneously. The set lists simply establish the 'primary territories' through which the music will flow, without pause, during the set; the movement from territory to territory being negotiated, in the main, via open improvisation.)*

Bemused as I am by the music's complexity, there is still plenty to savour, from the surging elation of *52* to the 'accordion sound space' of *115* where bass, drums and piano keep accelerating, then retarding, the tempo around the improvising saxophone; an experiment with time that reminds me of Thelonious Monk's offbeat humour and his delight in complex time formings.† Braxton has brought five instruments – clarinet, flute, sopranino, alto and C-melody saxophones – and he plays the complete spectrum of each one's sound range, from guttural honks to high squeaks. The quartet's level of rapport is incredible, both in the quiet wisps of sound with which they hold together large areas of tensile silence and in the headlong, zig-zag lines that characterize one (bebop-inspired) aspect of Braxton's composition, so fast and crazy, like four trails of light careering around each other down a spiral staircase and converging – FLASH! – at a single point in a single instant. Wonderful!

Post-gig audience responses vary from euphoria to puzzled dislike. 'It was so neurotic, all those jerky lines,' someone complains, 'I couldn't hear any feeling in there.' I groan. No swing, no emotion: the same old brickbats that have been hurled at Braxton's music for the last two decades. I find it inexplicable, though I guess one of the things I'll have to try to do during this tour is explicate it. Later, later.

I hurry home to bed, but I'm too excited to sleep. Tomorrow, the road.

---

*For more on 'primary territories', see p. 174 below; for more on 'collage form structures', see pp. 203–6 below

†Muhal Richard Abrams, one of Braxton's early mentors in Chicago, has also investigated the 'expansion and contraction of rhythm' and cites Art Tatum as his chief influence in this context. See Litweiler, 1985, p. 181

METAROAD

i

SWEET HOME CHICAGO — FACTORIES OF DEATH

Anthony Braxton was born at 2 a.m. on 4 June 1945 in St Luke's Hospital, Chicago – a city stained with history and myth. This was Al Capone's town, a sprawl of steelyards, stockyards and slaughter-houses: Meat City, USA, famous for its butchers, from the gun-toting hoods of Prohibition to more recent disrespecters of human flesh like Richard Daley and Hugh Hefner. A violent city, notorious for its brutal cops, and for its teenage gangs, 200 strong, who carved out their territories with switchblades; a racist city, where the black ghettoes of the West and South Sides were mocked by the obscene opulence of a white, business-class clubland. This was one Chicago: a chronology of bloodied fists and greased palms; a city of stench, where the smell of putrefying cattle carcasses comingled with the stink of city-hall corruption, poisoning the atmosphere despite the icy winds that swept in from Lake Michigan to scour the city's open spaces.

But Chicago, founded by the black explorer du Sable, was also famous for its music – its *Great Black Music*. A home for the New Orleans musicians displaced by the government's closure of Storyville in the First World War, Chicago became the jazz centre of the 1920s; here, the foundations of a tradition were laid down on record by artists like King Oliver, Earl Hines and the great Louis Armstrong. It was a gospel town too; base for Thomas A. Dorsey and Mahalia Jackson; the place where Sam Cooke grew up before he made the switch to pop. Even the classical tradition had its representatives: the black composer Florence Price settled in

Chicago in 1927, her *Symphony in E Minor* receiving its world première at the Chicago's World Fair in 1933. Chiefly, though, Chicago was a blues town; headquarters for the vintage OKeh, Paramount and Vocalion record labels, then later, in the black migration movements of the Depression and post-war years, the crucible in which raw Delta music from the Mississippi was amplified and urbanized in clubs, bars and South Side tenement parties. Blues giants like Muddy Waters, Howlin' Wolf and Sonny Boy Williamson all recorded for Chicago's Chess label – home too for Chuck Berry, the Dells, Bo Diddley, the Impressions, and a major catalyst in the transformation of blues into R & B and fifties rock'n'roll.

A decade later jazz too was transformed in Chicago. Sun Ra's cosmic capers had sown the seeds, but in 1960 the Arkestra had moved to New York, leaving Chicago's tiny avant-garde scene in the hands of a few local musicians. Prominent among these was Muhal Richard Abrams, a pianist/composer who in 1961 set up the Experimental Band, a rehearsal group for the city's improvisers; and in 1965 he became one of the six founder-members of the Association for the Advancement of Creative Musicians (the AACM), now recognized as the most important and influential musicians' organization of the last twenty-five years.

Initially the AACM comprised a pool of thirty to fifty musicians who would play together in every conceivable ensemble combination. Early members (not all of whom were native Chicagoans) included: Muhal Richard Abrams, Fred Anderson, Thurman Barker, Lester Bowie, Anthony Braxton, Charles Clark, Malachi Favors, Christopher Gaddy, Fred Hopkins, Joseph Jarman, Leroy Jenkins, Lester Lashley, Wallace MacMillan, Steve McCall, Kalaparush Maurice McIntyre, Roscoe Mitchell, Amina Claudine Myers, Leo Smith and Philip Wilson. Soon regular ensembles began to emerge: notably Braxton's group (with Jenkins and Smith), which later became the Creative Construction Company; Jarman's group (with Anderson, Barker, Clark and Gaddy); and Mitchell's group (with Bowie, Favors and, sometimes, Wilson). At the end of the sixties, when both Clark and Gaddy died suddenly, within months of each other, the former from a brain haemorrhage and the latter from heart disease, Jarman joined Bowie, Favors and Mitchell to form the Art Ensemble of Chicago. In 1969 the Art Ensemble moved to Paris, followed weeks later by the Creative Construction Company; but whereas the CCC were not well-received in France and broke up there, the AEC prospered, found a new drummer in Famadou Don Moye, and have remained together ever since, becoming the best-known and most fully-documented of all the AACM ensembles.

The AACM worked as a co-operative, with the ideal of musicians helping each other and serving the community. They organized festivals and concerts, studied and practised together, and set up educational programmes for local children. Their aim was to become a social, as well as a musical, force; and soon similar organizations like the Black Artists Group (BAG) of St Louis and the Detroit Artists Workshop sprang up, inspired by their example. Though this aspect of their work was not unique – Horace Tapscott had established the Underground Musicians Association, later the Union of God's Musicians and Artists Ascension, in Los Angeles as early as 1961 – the AACM's political goals, notably their emphases on independence, self-help and researching black culture, exemplified the mood of an era when the struggle for Civil Rights and the aspirations of black nationalism were at the forefront of events. The additional factor that really underlined the AACM's status as a turning-point in the evolution of African-American music was their experimental approach to sound, space, structure. In Chicago, the outlines of new musical languages were beginning to take shape.

During the early sixties the new jazz had flown thick and fast. New York was the eye of the hurricane and John Coltrane its presiding spirit. His music, as the decade progressed, seemed an ever more urgent quest for spiritual apotheosis, pursued, on an LP like *Ascension*, via dense wedges of ensemble free-form where players blew themselves frantic on the thin line between bliss and cacophony. This was a truly high-energy music, racing too through Albert Ayler's dervish tenor cries and Cecil Taylor's molten arpeggios. Wailing, intense, claustrophobic, it crashed around you in mountainous waves, whisked you like a cork along its headlong torrents.

Then, just as it seemed that jazz might dash itself to pieces on these walls of febrile noise, Chicago's new music reasserted the fundamental values of space and silence. Roscoe Mitchell's *Sound* and *Congliptious* LPs and Anthony Braxton's *Three Compositions of New Jazz* breathed rather than screamed: sounds floated in and out of silence, cries and whispers rose and faded in a kaleidoscopic mix of colour and space. The mood was calm, playful; the music often pointillistic. Though revolutionary in its emphasis on *sound* rather than notes or chords,* it certainly didn't reject the past, but took an affectionate stroll through history, emphasizing the continuity of the black tradition and reclaiming all styles and genres as departure points for exploration. Musicians could now embrace a heritage that reached back beyond New Orleans, minstrelsy, gospel to Africa itself, the original source. (This sense of achievement-through-time was later given graphic expression in the Art Ensemble's famous slogan 'Great Black Music – Ancient to the Future', as well as in their logo, a pyramid, and in their onstage garb: African robes and facepaint for Favors, Jarman and Moye, a scientist's lab-coat for Bowie.)

If Roscoe Mitchell's *Sound* had caused the initial shock, being the first example of the new Chicago music on record and a blueprint for the realignment of ensemble dynamics,† Anthony Braxton's *For Alto* was the second truly startling artefact to come from the Windy City. Whereas his earlier *Three Compositions of New Jazz* had been a group record, *For Alto* presented a double album of solo saxophone tracks: an unheard-of project at that time. Several reeds players (Sidney Bechet, Coleman Hawkins, Sonny Rollins, Eric Dolphy) had already pioneered the occasional unaccompanied performance, but the idea of developing an entire solo language for a single-line instrument was particular to Braxton (and the AACM). It proved enormously influential, however, and solo LPs and concerts by single-line instrumentalists became commonplace in the 1970s; Steve Lacy being one example of a noted solo practitioner who has cited Braxton as his original inspiration in that field.

AACM members also began to explore the possibilities of large, and unusual, ensembles and to reinstate neglected instruments of every shape and size. Multi-instrumentalism became the Chicago norm, with horn players like Braxton, Jarman and Mitchell learning the whole range of the saxophone family, from contra-bass to sopranino, as well as various clarinets, flutes and percussion

---

*John Litweiler points out that on the track *Sound* the instruments' customary sounds are never played: 'instead, distortion is the medium of communication, as the players create in overtones, harmonics tones, imprecise pitch, high and low tones that extend the ranges of the instruments' (p. 175). Cf Braxton's statement that 'we don't need *notes* any more. I'm looking for instruments that are not concerned with actual fixed pitches, instruments with *whorls of sound* in them.' (Wilmer, 1977, p. 114)

†*Sound*'s first track, *Ornette*, indicated that, of course, the Chicagoans' interest in space and structure was not without precedent; and Bill Dixon's work, particularly "*Intents and Purposes*", showed they were not alone

instruments. 'Found' instruments became an integral part of ensemble equipment: the Creative Construction Company used hammers, dustbins and similar 'sound tools'; the Art Ensemble collected bells, gongs and 'little instruments'; saxophonist Henry Threadgill would later build his percussive hubkaphone from discarded hub-caps, and Braxton's *Composition 9* was scored for four amplified shovels and a large pile of coal. The Creative Construction Company also recorded several 'environment' pieces, which incorporated traffic noises, waterfalls and other 'found' sounds. These things didn't all happen at once, but they were all rooted in the flurry of activity – of study, research, experimentation – which characterized the early years of the AACM. Suddenly, it seemed as if everything was possible. And yet nothing was: because if the musical challenge had become, how to proceed?, the economic challenge was just as basic: how to survive?

Two major problems which AACM members faced were the poverty and racism endemic to American capitalist society. One solution favoured by many musicians was exile in Europe; and in 1969 both the Art Ensemble and the Creative Construction Company fled to Paris because, in Braxton's words, 'we were dying in Chicago'.* What proved inescapable was the indifference of the American music business, most of which was based in New York City. It's ironic that in an age of instant global communication the AACM's initial music revolution was one of the most patchily documented in jazz history. All of their (relatively few) early LPs were on the local Chicago labels Delmark and Nessa; and though the Art Ensemble made two LPs for Atlantic in 1972–3, and several Chicagoans (Abrams, Braxton, Threadgill) appeared on Arista later in the seventies, the big guns of the American record industry have generally missed out on the continuing history of the new Chicago jazz. To reconstruct it, you have to track down records on numerous independent labels, many of them based in Canada or Europe. (This is still the case: for instance, the Ethnic Heritage Ensemble's first three LPs were on the German Moers label, the Italian Red label and the Finnish Leo label.) The most extensive

---

*Mal Waldron, who left America in 1965, explained it thus: 'The attitude in America at that time was that the musician, and particularly the black musician, was like the lowest man on the totem pole. The highest man was the white man with lots of money in the bank. That was their scale of achievement . . . I thought, well, I'm black, I'm a musician, I don't have any money, why should I live in a society that thinks I'm the *worst*, let's get *out* of that society.' (Lock, 12/83)

collection of new Chicago music is on Giovanni Bonandrini's Milan-based Black Saint and Soul Note labels which, over the last decade, have built up an impressive roster of black creative music, including many records by the AACM pioneers. However, Black Saint did not exist until 1976, nor Soul Note until 1979, so perspectives on AACM history have inevitably been distorted by the fact that so little documentation from the first years has reached the public. In particular, the role of Muhal Richard Abrams as mentor and spiritual guide is only hinted at by his three Delmark LPs and by guest appearances with the Art Ensemble and the Creative Construction Company; while the contributions of many musicians like Lester Lashley, Wallace MacMillan, Kalaparush Maurice McIntyre, have gone largely un- or under-recorded.*

Yet if the musicians suffered from the neglect of the record industry, they were even more distressed by the attentions of the mass media which, they say, have consistently misdocumented the history and purpose of the music.† In reply, artists like Braxton and Leo Smith have written their own accounts of the music, developing new philosophical and analytical perspectives to describe better their understanding of the music's various aspects: where it's from, how it evolved, what it's for. This act of naming, of reclaiming, not only challenges the right of the European and European-American critic to impose inappropriate Western criteria on African-American culture, but threatens to render the bulk of jazz journalism, past and present, completely redundant. In particular, Braxton's *Tri-axium Writings*, a massive philosophical/historical/spiritual discourse on black creative music and its relation to world culture, seeks to transform our basic understanding of what creativity *is*. Reading it, the continuity of the African-American tradition becomes clear; because if the *sound* of the new Chicago music was very different from that of the Ayler/Coltrane high-energy axis, its intention, on a fundamental level, was very similar: to affirm and explore the spiritual dimensions of the music.

*It was not until the end of the 1970s that records by Abrams began to appear with any regularity. Other 'regional' centres of alternative music fared no better. There are few, if any, records from early BAG or Detroit Artists Workshop ensembles available, while Horace Tapscott's work in Los Angeles went largely undocumented for more than fifteen years before Tom Albach began, in the late seventies, to record Pan-Afrikan People's Arkestra concerts for his Nimbus label

†In the early seventies Leo Smith even requested that his work no longer be reviewed in the music press

Malachi Favors's claim that he came 'into being in this universe some 43,000 years ago. Moved around and then was ordered to this Planet Earth by the higher forces, Allah De Lawd Thank You Jesus Good God a Mighty . . . for the purpose of serving my duty as a Music Messenger'* may smack of Sun Ra's droll mystic-isms, but the underlying seriousness of the AACM's spiritual concerns comes through repeatedly – in LP titles like Maurice McIntyre's *Humility in the Light of the Creator*, in poet Amus Mor's sleevenotes to Muhal Richard Abrams's *Young at Heart, Wise in Time* LP, and in Anthony Braxton's declarations that: 'we're on the eve of the complete fall of Western ideas and life values. We're in the process of developing more meaningful values, and our music is a direct expression of this,' and: 'You are your music. If you try to vibrate towards the good, that's where your music will come from.'†

Seen in this context it's not surprising that the AACM has remained separate from the commercialism of American main-stream culture, nor that when the two currents have crossed – as in Braxton's dealings with Arista – the proceedings have often been extremely turbulent.

The AACM has certainly paid a price then, but the fact remains that, like Sun Ra and his Arkestra, it has survived in an alien America without compromising its ideals. A new generation of talented musicians has come from Chicago – Douglas Ewart, Chico Freeman, 'Light' Henry Huff, George Lewis, Edward Wilkerson, Kahil El'Zabar – and members who have long since left the city still uphold the AACM values. These artists have spread AACM music and AACM philosophy around the world, and the world has listened with delight. It seems that only American corporate capitalism remains impervious.

Let me conclude by stressing that Braxton, Smith and their AACM colleagues are certainly not alone in their disgust at the US music establishment and its failure to recognize the true value of the music. Here is Cecil Taylor speaking in 1983:

> The music is simply *not* encouraged. Its growth is not encouraged, its place in the American culture is ignored, there is no *real* information made available as to the aesthetic principle within the structure of the sound.
>
> One could say that given the world recognition of the kind of constructions that Black Americans have given the world, for it *not* to be enshrined in America

---

*From the Art Ensemble's resumé, circa 1969. Quoted in Litweiler, 1985, p. 176
†Quoted in the sleevenotes to *Three Compositions of New Jazz*

is the indication that the establishment has problems dealing with the rituals involved.

It is, if anything, *more* difficult today to find one's centre because of all the defections within the music, the perpetual mountain of false idols, the propagating of values attendant on the most *shallow*, and because of the menial attitudes of most executives in the music; the refusal of these men to recognize anything beyond their economic reasoning – which at the same time allows them to assault the integrity of some of the most creative people in the world – indeed, in this area, this music, *the* most creative.

It is always an embarrassment to realize that one has to live in spite of perpetual harassment, and it's at a point where their insensitivity is simply *there* – they don't even recognize their inability to think, to feel.*

It would be hard to imagine a more comprehensive vindication of Leo Smith's argument, published a decade before, that if musicians are to attain higher levels of creativity, it is vital that they first: 'cut-connection with this factory of death . . . (commercial business-production-journalism and the likes of the POWER-MAN)'.†

ii

BIOGRAPHY 1, 1945–69

BLACK AND POOR IN AMERICA

L: Can we begin with some family background?
B: Well, I was the middle child of five. Only two of us are Braxtons. There's LaFayette, his last name is Samuels; then Clarence Braxton Junior, we called him Juno – he passed about two years ago at forty-two years old; then there's me; then Donald, Donald Fouche, he died a week after Juno, he was thirty-two; and after Donald is Gregory Fouche, he's living in Toledo, Ohio, he's married with two children, and he's working in the environmental field, in air pollution.

*Quoted in Lock, 6/83
†Smith, 1973, no page numbers given

L: The brothers who died – how did that happen?

B: Donald never recovered from Vietnam. He went over and actually saw battle, and when he came back he was never able to pull his forces together and get on with his life. I don't really know what he experienced. And Juno, I see him as a casualty of the South Side of Chicago, especially between 61st Street and 79th; well, actually 61st and 63rd.

L: You'll have to explain that to a non-Chicagoan.

B: The African-American community in Chicago, the socio-political structure that surrounds life in that community . . . there are a great deal of lounges and taverns, places for you to go and have fun. Juno, in my opinion, was seduced by some of the forces that are aligned on, and very intense in, the black community. Plus, there's the hopelessness and the narrow information scan that are prevalent in poorer communities.

I think the only thing that saved me was music. At an early age I discovered I loved music. But as a very young child I was really interested in rocket ships – Wernher von Braun, the V2 scientist, was one of my heroes – and in technology, television, space. I was very fortunate in that I had two good friends, Howard Freeman and Michael Carter, and we did not join the gangs, we were interested in building things. Thanks to those guys I had a wonderful childhood, because even though we had no money we had our imaginations. We were always dreaming up projects, writing books: we tried to build movie cameras and TV systems using mirrors, we had a magazine called *The Joke Book*, we turned out an issue a week. Of course, nobody bought 'em but it didn't matter, we gave 'em away.

I didn't realize at the time, but those experiences would help me much later on when I began to encounter such a spectrum of reaction to my music. In fact, I turn around at forty years old and I find myself thinking, hmm, my life isn't that different from what it was when I was a child. I was always drawn to science and the world of thought; and I think music especially would be the major factor that would change the direction of my life from what my brothers were dealing with.

L: Were these projects happening at school? Were they encouraged?

B: I don't know if I could say we were encouraged in school, but we were never told not to dream the greatest dreams . . . you know, we kinda came up with the mentality that we could accomplish anything we wanted to accomplish. We never realized that we were black and poor in America and what that meant, even though all around us . . . For instance, four years, say, after graduating from grammar school (I went to Betsy Ross Grammar School) maybe thirty or forty per cent of the people I graduated with would be dead or in gaol. And maybe ten to fifteen years after grammar school, I'd say seventy per cent of the young men and women I grew up with were either dead or in gaol; and of that surviving thirty per cent, maybe two-thirds of them would be living in serious poverty, never finishing high school, their lives reverting back between 61st and 63rd, that mentality.

As a young man I didn't quite understand all of that. But I didn't join any of the gangs, for instance; I was frightened of the levels of violence that were taking place. So, I don't know . . . I look back on it now, and it's like 'Wow!' I don't know how to see it any more. Not many people survived from my generation, yet I grew up thinking I was a very unlucky person – I'm the darkest child, and in the black community in that period the darker you were the uglier you were perceived. I tried to make up for being ugly by being smart, though it wasn't always on the conscious level.

L: Was there a particular time when you did realize you were black and poor in America?

B: My first exposure to white Americans would be in high school. I went to Chicago Vocational High School when I was about twelve or thirteen. Not to mention the television set would reinforce the fact that there were other realities happening. There was a TV show called *Ossie and Harriet* – they lived in California, with beautiful trees, a completely different lifestyle. So it wasn't like I grew up not being aware of white America, because the media are based on white Americans' image of themselves.

Later, after high school, I went to Wilson Junior College for a semester, which is where I met Roscoe Mitchell, then I went into the army and later I was stationed in South Korea for a year and a half. So all of those experiences would help me to open up a broader world perspective than I received in the South Side of Chicago. Let me say this too – the more I was able to learn about humanity from a universal standpoint, the better I was able to feel about myself. Because – how can I say this? – I was looking for something in my life that I did not see in the South Side of Chicago, especially when I discovered the power music had over me. The music kept telling me there was something more than Chicago, though at that point I had no thought of becoming a professional musician. I just wanted to be involved in something that made a little more sense. Because I was never, for instance, very *hip*. I was never drawn to the real hip school. In fact, when as a young man I tried to be hip, I was always late (*laughs*). Like, when I got the shoes with the nickles in them, they were out of style. So I gave up on that concept.

L: You said Juno was a casualty of the South Side. Could you explain that a little more? What happened to him?

B: (*softly*) Ah . . . Juno never discovered what he wanted to do with his life. He was never able to find something that could give him a sense of . . . evolution. He was a very nice man. He drank too much. He just kinda lived to forty-two, then his heart gave out, his lungs – he just died. He never hurt anybody. He fell victim to the illusion of sex and sensuality and pleasure . . . I say he fell victim, actually he was very happy with his life, or so he said. I did not understand my brother; we were never close. We loved each other deeply, though, and whenever we saw each other we went and played pool or something. We were not able to share too much. In fact, I've never been able to share too much with my brothers, with the exception of Gregory; and it's only in the last three or four years that we've been able, as grown men, to have a healthy dialogue and communicate. I think all my brothers thought I was somewhat crazy or strange or far-out: they never really listened to my music, for instance.

L: They thought that because of your music or because of the earlier projects?

B: I think I became aware of it somewhere around four or five.

L: (*laughs*) You were crazy at four?

B: (*shrugs*) It didn't seem crazy to me, I was just involved in the things I was interested in. By the time I was twelve, thirteen, fourteen, it was pretty clear that everyone in the family thought I was different. But I can say this about my family – at no point did they ever tell me that I could not achieve what I wanted to achieve. When I began to take music lessons, about eleven I think, my family never told me that I could not succeed in music; and later, as it became apparent that my music was moving in areas that they were not too excited about (to put it mildly), they never tried to discourage me or make me feel that what I was doing was not of value, just that they could not relate to it. And I thank them for that.

FRANKIE LYMON, JAMES BROWN,
LIVE AT THE REGAL

L: The first music you liked was doo-wop and rock'n'roll?

B: My first big hero was Frankie Lymon, Frankie Lymon and the Teenagers. Their early records were *Why Do Fools Fall in Love?*, *I Want You to be My Girl*, *The ABCs of Love*. He was a very special singer and the group's arrangements were restructuralist,* as far as I'm concerned. Mr Lymon would die when he was twenty-five years old, I think, but in his brief career I *lived* for each new record.

There was a record store on 58th Street, a very good store – had it not been there I'm sure the course of my life would've been very different – and I would be there every week. I would save up all my money, in high school I would save my lunch money, to buy records. I became a real collector by the time I was thirteen, fourteen. I was also influenced by Bill Haley and the Comets, I really liked *Rock Around the Clock* and the movie *Blackboard Jungle*. Little Richard I kinda liked too, though he was a little far-out for me.

I had a vocal group back in that period, in grammar school. I'd write songs and we'd sing 'em. There was a song, *Earth Angel* –

L: The Penguins!

B: Yeah! I took the melody line and wrote a song called *Sun Flower*. We sang it a lot at grammar school.

L: Can you remember how it went?

B: (*laughs*) Yeah, it wasn't very creative. (*Sings*): '*Sun flower, sun flower, will you be mine?*' It went someplace, but I can't remember where (*laughs*).

L: You say on the sleeve of your first LP that James Brown is a favourite of yours.

B: Yes, Mr Brown! I've always loved his music. I had the opportunity to work with Sam & Dave, the Impressions, the Del-Vikings – this would be later, after the army – but I never had the opportunity to work with James Brown and I always found myself wondering what it would be like to be in the Famous Flames. James Brown is a restructuralist. The music of the seventies and eighties is very indebted to what he brought to the music, especially rhythmically.

---

*For Braxton's definition of restructuralism, see pp. 162ff below

L: How did you come to play with Sam & Dave and the Impressions?
B: I was playing alto and tenor with . . . whose big band was this? I think it was George Hunter's. There was a theatre in Chicago, the Regal, like the Apollo in Harlem: all of the acts would come through, and there'd be a houseband that played with all the various people.
L: How long were you in the houseband?
B: About six months. Until I became so radical I decided to take my own solos and play the way I wanted to play. In other words, I was becoming an arrogant young man who would not play in the closet the music he was getting excited about. I wanted to demonstrate what I was learning and what I believed in. My convictions were forming in that period. I've always been very *narrow* once I've made a decision about my beliefs (*laughs*).

PHILOSOPHY – *PIANO PIECE 1*

L: Let's turn to your interest in philosophy. How did this begin?
B: Oh, I studied philosophy at Roosevelt University, but in fact I grew up in the sixties, so . . . for instance, my cousin Rafiki was very involved in CORE and SNCC and because of him I was able to get some kind of political consciousness. Through him I met people like Shosana Ori: this was an Asian woman intellectual, and she turned me on to reading Freud and some of the Russian writers, Dostoevsky, Chekhov. My interest in philosophy was based on just trying to understand – life, you know (*laughs*). Like, *what is* this experience? I began taking philosophy classes at Roosevelt, Greek philosophy. I was not happy with that, but it was better than the Music School.

I recall writing *Piano Piece 1* – did Marilyn play it last night? Maybe not – I took it to one of my music teachers and he pointed out all the parallel fifths, so I took it to the philosophy teachers and they found it very interesting. I said, OK, it's clear where I should be: the Philosophy Department was more interested in my music than the Music Department. I became very – not angry – in college, but I found myself very affected by the fact that there was no mention of black people, or Asians, or women. There was no real respect for Stockhausen or John Cage. They were still debating whether or not Schoenberg was valid! I didn't have any patience with that as a young man.

RACISM IN THE ARMY – KOREA

L: Were you at Roosevelt before or after the army?

B: I was at the university while I was first in the army, then I went back later after I left the army.

L: You were drafted about 1963?

B: No, no, I wasn't drafted. I joined the army.

L: Volunteered? Why?

B: Well, because . . . see, I was in Wilson Junior College, and up until then I'd only been listening to Paul Desmond, Lee Konitz, Warne Marsh, Miles Davis, a handful of people, I was just discovering Jackie McLean – then suddenly I began playing with Roscoe Mitchell, Jack DeJohnette, I was getting really excited about the music. But I was having a great deal of money problems, my family were not able to send me to college. I talked it over with my music teacher, Jack Gell, and then I took, and passed, a test for the Fifth Army Band. This was an Area Band, the bands that the generals use, so they always keep their instruments, they don't do any fighting. I went to basic training first, then I was stationed with the Fifth Army Band in Highland Park, Illinois, for about a year and a half. It was an excellent group, some of the best musicians I ever played with, even though it was a very *racist* organization: I was only the second black person in it.

L: The army was racist, or this particular group?

B: This band was made up of very upper-class European-American soldiers and, of course, they were not used to being around a black person and I was not used to being around them. But they . . . it was difficult. I felt – not oppressed, but I was very much aware that I was not accepted: lockers turned upside down, 'Nigger Go Away' signs, all that kind of stuff. It was an, ah, interesting experience.

Later, as I began to meet some of these people and get to know them, I would find and I think they would find that we were just human beings. It's indicative of America's social reality that you have people growing up right next to each other, yet they don't even realize it.

L: The racism decreased?

B: It began to decrease, yeah. In my second year I would even say I had some friends, or almost-friends. Certainly the hostility relaxed. And I learned a lot from those people, the level of musicianship was incredible.

L: What music were you listening to then?

B: I was still fascinated by vertical harmony, but it began to open up. It was in the army that I discovered Arnold Schoenberg's music, and that had as powerful an effect on me as John Coltrane's did. Up until that point I didn't have any relationship with composing – well, I was becoming excited with the composing of Ornette Coleman and John Coltrane, their music really opened up all kinds of thoughts and feelings for me – but Arnold Schoenberg crystallized what that would mean. The world of composition.

L: What music did the army band play?

B: A lot of John Philip Sousa, marches . . . The Fifth Army Band had a radio show; every week they'd play different kinds of music – Broadway musicals, arrangements of *Tristan and Isolde*, *The Sound of Music*. It was very educational for me.

Then I went into the Eighth Army Band and was stationed in Korea under General Westmoreland. I met a lot of good musicians who were interested in improvised music, so there were sessions, I had my own group in Korea – it was very nice. I was finally away from my mother and father, eighteen, nineteen, coming into my own. I practised ferociously – eight, nine, ten hours a day – because I was feeling, like, I was getting better, but I was frightened. Frightened of the time going by. So I was desperate to get this instrument to come through. Oh my God, I remember that cycle in my life! It seemed like I was never gonna be able to play the instrument. Suddenly, just as I was ready to commit suicide, I'd notice a scale coming in (*laughs*).

L: After the army, you returned to Chicago?

B: I went back to Chicago, called my cousin; he told me about this AACM organization forming and he was sure I'd be interested. I went to a concert that Sunday at a place called the Lincoln Center – it's been torn down now – and it was the Muhal Richard Abrams Sextet: Maurice McIntyre, who's now Kalaparush Difda; an altoist called Virgil Humphreys, he's now Absholom Ben Shlomo; Wilbur Campbell and Steve McCall on percussion; Charles Clark on bass and Muhal on piano. The first half of the concert, the curtain stayed *down* (*laughs*). They never opened it up, just played behind the curtain! It was like, for the first time in my life I met a group of people who would not call me strange. Up until the AACM, as my interest in contemporary music developed, I noticed I was isolated from more and more people. I was feeling like I did in my family, where my brothers eventually gave up trying to appreciate what I was doing 'cause they felt it was just – you know, too different.

L: You say in Michael Ullman's *Jazz Lives* that it was bringing home a Cecil Taylor LP that caused the first serious rift with your family.*

B: That's right. And in the Eighth Army Band they had a rule saying I could only play my records during certain hours, like from six to eight, when everybody was out eating; so I bought a small record player and a headphone set, I had a guy drill a hole in it, make a connection, like a Sony Walkman, then I could play my music in barracks. 'Cause no one liked it. They hated it. My mother sent me John Coltrane's *Ascension* when I was in Korea, Albert Ayler's *Bells*. I played five minutes of those records . . . everybody went crazy!

It got to be very difficult in the army in, say, the last year. I was just living for each new John Coltrane record and, in fact, each new record in that period would demonstrate another step in evolution: *Impressions, Crescent, A Love Supreme*, that record with *Brazilia* and *Chim Chim Cheree*.† It touched me so deeply, I can't begin to tell you. Plus, I was hearing about Archie Shepp, Marion Brown. I knew something was happening.

THE AACM – MULTI-INSTRUMENTALISM

After that first AACM concert I met Roscoe Mitchell again; he told me to come down and practise. He brought me into the organization.

L: They'd just started then?

B: They'd been together for two months or less, I think.

This was a very powerful experience for me, one of the major life markers. My association with the AACM would clarify what I wanted to do for the rest of my life. Especially the conversations that I would have with Leo Smith; Leo and I were very close. Later, my work and Leo's would be viewed as not as 'black' as some of the musics that were reaching into Africa. It was in this period that that controversy began to ensnarl me, even in the AACM; because I was not interested only in Africa, I was interested in Africa *and* in Europe *and* in Asia – for instance, I was very much into the music of Ali Akbar Khan and Ravi Shankar. So my work

*Ullman, 1982, p. 204
†*The John Coltrane Quartet Plays*

with Leo Smith would be invaluable to me. We learned a lot together. We were always interested in composition and structure and different kinds of improvisation.

L: Which instruments were you playing then?

B: Initially, what I really wanted to do was just play the alto saxophone. But I'd played clarinet in high school because they didn't have any saxophones, I'd played clarinet and alto in the army. In the AACM Roscoe and Joseph Jarman were starting to develop multi-instrumental possibilities, so I was influenced by them but I wanted to find my own way. For instance, they were integrating bells and things into their music, so I started trying to integrate sound tools, hammers . . . going to more direct sources. I was discovering John Cage in this period too, trying to integrate all of this into a music that would respect my sources but not imitate. I didn't want to imitate anyone, I never have. Though I remember thinking I could be quite content playing like Paul Desmond for the rest of my life (*laughs*).

I began to investigate very low-register instruments too. Suddenly, in that three-year period, '66 to '69, everybody understood that something was really happening. Everybody started to examine everything they could possibly examine! It was like, there's so much to do! I started my solo concerts in that period; Leo Smith and I gave a lot of concerts with tape – we didn't have a synthesizer, so we'd go and record sounds, integrate them into the music. My interest in structure and in designing different environments dates from this time.

L: Why did all this happen in Chicago *then*?

B: It was a time of social upheaval, alternative movements were taking place. The state of consciousness in African-America was changing, people were starting to ask serious questions about their lives. Coltrane's music especially would generate a lot of thoughts about – everything! Cecil Taylor's too. The AACM came together from many different factors. Common interests, certainly. We were all seen as aliens or renegades because the traditional structure did not then – nor do they now – like the music. If you played what they thought was 'space' music or 'noise', you couldn't get a gig. So, in 1966, '67, everybody turned around and discovered there was no work. It was the right moment for a mutual support organization like the AACM to happen.

L: In *As Serious as Your Life*, Valerie Wilmer suggests that the different kinds of architecture, of space, in New York and Chicago were reflected in the music: that Chicago's music, like its buildings, had plenty of space in which to breathe.*

B: Oh yeah, I think that's definitely true. The atmosphere was very different too. In New York, everybody was ready to *make it*; in Chicago there was more time to practise, more communication between the musicians.

SOUND TOOLS, LIVE DUMP TRUCK, ENVIRONMENT STROLLS

L: Tell me more about your sound tools and environment music. You used to play with a couple of London dustbins, is that right?

B: Yes, there was a time – when I first came to Europe, in fact – I used to travel with about five piles of equipment. I had two different sizes of London garbage cans, I had three coat racks – one had the dustbins on, the others had power tools, washboards, things like that.

L: Power tools?

B: Hammers, saws, electric saws, all kinds of what I call sound tools, things I could use to make sound and play. I had an *arsenal* of noise, it was wonderful! This is an aspect of music I hope to resurrect now that I have a job. In this last period of my life I didn't have any money to make cases, plus I'm forty years old now, I couldn't even bring all my saxophones or the bass clarinet over for this tour. I can't carry all those things any more.

L: Your sound tools sound less flexible than the Art Ensemble's 'little instruments'.

B: The concept was very different. I wanted to be an instrumentalist who could function from the lowest to the highest register, use all the different instrumental possibilities, and as a composer I wanted to have the option of working in, or writing for, various settings. I was not interested in having my arsenal at every concert, for instance: what I wanted was the possibility of having all the instruments for one concert, then just have clarinet or soprano for the next concert, then conduct a chamber orchestra piece, then do some electronic music, do some dance, do a duo. That's the kind of flexibility I wanted.

Harry Partch and the European continuum would help me with understanding diversity in composition, and I also tried to learn

*Wilmer, 1977, p. 119

from the early orchestras that travelled around America, like 'Old Man' Finney's Band or some of the groups that criss-crossed the Mid-West in the twenties. They had very interesting instrumentations: ten saxophones plus trumpets . . .

L: I think you composed a piece to be performed in a steelyard?

B: Well, I have a composition for 100 tubas that was written to be performed in a specified environment. I have another composition from that period, the first to use a cell-structure notation I think, for dump truck, live dump truck, that would be modulated; the truck would dump a pile of coal and the score would be for four shovellers – and each shovel would have an electronic modulation on it. I have the score . . . I never had a performance, of course. I was trying to move into schematic and environment musics in that period. I also did a series of environment strolls that I still have master tapes for.

L: Strolls?

B: The instrumentalists would stroll in different sections of the city. I was doing a great deal of outside recording then, in various settings – near waterfalls, whatever. I just couldn't get anybody to release it. I had one record called *This Time* on BYG; they put some of the outside music on, but in fact what they put on were the tests. They threw away the real music in the garbage can (*laughs*).

FOR ALTO – A SYNTAX

FOR SOLO SAXOPHONE

L: *For Alto* was your most influential recording in that period – the first LP of solo saxophone music. What attracted you to that project?

B: I wanted to establish a piano music, but I didn't play piano very well. I was in love with solo piano music, especially Schoenberg's. Later I would discover Fats Waller, Stockhausen's *Klavierstücke IV, VI, X* – that *did it*! I decided it's time to create a vocabulary, a syntax, for solo saxophone. This would allow me to have a solo music.

L: Did you begin by transferring your piano music to the saxophone or did you start afresh?

B: I wanted to create a particular language for the saxophone. It wasn't as clear then as it is now. When I started the solo music, I did the first concert, just improvisation. It did *not* work; I was very unhappy. Separation was the only thing I could figure out: focusing on particular areas, parameters, I could work within; separating elements as a basis for establishing a sound logic. That seemed a practical way to continue, as opposed to the idea that whatever you play is interesting so you just keep playing. I wanted to create a music that *I* could listen to. I wasn't gonna kid myself . . .

The biggest difference between me and the total improvisation schools that have developed is – how can I say it? – it seems to me that structure gives one the possibility of defining the space in a way where it can be evolutionary. So, I was interested in developing a music and a music system and then, from that point, extending it. My last influences, those being Stockhausen and John Coltrane, showed me beyond a doubt how to do it: you establish a point, you work, you try to develop it. Let me elaborate on that because there are differences. Coltrane, to me, demonstrates a very clear linear evolution in his music. We can look at those very early Coltrane records and see how he mastered bebop, then got into a complex bebop on *Giant Steps*, then into the modal music, etc. That would be one demonstration of evolution. Stockhausen would demonstrate another evolution by establishing a particular piece with a language, then the next piece would be another language, another syntax, and it was, like, isolated, theoretical – well, I don't want to say theoretical – but, without trying to develop any one *line*, he would demonstrate this extended understanding of form and of putting events together.

I decided to take both of these approaches; to start first at several different points and then try to generate from those points. This would be in accordance with what I'd learned from Mr Coltrane and Mr Stockhausen. As a young man I didn't understand these things as clearly as I do now, but I understood after that first concert that *this* could not continue 'cause *this* was horrible (*laughs*).

ROSCOE MITCHELL, JOSEPH JARMAN, LEO SMITH

L: It seems that Roscoe Mitchell, Leo Smith and yourself are the three AACM composers to have established most clearly your own musical languages.

B: Roscoe Mitchell was one of my strongest influences in Chicago. Roscoe had developed a very advanced music in 1965, say. Albert

Ayler's records were coming out then, but in fact Roscoe had already understood what that music was and had erected his own language.

Roscoe has a very profound understanding of form, he's a restructural-minded person like I am. In the beginning, the first two years or so, I think I learned more from him than he would learn from me. Part of my fight would be not to copy Roscoe, not to let him influence me too much because he had a very strong music that he'd put together. That record *Sound* would really define the parameters of the music. And Roscoe . . . I have never known him not to be working on something. That's the ultimate compliment.

L: Would you say there are many similarities between his language and yours?

B: I think our musics *could not be* more different. Even though I feel he has an understanding of my work and I feel I have an understanding of his. But I was always more of a line player; Roscoe was more interested in sound. I think my music got very distorted under the weight of Roscoe's music in the early period. All of the critics would go wild over Roscoe, then they'd beat me over the head 'cause I didn't sound enough like him (*laughs*). It was very frustrating, because our musics have always been very different.

L: Surely there's a similarity in the way you both take things apart, break down your musics into the basic particles?

B: Yes, we have that in common. His solo music is like a study of the micro-elements of his language. I broke down my music, but I created a more visual base, the language music, that joined elements to create a different syntax or vocabulary. Roscoe's would be more like a Webern-type of restructuralism that focused on, like, a specific problem and worked with just that problem; then on to the next problem. It's like the difference between Webern and Stockhausen, that would be the difference between Roscoe and me. Roscoe tends to peer in through the microscope at those events he's looking for, particular sound combinations or whatever; I tend to put models together, stick them together and build greater and greater models. Our results have been very different, but it's only in this period that I feel maybe a handful of people are starting to understand it.

Joseph Jarman is another person who would affect me. His vision of the music was just as strong as Roscoe's – somehow that got lost in the press. But Mr Jarman . . . his work in the theatre in the early sixties was very important, but he's also a brilliant composer. This is the thing about the AACM musicians: I hate to sound, ah, chauvinistic, but it's a real characteristic of the guys who came out of Chicago that not only have they demonstrated a solo music, they've demonstrated ensemble music, orchestral music, music in the conventional systems, music in their own systems and their own notations. They each have their own sound, their own relationship to time and rhythm; for instance, I met Henry Threadgill when I was eleven years old, we studied together under Jack Gell, yet no one could ever mistake our playing. That's true of Roscoe, of Joseph . . . People talk about the AACM as if it represented one set of values or one area of research, but it was a dynamic spectrum: no one was interested in establishing a single collective voice. It was a restructuralist school, a union of restructuralist thinkers. That was the reason I liked the AACM in the beginning and it's the reason why, when I turn around now, I find myself still respecting all those guys.

L: And Leo Smith?

B: I think only in America could a person of Leo Smith's talent not be recognized. I think Leo Smith is a genius, and whenever the thrust of his work becomes known, then he will get the respect he deserves. I only hope it will happen while he's on this planet. Leo and I basically grew up together in the AACM. We would study scores, we were always writing, composing, day-dreaming about new projects. I have never known a time when Leo Smith was not developing something. Of course, I've just said that about Roscoe, but I could say it, oh, 100 times more about Leo. My hope is that someone will help him, give him the money to have some of his projects realized. The man is a genius.

DYING IN CHICAGO

L: Soon after *For Alto* came out, you, Leo Smith and Leroy Jenkins went to France.

B: Yeah, but the solo album was actually made in '67 or '68. It came out much later, 1969 I think. I recorded that material myself in the basement of the Parkway Community Center and basically *gave* it to Delmark Records – and they still wouldn't put it out *(laughs)*.

L: What were you doing between recording *For Alto* and leaving for France?

B: Oh, Leo Smith and I had a duo. We used to give concerts in lunch rooms while people were eating their lunch. They wouldn't pay any attention to us, but we'd still be there with our garbage cans (*laughs*). Joseph Jarman and I had a duo . . . This was a very special period for me. We were all young musicians who were excited and fearless, so we were trying to – you know, change the world. We thought we were the *baddest* guys in the world. Young twenty-year-old guys with their big dreams of change. Everybody was bouncing off everybody else, learning from each other – even though the first fifteen years of the music would be documented in a way that suggested the Art Ensemble of Chicago established everything in the music and the rest of us were simply students of theirs. I always resented that because it was not true.

L: Presumably that impression is due in part to the glut of recording the Art Ensemble did in Paris. I think they recorded twelve LPs in eighteen months in France, which is more than the rest of the AACM *in toto* were able to do in the first five years.

B: That's right. In fact, so much has *not* been documented, you wouldn't believe it. The AACM consisted of thirty, forty people and there's no way of looking at the work that transpired without transcending the concept of one person or one sector of people being responsible for all the changes that took place. I'm thinking of someone like Kalaparush Maurice McIntyre: he was not fortunate enough to survive the social and political wars of the past fifteen years, so nobody talks about his music. But he was very important too, many of his ideas would help us to understand the music better.

L: What do you mean by 'he didn't survive'? He's still playing.

B: He did not have the good fortune to record very frequently, he did not make the decision to leave Chicago and go to Europe . . . Because of a whole lot of reasons, there are not many records of his music and that's a shame because he's always been a special player.

L: I think he's playing now with the Ethnic Heritage Ensemble, isn't he?

B: Oh. I don't really know. I haven't seen Kalaparush in many years.

L: How did you support yourself in Chicago?

B: I lived on Hostess Twinkies, and every now and then I'd get some brown rice. I discovered eggs and rice would keep you going for a long while. In other words, we were dealing with *severe* poverty.

L: This is why you left for France?

B: It was a response to several different factors. For one, Charles Clark died, Christopher Gaddy died, twenty-two-, twenty-three-year-old guys, young men . . . I was determined not to die in Chicago, I could die in Paris. We'd give concerts, work all week or two weeks to get the music right, then maybe get three people turn up. So you couldn't make a living performing your music. Though, as a young man, you don't care so much about food – the most important thing was the cause. Not to mention that I was so damn excited by the music – just as I'm so damn excited by the music right now. That fills you up in another kind of way.

We went to Paris because it made no sense to stay in Chicago after 1969. We were dying. And I had been reading about Europe for years. I thought there was a possibility people would be more interested in the music. I went on ahead of Leo and Leroy. I took a plane to Paris; I had a one-way ticket and fifty dollars in my pocket. After the plane arrived, I took a taxi to the city, I looked out the window – *Steve McCall was walking down the street!* And the next cycle of my life began.

ROAD

THURSDAY 14, NEWCASTLE

Up at 6 a.m. It's *cold*, misty; a thick white frost sparkles on roads, cars, hedges. I've borrowed a spare coat for Braxton, but he arrives in the hotel foyer wrapped in a dingy yellow sack-like garment, trimmed with a moth-eaten brown-wool collar. 'Margaret Parker lent it to me,' he explains cheerfully, 'it's an old one of Evan's.'

The plan is that John Cumming from Serious will drive us to Newcastle, where Braxton has to lecture at 2 p.m. The rest of the group will follow later with Tony Cresswell in the tour van. Two hours out of London I find myself in a motorway cafe staring grimly at a plate of fried fish. I hadn't realized touring was such a health hazard.

'You'll be a meat-eater by the second week,' Braxton promises. 'Either you'll crack or I will.'

'You're lucky you're not with Steve Swallow,' says John Cumming. 'He tries to make people smoke – *go on, have another cigarette, it's good for you.*'

The road stories begin. Braxton describes tours where each gig has meant 'three flights, then two hours in the back of a truck, play the gig in the middle of the night, two hours back in the truck, three more flights to the next gig. That's an Ulli Blobel tour!'

(Mr Blobel is a German promoter whose tour itineraries are, it seems, legendary for their attempts to push back the limits of human endurance.)

'The Paul Motian Trio played a gig in Sofia,' John Cumming relates, 'then flew to Belgrade, changed flights, flew to Hamburg and played a gig there – all in the same night.'

'Ulli Blobel?' asks Braxton.

'Ulli Blobel.'

It's a dull, drab day: the views from the motorway depress the spirit, an endless procession of industrial and suburban wastelands. Low stormclouds and clinging mist make it much more dismal. Talk is desultory, although the topics of Stonehenge (which Braxton and Marilyn Crispell are keen to visit) and the music business raise a degree of animation. Braxton's latest quartet LP has just been released by Black Saint, but the records haven't been distributed in England in time for the tour: Polygram, the importers, claim that their copies have somehow become 'lost in the warehouse'.

'Just my luck,' sighs Braxton. 'The first copies had the wrong title printed on them too. That's the wonderful world of jazz for you, Graham. Boy, I'm glad I've got a teaching job now!'

Braxton's talk at Newcastle CAT follows a similar pattern to yesterday: a general introduction, then discussion of a specific aspect of his work – today, it's uses of repetition (see 'Postscript 3', ii). The two sets of students make a striking contrast, reflecting the UK's north/south divide: the Newcastle group, in faded T-shirts and patched jeans, are noticeably shabbier than their London counterparts; and they greet Braxton's strange terminology and his heady declarations of music's importance with the surly impatience of people facing a future on the dole. Yet, as in London, as he begins to talk about and play examples of his own music, their interest is kindled. The questions consolidate a mood-shift from hostility to agitated puzzlement.

Q: 'But what are you trying to express? I don't hear any joy in your music, only anger.'

B: 'I'm sorry, did you say anger or anguish?'

Q: 'Well, both. It seems very introverted.'

'No joy, huh?' Braxton frowns. 'OK, let me play you another piece, just to see your response.'

I can't help smiling. He plays *Composition 58*, from the *Creative Orchestra Music 1976* LP; a parade march which is one of the most gloriously joyful and celebratory pieces in all creative music.

B: 'I don't think you could categorize that as anguished or angry. But maybe these kinds of terms are too subjective. Schoenberg's music might be thought of as brooding, say, but it changed my life.'

Q: 'Aren't you afraid you're alienating people with your music?'

B: 'One thing I've found out is that you can alienate people by doing anything. Or nothing. Whatever I do or don't do, I'm guaranteed my enemies.'

Q: 'How exactly do you see your music? Is it an intellectual music?'

B: 'I'd say my music is an expression of what I think *and* feel *and* hope.'

Q: 'How do you see music in general?'

B: (*laughs*) 'That's a big question. I think what we have to find and deal with in this time period is *fundamental information*. What do I mean by that? All I can say is that no music is separate from its spiritual dimension or the forces it sets into motion. So-called jazz has been profoundly misdocumented because the critics have not understood this, and so its essence has become totally distorted by the media.'

Q: 'You say "so-called jazz". Do you regard the work you're doing now as separate from jazz history?'

B: 'No, not at all. It's the word I argue with, not the reality. I mean, if I had my past taken away from me, you'd have to put me in an insane asylum or something.'

Q: 'Do you think you're losing the quality of feeling in your music by being too philosophical about it?'

Braxton smiles grimly. 'A lot of people would agree with you. Fortunately, I don't.'

After the lecture I take Braxton to meet two friends of mine, pianist/composer Katy Zeserson and ecologist Malcolm Green. Some months earlier I'd sent Braxton a paper co-written by Katy and myself on the connections between ecology and feminism. 'Oh, I remember,' he says, when I remind him. 'I could see we were exploring the same areas. That's when I knew we'd have plenty to talk about.'

In the event, he and Katy talk about 'the feminine vibration' in music. (Braxton posits this notion in *Tri-axium Writings 3*, in a section on 'The Reality of the Creative Woman'* which examines sexism in terms of both the exclusion of many women from creative activity and the neglect of those who do contribute. He relates discrimination in music to the suppression of 'the feminine vibration' in most levels of Western and non-Western culture. The result is a world operating on only half-potential: unless sexism ·is eradicated, he concludes, there is no hope of world change.)

Katy points out that it's a big problem to define precisely what a

---

*T-a W3, pp. 428–68. See also 'Postscript 2', pp. 318–20 below

feminine vibration (or aesthetic, or consciousness) *is*. She tells us
that the women she plays music with in Newcastle have started to
question every aspect of musical language because most of the
music that's come down to us has been made by men: they've
developed the language, designed the instruments, set all the
parameters. But trying to work out which, if any, facets of the
tradition are inherently masculine, which can be appropriated by
women and which have to be rejected, is proving an almost
impossible task. 'We may even find that ultimately music can't be
separated out like that,' she says, 'but we need to try, just to find
out who we are, musically.'

'I think it can be separated out,' says Braxton. 'I think there's a
men's music and a women's music, masculine and feminine
vibrations.'

Katy nods. 'My hunch is you're right. But then we have to be
very careful how we use terms like masculine and feminine. The
danger is we'll exclude whole areas of experience, like violence,
which women do feel but which are traditionally deemed *not
feminine*. My feeling is we're only just beginning to unravel these
things.'

'You're really questioning every aspect of musical language?
That's an enormous task.' Braxton smiles appreciatively.

I ask him about a couple of women composers he's mentioned in
the lectures: Hildegard von Bingen and Ruth Crawford Seeger.

'Yes sir, those women are master composers, yet I was forty years
old, an old man, before I heard of their music. I can't remember
dates and those kinds of detail, but Ruth Crawford Seeger is an
American twentieth-century composer whose work I find very
special; and Hildegard von Bingen was in medieval times, I think,
she worked in the Church but she was a composer, a mystic, a
scientist, a philosopher. She travelled all over Europe, she helped
the poor people, she wrote about medicine . . . She was a real
visionary, and established her own mystery system too.'*

---

*Ruth Crawford Seeger (1901–53) was an avant-garde composer whose compositions used
techniques like 'expressive silence and spatial separation of performing groups' (Jepson) as
well as '"heterophony", allowing several unrelated events to take place simultaneously'
(uncredited sleevenotes to *Piano Works*). In 1921 she began a nine-year period of study at the
American Conservatory in Chicago, where she became acquainted with a circle of composers
that included Edgard Varèse, Henry Cowell and Dane Rudhyar, the last of whom introduced
her to the work of Alexander Scriabin. Her best-known works include *Nine Preludes for
Piano* (1924–8), *String Quartet* (1931) and *Suite for Wind Quintet* (1952). See Jepson, 1980,
pp. 38–43.

'Mystery system?' I ask. 'What is that, exactly?'
'You've never heard of the Egyptian mystery system, the Nile Valley mystery system?'
I shake my head.
'Well then, the first thing I would say is for you to get the Wallis Budge books on Egypt, read *The Egyptian Book of the Dead*, read *The Tibetan Book of the Dead*.' Braxton laughs. 'Start there, then we'll get you more books.'

NEWCASTLE CONCERT, PEOPLE'S THEATRE

First Set (Primary Territories)
Composition 105B (+96)
Composition 60 (+108C)
Composition 69Q

Second Set (Primary Territories)
Composition 69H
Composition 69N (+96)
Composition 40B
Composition 110A (+108B)

(*108B* and *108C* are from the *108 (A–D)* series of 'pulse tracks', that is notated rhythm tracks interspersed with brief spaces for improvisation: these are played, usually by bass and percussion,

---

Hildegard von Bingen (1098–1179) was Abbess of the Benedictine convent at Disibadenberg and later founded a new convent (Rupertsberg) near the town of Bingen, on the Rhine. A naturalist, playwright, poet, philosopher and composer, von Bingen was also – literally – a visionary who saw (and heard) revelations from God which she described in three illustrated books – *Liber Servias, Liber Vitae Meritorum* and *Liber Divinorum Operum Simplicis Hominis*. She also wrote books on natural history and medicine, one of the earliest mystery plays (with music), and a large collection of music and poetry, the *Symphonia armonie celestium revelationum (Symphony of the Harmony of Celestial Revelations)*, now reckoned to include some of the finest, and most experimental, music of the Middle Ages. 'The songs are conceived on a large – sometimes a massive – scale . . . The corresponding musical resources are immense, ranging from the most tranquil melody to an almost obsessive declamation at high pitch. Everywhere we sense a movement of the mind in music . . . in Hildegard's words, of "writing, seeing, hearing and knowing all in one manner"' (from Christopher Page's sleevenotes to the LP *A Feather on the Breath of God*). Von Bingen's cosmology was a variation of the Pythagorean model, while her medical theories employed many of the same mystical correspondences as Renaissance Hermeticism (see 'Postscript 1'). See also Alic, 1986, pp. 62–76; Grant, 1980, pp. 6–10; Warner, 1987, pp. 184–95

with various other compositions from the Braxton repertoire.*
Composition 96 is originally a work for orchestra and four slide
projectors, but Braxton inserts notated sections from *96* into the
quartet music, where they are played by reeds and/or bass and/or
percussion either in designated solo spots or as optional accompaniment 'under' the primary territory.)†

I can't get into the first set tonight. I'm sitting right in front of
the drums, and they're *loud*. Plus, I'm still trying to follow the
musical structures and getting hopelessly lost. For the second set, I
change seats, stop worrying, and become completely absorbed in
the music. There's a slowly unfolding tension to the set, like a held
breath that's gradually expelled in the tease and tug of group
interplay. Gerry Hemingway, in the middle of a hushed solo, is
joined by a baby crying in the auditorium; unperturbed, he turns a
potential disruption into a conversation, duetting with the cries,
maintaining the flow. The quieter passages tonight have a delicate,
almost serene, quality; then there are sudden bursts of sound, the
quartet sprinting forward like hares – *40B*, for example, one of my
favourite Braxton 'bebop' tunes, has a marvellously exhilarating
swing to it. Marilyn Crispell's speed is incredible; not just her speed
of playing, but her speed of response. She plays so hard and fast,
yet each note sounds unhurried, placed exactly *right*.

'It's so inspiring to see a woman play like that,' Katy murmurs at
the end.

I ask her opinion of Braxton.

'Oh, he was the heart of the music, of all its colours and
contradictions. He has a *generous* presence too, I felt like a guest in
his house.'

Backstage, I ask Braxton for the set list. He looks up in horror.
'Graham, I've forgotten it already!' He flips through the scores,
calling out numbers like a bingo-master, asking the quartet which
ones they've just played. Nobody seems quite sure. 'The last one
was the curved sound piece,' he mutters, frowning. 'Is that *110A*? I
get the numbers confused.'

Gerry grins. 'Huh, Anthony, you're still captain of the Space
Cadets.'

---

*For more on pulse track structures, see pp. 121, 195–206 and 261–4 below
†For more on this use of *Composition 96*, see p. 202 below

METAROAD

FOREGROUND MUSIC 1

PAUL DESMOND – 'ONLY THE ESSENCE REMAINED'

B: I have eight million heroes.
L: OK, let's take them one at a time. Paul Desmond was your first major influence?
B: Yes, Paul Desmond would open the door of the saxophone world for me.
L: What was the attraction?
B: What *is* the attraction, because I have never stopped loving this man's music. The first thing I recall that struck me about it was his sound. The sound grabbed me. Then, after that, his logic grabbed me – held me in its grip, in fact. I think Paul Desmond's music is widely misunderstood on many levels. He was fashionable for the wrong reasons and he was hated for the wrong reasons. In retrospect, when I look at his life, his is a kind of . . . what's the word? Kind of mysterious music, he's not always there.
L: Enigmatic?
B: Enigmatic, thank you. I understood that better when I met Mr Desmond. I met him in Paris, though actually I said hello to him in the street before. He turned around and looked at me – I said, thank you very much for your music, sir. He said, well – thank you. And suddenly I understood everything, because while I was talking to him I was aware of the fact that he was way over here. I mean, he was not *there*, in the sense that we talk of there. He had already plotted out five seconds ahead of time what he was gonna do, and you could hear it in his music. It looked like he was a very slow

62

player, but in fact he was making very quick decisions, and because he understood his craft so well his music has this air of easiness about it, as if it's just kind of floating. But, oh, the man is very ahead, a profound thinker. He was far ahead of what you heard: what you heard had been edited completely, only the essence remained. Desmond understood how to get to the point quicker than most players ever learn. This is a lightning-fast improviser, who understood sound logic and how to prepare the event.

THE TIGHTROPE OF 'IT' – MASTERS

Desmond too was a very good chess player; I hear it in his music. He actually had his personal language within the style of so-called jazz. He was never afraid to walk the tightrope. It didn't look like he was walking on the tightrope, but he was there – right on the line of invention, the line of *it*. His solo flights fired me up as a young boy, then later as a teenager, as a man, and now as an old cruster. It fires me up because it's all *it*. I'm surprised that people are not able to hear his influence – no saxophonist has put their stamp on me more than Paul. Well, I'd say Paul, Coltrane and Warne Marsh would put their stamp on me deeper than any other instrumentalists.

L: I know you've dedicated compositions to Coltrane and Marsh; are there any to Desmond?

B: The saxophone piece on *The Complete Braxton*, the overdubbed soprano piece, is dedicated to Paul Desmond. Is that right? – I think it is. I was afraid to tell him that, though, when I met him in the street, I didn't want to bother him. He was a strange man. He became very successful in the monetary sense of the word, but he never got what he wanted. He wanted the respect of the African masters; they denied him that, and they should not have denied him. Duke Ellington didn't deny him, Charles Mingus acknowledged him; but Miles Davis, I think it was, spat on him verbally in public, talked about Desmond's sound insultingly. It was very fashionable not to respect Desmond, but he touched a lot of people's hearts. That's the thing about the masters that's so interesting: you can say what you like, but masters can touch your heart and change your life. In the case of Desmond, I *know* that's true.

L: Do any of your records particularly show Desmond's influence?

B: *All* of my recordings show the influence of Paul Desmond. But remember, I never wanted to imitate anybody because that would insult the masters. What I liked about them was that they found their own way. You have to do that; and the only way you can do that is, you have to know yourself. You have to know what you believe in and you have to set out on a path and develop it. It's the only way. You can't theorize it, even. You can theorize some of it, but you've got to live it, and experience it, and you have to be tested to make sure that you believe what you say you believe.

Desmond understood that he couldn't deal with Charlie Parker's dynamic, electric brilliance – he knew he couldn't out-Charlie Parker Charlie Parker – but he also knew he could create the same aura by playing slower. So you go to the opposites. You've heard the old saying, listen to everybody so you know what *not* to play. As soon as I hear the pentatonic scale or the Parker licks or the Coltrane licks, I say, OK – bang! – next! It's the ones who've put together their own language, their own syntax, their own way of being – those are the ones I'm interested in. That's why I love Paul. Plus, he understood how not to let even ruffles and flourishes get in the way of singing from the heart.

CHARLIE PARKER – TALKING

OF THE UPPER PARTIALS

L: It was later, after Desmond, that you began to listen to Charlie Parker?
B: Yes. Charlie Parker's effect on me would not be so apparent in the beginning. When I first heard Charlie Parker – the record was *Bird on 52nd Street* – that record frightened me. It frightened me, and it was the most exciting music I'd ever heard, and it was also talking of partials that I could not, as a young man, understand exactly.
L: Partials?
B: Spiritual partials, vibrational partials, upper scientific partials – different levels with respect to a given subject. Charlie Parker solidified all of the language dynamics that took place in his time period and, like Louis Armstrong before him, his language would express the – what's the word? – the *brilliance* of the era and all the people who had worked to solidify bebop. I've always disagreed with the concept that Charlie Parker was, like, the only

restructuralist, at the expense of Wardell Gray, Lester Young and Coleman Hawkins: all of those people are part of a continuum. But Charlie Parker is one of the masters. His work made it possible for the intellectual and vibrational dynamics of African-American creativity to be carried further. It's because of Charlie Parker that we have the lineage moving into John Coltrane, to Albert Ayler, later to Roscoe Mitchell and Joseph Jarman. There was more in his music than just the notes: I mean, his notes, his ideas, would set the stage for the projectional possibilities of trans-African and world culture information dynamics. His work personified the next juncture of the post-existential African-American, vibrationally and intellectually, after the Second World War.

L: What do you mean?

B: Well, Charlie Parker's music and the solidification of bebop would represent many different things. Bebop would represent a serious break between the black middle-class community and the restructuralist revolutionary intellectuals and intellectual thought that was gathering in that period. For instance, bebop would extend separately (in terms of what I call the affinity insight principle)* from the Baptist Church continuum that had solidified; I'm thinking of the gospel and spiritual musics that developed as a direct affirmation of, and linkage to, the community and in that context men and women would go to the church and participate in shaping that music. It became a profoundly important music that contributed to the information feed of American culture on several levels. But bebop was different. It emphasized the individual, the solo; and it was existential in the sense that musicians would look for God, for meaning, on a personal level, in the music. Also, bebop took place in the back rooms, the smoke-filled rooms . . .

Of course, the gangster community in America has always had its relationship to so-called 'black exotica' in every period. You can't talk about New Orleans, for example, without talking about the political forces that affected, or even caused, the situation where early jazz was associated with the red-light districts, and the separation between the rich blacks and the house blacks. You can't talk about Kansas City without looking at the Pendergast political machine that ran the town, and its relationship to the music's formings. There's a long history to how black culture has been

*For more on the affinity insight principle, see the footnote to pp. 312–13 below

reduced to terms of 'black exotica', and black people seen only in terms of their sexuality. It's happening to white women too in the Western media today. The music has always been associated with the red-light district and all of that mentality, as if the music was an affirmation of lower partials, or sin,* when in fact in every phase all of the masters had a viewpoint about humanity, and the music that was solidified – the science and vibrational dynamics of that music – held forth the most positive alternatives for the culture.

So Charlie Parker's music would shape the vibrational . . . *bridges* that were operating in his time period, and set those forces into motion. His language especially would be so dynamic that all the saxophonists would be blinded by him for a period of twenty years, and even now many people have not been able to think in terms of establishing their own vocabularies because of the brilliance of his language. Unlike the people who would take his music, Charlie Parker didn't repeat himself. His music was always living, always fresh, always trying to be honest.

THE POST-PARKER CONTINUUM

L: You've used the phrase 'the post-Parker continuum' in the lectures: presumably you're referring to those people still playing Charlie Parker's language?
B: Yes, but let me be clear. When I talk about the post-Parker continuum, I'm talking about a continuum of stylists and I have respect for that continuum. The master stylists who would take Charlie Parker's music as a point of departure and within that vocabulary try to make something special happen, people like Cannonball Adderley – they can still be original. But the music that is now coming from the universities – the assumption there being that the technical solutions and scientific dynamics of bebop are now understood, which I say is completely untrue – those people are fundamentally misusing the music, as far as I'm concerned. They're not really playing bebop, they're playing other people's solutions and other people's versions of Charlie Parker. But Charlie

*See, for example, Scott, 1976, who attributes the appearance of jazz to 'the Dark Forces' and blames a variety of modern ills, from 'a marked decline in sexual morals' to an increased 'love of sensationalism' on the music, which, he claimed, 'inflamed, intoxicated and brutalized' and was 'entirely divorced from any more exalted musical content' (pp. 142–4). Scott's book on music is one of the best-known from the Western mystical tradition; and his view of jazz appears to be the standard one in such circles

Parker was participating with affinity insight dynamics, with respect to his own life, to what he set into motion, to what he was thinking about. There's a big difference between what Mr Parker was playing and how his music is currently being used.

'BLACK EXOTICA' – THE CONCEPT
OF AFRICAN INFERIORITY

L: You said in a 1984 *Cadence* interview* that you felt the *intellectual* content of Charlie Parker's music had been completely neglected. Could you explain that a little?

B: Well, what has happened . . . This is part of the misinformation that African-Americans are dealing with, and the position of powerlessness that we are in as regards having the possibility to make our definitions stick. Charlie Parker's music is separated from his actual thoughts. It's as if the notion they're trying to perpetuate – they being the power structure and the collective forces of Western culture – is that this man is sticking all of this dope into his arm and just playing, without making any kind of intelligent decisions about the music.

L: You mean the glamorization of pain? Like a kind of intellectual pornography?

B: Well, it's all a part of what I was just talking about, 'black exotica'; that being the notion of separating the results of the music from what the person was thinking, and portraying the person as a dope addict or as incapable of establishing a thought that's valuable enough to be respected, that comes with its own value systems. What the Europeans have done, I think, is to undercut trans-African, even world culture, value systems; and this is not separate from the moves that have taken place in the last 300 years to justify what has happened in Africa, and to justify the present notion of human beings . . . the idea that a person's IQ is a justification for saying he or she is a better person, or not a better person, and from that point to say that some lives are better than other lives, and then to say let's get rid of those lives which are not as good as the other lives . . . the concept of African inferiority.†

I'm sorry, we're getting away from my eight million heroes (*laughs*). But all these matters are connected.

*Carey, p. 6
†See also 'Postscript 2', pp. 313ff

ERIC DOLPHY – BEBOP TO EXTREMES

L: OK, I wanted to ask you about Eric Dolphy. A lot of people see you as the heir to his musical explorations, but you haven't mentioned him as an influence at the lectures.

B: Oh, my work has constantly been compared to Mr Dolphy's and, of course, in my late forming period, just before I began to move into my own music, I did listen to Eric's music. But, in fact, his music was very different to mine, in the kind of . . . I don't know, his music was just different! (*Laughs.*) I recall buying the *Out There* record; I thought I was listening to a violin – that's how strange his sound was to me, and how incredible the facility he had. For instance, Ornette Coleman, who we'll probably get to, his music would really open up my world on another level; Eric's reaffirmed what I was already learning.

L: Was his multi-instrumentalism an influence at all? His solo performances?

B: His work with bass clarinet and flute would certainly up the *ante* for multi-instrumentalism, and that he was such a virtuoso on all of his instruments would help me to aim for achieving the broadest range I could possibly achieve; I enjoyed his bass clarinet solos but in fact I see my solo music as being very separate from that. I was always impressed by Eric as a musician, but I was not as influenced by him as people have thought. I look back on it now like Eric was kind of an extension of Charlie Parker: his music makes a lot of sense if you look at Charlie Parker's language and gravillic* formings, but suddenly stretched to extremes. It's like a disjointed, extended bebop vocabulary that would stress extreme intervallic distances but basically used the same language (though his later records, like *Out to Lunch*, show his language evolving too). I was coming from a Lester Young forming affinity continuum: from Lester Young on through Bird to Konitz, to Marsh, then into Jackie McLean. Then, I think I was always more influenced by ametrical formings than by the type of metric formings that we now associate with Charlie Parker. It's funny, because I learned about Lester Young after I'd heard Warne Marsh and the power of his music would clarify a lot for me in terms of progressionalism and vocabulary dynamics, because Lester was the root that Konitz and

*For an explanation of gravillic formings, see pp. 99ff below

Marsh would adopt. His solutions to language and to formings would open up that whole continuum. So Eric Dolphy's work was very exciting to me, but I never felt that his way was my way.

JACKIE MCLEAN, ROY HAYNES
JIMMY GIUFFRE

L: You've mentioned Jackie McLean a few times. Was he a big influence?

B: Oh Jackie McLean, yeah! I had thirty, forty records by Mr McLean. I lost them all when I went into the army, and also when I went to Europe; each time I lost probably 1,000 records. I like Jackie McLean, I like the feeling of his music, his sound, and I like the way he can play blues. There's a record I remember called *A Long Drink of the Blues* where the musicians start to play, then they stop and begin to argue – on the record – then they play again. It was a strange record, but, boy, the music goes right to *it*. It's *real*; frighteningly beautiful. On the second side Jackie plays three ballads, *I Cover the Waterfront, Embraceable You, These Foolish Things* – it's a very special record. I recall being greatly affected by his music, his sense of timing. I liked *Let Freedom Ring*, when he was changing his music, and later too, as he moved into his modal period, the records with Charles Tolliver and *It's Time* with Roy Haynes, who is a master percussionist. I played with Mr Haynes as a young man but he would never remember it;* since becoming an adult I've never had the opportunity to play with Mr Haynes and I love, *love*, his music.

I tell you who else I'd like to mention – Jimmy Giuffre. I learned a great deal from Mr Giuffre. The work he did in the trio format with Paul Bley (who's another special one) and Steve Swallow is very important to my evolution. Not only that, his arrangements behind Lee Konitz, Sonny Stitt, his work with the Modern Jazz Quartet . . . I think he also has a couple of records with a symphony orchestra playing his chamber music or orchestral music. I've always greatly respected Jimmy Giuffre. I forgot to mention him in my own book! I feel horrible about it, but I'd have never got the book out if I'd mentioned everybody in the world I wanted to mention. I hope I've got him into this book (*laughs*).

*On Dave Brubeck's *All the Things We are* LP

ORNETTE COLEMAN – REAFFIRMING
THE AFRICAN COMPOSER

L: Let's finish today with Ornette Coleman.

B: Mr Coleman . . . his work was a landmark for me. In grammar
school I had two friends, Pierre and Tommy Evans, they lived
about two blocks away, and one day – I had been well into my
Desmond records in this period – one day I went with Tommy over
to their house and Mr Evans, he was like one of the guys in the
neighbourhood who listened to jazz, not hip but *maybe* hip, a nice
man, though, he knew about the music, he told me, look, take this
record home, this is where the music's going, you listen to this. The
record was *The Shape of Jazz to Come*, I put it on – G-o-o-o-o-d-d-d-
d-a-a-a-a-m-m-m-m!!! This saxophonist!!! . . . I mean, he doesn't
sound like Desmond, this is not a Desmond sound, this isn't where
the music's going! There must be some mistake! I took the record
back – Mr Evans, please, that was the strangest shit I ever heard in
my life. Then, over the next couple of weeks – Wow! That was a
strange record! Let me borrow it again. I put it on – hmm, this is
not music, it's just *not* music. I took it back. The next week I'd be
listening again – hmm! His compositions *Lonely Woman* and *Peace*
were on that record, so it was like – Wow, this is really beautiful,
I've never heard compositions like this. And the solos Ornette took
on that record were so special.

So I went through a period of about six months saying, you
know, I don't like this music. Maybe I like it a little bit. OK, this
part is interesting but this part I definitely *don't* like – I mean,
what're they *doing* there? Finally, it was – Yeah! There's something
happening here I don't know about.

I think Ornette Coleman . . . Oh my God, he's a dynamic
master. I think the press has still not been able to convey to people
the significance of this man – what he really *did*. Ornette Coleman
re-established the affinity dynamic implications of trans-African
functionalism. He would solve the problem of complicated vertical
harmonic progressions, which were either interesting or not
interesting, but his work re-established the fact that the music is
not about any one way of functioning. He would also extend the
existential implications of trans-African information dynamics; I
mean, his work set into motion so many variables that people are
still dealing with him and they'll be dealing with him for another
1,000 years.

As a composer, his *Skies of America* is a dynamic piece, as are the quartet musics in all of the various periods. This is a unique composer. His work would open up the world of composition to me on another level. Before, I was beginning to enjoy Brubeck's composition (Brubeck, I might add, is a very good composer), and the Lennie Tristano school, with their wonderful melodic lines, I was always seduced by them. But Coleman had that in his music, he had a line-forming music, he had a chamber music, his string quartets. He would open up the lid of the genie lamp for the next generation of African-American composers and intellectuals like myself. None of my work would have been possible were it not for Ornette Coleman. Mr Coleman would re-establish the concept, reaffirm the existence, of the African composer; *and* he defined his terms with respect to *his* value systems.

L: Looking back, it seemed in the sixties that Ornette Coleman's music became overshadowed rather by the impact of Coltrane and Cecil Taylor – that emphasis on energy music. Then the AACM reasserted the sense of space and flow which Ornette Coleman had.

B: That's right. We were more attuned to the structuralists, Coleman and Charles Mingus, and what they were doing. We were aware that the spectrum range that many of the New York musicians were dealing with was narrow: everybody was ready to take Coltrane's language and just stay right there, as if evolution stopped at Coltrane. The musicians were not thinking in terms of establishing syntax or structure, they were responding to the emotional dynamics of that music. And, of course, their response was dynamic; their music certainly helped me. But in Chicago, our emphasis on structure and the mechanics of the music would, in terms of what has transpired in the last twenty years, mark the difference between the AACM and the New York school. I have a great deal of respect for that first wave of musicians to begin practising the music of Coltrane and Taylor – people like Marion Brown, Archie Shepp, Giuseppi Logan – but it was the Chicago school who supplied the structural and scientific dynamics of what that revolution implied.

ROAD

FRIDAY 15, MANCHESTER

We meet in the hotel lobby at 11 a.m. Mark has bought *The Times* and, slumped in an armchair, is reading a review of the London concert.

'What's a Heinkel?' he frowns, pointing to a phrase in the paper: ' *"Dresser's imitation of a droning flight of Heinkels"*. Is it a bird?'

Marilyn, reading over his shoulder, gasps in disbelief. 'It says Anthony left "no space for emotional projection". This guy has to be joking!'

Braxton appears, swaddled in Evan Parker's yellow overcoat. 'Is that a review?'

'Yeah, but it's a weird one,' Gerry warns.

'One of those, huh?' Braxton reads. When he reaches the sentence *'Braxton is using a traditional line-up to create a formal context for the vocabulary of sounds developed by the community of free improvisers – and the Europeans in particular – in the 1970s'* he hits the roof. 'That's a lie, that's completely untrue. I had my own language in the 1960s, long before I came to Europe. We were developing our own vocabularies in Chicago. Europeans just can't believe that somebody else could have done something before they did.' His face tightens with anger. 'This is the kind of nonsense I get all the time from so-called jazz critics.'

Oops. I sink into my chair, trying hard to be invisible. It's no easy task to review music as structurally complex as Braxton's, but in this case my sympathy is tempered by the thought that anyone who merely trots out the old clichés about 'European influences' and 'no emotion' deserves all the flak that's going.

Mark is still puzzled. 'Do you know what a Heinkel is, Anthony? It says I sound like a flight of Heinkels.'

72

Braxton lays a hand on Mark's shoulder. 'You better leave the group, Dresser. Your reputation will be besmirched if you play with me. Already they're calling you a Heinkel.'

The drive to Manchester, skirting the edge of the Pennines, is pleasantly sunny. Already everyone has their own seat in the tour van. Tony Cresswell drives, Braxton sits next to him, rarely speaking; Marilyn and Mark occupy the middle seat; Gerry and I are at the back with Mark's bass. (The only variation in the next two weeks will be that Mark and I sometimes change places.) Gerry has brought a Walkman, two sets of headphones, and several boxes of cassettes – reggae, gospel, C&W, everything! He tells me he began as a rock fan, particularly of British art-rock bands like King Crimson and May Blitz; in the seventies he lived in New Haven, playing a lot with Leo Smith and Anthony Davis; now he's in New York, with a small recording studio in his apartment and his own record label, Auricle, which he runs on a zero budget. Before long, we move on to politics, exchanging mutual bewilderments. How can Americans have failed to ratify the Equal Rights Amendment? How can the British go on building nuclear power stations? You re-elected Reagan? *You* re-elected Thatcher? Aaarghhh! I shake my head: I thought we were supposed to get wiser as we got older, instead things just become more inexplicable.

Mark brings us back to basics, turning around to prod at his instrument like an anxious parent. 'It's a lot tougher to play than the bass I have in San Diego,' he complains. 'You can *swear* on that bass; this one is less responsive, more hard work. You really have to carve the sound out.'

'Is it a problem on those faster pieces?' I ask.

He nods. 'Some of the scores are pretty complex, you really have to move.'

Braxton turns around. 'Yeah, but once you get through the agony and sweat, it's fun. Just don't blink or cough, or you'll miss five notes.'

'Don't you ever get nervous counting some of those times?' Mark asks. '13/2?'

'Yes sir,' says Braxton. 'The problem is, when I get nervous I count it faster.'

Gerry laughs. 'That's typical Braxton – when in doubt, count faster.'

'How *do* you count 13/2?' Mark frowns.

'You just stuff it in,' Braxton says. 'Count the two strong, and

just stuff the rest in. That's all you have time to do.' He grins:
'Then, when you're comfortable with 13/2, it's time to move on to
17½/2!'

We arrive in Manchester, check in to our hotel, then look for
lunch. Tony discovers there are a couple of vegetarian restaurants
nearby, so Gerry, Mark, Marilyn and I opt to try one. Braxton is
disgusted. 'Eat with Hemingway! I once spent *two hours* walking
around with Gerry Hemingway before we found a place he'd *deign*
to eat in. I'm an old man now and I've still got a lot of work to do; I
don't have *time* to eat with people like Gerry Hemingway and
Graham Lock!' He hurries off to the nearest McDonalds.

'We have to convert him,' I say to Gerry.

He shrugs. 'No chance. I've been trying for the last two years.'

'We tried to take him out for a meal, the evening before the
London concert,' Marilyn relates. 'When he realized we were going
to a real restaurant, he ran away.'

Braxton's words prove prophetic. We find the first vegetarian
restaurant; it's not open until the evening. We fail to find the
second; eventually a passer-by tells us it closed down six months
ago. Crisis! I'm due back at the hotel to interview Braxton in less
than thirty minutes. Starving for art, yes; but starve for *journalism*?
We split up: Gerry and Mark head for Chinatown, Marilyn and I
hurry into a handy Baked Potato Bar.

Between mouthfuls, I ask her what she thinks of Braxton's
theory of the feminine vibration. She looks startled.

'Oh, I haven't read his books. But I'm not a feminist.'

'How come?'

'I guess I've never needed to be. I've always gone out and done
what I wanted to do.' She toys with her potato. 'I was asked to play
at a women's concert recently, but I said no. I wasn't very popular
after that.' Her voice is quiet; there are hesitant pauses between
each sentence. 'I guess I don't really believe in women's music or
men's music. I just think . . . music is music.'

I decide I'd better make my sympathies clear, so I explain about
Katy's examination of music as a male language. 'Writing about
music too,' I add, 'I've found there are lots of words for male
strength – virile, masterful, even seminal – which are all praise
words, but there are no equivalent words for female strength. Some
rock writers have been reduced to saying a woman performer has
balls!'

Marilyn stares at me. 'Maybe female strength is less obvious; but in many ways women are the stronger sex – women give birth, live longer. I mean, people often say to me "you play like a man" because I'm so physical on the piano, but they mean it as a compliment.'

'That's what I mean. They're applying male standards all the time.'

'Yeah, but I can't get upset about it. I just think it's funny.' She shrugs, with a private, dreamy smile. I ask her if she makes any money from her music. She shakes her head. 'So how do you survive?'

'I get help from my parents. Sometimes I work as a hostess in a French restaurant in Woodstock, near where I live. You know, serving drinks, making up bills, showing people to their tables.'

I remember that back in the early sixties Marilyn's great hero, Cecil Taylor, used to work in a restaurant when he couldn't get any gigs. What was particularly galling was that they'd play his records over the restaurant PA while he was stuck in the kitchen, washing dishes. History repeats itself, not so much as farce as entrenched philistinism.

When I return to the hotel, Braxton is already waiting outside my door. I apologize for being late. 'We couldn't find anywhere to eat,' I explain. His eyes gleam, but he says nothing. A true gentleman.

The soundcheck is at 6.30. To my surprise, the group run through a standard, *Tune Up*, plus a few Braxton charts. Then we retire to the dressing-room and sip Perrier water. Braxton shuffles his scores, compiling the sets. 'OK, let's begin with *23C*, then, ah, *69B*, *69J* . . . no, let's open the second set with that . . . *69(O)* after *69B* then . . . have we done *40M* yet?' Blank faces all round. 'I don't think so. OK, *40M* to close the first set.' And so on.

Everybody sorts through their parts. Mark, still a new boy, looks worried. 'The up arrows mean *no play*, the down arrows mean *play*, right?' he asks Gerry.

'Either that or *vice versa*,' Gerry grins.

Just before they go onstage, the quartet sing through the opening of *23C* together. 'So we all get the rhythm right from the outset,' Braxton explains.

MANCHESTER CONCERT, OPERA THEATRE, ROYAL
NORTHERN COLLEGE OF MUSIC

First Set (Primary Territories)
Composition 23C
Composition 69B
Composition 69(O)
Composition 40M

Second Set (Primary Territories)
Composition 69J
Collage Form Structure (Piano *31*, reeds *96*, bass and drums *108A*)
Composition 34
Composition 69F
Composition 69G

(Curiously, the only concert in which Braxton didn't include any
of his more recent quartet compositions. With the exceptions of *34*
and the collage form structure, the material all comes from the *23*
(A–P) series, the *40 (A–Q)* series and the *69 (A–Q)* series, which,
together with the *6 (A–P)* series, comprise the bulk of the quartet
repertoire.)

I'm still struggling to get to grips with the music, but at last the
outlines are coming into focus. The group's interactions are
mercurial: solos, duos, trios; support, reaction, opposition. A flow
of instantaneous realignments too rapid for my pen.

23C begins with Braxton on flute, skipping phrases, then long
notes, building into an intense solo while Gerry flails the kit with
bare hands. Braxton switches to sopranino, then alto, as the tempo
shifts from jaunty to ferocious through *69B*. A percussion solo
changes the kinetics again, and clarinet trills lead into the graceful,
almost courtly airs of *69(O)*. Bass and drums duet on scraping
sounds; then comes a chiming piano solo; Braxton's joining in on
sopranino heralds a complex ensemble section before Mark's dark,
swooning bass lines lead into *40M*, with flying solos from Braxton
(on alto) and Marilyn.

69J is frilly, spirited at first, then the music grows dense and
difficult, passing imperceptibly into the collage form structure; the
separate compositions hanging apart-yet-together in the space, like
interlacing fountains. This fades, and Gerry is tapping out little

runs on the tom-tom, then rubbing the skins with his palms, a barely audible squeak that begins a mesmerizing solo – tiny crumbs of sound floating in space. Braxton's sopranino guides the group through the repeating, descending steps of *34*, then Mark ushers in *69F*: hushed caesuras, low, eerie timbres, Gerry just clicking the rim of his cymbal. The alto whispers a change and the group realign, via a lovely ensemble improvisation, into the faster, boppish lines of *69G*, with more fierce solos from Braxton and Marilyn before the group slot back into the theme, rush it helter-skelter around the block and – *VROOOM!* – halt on a T.

When I get back to the dressing-room, Braxton looks up. 'Ah, Graham. How did the flute sound?'

'Well, it . . . fine, I think.'

'Was the sound differentiation OK?'

'Um . . . yeah . . . I guess so.'

'Was I standing close enough to the mike?'

'Uh . . . I . . . yeah, it was all right.'

Braxton raises his eyebrows. 'Thanks Graham. Not too much information at once, now.'

Everybody laughs. I wish again I were invisible. It's not been a happy day for so-called jazz critics.

The sound has actually been very good. The sound engineer, Paul Sparrow (who is travelling with us, but separately, in his own van, with all the equipment), is the best kind of specialist, very efficient yet sensitive to the group's particular needs. The only problem he will have is that some venues have better acoustics than others; but he invariably gets the optimum results in the circumstances. 'If the sound is bad,' he wryly notes, 'the sound man gets all the blame. If the sound is good, the band get all the praise.'

After the gig, John Cumming reappears, accompanied by Annette Moreau from the Contemporary Music Network who's here to check that everything is running smoothly.

Mark looks up hopefully. 'Hey, do you people know what a Heinkel is?'

'It's an aeroplane, isn't it?' says Annette. 'A German bomber.'

Mark frowns, then laughs. 'Damn, I still don't know if it's good or bad.'

We all go out for a Chinese meal. Someone asks Braxton what it's like living in California. Why do people risk living in an earthquake zone?

'If your job's there, if your home's there, what can you do? I guess most people can't afford to move. Plus, they don't have any place to go.'

He tells the old joke about the guy in San Francisco who's sitting in the house late at night smoking a huge joint. Suddenly there's an earth tremor: the walls tremble, the curtains flap madly, the ornaments dance along the mantelpiece. The guy looks on, awed. 'Hmm, this weed is *strong.*'

Later, the talk turns to astrology. Braxton and Marilyn are firm believers, and Braxton has used astrology and astrological correspondences in several of his compositions. He's a Gemini (Air sign), Marilyn and Gerry are Aries (Fire sign) and Mark is a Libra (Air sign).

'There's a lot of Air in this group, Mercury too,' Braxton declares. 'Things flying about all over the place. Air signs generally like my music, but Earth signs hate it.'

Knowing of Braxton's interest in astrology, I'd asked a friend who's also a student of astrology to draw up Braxton's birth chart before the tour (see p. 79). I hadn't told him who the subject was, just given a birth date – 4 June 1945 – and place – Chicago. (Unfortunately, I hadn't known Braxton's exact time of birth then, so a really detailed reading was not possible.) This is what he sent me.

'What I've done is to consider the more significant relationships on the chart, and note their ascribed attributes, paying particular attention to what seem to be the recurring factors.

1. Sun conjunct Uranus
If the time of birth was around 3 a.m. [*it was 2 a.m. – GL*], then the conjunct is almost exact, which is extremely rare, suggesting this person is involved in revolutionary or transformational activity of some sort. If not, I'd still say this is someone who's highly self-aware, who moves freely in their chosen environment, and expresses themself in a unique fashion, even though many people may think it eccentric. A wilful person too, shocked by attempts to restrain them, jealously guarding their right to be themself. They'll speak their mind without compromise, and fight for their freedom. Is intolerant of tradition, or rather of the limitations it imposes. An innovator with electrifying qualities, but may be judged unstable even by those who are sympathetic. Possibly an arrogant person, especially when young. Progressive in outlook. Interested in

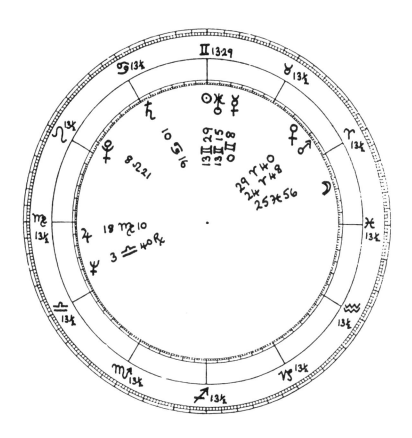

Birth Chart: Anthony Braxton

science, politics, education, technology. Very into *progress*. The
past is accepted only as a basis for continued development. Excited
by expectations for the future, but needs to be earthed by
companions or could easily lose contact with reality. Chance of
insanity in some extreme circumstances.

2. *Mercury trine Neptune*
Suggests someone very good at communicating, particularly the
unconscious or hidden things. Very intuitive. Very artistic,
sensitive, intelligent. Perhaps a person who's happiest when
creating.

3. *Uranus sextile Pluto*
Someone shocked by injustice, ready to protest. Perhaps resents the
fact that powerful forces can apply economic pressures or controls.
Uncanny ability to discern dishonesty. Determined to be free.
Again, in extreme instances, elements of madness.

4. *Jupiter square Uranus*
Suggests power, lots of energy. Perhaps too much. A tendency to
bite off more than they can chew. Someone who's very capable, but
tries to do too much at once. Needs to establish priorities or is ruled
by enthusiasms. Not motivated for success, though, in worldly
terms – i.e. not interested in social accolades.

5. *Sun square Jupiter*
Again, a tendency to overdo things. Creativity is so flowing, he/she
gets carried away. Communication is a strong talent. Also, possible
tendency to accidents.

6. *Uranus in Gemini*
Person who works with flashing genius, very quick, lots of
inventiveness. Possibly eccentric too.

7. *Venus conjunct Mars in Aries*
Venus here indicates ardent in love affairs. Has strong feeling for
beauty. Strong affections, but maybe tends to be self-seeking. Mars
suggests lots of energy, assertive, emotionally warm, generous.
Someone who may be easily misunderstood, but who doesn't
give up.
    'I don't have the time of birth, so I can't be more specific.

Looking at the above possibilities, though, I think a picture begins to emerge of someone who is powerful, energetic, possibly quite eccentric – the extreme case would be genius bordering on insanity. An innovator, communicator, very quick, very creative, yet with a tendency to be over-ambitious with their plans or swept away by enthusiasm. Someone who's also very fierce in their beliefs about freedom and justice, particularly regarding their own freedom to do or say whatever they feel strongly about. If I had to guess, I'd say this is a radical politician or perhaps an avant-garde artist of some kind. Am I close?'*

*Later, we also checked out Braxton's claim that there was a lot of Air in the group. This is the allocation of planets in the element signs on each individual's chart. (We were unable to include Ascendants too as we did not have everybody's time of birth.)

	Air	Water	Fire	Earth
Braxton	3	2	3	2
Crispell	3	4	3	0
Dresser	5	1	3	1
Hemingway	2	5	2	1
	13	12	11	4

The interpretation of this is that the high number of Air and Water signs suggests that the group will be exceptionally strong in areas like inspiration, speed of communication, empathy and intuition; the above-average Fire total indicates a high level of energy and enthusiasm; while the strikingly low Earth total means there will be very few 'grounding' or traditional elements in the music, such as, for example, a regular beat. This is definitely a music that 'takes off'

METAROAD

BIOGRAPHY 2, 1969–74

'PEOPLE WERE THROWING ROCKS AT US'

L: You'd just arrived in Paris.

B: Yes, I looked out the taxicab window and there's Steve McCall! I'd heard Steve was in Copenhagen or Amsterdam. It was as if God was looking out for me. I was a typical young man who never thought about practicalities. That has been one of my resounding . . . I don't want to say flaws, but I've never been a practical person – and I have *paid* for it (*laughs*).

But suddenly I'm staying at Steve McCall's place – he had such a beautiful family! That same day I went to Montparnasse and ran into Joseph Jarman and Don Moye – Joseph looked up right into my face, he could *not* believe it (*chuckles*). They thought they'd seen the last of Braxton! (*Laughs.*) I also met Kenneth Terroade, Claude Delcloo; the magazine *Actuel* was starting; there was a whole new political scene beginning in Paris. Then Leo and Leroy arrived, they'd taken a boat over. Steve McCall joined the group, playing percussion. We lived on one side of the city, the Art Ensemble lived on the other.

L: The Art Ensemble were well-received in Europe, but the Creative Construction Company didn't go down so well. Why not?

B: There was a great debate in Paris that lasted maybe six months, and the verdict was that our music didn't swing, while the Art Ensemble represented the real gains of the AACM – in fact, the two virtually became synonymous.

There was a lot of confusion in that period. Our music was viewed as cold, intellectual, borrowing from Europe or something. We were not acceptable African-Americans. The image that surrounded my music in late Chicago would stay with me all my life – that being the concept of the intellectual separate from what the essence of black African intellectualism should be. For instance, I never talked of my music as being 'Great Black Music', I was more interested in world music, but this was never fashionable in African-American intellectual circles, especially from the mid-sixties through to the seventies. Any talk of universality was viewed as possibly disloyal to Africa. And among the white community, musicians like myself were seen as a parody of the intellectual or as somehow trying to imitate something we were not – I don't know how to explain it. But certainly my music, in terms of its intellectual content, would never be looked at on the same plane as Cage or Stockhausen or the Europeans.

L: The Creative Construction Company split up in Paris?

B: Yes. The Art Ensemble – they've held the group together through thick and thin, and that's very admirable, I think. The Creative Construction Company were not able to do that. Leo and I were both really into composition, the reality of the composer, and we each had our own vision of what we wanted to do. Leroy was more flexible, he was the guy who really wanted to work for the group and stay with it. Leo and I . . . we're so much alike: he's Sagittarius, I'm Gemini; he liked Boulez, I liked Stockhausen. I feel we've learned so much from each other, but we could not stay in the same space for too long. We would each want to go and do our own work.

We played in Paris for a year or so. It was a wonderful cycle. One concert, I think it was the Angoulême Festival or maybe Actuel, we were playing and people were throwing rocks at us, rocks and bricks. We were fighting off the bricks and still playing (*laughs*). One half of the crowd said 'boo!', the other half said 'yay!' It was an incredible experience. We had a lot of concerts where the audience at some point would take over – half liking it, half hating it.

Then Leo and I separated and I was not very happy in Paris. Originally I had gone to Europe with the understanding that I would never come back to America. I was tired of discrimination, tired of the American mentality. But after a year in Paris I found myself thinking . . . (*sighs*) . . . I wasn't finished with America. So I went to New York. Ornette Coleman had come to hear us at a club in Montparnasse, he gave me his address and telephone number and when I came back to New York I lived with him. This guy took me in like a son, really. He was so beautiful to me.

L: What do you mean when you say you were not finished with America?

B: Well . . . for instance, it became apparent that for me to continue the work I wanted to do I would have to pursue my direction separate from the Art Ensemble. Not just from the Art Ensemble, but from the whole scene that was developing – using Africa, talking about Africa and African things in the morning, and then in the evening committing the vilest crimes against humanity. That's *all* I'll say about that!

L: Ah . . . that's very enigmatic.

B: (*shrugs, long pause*) Next question!

L: Why did you go to New York rather than Chicago?

B: In Paris I'd had a taste of what life can be like in a non-segregated environment. Chicago is a very politically and racially divided city. It's also a very oppressive city: if you're an African-American growing up on the West Side or many areas of the South Side, you can develop a very unhealthy outlook – especially about black people and white America, those political dynamics. Like, in Chicago, if you walk outside your community, you could be killed very quickly; in the area where Mayor Daley lived, an African-American could be killed just by walking down the street. Plus, there's the crimes that black people commit against themselves, the gang mentality – Chicago is a very *violent* place. It's a dynamic place too, but in the final analysis it's a city with a small-town mentality, whereas New York is a city with a city mentality, even if it is *sick* (*laughs*).

I knew I could never survive doing my life's work in Chicago, and as fond as I became of Hostess Twinkies and cupcakes, this was not the kind of thing you could build a future on. Later, I would find that whenever I went back to the city, I'd think of my father, who passed in . . . 1971, I think. No, I had too many memories of growing up in Chicago. I did not want to go back there.

CHESS HUSTLER – A LOST GENERATION

L: It was when you moved to New York that you gave up music and became a chess hustler for several months?

B: Yes. First I went home to Chicago to say hello to my family, then Leroy Jenkins and I drove up to New York and we lived in the basement of Ornette Coleman's house on 42nd Street. In that period, as now, I was always extremely broke, so I made my living playing chess.

L: How does a chess hustler operate in New York City?

B: You go down to Washington Square Park, which has been, historically, a chess venue for years – the chess boards are set into the tables in the park. All the hustlers go there. You sit down, find someone to play, and play 'em for a dollar or two a game, find out what they can do. Then you play 'em for five dollars, or whatever. If you're a gentleman, you make sure you lose sometimes, but you also try to win as much money as you can.

L: How much were you making?

B: I'd say maybe ten, fifteen dollars a day on average. My life at that period became: wake up at 4 a.m., buy the *New York Times*, get the chess game of the day, go down to Washington Square Park, spend an hour or two working out problems, then spend the rest of the day playing people. Maybe get enough money for lunch, then go back and play some more or go to the Manhattan Chess Club, work out more problems . . . who needed music? I had come to a juncture in my life where I had to decide what I was going to do: play chess or play music? I made what I considered to be the best decision – chess.

L: Yet in 1965 you'd made a life's commitment to music.

B: Yes, but I was discovering . . . I knocked on every door in the world, begging people to perform some of my notated music. One of the reasons I got disillusioned in Paris, it became clear to me that I could maybe become successful as a saxophonist there, but I could not have my notated works respected; that, in fact, it might be even more difficult because the area of notated music was closed to me. My work would only be considered with respect to the value systems and terminologies developed for what they called 'jazz', that is 'black exotica'. This wasn't acceptable to me.

I came back to New York, and again I found there was no way I could do what I wanted to do. I was viewed as an alien. If I would just play the saxophone and behave, there was a possibility I could be accepted, but . . . After 1966 I had no doubt what I wanted to do with my life, my parameters had been defined by the masters, as I've said, and there was no possibility of compromise. I don't compromise. When I saw it was going to be virtually impossible to get notated works performed, or even to present the kind of instrumental projects I wanted to do, I found myself thinking – who needs this?

I had problems with the various musicians' camps in New York. Free musicians hated the guys who played chords; the bebop musicians hated the free guys. The white musicians were angry about black people; the black musicians were angry about white people. The downtown guys – Philip Glass, Steve Reich, the people into repetition – were angry about the uptown guys; the uptown guys – Sollberger, Davidovski, the post-Babbitt serialists – were angry about the downtown guys. And they *all* thought I was crazy, just for being there talking to them. So, like, you know – I must be crazy!

I felt as if I would never have the possibility of achieving my dreams in music. Plus, I got tired of the political games. But with the chess players I got along just fine.

L: What political games?

B: Well . . . this was also a period when the Black Power concepts that were surrounding the music became rampant. People were talking about black, black, black, black, black. It got very complex (*sighs*). I don't know . . . I became very tired of all the dishonesty . . . Though to say it like that, I don't mean I was looking down on people and seeing they were dishonest, I don't mean it like that. I only mean that I watched what was a dynamic time period, with all kinds of fresh musical solutions and the hope of evolution, I watched it all suddenly – dissipate. It was painful to see what ensued in the next ten years. From a group of fifty to a hundred young musicians who converged on the city with all kinds of hopes, maybe only four or five survived the drug problems, the record-company suppression, the media manipulation. It was like a whole generation of lost musicians.

Where the concept of freedom at one point held the possibility for new political order, new dreams, suddenly we see a generation who used their freedom as an excuse not to take care of basic responsibilities. That was one of the sad truths that accompanied the post-Ayler dynamics. It was also manifested in the post-Cage continuum, where we would see evolution used as an excuse for not trying to deal with fundamentals.

L: Presumably you're talking more of musical freedom than political freedom – can you be more specific?

B: I can't be more specific without talking about individuals, which I would never do.

LIVING WITH ORNETTE

L: Can you talk about Ornette? Was he playing at this time?
B: He gave brilliant concerts in New York in this period. He had Dewey Redman with him. I used to go to his concerts . . . I admired Ornette Coleman and I still admire him: the one thing I feel sad about when I think of Ornette is the article in *Coda* where I criticized him. I regret that profoundly, I feel horrible about it. He was really fair with me, and he's a *good* man outside of being a genius. In three months he taught me everything I needed to know about New York, the political dynamics that surround New York. Because Ornette *knows* – he understands how the whole scene works. That he has been able to plot his own course through it, this African-American from Fort Worth, Texas, who came to New York and delivered his vision of the world, that's incredible – a testament to what a genius he is. So after living with him in that period I was able to understand what New York is all about. New York is the platform of deals: everything is based on how flexible you are.
L: What did you say about him in *Coda*?
B: Oh, there was one sentence where I said something like, Ornette is out of it now. It was something only a young, arrogant man would allow himself to say – this was in '74, I think. I'm going to reprint that interview in *Composition Notes A* and also apologize to Mr Coleman; that's how strongly it affected me.
L: Did you play music with him in New York?
B: We rehearsed together; I don't think I ever played a concert with him. But I listened to him a lot. He was in the final stages of formulating his concept of harmolodics; not only that, he had done *Skies of America*. I watched what they put him through to do that project. But they couldn't stop him; he worked night and day . . .
L: 'They' being Columbia Records?
B: The power structure, the power people he had to deal with to get that project through.* Like I've said, African-American composers

*For example: 'In 1969 he started work on an ambitious project entitled *The Skies of America* which he planned would be played by his quartet and an eighty-piece orchestra. Coleman was perhaps being a little over-ambitious for a so-called "jazz" musician. Despite the fact that he was under contract to a major American record company, he was forced to cross the Atlantic to save money on the orchestra and not allowed to take his sidemen with him' (Wilmer, 1977, pp. 71–2). Mr Coleman's problems continued right up to and even during the recording sessions – see Wilmer, p. 11

and intellectuals are taboo. We've been sacrificed; our viewpoints are seen as not even secondary in this period.

CIRCLE — SCIENTOLOGY

L: It was Leroy Jenkins who persuaded you to perform again?
B: Yes. Leo Smith was coming to New York; so Leroy said, 'Let's do a get-together concert.' He organized a concert at Washington Square Peace Church; we invited Muhal Richard Abrams and Richard Davis as guests, Steve McCall was in New York too, and we played. It was a very nice concert. Jack DeJohnette came along, and afterwards he wanted to go play, so we ran down to the Village Vanguard. Chick Corea, Dave Holland and Barry Altschul were there, working as a trio, and they were fantastic. We sat in with them in the second set; Chick gave me his address and asked me to come by and play. The four of us began to practise and right from the beginning it felt good. We gave a concert – I think one half was put out by Japanese CBS – then Chick told me we had tickets for California. We were a group! Those guys were very beautiful; they changed my life and gave me a new start, new hope for my life. I'll always be grateful. Later, Chick would join Scientology, and we all joined Scientology.
L: The whole group?
B: Yes. But Barry, Dave and myself went only to Grade Four. Then I found myself thinking, hmm, it's time to exit stage left.
L: How many grades are there?
B: As many as you can imagine (*laughs*). Chick changed after Scientology . . . He went to what's called 'Clear'. You go through so many grades, then you go into 'Clear', then you go into another set of learnings called 'Power', I think, I can't remember the terms. But Chick began to change . . . I found Scientology very interesting, especially some of the techniques they developed for having people brainwash themselves, but this was not what I wanted to be a part of. So, just at the point where the group had the possibility of being successful – I'll put it like that – the divisions that occurred between Chick and me made it impossible for us to continue.
L: What divisions?
B: Chick was becoming interested in what he called music that communicated more, whereas I wanted to continue with my work. Let me be clear on this, though – I've always wanted my music to

communicate: it was a question of priorities. The most important thing to me was my music: if it could communicate, great; if it couldn't, OK I accept the verdict, but I'm not changing my music in order to communicate. Because what would I be communicating? I mean, if you have to become somebody else to communicate, what is that? (*Laughs.*)

So we broke up in Los Angeles. The vibration between Chick and me had been going bad for three or four months. We could easily have broken up in New York, which is what I wanted to do, or in London, which would have suited Dave; but Chick asked us to stay together. Then he broke up the group, and I was stranded in Los Angeles.

TITLES – A CRACK IN THE UNIVERSE

But Circle, in its good period – we played the Lighthouse, we travelled around Europe, did concerts in Germany . . . also it helped me in terms of being able to get some of my projects done. The Freedom record was done in that period, *The Complete Braxton* – which was not my title.

This was another thing that was developing. People would start rejecting my composition titles and the titles of the records: each time I just wanted, like, the number of compositions on the record, plus the year, so it would be a clear title, not fancy. Historically, I've had nothing but problems and disrespect. If you would, in your book, put the fact that Werner Uehlinger, for instance, would reissue the *Performance 9/1/79* record and not put the titles on it. This is a profound insult and he knows it and I know it. And this is also normal in the jazz world, to get insulted like this.

L: Surely it's not normal for him. Your other records on hat Hut have had the titles and your sleevenotes on them.

B: Yes, but our relationship went very bad, and what we think of each other . . . believe me, you would never want to hear how I really see that man and I'm sure he doesn't feel good about me. But the difference is, I can't mess up his business or disrespect him, nor would I want to, but for him – he would put out my record and purposely disrespect me by not putting the titles on.* I would never

---

*The composition numbers – plus details of intervening improvisations – for *Performance 9/1/79* are listed in the Discography; the original diagram-titles appear in the 'Catalogue of Works', below

tell anybody what I feel about Werner Uehlinger because it would
hurt me, it would hurt him . . . it would cause a crack in the
universe! That's about the best I can say about the man.
Alan Bates called my record *The Complete Braxton* – I want the
world to know that is A LIE. I would never call my work 'The
Complete Braxton' or any of this nonsense. I've had nothing but
problems with record companies. I made no money from my music,
I allowed myself to be exploited because I wanted to get my music
out there. I've been fortunate to make so many records, but I
wouldn't want anyone to be fooled: Stockhausen has about as many
records as I do, but do you think we're in the same economic zone?
Mr Stockhausen is a millionaire, and rightfully so because he has
demonstrated mastership; I might have to borrow a pound from
you to pay for my coffee. That's the difference between Mr
Stockhausen and me.

CHESS – 'A WORLD OF FORCES'

L: Before we rejoin the narrative in Los Angeles, could you say a
little more about chess? Why does it appeal so much?
B: Chess is one of the most exciting games I've ever discovered; in
fact, it's one of the most exciting *things* I've ever discovered. I keep
away from it in this period of my life because I'm a grown man with
a family to support and I have to be more practical. But the world of
chess is really dealing with the world of forces – there's everything
in it, there's mathematics, there's the understanding of relationships, of pressures, of forms. A good chess game is like a
musical composition. There's so much there, it's incredible.
It's the kind of game that was made for a person like me. I like
understanding how things are put together, the creativity in the
game. And it's a very logical, *un*logical game! It's logical, but the
real masters have developed something that's past logic – it's
beautiful. Chess is logically and structurally beautiful.
L: You say in *Jazz Lives* that chess is 'a just universe'.* Is that part

---

*Ullman, 1982, p. 202. In his book *Total Chess*, David Spanier refers to George Steiner's
1972 essay, *White Knights of Reykjavik*, on the affinities between chess, music and
mathematics: 'All three, he notes, being non-verbal, seem to depend on the interaction of
highly abstract dynamic relations with a very strong emphasis on spatial groupings. Thus,
the solution of a mathematical problem, the resolution of a musical passage, the elaboration
of a winning chess position, can be envisaged as regroupings, as releases of tensions between
energy levels.' (Spanier, 1986, p. 64)

of the appeal, as opposed to the rest of the world being unjust?
B: Hmm . . . no. I just mean that the purity and absolute beauty of
form is expressed on the board and it's a wonder to behold (*laughs*).
What are you thinking?
L: That perhaps the appeal is that it is a *just* world, self-enclosed,
where you have full responsibility and control over what you do.
You don't have to worry about outside forces, unlike in the music
business, say, which is far from a just universe.

'SWING' – THE LITTLE BOX OF 'JAZZ'

B: (*laughs*) The music business is about as far away from music as
you could ever imagine. The problem with jazz, and this is a point
I'd like to stress, is that they're defining the music in such a way
that *you cannot do your best*. So there's something inherently wrong
with how jazz has been defined. They have it defined now where, if
you think of writing a piece for 500 saxophones, you're looked at as
having nothing to do with jazz. Or if you practise your instruments
to where you really gain the kind of facility you need, and create the
kind of language that expresses that, they say it's not jazz. Take
rhythm. How many articles have I read about the fact that my
music doesn't 'swing'? Yet all of the masters have developed their
own relationship to forming, to rhythmic contours, etc. The
situation now is designed so that jazz is framed in a little box and if
you don't follow in someone else's footsteps, someone who is
so-called 'jazz', then you're automatically excommunicated. But all
the masters followed their own steps, so it's a contradiction in
terms.
L: And the same accusations are always made. When Charlie Parker
started playing, and John Coltrane, people said it's anti-jazz, it's
neurotic, it doesn't swing.*

---

*See, for example, Russell, 1976, pp. 172–4; and this exchange from a *Downbeat* (21/4/62)
article, quoted in Simpkins, 1975, pp. 152–4:
'One of the charges is that what Coltrane and Dolphy play doesn't swing.
'"I don't know what to say about that," Dolphy said.
'"Maybe it doesn't swing," Coltrane offered . . .
'Well, don't *you* feel that it swings? [Dolphy] was asked.
'"Of course I do," Dolphy answered. "In fact, it swings so much I don't know what to do –
it moves me so much" . . .
'"There are various types of swing," Coltrane said. "There's straight 4/4, with heavy
bass-drum accents. Then there's the kind of thing that goes on in Count Basie's band. In fact,

B: Right. That's because 'jazz' is the word that's used to delineate the parameters that African-Americans are allowed to function in, a 'sanctioned' zone. That's what 'jazz' is. 'Jazz' is the name of the political system that controls and dictates African-American information dynamics (and also the European or trans-European information dynamics that come in that particular zone). For instance – how can I say this? – the European and Euro-American definers have defined the music to the point where it is now so-called 'understood'. And when this happens, invariably African-Americans will vacate the form. How many African-Americans do you see playing Dixieland today? You don't see many African-Americans at bebop concerts, for that matter.

I believe that many of the problems I've had to deal with are to do with the fact that I have defined my own terms from the very beginning. Look at that article in *The Times*: he talked about Braxton's use of European vocabularies. Is that right? I've defined my vocabularies at every point – that's why I've written the *Composition Notes* – and, yes, I've been influenced by Europe, but I've also been influenced by Africa, by Asia . . . And the final definitions which have come to make my music have come through me as a human being, are based on me making decisions about what I wanted to do with my life. For him to call my music European-based, in terms of vocabulary, is profoundly mis-documenting my music.

But the whole thing is . . . I mean, it's taken for granted that a European or European-American jazz musician has borrowed some aspects of African-American language: why should it be such a big thing that I've learned from Europe? I'm a human being, just like Ronnie Scott or Derek Bailey. Why is it so natural for Evan Parker, say, to have an appreciation of Coltrane, but for me to have an appreciation of Stockhausen is somehow out of the natural order of human experience? I see it as racist.

AFRICAN INTELLECTUAL DYNAMICS –
THE BLACK SPANIARD OF BONN

L: Yes, it's curious. I remember Randy Weston telling me that all

---

every group of individuals assembled has a different swing. It's the same with this band. It's a different feeling than in any other band. It's hard to answer a man who says it doesn't swing.'"

the early beboppers – him, Bird, Monk, Max Roach – would listen avidly to modern composers like Stravinsky and Shostakovich. And, of course, a lot of European composers were inspired by aspects of jazz, too. But Charlie Parker, for instance, was a big fan of Bartók, of Varèse – he wanted to be a 'composer' as well as a 'jazz' player.* This just isn't talked about very much.

B: Right. That's part of the dilemma of the African-American intellectual. James P. Johnson wrote several operas – I think there's been *one* performance in North America and that not too long ago.† Most of the performances he had in his lifetime were in South America. Why isn't this information known? I'll tell you – because there's a real interest in suppressing African intellectual dynamics. As I said just now, it's a taboo subject; and we have all paid for it.

There is a whole group of African-Americans who have been interested in achieving, but they are not talked about, those are not the images being held up to young people. The average young African-American today is growing up with an information scan of the Top Ten. The fact that the intellectual weight, the history, of African musics are not commented on and the children aren't able to learn about them is a *tragedy*. The images are all of the superstud, the real sex man, or the boxer, the real tough guy – those zones are open for us. But we don't get the opportunity to have our children see the black physicist, chemist, doctor, educator.

Everybody else knows more about African-Americans than they know themselves! That's true of me, too: I learned more about Fats Waller's music in Paris than I ever did in Chicago. The fact that James P. Johnson was a composer, that Beethoven and Haydn were black Germans – this information has been known by Europeans, but they don't talk about it.

*For example: 'Bird had all sorts of musical combinations in mind. He wanted to make a record with Yehudi Menuhin and, at least, a forty-piece orchestra. He mapped out things for woodwinds and voices, and Norman Granz would holler, "What is this? You can't make money with this crazy combination. You can't sell this stuff."' (Max Roach, quoted in Reisner, 1974, pp. 194–5); and: 'He stopped by my place a number of times . . . He'd come in and exclaim, "Take me as you would a baby and teach me music. I only write in one voice. I want to have structure. I want to write orchestral scores." . . . He spoke of being tired of the environment his work relegated him to, "I'm so steeped in this and can't get out," he said.' (Edgard Varèse on Charlie Parker, quoted in Reisner, pp. 229–30.) Even Duke Ellington had similar problems: 'After his first Carnegie Hall concert in the early forties, one manager dismissed his extended compositions as valueless (as did some critics) and is supposed to have told him to get back to "nigger music".' (Gleason, 1975, p. 157)

†Other African-American creative musicians (besides Braxton and Johnson) to have written operas include Albert Ayler, Anthony Davis, Andrew Hill, Scott Joplin and Leo Smith

L: Hold on! I didn't know Beethoven and Haydn were black. What's the evidence?

B: Let's go back to the formation of classical music, that period of time. There were two Moorish invasions of Spain, one by the Arabic Moors, one by the African Moors; then there were migrations. The Beethovens are documented as living in Brussels in a very integrated sector of the city. Later, his grandfather got a job in Bonn, became *kapellmeister*, and Beethoven was known as the 'black Spaniard of Bonn'. There's a black scholar who did work on this, J.A. Rogers; but Thayer too mentions it in his book on Beethoven.*

In the final analysis, whether he was black or not is irrelevant. My point is that there were, in the early period of the solidification of Western art music . . . well, there has *always* been a tradition of African instrumentalists and African composers, men and women, and this is documented. I might also add there's a lineage of trans-Europeans who've been improvisers, what I call creative musicians, and that's been documented. But people are not given this information. People are given *one* criterion of information that addresses itself to *one* spectrum of value systems which is conducive to *one* set of political dynamics. That's what's happening in this time period.

STUCK IN LA, DAMNED TO HELL

IN *DOWNBEAT*, PARIS

L: I think we're running out of time today. Can we just nip back and get you out of Los Angeles? You were stranded there?

B: In Los Angeles I discovered *Star Trek* (*laughs*). Captain Kirk and the gang! That's the only redeeming thing I can say about Los Angeles, it's second only to Chicago in the list of cities I hate. I got stranded in Los Angeles . . . this was the period where Phil Woods put me down in *Downbeat*, the 'Blindfold Test' where he talked about me like I was a dog. And Leonard Feather had other articles

---

*Thayer's nineteenth-century *Life of Beethoven* is still the definitive biography. Rogers's work is based on contemporary illustrations and descriptions of Beethoven. Checking this, I found in Sonneck (ed.), 1967, that Gottfried Fischer, Beethoven's landlord in his childhood, describes him as having 'a dark-brown complexion' and says his nickname as a boy was 'the Spaniard' (pp. 8–9); while other contemporaries refer variously to Beethoven's complexion as 'brown', 'dark', 'dark red' and 'red'; to his 'brown' eyes, and to his 'coal-black' hair

putting me down, so I couldn't get any work to get out of Los Angeles. I was stuck there for six months. Dave Holland's family fed me, but I was just sitting around . . . That was one of the worst times in my life. My father died in that period, my fiancée and I broke up, Phil Woods damned me to hell.

Finally I got a gig in San Francisco thanks to Ted Gurkey, who's been a friend for years, and then I went back to Paris. I said, to hell with America. And what did I do in Paris? I started working at the American Centre, that's what! (*Laughs.*) I worked in the electronic music department with Jorge Arriagada. That became a nice period for me. I did a lot of concerts in Paris, though again I would constantly run into the wall of definition which said 'No performances of notated music for you, nigger!' The 'jazz' yoke around my neck would limit my options. But even so this was the period where I met Laurent Goddet and we would be like brothers, and I worked with Sheila Raz, the dancer, and with George Conley who changed his name to Kunle Mwanga. I did *Composition 25* at Chatellerault because of Mr Mwanga's help.

Also I was able to bring in Kenny Wheeler, who I'd met in Hamburg with Circle – there was a big workshop there, which is where I met Evan Parker too – and we started to do some quartet projects. I was also doing concerts with Oliver Lake and Baikida Carroll. We had a good time.

L: Were you still playing with Dave Holland and Barry Altschul?

B: Sometimes. They would be more in America. For instance, I went to New York for a few days to do the *Conference of the Birds* record with Dave. He was in New York a lot. I used J.F. Jenny Clarke on bass in that period, Charles 'Bobo' Shaw on drums, Kenny on trumpet – that was a nice group.

IRCAM: 'BUSINESS AS USUAL'

Then I started noticing something about the record companies. None of the larger ones like ECM wanted to deal with me, I could only find some of the smaller companies and basically give them my music (*sighs*). I was always on the outside. So I spent my last year in Paris in the house, writing piano music.

I got disillusioned again with Paris. I started learning the language and seeing that Paris had its own problems. Plus, there was no hint of advancement for me in Paris. To this day, IRCAM has never tried to help me do anything. I wanted to study electronic music there, but they wouldn't let me in. I think Boulez himself probably doesn't have any respect for me. He would later bring in people like – who's that rock performer? Frank Zappa? – and give him the opportunity to have a symphonic work performed which Boulez himself conducted; but they wouldn't even let me walk in the place. That's the nature of the political dynamics at IRCAM.

It's not that I want to accuse any one individual of racism, it's just that when it comes to dealing with Africans and African-Americans it's *business as usual*. They can use black people in the Pigalle section where there's a lot of, you know, good fun and 'black exotica'; but because I had the same kind of visions as a Stockhausen, in terms of the projects I wanted to do, I was seen as an arrogant nigger. The so-called liberal white community would pat me on the head, but twenty years and no performances . . . Oh, I won't go into that again.

So I stayed in the house and wrote piano music, and again I felt like I was dying. Everything was drying up. Then there was a phone call from Michael Cuscuna and Steve Backer: *come to New York*.

ROAD

SATURDAY 16, MANCHESTER

The first of the tour's two rest days. It rains, of course; a steady, remorseless downpour. I interview Braxton from one until four. He says he'll spend the evening composing and practising. He's having trouble with his embouchure on the flute. 'If I don't get more time to practise, I'll have to drop it for this tour,' he complains.

I ask what he's composing.

'I've started on a new piece for the quartet. I hope we'll be able to play it before the end of the tour.'

'How do you compose?' I ask. 'What's the process?'

He shrugs. 'Oh, I just sit down and start writing.'

'You never get stuck for inspiration?'

'Composition's not the big deal they make it at colleges. They paralyse people with rules. I just sit down, write out an idea, and work on it.'

He adds that he's also transcribing a couple of the brass parts from earlier quartet works so that Marilyn can play them before the tour's over.

Fired by this dedication, I haul out the weighty volumes of *Tri-axium Writings* which Braxton had presented to me in London. *Tri-axium Writings* comprise over 1,500 pages of densely argued, very abstract perspectives on the history and philosophy of music: Braxton took seven years to write them, another five to raise the money to publish them himself. Even now only fifty or so copies of the three-volume sets are in circulation.

I skim the pages; gulp. Braxton has not only evolved a personal philosophy of music, he's devised a personal terminology in which to describe it. The chapter-headings promise fascinating reading – 'Creativity and Science', 'Black Notated Music', 'The White Improvisor' – but browsing is frustrated by my constantly needing to refer to the glossary to look up mysterious terms like 'Affinity Postulation' and 'Multi-transfer Shift Activity'. After an hour, I feel much as Tony Hancock did faced with Bertrand Russell's *Human Knowledge – Its Limits and Scope*: 'Well, we've soon found out my limit, haven't we? Three sentences.'

Time to eat.

I spend the evening writing up notes and jotting down first impressions of the group. Mark – tall, full beard, thick-rimmed glasses, looks formidably serious until he smiles; onstage, very *engrossed*, still learning the music – but beginning to use his space to explore intriguing timbres: seems amiable, relaxed, a nice guy. Gerry – wiry, loose-limbed, laid-back; laconic and shrewd, with an NYC (I guess) streetwise wit; his solos intimate extreme sensitivity; more knowledgeable about more kinds of music than anyone I've met. Marilyn – compact, quiet, a kind of *distracted* presence yet can fix you with an intent, inscrutable stare; the transformation when she plays is startling, as if a switch is flicked and she suddenly radiates power; bit mysterious – or am I stereotyping? Probably just wary of a strange journalist questioning her politics, though some of her composition titles – *Spirit Music, Spaces and Elements, Into the Blue, Opium Dream Eyes* – do seem in-character.

Later I try *Tri-axium Writings* again. I'm just settling into 'The Reality of the Creative Woman' when there's a thunderous din from above, and what sounds like a roomful of drunken businessmen start singing pornographic songs. In desperation I switch on the TV and find solace in the late-night film: *I Married a Monster from Outer Space*. About a bunch of aliens who show no emotion and can't even swim, let alone swing.

METAROAD

FOREGROUND MUSIC 2

THE UNSUNG MASTERY OF WARNE
MARSH — GRAVILLIC CONTOURS

L: You said earlier that the three instrumentalists who have most left their mark on you were Paul Desmond, Warne Marsh and John Coltrane. Can we talk today about Coltrane and Marsh?
B: Warne Marsh, I think, along with Lucky Thompson and Von Freeman, has been one of the most misunderstood, undecorated, under-respected saxophonists of the last thirty years. It's a damned shame so little recognition has come to this great man. I think he is a *great* man. I don't mean to say that Warne Marsh is a restructuralist in the sense of Coltrane – he isn't; he's a stylist from the Lester Young/Lennie Tristano school – but he's demonstrated an understanding of the music that's unique. His sound, his phrasing . . . the gravillic weight of Mr Marsh's solos used to drive me crazy.

By gravillic weight I'm talking of the gravity that underlines how a given forming is established in space. That being . . . Suppose I did a visual imprint, with respect to the gravillic contour; I would take one particular shape and section it off, then talk of the gravity points in the forming as a way of understanding how that vocabulary works. Bird's music would be like: (*hums Parker solo and traces shape in air*).

Charlie Parker – Gravillic Contours

Take Eric Dolphy's language: the intervallic relationships between distances would be part of the contour of his music: (*hums Dolphy solo and traces shape in air*).

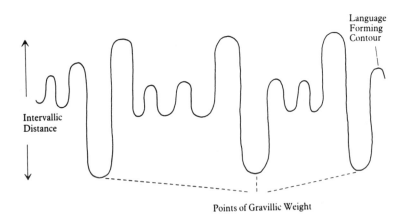

Eric Dolphy – Gravillic Contours

Coltrane's music would be – well, in different periods, it would
have different shapes, but he was always a restructuralist. I'm
thinking of his solo on *Bye Bye Blackbird* with Miles Davis★ (*hums
it*). If I were to draw that visually, and fill it in in terms of colour,
shape and mass, we could take a look at a new, kind of furling,
shape in Mr Coltrane's music. Desmond's music was more –
beams, sound beams, architectural music (*hums Desmond solo*). This
was another way of construction, that extends from the Lester
Young school in terms of the gravillic inter-relationship of those
formings to the metric pulse beneath it.

L: More of a flow than Dolphy's extreme leaps?

B: Yes. Now Warne Marsh . . . if you look at that solo on *The Song
is You* from the *Lee Konitz Meets Jimmy Giuffre* record, that solo is
completely . . .!!! I burned up three copies of that record just
listening to the Warne Marsh solos, especially on *The Song is You*
(*hums it*). If we break down one of Marsh's solos with respect to the
time, we find all kind of inner gravillic – *pockets!* – completely
ametrical, completely outside of the time, which rebalance his
phraseology, the nature of his construction, in a unique way. He
demonstrates this in every period of his music: his vocabulary, the
relationship of his forming to gravillic balances, has always been
unique.

Once I understood these things I would begin to build my own
music. It was like, oh no one's using angular kinds of weights, so
let's try angle attack languages: (*traces in air*).

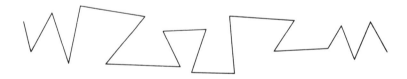

Angle Attack Contours

Then, let's try intervallic languages.

It's for that reason I became a restructuralist: well, one, it was my

★On Miles Davis's *Round About Midnight* LP

natural tendency, but two, because as I began to grasp everybody's
solo formings and began to look at them with respect to their
contour nature, their gravillic dynamics, their element criteria or
specifics, I would begin to isolate not only vocabulary studies but
also structural attacks. So I arrived at the language music as a
context, a platform, from which to create vocabularies.

But Warne Marsh, yes. There's a record of Mr Marsh with Philly
Joe Jones, Paul Motian, Paul Chambers and Ronnie Ball, they're
playing a piece called *Excerpt*, based on *I'll Remember April*, and his
solo is *out* – it's OUT, OUT, OUT!* He could've been hung for a
solo like that! It's so inside of the chord changes, he's really
somewhere else. It's like you know the context so well that you're
free: you're free because you understand the rules to such a level
that you can do anything you want. That's what freedom is. You
can't be free unless you have a context to be free in. Existential
freedom is not evolutionary, that's what we're seeing now.

So Warne Marsh meets my final criterion. I don't like listening to
saxophonists unless they do something that makes me say – *huh!*
That's all I ask. Warne Marsh, every time I hear him play he does
something; I find myself saying, *hmmmmmm!!??* Steve Lacy does
that to me too.

CAPABLANCA'S LINE

L: There's a very intricate quality to their musics at times, yet
they're both very terse players too. If I traced the way I hear Warne
Marsh, it's like he'll dance very closely around the line of the tune,
then take sudden, strange, sideways leaps (*waves arm in erratic 3-D
weaving motion*).
B: Yes, yes, yes! I used to love to draw diagrams to understand
better what I call forming. Mr Marsh's music is right in there. And
he's looking only for what he's looking for, that's why I like him.
He's not playing somebody else's music, he's playing his music. He
knows what fascinates him and he does *that*. That's what I love. He
was never seduced by the image of the music, he was seduced by
the music.

The first time I heard him live, oh I couldn't believe it!
Sometimes, when he was playing, he was looking around at the
people . . . he's a Scorpio, see, like Desmond, so he wasn't *there*. I

*On the LP, *Warne Marsh*

mean the music he was playing was so profound, so thought out, yet he was still looking around. I was, like, OK, there's something happening here, some decisions going down that I know nothing about outside of saying, this man can play! (*Laughs.*) And harmonically he always finds a new line. It's like a chess move, like Capablanca – he understood where to find a line. Marsh knows where to find a line.

L: Have you ever played with him?

B: I had an evening of sitting in with him and Gary Foster in 1970. I gave him the *For Alto* record and the next week I came back and sat in with him. I asked him, you know, what did he think of *For Alto*? He gave me this – long, hard *stare*. He tried to be nice, but he didn't like it. Probably thought it was complete junk.

The first time I met Mr Marsh, I'll never forget it – this was just outside Los Angeles during that period I was stranded there. I went up to him, and I'm shaking 'cause I'm going to meet one of my *heroes*, you know. I say, how are you doing, sir? I'm very happy to hear your music. So he kind of *looked* at me; he said, *why* do you like my music? I said, ah, well, I've been listening to you for ten years, I really appreciate what you're doing and I really care about your music. He just looked at me: but *why* do you like my music? (*Laughs.*) He had a very forbidding exterior, but he's really a very nice man.

THE EUROPEAN MYSTIC LINEAGE

L: Why do you think he's been so neglected?

B: Because he's from the European mystic lineage. Like Desmond, and Lee Konitz, his music has in it his heritage as a trans-European man: all of his solutions do not come from Africa. He's not respected in the black or white 'jazz' communities because his music has never lent itself to the political games that have been played, that *are* being played, around the music. He was interested only in the music and in developing an evolution . . . so they, the powers-that-be, couldn't use him. They could use someone who, for instance, would take Charlie Parker's language and function under the mentality of the 'jazz musician' that has been perpetrated in this time period. Marsh, by contrast, was talked about as being cold and academic, no feeling, not swinging. Fortunately I'd read all those reviews of Warne Marsh, so when I started getting the same reviews that didn't hurt me too much. Because, by every criterion, he is a master instrumentalist.

I saw his picture recently on the cover of a Chet Baker record, *Blues for a Reason*, and he looks like he's getting older, his hair is grey . . . I wonder if he's ever going to experience just a little bit of the success that one would have thought he'd have had twenty, thirty years ago. You know, I have more records out than Warne Marsh by a long shot; it saddens me to think that so gifted an instrumentalist has so few records, so little exposure. It's indicative of what the 'jazz' world is all about. Remember, 'bebop' is back, 'jazz' is back! Well, Warne Marsh meets all the criteria of a master *jazz* musician, but somehow they are still not talking about Mr Marsh – the reason being that this period is really about something else. Lucky Thompson is still alive, he's living in America, but there are no records of his music, people don't do articles on Lucky Thompson.

L: Oh, I love his *Lucky Strikes* LP, and *The Jazz Skyline* with Milt Jackson . . . Is Lucky Thompson still playing? Or what is he doing?

B: I don't know. I think maybe he has a regular job, but I really don't know.

JOHN COLTRANE – A NEW LEVEL OF SOUND
WONDER – 'SIT IN WITH GOD!'

L: Shall we move on to John Coltrane?

B: This man . . . I don't know how to talk about John Coltrane because he is such a master, a restructuralist master, which is the highest degree of mastership as far as I'm concerned. Every period of Mr Coltrane's music demonstrated a unique personal vision. The fact that he was an evolutionary musician would be profoundly important to my later forming aesthetic: because of him I began to learn about evolutionary thinking. His music is overwhelming, awesome. As a saxophonist I can only marvel at the ideas he was able to execute. He brought another level of technical dynamics to the instrument, sheer technical brilliance. My final decision to make the world of music my life's work came after seeing John Coltrane live, when I experienced the next level of what I'll call sound wonder.

L: It must have been a terrible blow when he died so suddenly.

B: Oh . . . it was so great I thought *I* was going to die. I mean, basically, I wanted to follow him around, carry his horn if he would let me. He was like a god to me, like Martin Luther King; and his death, that whole period – the three assassinations, Dr King and the two Kennedys, then Coltrane dying too, and Albert Ayler soon afterwards – it was very shocking. When Coltrane died, I felt like I'd lost a father. I stopped listening to his music for ten, fifteen years; I couldn't bear to hear it. His death was so catastrophic that I quickly had to move away from him, 'cause I knew I couldn't follow him. I'm only now starting to listen to him again.

L: Did you ever meet Coltrane or play with him?

B: Yes. Well, I met him. The first time I met him I was crying, with my nose smudged against the glass outside the Plugged Nickel. They wouldn't let me in – I was too young, about nineteen I think, you had to be twenty-one – so I stayed outside, listening through the glass, crying. At the end of the set the group came out and talked to me, they were very nice.

Later I got the chance to see him again. I asked him dumb questions about the saxophone or, like (*falsetto*) '*What key was that tune in, sir?*' (*laughs*) but I didn't try to sit in with him. Coltrane was a very nice man and he let a lot of people sit in, he was trying to help the younger musicians – something which isn't done that much in this period. Coltrane was sincerely interested in young people and in helping them. I had the possibility, I believe, of sitting in with him but I didn't even try. Sit in with Coltrane! Sit in with God! Not me. I was just a student then: I actually thought I was pretty good, but not good enough to play with Mr Coltrane.

ATTACKED WITH AN UMBRELLA

– SPIRITUAL POWER

I learned a lot about power from John Coltrane too. He was a humble man. I saw a woman come into a club and with the hook of her umbrella try to grab him around the arm while he was playing with the quartet. I could have killed that woman! But after the set, when she came up to scold John for playing this loud, crazy music, he was so kind to her, so understanding. I could *not* believe it.

L: She just walked into the club and attacked him?

B: Yeah, she came in off the street. She said, stop playing this crazy music, it's too loud and the drummer's tired, just stop it! And she took her umbrella and began poking at him. You can imagine how I hated her. To see Mr Coltrane talk so nicely to her taught me that you have to develop more understanding, and the more understanding you develop the less prone you might be to involvement in anger and negative vibrations. There was none of that from Mr Coltrane, no hip ego looking down on you, like *I'm the baddest cat and you ain't shit.* He was a very spiritual man, you knew it immediately.

L: This is what you meant by 'power'?

B: The power of conviction, spiritual power, the power he projected in his music. I used to play very much like Paul Desmond and Warne Marsh before I began to digest and learn from Coltrane's music. Whatever intensity I've been able to generate in my music, that region is directly related to what I learned from John Coltrane. Before that the percussionist had to go to brushes when Braxton played (*laughs*).

The mystical and spiritual implications of his work would also be very profound, not only for me but for the whole of that time period. He affected the next generation of saxophonists, pianists, percussionists . . . everyone would have to deal with the vibrational and empirical weight of his music. In John Coltrane we're not talking of one area of focus, we're talking of a world musician.

CECIL TAYLOR, A *GENIUS* GENIUS

L: Your other major influence in terms of power and intensity was presumably Cecil Taylor?

B: Ah, Cecil Taylor is a *genius* genius at the piano. But what's really amazing about Mr Taylor to me is that even in 1985 there are pianists who are still trying to figure out whether or not he can play! It's incredible. I've had people recently ask me my opinion of Mr Taylor because they weren't sure what to think. Mr Taylor is a master of masters: I mean, how could you be more dynamic or demonstrate a more brilliant music than Cecil Taylor? It's unfortunate that we've not been able to hear the whole spectrum of his music. I recall being at a concert in New York in 1970, '71, of his creative orchestra music – an incredible concert! That whole area of his music has never been on record, but you can *believe* it's exciting.* It reminded me of Varèse, though of course if Cecil were

*An LP of Cecil Taylor's creative orchestra music, *Winged Serpent* (*Sliding Quadrants*), was released on Soul Note in 1986

to read that he might buy a gun and shoot me! It wasn't all Varèse, it was like an African Varèse or something – not to mention that Varèse probably learned from Africa too. It was a very, very special music.

I'm sorry we have never played together. Cecil likes me – every now and again! Especially when I was a young man, I don't think he liked me very much; I think he thought I was too European-tainted. I was never able to penetrate his inner circle of friends, so I have learned to love him from a distance. The first time I saw his music live was in Paris: before the concert was over I'd almost fainted! I thought I knew what to expect, but hearing it live was awesome, awesome. There has been no language more brilliant than Mr Taylor's.

L: I think Cecil Taylor has finally, after years of racist – or just stupid – abuse, won respect as a player, but his importance as a composer is still overlooked. Many people seem to assume his music is chiefly improvised, but Sam Rivers told me that when he played with Mr Taylor in the late sixties about seventy-five, eighty per cent of the music was composed.

B: Oh, he's a master composer. His compositions are *very* interesting – very long, winding kind of compositions, something that's peculiar to him. It must be terribly exciting to play with Cecil Taylor, to be in the middle of that music and see how it works! He's a complex man, complex . . .

THE TENTH FLOOR –
'INVISIBLE THINGS'

L: Are there any other aspects of his work which have particularly influenced you?

B: Well, the rate of information in his work is frightening. But, in fact . . . Mr Taylor is a mystic, he's dealing with mysticism and forces, setting forces into motion.

L: Could you explain that?

B: I can't, because I would be violating what it's possible to communicate at this point in time. But I believe Mr Taylor . . . it will be fifty, a hundred years before people can deal with his music.

L: What forces are you talking about?

B: I can't elaborate on that outside of saying I believe Cecil has real insight into what he's doing. It's not just a question of him playing the piano; the man has real insight into what he's generating, as a master should.

L: Why can't you talk about this?

B: It's not something I can talk about. *He* would have to talk about it. I can't talk about his work on a level that would possibly disrespect him. Cecil Taylor could tell us more about his music than I ever could.

This is why I've gone to such lengths to do my analysis books, the *Composition Notes*, because I know what my work sets into motion; or at least I have not built a music system separate from what it sets into motion. My hope is that in the next ten, twenty years I will begin to talk about the upper partials of my own work. As it is now, we're only talking about the first floor of my music and we can't talk about the tenth floor until the first floor is in place and people can understand the basic mechanics, the fundamentals, of what is being extended and how it's being extended. But there *are* upper partials. Let me put it like this: there's information that's related to anything you can think about, any area you want to enter. For those things that are vibrationally focused or based, you can't simply talk about them without first establishing a proper kind of context. This information has not been available because of the manipulation that surrounds the music and also because of the social reality dynamics that African-Americans are dealing with.

L: When I interviewed Cecil Taylor, he was talking of 'invisible things' – beauty, love, voodoo, ritual.* I think maybe he's already on the tenth floor!

B: Please don't misunderstand me. I've not meant to imply that Mr Taylor can't talk about what he's doing. My hope is that some of this information will be put into books, that the musicians will write about the music and tell people what they're doing. This will help the culture, help young people. In this period musicians like myself are looked at as being very esoteric, crazy guys who just want to play strange sounds, as if that's all there is to it – and, of course, that's not all there is. It's important in the future to have this information documented so people can enter into the system of the music and understand exactly what it means, how it works, how it can be used to help humanity.

---

*Lock, 6/83. For more on Cecil Taylor's views about 'the methodological concepts of black music', see his poem 'Aqoueh R-Oyo'

ROAD

SUNDAY 17, BIRMINGHAM

Thick mist, then sunshine. In the van everyone is cheerful and relaxed after the rest day. 'Did you see that TV movie last night?' Mark asks. '*I Married a Monster from Outer Space.*'

'Yes sir, I must've seen it fifty-one times,' Braxton enthuses. 'I like those monster movies. The last time I stayed in England I went to see *Attack of the Giant Spiders* with Evan and Margaret Parker and their kids. That was a good one!'

Marilyn, who missed *I Married a Monster*, wants to know the plot. Braxton explains: 'Well, these aliens come down from outer space and take over the bodies of some American men. But then the real Americans find out because the hero – see, his wife can tell he's become an alien because he's so *cold*. So they round up some real, red-blooded American men – they know they're real men because their wives are pregnant! – and they go stomp on the aliens. Yay!' He purses his lips and chuckles quietly. 'Oh boy, America.'

Gerry has the headphones on and is singing along to Screamin' Jay Hawkins's *I Put a Spell on You.*

Braxton smiles. 'I remember that; that was a *baaad* record.'

'You're an old rock'n'roller then, Anthony?' inquires Tony.

'Yes sir! Frankie Lymon was my man.' He starts to sing *Why Do Fools Fall in Love?* in falsetto.

I wonder idly about Braxton's liking for Frankie Lymon. One of his hits – *ABC's of Love* – is based on letters, another – *Baby Baby* – on numbers. Coincidence? Minor curiosity? I guess it's nothing more.

Mark announces he's feeling sick. 'That English Breakfast was real greasy,' he groans. (The Continental, I might add, was a slur on Europe.)

Tony stops the van and Braxton takes Mark for a stroll. Tony and I also get out to stretch our legs: he's wearing an alarmingly bright lime-green suit which I suspect has played no small part in Mark's nausea. He tells me he used to drum with a Manchester rock group called Sad Cafe, then he worked as a tour manager for Jazz Services until the constant touring began to wear him down. He's now a writer, working with community theatre, but he still does the occasional tour to supplement his income. This one is his Xmas bonus.

I ask what he thinks of the quartet's music.

'Well, it's not really my area,' he says dubiously. 'They're obviously great musicians, but I find it very intense. I can only take, like, half a set, then I have to nip outside for a fag.'

Mark returns, feeling better, and we set off again. Everyone tells horror stories of having to play while at death's door. Braxton recalls a concert he played with trumpeter Jacques Coursil in the late sixties. 'I think it was at the Avignon Festival. We went to the mountains and the water or something didn't agree with me. I was so sick I had to play the gig lying on the stage. I'd stagger to my feet, take a solo, then lie down again and *die* until my next solo.'

We reach Birmingham in the early afternoon. The hotel is also the venue for tonight's gig, which is very convenient though when I see the playing-space my heart sinks: a large, anonymous room, bar in the corner, rows of hard-backed chairs. It looks decidedly downhome after the opulence of Manchester's Opera House. Michael Gerzon, a freelance sound engineer and Braxton fan, has turned up with his own digital equipment to record the concert for his extensive new-music archives. The soundcheck seems fine: Marilyn and Mark duet briefly on *Ruby, My Dear*, then the quartet play *All the Things You are* and *On Green Dolphin Street*. Afterwards, though, Braxton is clearly unhappy.

'I wish we hadn't played *tunes*,' he grumbles. 'I've played enough tunes to last a lifetime. I mean, I'm interested in harmony, but there has to be another way.'

BIRMINGHAM CONCERT, STRATHALLAN HOTEL

First Set (Primary Territories)
Composition 69M (+ 33)
Composition 110A (+ 108B)

Composition 60 (+ *108C* + *96*)
Composition 85 (+ *108D* + *30*)

Second Set (Primary Territories)
Composition 105B (+ *96*)
Composition 87 (+ *108C*)
Composition 23J
Composition 69H (+ *31*)
Encore
Composition 40(O)

(*Compositions 30–33* are all works for solo piano, comprising 250+ pages of music; Marilyn had these, plus *Piano Piece 1*, at every concert with a brief to play from them whenever she deemed it appropriate – that is, at any time when she was not playing notated material from the primary territory or improvising on that. Braxton did sometimes specify which piece was to be played, though usually only in the case of a designated solo spot, as at the London concert. It wasn't possible to document these details with 100 per cent accuracy because Marilyn could not always recall after the concert which pieces she'd been playing – her scores were not numbered – nor exactly at which point she'd been playing them. The same was true of the other three players with regard to *Composition 96* which, like the piano music, was available as an *option* to be played at certain times during the primary territory. I have included it in the set lists only when I knew for certain that it had been played by someone, but there were undoubtedly numerous other instances which I have failed to list.)

The group play the theme of *69M*, one of Braxton's most maddeningly catchy and convoluted tunes, then his sopranino snakes over the fast pulse while Marilyn hammers out extreme intervals from *33*. Mark takes over, his quiet bass solo using glissandos, then we're into the ebb and flow of open ensemble interplay. Four blasts on C-melody sax cue a realignment to *110A*, which Braxton describes as 'curved sound dynamics as a base for extended improvisations' (in lighter moments, he also refers to it as his piece 'for lovers'). He plays a series of jittery wails while Mark returns to glissandos, the bass sounding like a slide guitar: suddenly the sounds feel intensely sorrowful – I think of Albert Ayler's cries, of ancient country blues, of a deep, solitary sobbing – then the piano trickles in and the feelings shift. Braxton plays scrabbling phrases on alto; Gerry takes a solo, flitting all over his kit, tapping with fingernails, rubbing with palms; then *60*, originally a duet for clarinet and piano, collaged here with the *108C* pulse track. Braxton's clarinet trills lead into a tense space of stop-start, cross-duo dynamics before he moves to alto, accelerates the tempo and the rhythm section switch to *108D* ('my bebop pulse track') and we're into *85*, originally a duet for woodwind and string bass. I can't fathom how Braxton's adapted it for quartet – but it's great! The theme is like a relaxed bebop line that half floats, half scampers over the choppy pulse track, and Braxton extends it via a long, intense solo that climaxes in retching squeals. Marilyn follows, her solo an explosion of carnival effervescence, before Gerry rumbles around the beat, hits a wash of cymbals, then subsides gracefully as Mark escorts him into a gentle fade-out.

105B opens with a notated theme, then long clarinet notes lead into whirling runs and a variety of ensemble exchanges, notably Marilyn's splattery right-hand decorations of the rhythm section pulse track (*105B* is one of several compositions with its own 'in-built' pulse track). *87*, originally another woodwind/bass duet, conjures an eerie solo from Mark, full of bent notes and dramatic pizzicato flurries; Braxton joins him, leading the ensemble into a lovely sprinkling of sound textures across the space – squeaks, scrapes, sighs, whimpers. Urgency creeps back as the group realign for *23J*, a fast line that kicks into sudden exhilaration. (Michael Cuscuna's sleevenotes to *The Montreux/Berlin Concerts* LP report that the performance of *23J* on that record includes 'one of Braxton's most exciting solos to date'. The same happens tonight, which must say something about what Braxton would call 'the vibrational lining' of *23J*'s structure.) Braxton blows superb alto, very fast yet perfectly controlled, burning up the time, breaking into snarling phrases that leap into screams. The group are right with him, raising a thunder of support, until Braxton hits a peak with electrifying screeches that he abruptly reins in, and Marilyn, grinning madly, hands racing up and down the keyboard, takes up the intensity like a baton, holds it with frantic runs and crashing left-hand clusters, then subtly starts a dynamic shift that, via a plummeting bass solo and soft percussion, revolves 180 degrees into a totally different space, the only sound now Gerry flicking a cymbal rim with his fingernail. Braxton adds sopranino mewls and we're into a gripping silence, its surface scratched by minuscule sounds. This hush is torn by the sudden ringing of a till, and the barman begins to empty his night's takings, coins noisily jangling. I feel a wave of fury rising from my stomach – then it's gone: Gerry has taken a handful of loose change and is rolling it across the snare drum; the web of resonance mends, the sound flow resumes.* The ensemble move into *69H*, a 'fast pulse structure for extended improvisation' and we're into another sequence of brilliant ensemble nuance, brief episodes of manic ferocity interspersed with reflective pauses that lead finally into a quiet close.

The applause is long and loud and the group, with no dressing-room to hide in, return for the tour's first (and only) encore. I don't know if Braxton has a policy about encores – I suspect he's not too keen on showbiz games – but in this instance it would have looked very churlish to sit in the corner of the room and ignore the fervent cries for more. The quartet play *40(O)*, a Kelvin repetition structure,† its complexity rendered here with such a furious rapidity that it fizzes like a short fuse for two minutes, then stops – ZAP! (As if you've just walked into a glass door!) ('Hey, we really kicked ass on that,' Gerry grins later. 'I think that's the best we ever played it.')

The musicians wander out of the playing-space, beaming, dazed. The energy really flew tonight; *85* and *23J* in particular had the audience shouting and cheering. A fantastic concert.

'That was the best sound yet,' declares Mark, slumping exhausted into a chair.

'Yeah, it was the first time I could hear everything clearly,' Marilyn says, 'so I felt I could really cut loose. I enjoyed that piece that closed the first set.' She turns to Braxton. '*85*? I never played that before.'

'Oh, you didn't?' He looks surprised, his brow still glistening with sweat.

'Me neither,' says Gerry. 'We haven't played it since I've been in the quartet.'

'You'd never seen it before you played it tonight?' I ask, astonished.

Marilyn shrugs. 'I guess not.'

'I'm sorry. If I'd realized we could have run through it at the

---

*'I knew everybody would be aware of the cash register and feeling that it didn't fit, so I tried to make it part of the music,' Gerry told me later. Ironically, twenty years earlier, John Coltrane was complaining about exactly the same insensitivity – see Kofsky, 1970, p. 147

†For more on Kelvin repetition structures, see 'Postcript 3', ii, below

soundcheck,' Braxton frowns. Then grins. 'Hmm, I guess in the circumstances we didn't play it *too* badly.'

The musical and emotional dynamics have been different every night: coolly intense at London, almost serene at Newcastle, visceral and sweaty tonight. The latter qualities may be those closest to how 'jazz' is 'supposed' to be played, but they're not priorities for Braxton. On the contrary. In *Tri-axium Writings 3*, as part of a comprehensive critique of jazz-journalistic practices, he attacks the critics' use of what he terms 'the reality of the sweating brow' as a signifier of musical *realness*.* This notion is, he says, a cliché of jazz commentary and indicative of the mistaken Western emphasis on *how* something is played rather than on *what* is played. He relates it to both the 'spectacle diversion syndrome' (by which the Western media subvert the spiritual dimensions of non-Western cultures by focusing on their surface particulars rather than their essence)† and to the concept of 'black exotica'.

> 'The reality of the sweating brow' has to do with how white writers have come to interpret whether a given black musician is accurately 'doing the best' he or she can or whether that musician is merely 'coasting' – or not 'really trying to be creative'. What is interesting with this concept, however, is that 'the reality of the sweating brow' is not so much dependent on the actual music but instead on 'how' the actual 'doing' of the music looks.‡

This criterion, he points out, is rarely employed to the same degree when white music is under scrutiny: here, while 'a performer is expected to have some emotional involvement with his or her activity . . . white people recognize that there is no one way to be emotional . . . Some people are naturally demonstrative . . . other people are emotional in more subtle ways.'‡ However, jazz commentary since the Dixieland era has asserted a different line, namely:

*T-a W3, pp. 235–308. See 'Postscript 2' for more about the context in which this critique occurs. (I'm reminded of Barthes's critique of Mankiewicz's *Julius Caesar*, in which he points out that all the characters are wearing fringes, as a sign of Romanness, and are always sweating, as a sign of inner torment. What Braxton argues is that the process can be reversed, that jazz critics can *demand* sweat as proof of authenticity and even *define* the latter in terms of the former. Barthes too notes that: 'It is both reprehensible and deceitful to confuse the sign with what is signified. And it is a duplicity which is peculiar to bourgeois art.' (Barthes, 1973, pp. 26–8)

†See 'Postscript 2', pp. 311–14 below

‡T-a W3, p. 297

‡T-a W3, p. 298

the idea that there is only one type of black person, and also that there is only one level of 'involvement' by black people . . . Jazz musicians are simply supposed to sweat – if they are serious, and this is especially the case after bebop solidified. Ensembles like the Modern Jazz Quartet have long been viewed from a distance – not because of the validity and beauty of their music, but because the dynamics of their involvement challenged the most sacred observation position that has emerged in black music commentary – that being the reality of the sweating brow.*

Closely linked to this, Braxton argues, are 'the concept of the good night' and 'the concept of non-sequential credibility', two more Western criteria that are misapplied to black creativity and used as a means of 'not acknowledging the wholeness of a given individual's offering'. By focusing on an isolated concert, or record, or even solo, Western critics have been able to ignore a musician's composite work and the context in which it has evolved.

This is not to say that one is not free to so-call like or not like a given piece of music – because everyone has his or her own taste. But the reality of a given participation must be viewed in its total context – because the realness of an individual's music is not about one aspect of a given offering.†

Yet instead of there being any such awareness of the music's multi-faceted nature, Braxton says, 'jazz' musicians are 'still viewed from the so-called "cutting" mentality where whoever plays the longest and strongest will "win" '. This kind of criterion not only distorts the musicians' creativity – because some people will be tempted to play up to the image – it also reinforces 'the already over-accented position of the masculine affinity slant of present-day black creativity'; that is, the music is reduced to empty displays of fake 'soulfulness' and pyrotechnic machismo, or 'what is called "power" – even though in actual fact, this phenomenon retards the real power of the music'.

The relationship to 'black exotica' is clear: the stereotype 'jazz' musician who swings, blows and gets down all night long is not so far removed from the stereotype black stud or 'sex man'. (Ironically, this same perspective is used against white musicians who are often reputed to play 'with no balls': Braxton doesn't use that exact phrase, but he does note that 'West Coast jazz has long

*T-a W3, p. 299
†T-a W3, p. 307

been viewed in mocking terms because "obviously those white musicians could never 'get down' like those good old black musicians".' And, of course, women musicians, of all races, are also particularly vulnerable to this critical perspective/prejudice.)

Allied to the concept of 'black exotica', and a further factor in Western criticism's espousal of 'the sweating brow', is what Braxton calls 'the across the tracks syndrome'. This refers to his observation that many white critics adopt 'jazz' as part of a personal rebellion against the stifling respectability of their own mainstream culture and, consequently, value and define the music not on its own terms but in terms of their argument with establishment values: so, they brandish 'jazz' as a *sensual, soulful* and *goodtime* music, ignoring its scientific and vibrational facets. Black music thus becomes the victim of a white civil war: shunned by the establishment (grant bodies, Pulitzer Prize committees, etc) because it is *too sweaty* and *not serious enough*, yet attacked by the critics whenever they think its practitioners are being *too serious* and *not sweaty enough.**

---

*Many other African-American musicians have made critiques similar to Braxton's. Here, for instance, is Bill Dixon eschewing machismo and unnecessary sweat in the sleevenotes to his *Considerations 2* LP: 'An early criticism of, and objection to, my work centred around what was thought and advanced as my not being a "strong leader" type or "strong soloist". The fact of the matter is that in a great deal of my work I have never considered it to be a drawback to allow other members of the group to speak at length with their own voices in my music. On the contrary, I have felt that that approach revealed more of the totality of the situation and focused and attempted to show the entire scope of approach to both composition and the ultimate realization of that composition, performance.

'When one is responsible for the creation and design of a composition/the composer/ it hardly seems necessary whenever one takes a "solo" – as long as that solo is within the aesthetic confines of the composition – to separate that solo from the totality of the situation. In other words, it has always, to me, seemed a redundancy to write a composition and then use musicians sparingly simply because it was felt that I, as the leader, should blow my brains out to show some uncomprehending and insensitive critic that indeed I did have the capability of sustaining a large amount of hearing time through an overt use of physicality.'

QUARTET

MARK DRESSER, BASS

The double bass, laid carefully on its side, takes up most of the floor space in the tiny hotel room. The tall figure of Mark Dresser hunches over the electric kettle while I perch on the edge of a chair, a tape recorder balanced on my knees. It's 11.30 p.m.: the Birmingham concert finished an hour ago, and Mark has had the chance to wind down a little. He pours the tea, then sits on the bed, with the tight-lipped apprehension of a man about to have his teeth extracted.

This is Mark's first interview, and he's worried; inexplicably, when you consider he came through a harrowing Braxton quartet debut with flying colours. This happened some four months ago, in the summer of 1985. John Lindberg and Braxton had rowed, the bassist parted from the group in the middle of a European tour, and Gerry Hemingway suggested Dresser, then studying in Italy, as a replacement.

'They called me up and asked if I could come. I said I'll be there yesterday! My first time was sight-reading the concert at Ljubljana in Yugoslavia. The others arrived a half hour before the gig; they gave me these charts – Braxton pulls off the hardest charts in the book! – and it was like *total shock*! The amp was humming, the sound was terrible that night, I was not playing my own bass. It was like being thrown into the cold shower.

'Anthony has this composition, *121*, it's a fifty-page piece, all separate pages . . .! Plus, I wasn't ready to do these segues between pieces, pieces that I'd never heard before; so I wasn't sure when *121* actually began. By the time I realized it had started, they were on page two and I was scrabbling to find my place, like (*hisses*): "Gerry, what page are we on?" "Four." So I'd find the spot and *da-da*, play two bars, then there'd be a page turn. Every fifteen seconds there'd be a page turn! But it was fantastic to play that music. Things started happening right away, even though that first night was crazy.'

Now that you're a veteran of a dozen concerts, I say, what have you found to be the particular challenges of Braxton's music?

Mark leans forward thoughtfully, a large forefinger holding his glasses in place. 'Well, you gotta read your ass off. Your reading thing has to be formidable. And you really gotta be able to improvise. Think orchestrally, think soloistically . . . For me, it's a fantastic opportunity to play to my potential. When I was in Italy, I was getting a feel for reading weird scores, playing non-traditional music, but that was just using one side of my ability. Here, I got a chance where everything I could do, I was asked to do: play time, play many different levels of time too, play ensemble, independent, support, lead . . . After that first tour, it was the most alive I'd felt in years because I had to use so much of my ability.'

Is it still like that? I ask.

'Oh yeah. It's like every night is the absolute best I can do. Every night takes me to my limit.'

Mark Dresser was born in Los Angeles on 26 September 1952, and began to play bass ten years later. In his early teens he played in rock groups, though his first mentors were the classical bassist Nat Gangursky and jazzers Bill Plummer, Red Mitchell and Ray Brown. In the late sixties he studied music at Indiana University, but left after one year because 'it was too straight for me, like a music factory' and settled in San Diego. Here he began to study bass with Bertram Turetzky. Later, when Turetzky introduced him to drummer/writer Stanley Crouch, Dresser found a new world opening up for him. Every Saturday he'd drive from San Diego to Los Angeles to play with Crouch and trumpeter Bobby Bradford, a long-time associate of both John Carter and Ornette Coleman.

'That was a revelation. They were playing in a way I'd never heard. I didn't understand it, but I really liked it. Being in that environment was so rich, like I was the only white kid there, with cats much more sophisticated musically, much more experienced, and I was treated as an equal. Also, I was really being educated about the music. My listening had been very limited – Miles's *Silent Way*, *Bitches Brew*, some late Coltrane; when I started playing with

Bobby and Stanley, it went to Ornette, Bird, Louis, Duke. It went backwards as the music went forwards! Stanley would explain things in terms of political, social forces; Bobby would break things down musically, tell me about the changes.'

Flautist James Newton and reeds player David Murray, both in their teens, joined the group shortly after Dresser and they'd all rehearse together every weekend, although work prospects were practically nil. 'We'd do maybe two concerts a year,' Mark recalls.

Dresser found his commitment to the new music made him virtually unemployable in San Diego, where West Coast cool bop was still the chief commercial sound. A stint with the city's symphony orchestra only provoked an identity crisis – 'did I really want to be a classical bassist?' – so, in desperation, he moved to New York, where he began to play a lot with a young Chicago trombonist called Ray Anderson. Rather than live in NYC, which he hated, Dresser settled for a while in New Haven, Connecticut, where he found a flourishing musical community. 'I was neighbours with Gerry Hemingway, across the street from Pheeroan akLaff and Dwight Andrews, down the street from Jay Hoggard and about two blocks away from Anthony Davis. Mark Helias was there too, and Leo Smith – I got the chance to play some wonderful music with Leo Smith.'

This community dispersed, though, when several of the New Haven musicians moved to New York City. Dresser followed, but work proved scarce; he found his options closing down. I ask if there were any hassles being a white player in what was and is predominantly a black music scene.

'There were problems with that, but – shit – some things I can't do anything about,' he sighs. 'I don't know . . . I don't have an answer. All anyone can do is be themselves, that's the only thing I really have to offer.'

(The context for this situation, as Braxton explains in *Tri-axium Writings 1*,* is that because in a racist society white players are favoured by record companies, promoters, etc, many black musicians retaliate by forming cliques that exclude white players. It's notable that this didn't happen to Mark in California or New Haven, only in New York where the split between the music and the business is at its most exacerbated.)

Disheartened, Dresser returned to California; but the scene there

*See 'The White Improvisor', *T-a W1*, pp. 283–317

was so unstimulating he even blew his unemployment money to sponsor a mini-festival, Music Forward, where he put on Bobby Bradford and John Carter, George Lewis, Evan Parker, and the great Horace Tapscott, still a giant of the LA underground. Luckily, he'd kept in touch with Ray Anderson and Gerry Hemingway, and the former – now a member of the Braxton quartet – recommended him for his first gig with Braxton, at a special memorial concert for Eric Dolphy in San Jose in 1978.

'I played that concert with Braxton, Sonny Simmons, Barbara Donald, Eddie Marshall; that was like the high point of my career then. We played Eric's music, we had charts written out in his own hand, his parents were there; it was very meaningful on many levels. Braxton was very, very nice, complimentary, open; he made me feel at home. He said, "Well Dresser, we'll hook up one day." I kept sending him tapes and letters, but he was based on the East Coast then and I couldn't move back East just on speculation.'

Mark resumed his LA connection with Bobby Bradford and James Newton; he formed a trio in San Diego with Diamanda Galas (then a pianist) and reedsman/instrument-inventor Jim French; and he gradually got poorer and poorer. In 1980 he toured Europe with the Ray Anderson quartet (Gerry Hemingway was on percussion) and they recorded the *Harrisburg Half Life* LP for Moers. (His recording debut, though, had been in 1977, on James Newton's *Binu* LP.) When he returned to San Diego, there was still no work; he discovered grants were easier to come by than jobs so he went back to college to further his musical education. During his years of study, he played in a quartet with altoist Charles McPherson; recorded on Bobby Bradford's *Lost in LA* LP; and released his own solo tape, *Bass Excursions*, which included a version of Gerry Hemingway's *Threnody for Charles Mingus* as well as his own compositions. He'd already progressed to graduate school when in 1983 he got married, and then won a Fullbright scholarship to study in Italy with bass maestro Franco Petracchi. Two years later the call came from Braxton. Dresser had already been thinking of returning to the States again, and after that tour he made his move.

'I had a wonderful time in Italy, but I felt if I stayed there any longer, I'd be there for twenty years. And home is home, no matter how you feel about it.' A sour grimace intimates how he does feel about it, at least in the Reagan era. 'I went back to San Diego a few months ago. Now I want to finish my Master's, hopefully make a new solo tape, then maybe we'll relocate to the East Coast.'

How will you survive? I ask. Teaching? Playing?
'If I can get some teaching work, I'll do that. I'll play as much as
I can. God willing, it'll work out.' He smiles doubtfully, not exactly
confident of divine support.

After Mark has made us both a second cup of tea, I ask if he's
played any of Braxton's colour or shape notations.

He shakes his head. 'My scores are mostly traditionally notated.
There are some graph symbols, where you have to use extremes of
register, but graphic notation is common in contemporary music.
The things that *are* different are the pulse tracks, where you have to
play specific notes, specific rhythmic figures, then have maybe six
beats of improvisation, then you go to the next figure.* I've never
played any music that asked me to do that before. At first all I could
do was just count the beats,' he laughs; 'but it created new ways to
think. In fact, the more I'm getting into it, the more I'm finding.
The music is not easy, that's for sure; it's not even easy just to play
the surface, but I'm really digging and trying to go behind the
notes. That's when the music really begins – when you start
understanding what those notes, those figures and shapes, mean:
and it's fun digging because there's a lot of meaning there.

'To get with Braxton's music . . . There are a lot of beautiful
implications to it. People being independent but working together.
I mean, it's a wonderful formula, it has social ramifications that are
very beautiful, and . . . socially, what he makes the group do –
no, not makes, *requests* – is very exciting. Man, I'm as happy as I
can be.'

*E.g. from pulse track *108A*.

His beatific smile gives way to a puzzled frown when I ask how he feels about the criticisms that Braxton's music is too cold, too intellectual.

'There's definitely an intellectual component, but I don't think it's cold music, I don't think the performers are cold people. It's not easy to sit and listen to that music every night, perhaps, but a night like tonight, I don't think the people here thought that music was cold. We got a very *warm* response. I hate those terms, warm, cold . . .' (a shrug of displeasure). 'I think when the music's happening, it's *happening*, and it's self-evident.

'There's a really anti-intellectual trend that's happened in jazz . . . and if you look at the political scene in America right now, there's an anti-intellectual feeling: anything that isn't visceral is gonna be dismissed.'

So, for you, there is emotion in the music?

Mark casts an anguished glance at the ceiling. 'Oh, what's it look like, Graham? I mean, *clearly*. Anything that demands that much from a person, you gotta put everything you've got into it.'

How many rehearsals have you had? I ask.

'Since I started with Braxton? Two!' Mark shakes his head incredulously. 'When I joined the tour in Yugoslavia, I did five concerts without a rehearsal. I feel badly about that because this music deserves rehearsal, but you know what it's like on the road, the economic situation; there's no time, no money. We had one rehearsal before a concert in San Francisco last month, and one the night before the London concert. A piece like *121*, fifty pages of notation, that's hard to perform because it needs the kind of communication and clarity that a string quartet has. My feeling – and it's because I'm green to the band – is that we're still scratching the surface: I can't wait to get to the nitty-gritty of *121*, and . . . well, I can only speak for myself, but the more I know the music the less I have to think about what I'm doing. It demands so much instrumental finesse that sometimes – not on the best nights – you hear that effort. You've heard the music over several nights and I'm sure certain nights strike you as being . . . more *happening* than other nights?'

I nod assent.

'And what makes it happen, maybe we can dissect it, but when it *is* happening, the feeling level is much stronger, the group *breathes*, there's a real conversation. But you can't orchestrate feeling, that's a thing the musician has to bring to the music, and it's to do with who they are, how they're able to translate the experience – and you have to *know* your instrument, *know* the score, to get to the music behind the notes. That's the hardest for me: trying to learn this music well enough to where I can *play*.'

Mark slumps back, looking drained; the exertions of the concert are catching up with him. But he's still caught up in his thoughts.

'Like tonight,' he begins again, suddenly animated, 'there were moments when I was hearing myself, hearing Gerry, we were playing a completely independent thing to Marilyn and Anthony, but at the same time I heard us and I heard them and it was as if it was completely scored, we went together like hand and glove. And it was to do with our . . . with that extra element, that thing that's not written; making decisions, relating, leaving spaces for each other. I mean, there's a heavy human thing happening.'

One last question, I say. The feeling between the group seems to be very good, onstage *and* off. In your experience, is this degree of rapport common or not?

'Well, there is a high level of respect and co-operation here, people looking out for each other. These are the kinda people . . . you know, they're so gifted *and* they're like your family.' Mark strokes his beard thoughtfully, then looks up with a tired, happy smile. 'So, no; most musical situations aren't like this, most gigs aren't. This is a gas!'

ROAD

MONDAY 18, LIVERPOOL

Flipping through *Tri-axium Writings 2* I notice that, in his section on British jazz, Braxton mentions Joe Harriott only to say that he regrets he was never able to hear his music. By chance I have a tape of Harriott's long-unavailable *Abstract* and *Movement* LPs with me, but when I offer it to Braxton in the van he shakes his head: 'Maybe later, when I can really listen.'

I show him the photocopy I have of Harriott's sleevenotes to the 1963 *Abstract* record. The Jamaican-born Harriott, a misunderstood innovator (who evolved a concept of 'free music' contemporaneous to, and independent of, Ornette Coleman),* faced many of the problems that later afflicted Braxton in the way his music was perceived by critics and 'jazz' fans:

> So far as my own Free Form music is concerned . . . hardly a writer has come near me to try to find out exactly what we *are* trying to do. Instead, they have used conventional yardsticks to measure a commodity of which they know nothing . . .
> [The music] is best listened to as a series of different *pictures* – for it is after all by definition *an* attempt to paint, as it were, freely in sound . . . And the fan who came up to us after listening to a number at a date in Liverpool to complain that the music 'didn't swing' had better listen again; it wasn't meant to swing!

Braxton hands back the notes with a sigh. 'Plus ça change,' he mutters, staring gloomily out of the window. 'Plus ça change.'

I ask him what music he listens to at home, for pleasure.

*In this context perhaps I should mention Mr Coleman's comment (made at a lecture which he gave in London in 1987) that he had never liked the term 'free jazz'; it had, he said, been foisted on him by his record company and bore no relation to how *he* saw his music

124

'The last four years or so I've cut right down on all the information coming in. I just listen to my own recordings, to Warne Marsh, Sal Mosca, Mingus, Stockhausen, Wagner, Steve Lacy . . . that's about it.'

We reach Liverpool in the early afternoon. A thriving city at the height of Beatlemania, it's rapidly becoming a ghost town, full of gutted buildings, bricked-up windows, deathly tower-blocks. It's a city on the verge of bankruptcy too; this week the council is due to run out of funds for public services. The government cut-backs have hit northern inner-city areas particularly hard, all part of the Tories' assault on the Welfare State, or what Braxton acidly calls 'the Reagan/Thatcher mind-set' – 'Yay! Let's go stomp those poor people!'

Our hotel is right beside the river and from my window I can see a ferry pushing through the grey, choppy swell of the Mersey. While I watch, I say a silent prayer for John Lennon: the Beatles played the first music I really loved, where it all began for me; and John, dreaming war is over, was my last hero. The quartet are Beatles' fans too, especially Marilyn, and while I interview Braxton, Tony takes the others on a search for memorabilia (but a plaque commemorating where the Cavern used to be and a shop selling Ringo Starr underpants are about all they find!)

At the soundcheck Braxton produces the new piece, *Composition 124*, which he's just finished. The group run through their parts several times, and also play through *6A* and *40N*. Marilyn finds her part for the latter has been written out for brass rather than piano. 'I'll have to transpose it down a major third,' she says, peering at the score.

'OK, we'll leave it,' says Braxton. 'I'll write it out for you tonight, after the concert.'

'I can transpose it in my head,' she offers. 'We can play it if you like.'

I gulp. My God, sight-transpose a Braxton chart! Is this woman human?

LIVERPOOL CONCERT, EVERYMAN THEATRE

First Set (Primary Territories)
Composition 6A
Composition 114 (+ 108A)

Collage Form Structure (Reeds/bass *96*; piano/percussion *108A*)
Composition 40F
Composition 124 (+ *96*)

Second Set (Primary Territories)
Composition 40N
Composition 69Q
Piano solo (from *30–33*)
Composition 86 (+ *108C*)
Composition 40B

(Tonight's sets typify the structural variety of a Braxton concert. *6A*, Braxton's first-ever quartet composition, is built around a bass arco march; *114*, played with the *108A* pulse track, uses the C-major scale as a 'jumping off' or 'centring' point for extended improvisation; *40F* is based on chromatic phrases – plus its fast, rising-falling central motif is reminiscent of both the *Batman* theme and a snippet of Thelonious Monk's *Skippy!*; the new *124*, a very slippy-slidey piece, with Braxton on sopranino, is a 'multiple line' complex with its own pulse track; *40N* revolves around a bass drone; *69Q*, which has a distinctly jaunty feel to it, uses repetition, specifically a 'repetition phrase pattern' for 'structured improvisation'; *86* is another of the woodwind/bass duet series; and *40B*, dedicated to altoist Lou Donaldson, is one of Braxton's post-bebop extended lines, a dashing piece, its rhythmic changes superbly crafted, and designed – in typical Braxton fashion – with a variety of built-in options for the players – a fine example of restructuralist bebop.)

Though the music is never less than absorbing, I feel an inevitable air of anti-climax after last night's excitement. The venue itself is a contributory factor: chilly, run-down, two-thirds empty (eighty-seven people, the lowest attendance of the tour),* it seems to replicate the despondency of the city outside. The group's energy seems more diffuse than usual too, though by the second set the focus is sharper. In fact, *40N* is riveting, the three instruments creating a rich sense of spaciousness around the dark core of Mark's

---

*The highest attendance was 504 at London; other attendances all fell into the 100–250 range. (Information courtesy of the Contemporary Music Network. Figures refer to number of tickets sold, not including press tickets, guest tickets etc, so actual attendances will have been slightly higher)

Anthony Braxton, 1985

Above and opposite: Braxton conducting a performance of his *Composition 100* at the Huddersfield Contemporary Music Festival

Anthony Braxton, reeds

Mark Dresser, bass

Marilyn Crispell, piano. Through time...

. . . into space

Gerry Hemingway, percussion

bass drone. And the faster tempos of *69Q* and *40B* elicit some lightning ensemble interplay plus, in the latter, swashbuckling solos from Braxton (on alto) and Marilyn, who really seems to relish the chance to open up on the quicker pieces.

Later, in the dressing-room, she confirms my feeling of a slight loss of *rapprochement*. 'I think I preferred last night. There were times tonight when I thought, huh, where is everybody?' She turns to Mark. 'Did you hear my Beatles quote?'

'No, when was that?'

'I quoted *Yesterday* behind your drone piece.'

'Yeah?' He smiles. 'Well, you're sure subtle with your quotes, Marilyn.'

'You should've started singing "*yeah, yeah, yeah*",' Tony laughs.

The group's catholic tastes surprise and delight me. We have the same pop heroes!

'You know the two things I most regret?' Marilyn is saying. 'That I never saw the Beatles live and I never saw John Coltrane live. They were my big heroes in the sixties, with Jimi Hendrix.'

GL: 'Did you see Hendrix?'

MC: 'No, only on film a couple of times. He was fantastic.'

GH: 'I've never met anyone into music who wasn't into Jimi Hendrix.'

GL: 'Steve Lacy's into Hendrix. He told me Hendrix was like a god to him. And he liked the Beatles.'

GH: 'Have you seen that Devo video of *Are You Experienced*, with Hendrix coming out of the grave? That's great – a real satire on all the record-company necrophilia.'

AB: 'That's right. I remember once he died they released everything he ever played on: rehearsal tapes, jam sessions, demos . . .'

GH: (*laughs*) 'Yeah, there's nothing like dying to up your market value.'

AB: 'That's the record business for you. First they *kill* you, *then* they put out your records!'

GL: (*to GH*) 'So who do you like in recent pop?'

GH: 'Well, there's been no one of Hendrix's stature since then. I kinda go for the *weird* groups now – Devo, the Residents . . .'

AB: 'Hey, I liked that guy – Captain Beefheart! You ever hear him singing "*give me that old time religion*"? (*sings it in deep, croaky Beefheartian voice*). I heard that, and like – who *is* this cat? (*Laughs.*) He played some real *out* sax solos too. Somebody told me he didn't know anything about music, but I can't believe that. He was a *baaad* cat!'

GH: 'Yeah, that's his version of *Moonlight in Vermont*. It starts off with crickets, I think, people talking . . . I forget what they do to the tune exactly, but they completely *destroy* it. Wonderful!'

METAROAD

BIOGRAPHY 3, 1974–85

THE EUROPEAN IMPROVISERS

L: Before we go to New York, could we talk about the European improvisers you've played with – Derek Bailey, Evan Parker, the Globe Unity Orchestra? You played with them throughout the seventies, but presumably your relationship with them began when you were in Paris.

B: Yes. I invited Derek Bailey to Paris. In fact I wrote a piece for Derek: at the time I didn't realize he was totally not interested in notated music. I heard Derek's music the first time I came to London, with Circle. We stopped over for a couple of days and I played at the 100 Club with Mike Osborne, that was my first performance in London. Thanks to Dave Holland I'd already heard Derek's records and later that week I heard him live at the Little Theatre. He did a solo gig and, boy, his music excited me. I felt I could really play with this man.

L: You've said that you'd developed your language before you came to Europe, but did the European improvisers not have any influence on you?

B: That's a complex question. For the most part I don't think I've been influenced by the European improvisers. Well, I've learned from Evan Parker as a saxophonist – he taught me to circular breathe – but my ideas about music had formed six, seven years before this period in Paris.

In fact, in the early seventies, nobody – black or white – had any respect for Europe, for the European master composers tradition: I remember Peter Kowald got very angry when he heard I appreciated Wagner's music. The improvising schools that developed since 1970, say, many of them would reinforce the narrowest spectrum of the music: if you weren't involved in improvisation then your work wasn't respected. Fortunately, that wasn't the case with the masters who solidified their work after Coltrane's death; I'm thinking, say, of Evan Parker and Derek Bailey. But there was a real sentiment in the air against notated music, even from Derek and Evan in that period, although Evan has always been broader than most people think about matters of pedagogy and methodology.

To return to your question – it's difficult to answer. I think of, say, Dudu Pukwana, the Brotherhood of Breath . . . I found these people very interesting, though not from the same restructuralist criteria that applied to Derek and Evan: their work is important, yet it's not mentioned. And Willem Breuker's group in the Netherlands, Peter Kowald, Peter Brötzmann – I have a great deal of respect for those people. It's like we've all grown up together; there was a sense of solidarity in that we were all fighting for our music. But if you ask me what did I *learn* from those people . . . well, they were getting their solutions listening to the same people I was listening to.

I notice now, looking back over the years, you can see who's still generating, whose music is demonstrating evolution. There's a big difference between 1985 and 1965 in terms of what's been demonstrated.

L: Meaning?

B: Let me say it like this: many people talked of many things in the sixties. From a vantage point of twenty years, it's possible to look back and see who was talking and who was working; who really believed in what they were talking about and who took advantage of the moment to leap aboard what was thought to be current, like bossa nova or something. The time speaks for itself: what has been demonstrated clarifies everything.

L: So who jumped aboard the bossa nova?

B: Oh no, I could never go into that. But I am still a great fan of Steve Lacy, of Evan Parker, of Leo Smith, of Stockhausen, Cage, Cecil Taylor . . . there are probably more (*laughs*). The difference between those who planted seeds and those who didn't is that in this period there are trees.

THE ARISTA PERIOD –
'UNDER THE RUG'

L: OK. You had a phone call from Michael Cuscuna saying, come back to New York. You already knew Mr Cuscuna?

B: Michael is a special friend, I met him in Chicago in the sixties. We see each other every now and again; three or four years can go by, then we'll get together and it's always good. Anyway, he was part of the new structure that was forming at Arista Records. This was a period of change for me. I would meet Nickie Braxton, Nickie Singer as she was then, in Paris and she came back to America with me and we started a whole new life in 1974.

The challenge of the Arista association was to feed them the quartet music and slip them some of my other projects 'under the rug'. So for five or six years I was able to document some of the traditional quartet material as well as slip in the piece for four saxophones, the duo with Richard Teitelbaum, the chamber orchestra piece from Berlin, the piece for two pianos, the piece for trio and the piece for four orchestras,* which was the crowning project of that time, where Nickie and I went $25,000 into debt. It took us three years of poverty to work it off. This was before we had children: I could never do that now. But I wanted to use that platform while it was there: I knew it wouldn't last.

L: Why was that project so expensive?

B: There were 160 musicians. They were students, so I could pay them a cheaper rate; but the scores alone cost over $20,000 – and that was cheap! I mean, parts for 160 people! Plus I used colour and shape in that score.

L: Slipping these projects 'under the rug' – was that a strategy devised by you, Michael Cuscuna and Steve Backer?†

B: They understood, yes. They were very beautiful and understanding.

L: Who didn't understand? Why did you have to go 'under the rug'?

B: We're talking about the company, the upper business people, in particular the president, Mr Clive Davis. We tried to work within the structure to get the most out of it. I'll be grateful to Michael and

---

*Compositions 37, 38A, 63, 95, 76 and 82 respectively

†Michael Cuscuna was the producer of Braxton's Arista records, Steve Backer the executive producer

Steve for the rest of my life because I had the opportunity to document a cross-section of my music. Of course, I wanted to get more notated pieces out, but I understood the only possibility for me to maintain momentum was to keep playing the saxophone – that was the channel the company would give me. It was interesting . . . as the records came out, my name would go up in the polls, but when it became apparent what I was *really* about, I dropped from maybe third or fourth in *Downbeat* down to 500th! (*Laughs.*)

L: Your last record for Arista, the piece for two pianos, was never released in the UK.

B: It was barely released in America! They might have pressed 500 copies. I tell you, the piece for four orchestras – I doubt if they pressed 1,000 copies, then they deleted it! They realized it wasn't a big-band record – they were expecting something like the *Creative Orchestra Music* project – so . . . they showed me! I'd invested $25,000 in a record that stayed out for maybe six months.

L: How come Arista didn't pay those expenses for you?

B: For an African-American, you know, a young man . . . I was thirty, thirty-one, with visions of a piece for four orchestras, a three-record set: how many projects like that do you see released? The record companies are not going to do it. They're not interested in music, they're interested in getting something out that's very cheap. So if you want something done, you have to do it yourself. I had not planned on this, but I've always been ambitious in the sense of having ideas and wanting to get them executed. I was profoundly inspired by Stockhausen's *Carré* and *Gruppen*, by Xenakis's *Polytope* – there was no way I was not going to enter that region. If I'd waited for somebody to give me $100,000 for a project, I would still be waiting and the piece would not be written. I decided the only way to keep evolution going was not to think in terms of somebody helping me, I just had to do it myself. I mean, I specialize in not getting projects out! But I'll be damned if I'm not going to write the project just because they're not going to give me a performance or a record. If nobody ever performed it, it's fine by me! Well, I don't *mean* it's fine . . . but I am prepared to accept that, I'm prepared to write twelve operas and never get one performance. And the thing is, you can't complain if you don't write it. So first I'll write my twelve operas, *then* I'll complain. And if somebody performs it, I'll complain about something else (*laughs*). But with the piece for four orchestras, I'm just sorry that the records were not really distributed or made available for long.

NOTATED MUSIC – 'YOU TAKE WHAT YOU CAN GET'

L: I've read that the classically-trained musicians who recorded your notated music have not always been very co-operative or receptive to your ideas. Is that true?

B: The Berlin New Music Group, who did *Composition 63*, they were actually very nice. The tuba ensemble on *Composition 4* – it was ridiculous!* The performance of the piece is . . . I just took what I could get. You're paid like $1,000 a record or some such nonsense and in that period, as now, I tried to invest all my money in the music. So I hired these people . . . And, of course, I have *never* had proper rehearsal time on any of my music nor, with the exception of one or two pieces, have I ever been commissioned; and if I have been able to get some of my notated pieces represented on record, I can say it's not *their* fault – they being the record companies and the people I've had to deal with. I've tried to take advantage of the moment, but what that would mean is – *not* the best performance. But either I was going to get a bad performance or no performance at all.

L: Why do you say the tuba piece was ridiculous?

B: If I showed you the score . . . as far as an accurate performance, it's *ridiculous*. Not good enough!

L: Was that through lack of rehearsal time or the musicians' antipathy?

B: Oh . . . (*sighs*) we had little rehearsal time, which was normal, but I felt they could have worked harder and gotten better results. Still, that's fifteen years ago; I'm not as angry as I used to be. On a gradient scale of five billion to zero, I would say I'm only four billion 999 million, 999, 909 degrees angry compared to what I used to be!

L: How about the piece for four orchestras?

B: Well, we had about three hours' rehearsal time –

L: That is ridiculous! Three hours?

B: Something like that. But there's no unhappiness there, I appreciate the fact that they even did the piece. We had students, the score is 303 pages long . . . the record only has about two-thirds

---

Composition 63 is on *The Montreux/Berlin Concerts* LP; *Composition 4* is on *The Complete Braxton* LP

of the piece, I had to throw a third away because it wasn't right. But I say that not to indict the students or the people who worked to make that project happen – they in fact did the best they could possibly have done.

L: Michael Cuscuna told me that the piece was recorded, like most classical recordings, a few bars at a time, in thirty-second, sixty-second bursts, and spliced together later. He said the editing was a nightmare, about 700 little bits of tape to stick together.

B: Yeah. Basically we had to rush the recording because the record company, of course, thought it was going to be a 'jazz' record, and we kind of *snuck* it in. But the four-orchestra piece should be faster – the record is noticeably slower than it actually should be. I took what I could get, and I'd do it again.

RECORD COMPANIES – 'AARRGGHH!!!'

L: How were your relationships with the other record companies you've worked with? Moers, for instance.

B: Well, I developed a relationship with Burkhard Hennen in the early seventies, he was establishing his festival at Moers in Germany and he was interested in my music in that period. My association with him would result in four or five records, then our relationship broke up: probably we'll never even speak to each other any more. The only thing I would say about Mr Hennen here is that I feel fortunate to have had his friendship at that time. When he was my friend, he was my friend; and when he was my not-friend, he was my not-friend. I can relate to that.

L: That sounds similar to your dispute with Werner Uehlinger and hat Hut. The fact that it's happened twice . . . how far do you feel *you've* been responsible for the break-up of these relationships?

B: Oh, it's happened more than twice (*laughs*). I think I'm definitely responsible 'cause I keep thinking that people should deal with me like I'm a human being, so from the very beginning the axiom is wrong. When I look at the music business and some of the things that are happening – there's nothing to be said. I mean, *aarrgghh!!!*

L: How about Antilles? You made the *Six Compositions: Quartet* LP with them.

B: That was another example of my wonderful relationship with a record company. They said they were interested in my music, that for the first record we'd have to do a quartet record and after that we could do a small opera. Have you seen the opera record? No, OK!

L: Did they give any reason?

B: They dropped my contract right after the first record came out, so it wasn't even about sales. They just dropped it, so . . . I don't know.

L: To come up to date, you're recording now for Black Saint so I guess that's a satisfactory relationship.

B: Giovanni Bonandrini? I have the utmost respect for the man. I only wish I could make more records with him, but in this period where there are so few people documenting the music he's recording a lot of artists. We have our disagreements, but he's a very respectable gentleman; I hope we'll do more things in the future. Also Robert Koester from Delmark Records – we've fought and laughed and cried, whatever, but I'm grateful for my relationship with him.

L: When we talked last year, you said you would like to start your own record label. Is this still the plan?

B: This is my dream, yeah. I want to put out my own writings, my own records, and have it not depend on how many people want to buy them. So far I've printed about fifty of my books, that's 150 volumes; I think I've sold seven, eight, nine sets and given the rest away. In the future I guess that'll have to change, I can't continue to lose money. But I'm not that good a business person, I've got to figure out how to get better at that. I'd like to have a record company, put out two or three records a year, and if nobody buys 'em – I'll buy 'em (*laughs*). But for that small group of people who're interested in my work, I'd like for them to be able to hear it, that's all.

FOUR BILLION PROJECTS

L: If the chance comes along, you'll still record for other labels?

B: I'd like to have 5,000 records, like Duke Ellington! This is the medium we're dealing with in this time period and I'd like to document as much of my music as I can. I'm trying to learn from Steve Lacy, but frankly it's hard to keep up with Mr Lacy – he's a virtuoso in the art of putting out records (*laughs*). But if I make 5,000 records, there's a chance two or three of 'em will still be available after six months (*laughs*).

L: You've mentioned to me a series of solo music LPs that you'd recorded in France for the Stil Editions label.

B: Yes. I recorded a lot of my recent solo material in a church in Paris, I think this was some of the best playing I've ever done in my life, and they were going to put it out as a fourteen-record set. I drew up all the titles, worked out a running order – because there are some long pieces: *119F*, I think it is, takes up five sides – then the last time I spoke to them they said they were thinking they'd maybe do *one* record! That's the 'jazz' world for you, Graham!

L: You were also talking about other projects you'd like to do: Coltrane compositions, Mingus compositions.

B: This is what I would like to do in the future. I'd like to make at least one two-record set of Mingus compositions; one two-record set of Coltrane compositions; a set of Tristano compositions; a set of Charlie Parker compositions; maybe even a set of Dave Brubeck compositions. I'd also love to do a two-record set of Dixieland music, some of the old pieces like *Basin Street Blues* and *Royal Garden Blues*, oh boy! Maybe a set of Sousa's music . . . Oh, and a two-record set of, like, the classical repertoire: I'd love to record Varèse's *Density 21.5*. These are among the four billion projects I'd like to do before the year's out! (*Laughs.*) Not to mention my twelve operas, my multi-orchestral series . . .

IN THE TRADITION, THE

INFLEXIBLE GROUP, VALIUM

L: Tell me about your records in the post-Parker continuum, the two *In the Tradition* records and the two *Seven Standards* records. Why did you want to record this material, and why wait eleven years between the two recording sessions?

B: OK. One, I did the music because I love that music, I love that period, that is my lineage and it's a wonderful colour to be involved with or at least to document. I've always said my work is not a rejection of vertical harmony or of bebop. Two, my original plan was to document say every seven to ten years a two-record set of material from that tradition; and I made the decision to wait seven to ten years because I understood that to make a bebop record would also make life more complex when it came to putting out my own projects. For instance, I have three bebop records – four next year when *Seven Standards Volume Two* comes out – but I can't get my orchestra music out, I can't even get my chamber music out. One would not have to be a philosopher to understand that if a record company can get you playing *How High the Moon* rather than *Composition 116*, they'll ask for *How High the Moon*. So I decided not to do too many bebop records to protect my real work; which is not to say that bebop is separate from my work, but I haven't spent twenty years generating a music only to throw it away because 'bebop is back' – then, of course, next week bebop will be thrown out and bossa nova is in . . .

But to have the chance to play with Mr Hank Jones, my God! Rufus Reid! These people are incredible musicians, and it's a pleasure to function in that context *every now and again*: when I make the decision to do it. I'd rather die than play a standard just because somebody else wanted me to. I don't have that kind of flexibility, I don't *like* that kind of flexibility. I'm from, let's say, the *inflexible* group (*laughs*).

L: Why was the first *In the Tradition* LP dedicated to Roche Pharmaceuticals?

B: The makers of Valium. I lived on Valium for about five years, I was taking 100 milligrams a day.

L: Why?

B: Because . . . I was living in severe poverty, and . . . oh, every time I picked up a music journal, somebody was attacking me as if I'd done something personal to them. My life was very difficult, there was a lot of stress, and the Roche Pharmaceutical Company – because of their technology I would be able not to jump out of my skin.

TAKING THE LUMPS

L: From what you say, I gather that even when you were with Arista you weren't making a lot of money?

B: I have never made any money from my music. People think I've made money, but as far as what money really is . . . let's be honest, *money* starts at the zone where you have enough to live comfortably. That's not what's happening in the jazz world. People like myself, travelling all around the planet on two-month tours . . . you get home with $500 or $1,000 and the bills have piled up to $3,000. The life is not as glamorous as it might appear. There have been periods when I've been able to pay the rent, especially from 1974 to, say, 1979; but not *money*, you don't get *money* from this. When you talk about the Rolling Stones, or even the average rock group who get a hit after six months together, they'll make more money in two years than maybe I'll make in my whole life. That's why I feel fortunate to be at Mills now, with the possibility to have a profession I can make a living at.

L: Ah, that reminds me! One of Bill Dixon's Soul Note LPs includes an interview in which you're mentioned as someone who had spoken very antagonistically about the notion of musicians working in the education system. Is that right?*

B: (*grimaces*) Uh-huh, that sounds like me! I had never planned to teach professionally, but my value systems began to change in the last five years. We've been living on a subsistence, a survival, level for the last five years. I'm forty years old now, we have three children, my wife and myself: my priorities had to be re-examined. It's one thing to fight for your music and take the lumps and starve and die when you're only dealing with yourself. It's quite another thing to have the responsibility of children, and Nickie and I – it was like, *wait a minute*, you know? Charles Ives understood this problem a long time ago: what am I doing banging my head against a wall? I'm not working; then when I do work, I come home with no money. What about my family?

Our electricity was off for a month, then for another couple of months, three or four times in one year. The telephone was off basically for the whole year. Those kind of experiences helped me to re-evaluate my plans. So I'm grateful to be at Mills. It's not as if I'll be an academic in the sense of never having played music: I have, for the last twenty years, *lived* my music. My feelings about the academic community have changed completely – when I look at what was taking place in my life, they had to change.

A FORTUNATE STRUGGLE

L: I know that for many African-Americans, especially those involved in creative music, poverty is a fact of life. But the extreme poverty you've endured – do you think you've been very unfortunate or is that degree of hardship commonplace?

B: I would say that the poverty that I dealt with in the last five

---

*Bill Dixon in Italy, Volume One. The interview also includes Mr Dixon's caustic comments on the notion of 'swing'

years, in my whole life, is a *luxury*. I'm a very fortunate man to have had the experiences I've had, and when I turn around and look at the last forty years of my life I'm amazed at how fortunate I've been. I mentioned before Kalaparush Maurice McIntyre, his life has not been easy; Leo Smith – no one has dealt with this man's music on the level it deserves and he has not had the good fortune to have as many recordings out as I have; Douglas Ewart . . . I mean, there are a lot of people functioning who have experienced poverty.

We are now seeing many of the post-Ayler musicians change their music to a more commercial kind of music, and it's a tragedy . . . well, I won't say tragedy, but who can blame these people? Because the economic pressure to survive is terrible, especially when you have a family. And it's like, poverty is not only inhibiting, poverty is boring – and there's nothing worse than that. This is not to mention, of course, the *profound* levels of poverty that are taking place on the planet, the starvation poor people are dealing with in Africa, in South America. So the poverty I'm dealing with, it's like part of the context for people who decide to go on this particular route. And it's a luxury because I'm involved in something that I *love*, and I love it so much I'll do it whether anybody listens or not.

How fortunate it is to fight and struggle for something that you believe in, as opposed to, say, being involved in a job that means nothing and losing the flame of excitement. At least I know what gives me enjoyment, I understand the source of my excitement and I've tried to stay as true to that as I could – and that is an honour.

'KEEP AWAY FROM MUSICIANS'

L: Can we end today with a few details about your family life? I know you and your wife have three children, but you told me you had an older daughter too.
B: Yes. My first child, Terri, her mother's name is Darlene; it's Darlene Palmer now, back then her name was Darlene Talbot. I was in high school and, well, this was my first great love, but our families would not let us get married, we were too young, and . . . they were probably right. I recall Darlene used to say to me that the first thing she would do when we get married is throw away this danged saxophone because it seemed that I loved it more than I loved her. She was interested in the middle-class, the American

Dream – which made sense, we were all programmed for that. I wanted to play music, she wasn't really interested in music, but, of course, I was in love . . . I thought. Ah, it's a long time ago. Now my daughter has two babies. I'm a grandfather, at forty!

L: You met Nickie in Paris?

B: Yes, in 1973. She was with a friend of mine, and I was with another lady, so we just knew each other as friends. Then she broke up with her guy, I broke up with my lady – this was a period of transition – and we came together in Paris just before I moved back to America. When she made the decision to come to America with me, we were starting a whole new cycle in our lives, even our relationship with each other was very new. So we've been together now for eleven years, we have three children, and my family life has been a source of strength to me.

L: How old are your children?

B: Tyondai is seven, my daughter Keayr will be five in about two weeks, and Donari is three; so they're two years apart – and getting bigger!

L: Nickie has been involved in several of your projects?

B: Nickie Braxton is an incredibly creative person. She has a calligrapher's hand, she copies scores for me – they look as good as Stockhausen's. She's an excellent photographer, she did the photography for *Composition 96*, for orchestra and four slide projectors. She did the costumes for the two-pianos piece, she's doing the costumes for the *Trillium* operas; she's studying violin, she's studying music with me. Part of her problem is that she can do so many things well, she can't make up her mind what she wants to do. I try to have her in as many projects as possible because *life* should be creative, especially when you have as much talent as Nickie.

Having the opportunity to be with Nickie, the possibility of having a family, would fulfil my life and bring meaning to my life on levels I knew nothing about before. Some of the articles portray me as being a very far-out guy, but I'm actually a real traditionalist, I'm not very far-out at all. At home we have a very normal family life – I don't mean it's unexciting, in fact it's very fulfilling, at least that's what we work for; I don't mean to paint Utopia either. Nickie and I are human beings and we're dealing with trying to understand how to be together too. But, for instance, I was never interested in being on the scene, I wanted a conventional life; I wanted to be separate from the musicians – put that in capitals, SEPARATE

FROM THE MUSICIANS – and be with my family.
L: Why separate from the musicians?
B: Because the social reality that surrounds the scene is not healthy.
Not only that, I wanted to do my work, and you can't hang out on
the corner and talk talk talk and be composing music at the same
time. There's too much nonsense out there. Keep away from the
musicians! That's one of the primary axioms – and keep away from
the political scenes that surround the music. It's so ridiculous . . .

THE HEAT OF LOGS –

IN THE BASEMENT

I hope never again to make my living from performing music. I
never want to be in a situation where my family might have to
undergo the kind of poverty we've had in the past five years. I'll get
a job, I'll drive a taxi or work at Sears, whatever it takes. We had a
winter where we had no heat, I had to go out for firewood every
morning. We lost our home . . . we bought a home in '79, '80 – we
could not make the first payment! So we had a winter of living by
the heat of logs. We had a fireplace, thank goodness, but I had to go
out every day looking for wood.
L: Where were you living then?
B: Woodstock.
L: So there was wood around?
B: There was wood around, but after a month or two it was getting
hard to find. And if I didn't find it, my children were going to
freeze. Those were the parameters I was dealing with.
L: You say now you'll drive a taxi – people may wonder, why not
then?
B: Well, because . . . I had one other goal, and that was to complete
the theoretical and the aesthetic foundations of my music, the
Tri-axium Writings and the *Composition Notes*. This was very
important to me, to solidify my foundation, and . . . my babies
were not in school yet, so I made the decision I had to have that
finished before I was forty.
   I can only say that Nickie and I have tried to hold our family
together, and we have gone through our difficult periods. I've tried
to be a responsible father, but I know my family was definitely
committed to a hardship course because of the nature of my work.
My children are still healthy and alive, so I think they're OK, none

the worse for what we've gone through.

L: Do they like music?

B: They're very interested in music. They're normal children, into their robots and cars and trucks. I don't know . . . see, I know now that I will always be involved in music and music evolution, no one can stop me from playing. I might not get a gig, I might not get a record, but I'll do it in the basement.

L: The multi-orchestral series? *Trillium?*

B: If somebody performs them, I'll be very happy. If they don't, I'll maybe sneak downstairs to the basement once a month, look at the scores and imagine, yeah, it would've gone like *this*, then *this* would've happened . . . Like I said, you take what you can get.

ROAD

TUESDAY 19, SHEFFIELD

In the van Mark and Gerry are reading newspaper reports of the newly-convened Geneva Peace Conference.

'I think the Soviets have come to it with their position upfront,' says Mark. 'The US position seems kinda vague.'

'That's 'cause they're a bunch of mushy-mouthed motherfuck-ers,' Gerry grunts.

'Yeah, but it's also 'cause the US doesn't wanna give up shit. It's all theatre – part of Reagan's bid for immortality.'

'The BBC put it neatly,' Gerry drawls. 'They said the Americans are coming in playing poker, the Russians are coming in playing chess.'

I put on the headphones and listen to some of Gerry's tapes: Eck Robertson, a 1920s C&W violinist; Aiza Anaiak, a Basque percussion duo; Billy Pigg, legendary player of Umbrian pipe music. Gerry's tastes put eclecticism in the shade.

The drive across the Pennines treats us to the most spectacular scenery of the tour; the road winds above little valley towns with their tall, abandoned, factory chimneys, then up into the hills, russet, bottle-green, and higher still, across Snake Pass, the rocky ground dappled with snow, the sky slate-grey: a solarized landscape of shiny blacks and whites. Descending towards Sheffield, we drive along a river valley, its hillsides lined with pine trees, some thick with needles, others bereft.

'Hmm, the scenery here is beautiful,' Braxton sighs. 'I like those bare trees.'

'That's acid rain,' Gerry declares.

'Are you sure it's not just winter, Gerry?' Braxton asks mildly.

'No, I've read about the acid rain in Britain,' Gerry says. 'You get black snow falling in Scotland, right?'

143

I shrug. 'I thought most of our acid rain fell in Germany and Scandinavia. I know we've practically killed the Black Forest.'

'Yeah, but you get acid rain here too,' says Gerry. 'Your own lakes are starting to die. Those trees definitely look unhealthy.' He launches into an authoritative account of the history and causes of acid rain. A mood of gloom descends on the van.

'You saw this on Channel 125?' Braxton remains sceptical.

'Pines don't go brown, they don't lose their needles,' insists Gerry. 'That's why they're called evergreens, right? Because they stay green.'

'There are some pines that look OK.' Mark peers through the window dubiously.

'Yeah, how come there are *blocks* of green trees and *blocks* of brown trees?' Braxton asks. 'Does it rain from square clouds?'

'Well, that's kinda strange,' agrees Gerry. 'But they sure look dead to me.'

'I think they look nice,' Braxton demurs. 'I'm gonna check this out, Hemingway. We'll see what we will see.'

As we drive on I ruminate on the destruction of the forests and the curious historical analogies between freedom and space. How the enclosure of land in the seventeenth and eighteenth centuries coincided with the enclosure of European music in notation and a tempered scale that required the diminution of sound into precise pitches (and how the landowners came to own the musicians too); how this in turn was part of a greater *zeitgeist* of separation and individuation, exemplified in the rise of capitalism, of Protestantism, of clock-time, of perspective (the single viewpoint) in painting, and a Newtonian physics that saw nature as lifeless matter and the universe as a collection of objects floating unconnected in the dead vasts of space. Curious too how in the twentieth century the rise of a New Physics, with its view of the universe as a dynamic network of vibrations, has accompanied a new ecological consciousness, a new multi-faceted art (Cubism), the rise of different kinds of collectivism (as political and personal philosophies) and a music, jazz, which insists on both freedom for its individual voices *and* the reality of their interdependence. In fact, the music's history can be seen as a process of democratization, from the polyphonic ensemble lines of Dixieland, through the personal flights of bebop, to the harmolodic freedoms of Ornette Coleman and Braxton's collage form structures, where all the players are simultaneously independent *and* connected, free *and* responsible, expressing their self-awareness *and* their relationship to the ensemble/family/community. Like Mark says, a paradigm of how to live. (And, boy, do we need it!)

We check into our hotel, then Tony, Braxton and I drive to the Leadmill, the community arts centre where Braxton is lecturing this afternoon. (It's also the venue for tonight's gig.) We arrive in a snowstorm to find the upstairs room allocated for the lecture has no heating; we move to the main auditorium, which is slightly less freezing but far from ideal since it's the building's central space and people are constantly walking through. More disappointing, only a dozen people have turned up for the lecture. Braxton grits his teeth and gets on with it, but I notice that for the first time on the tour he's looking tired.

He begins by talking about vocabulary dynamics. He says his music is visually based and that he finds his solutions in the actual playing. In Western art music now, they only play the notes – the empirical at the expense of the spiritual. 'Correct players are some of the most boring players on the planet' because they emphasize process not personal potential or metaphysics, and their notion of development is existential rather than spiritual. But different structures tap different information zones; form has its vibrational aspects too. 'Understanding humanity is what I'm interested in, not just the evolution of process.' Braxton pauses and wearily surveys his silent, shivering audience. 'Is that clear? I don't want to assume that for once in my life I've said something clear enough that everybody understands it.'

He moves to the significance of repetition, particularly on a vibrational level, as in mantra. 'Let me say this, then I'll see if I agree with it: repetition is the most direct vibrational factor in music. Look at African, Indian musics; look at Gregorian chants.' There are musics for all functions, events, incidents – this information is known all over the world, but has been lost in the West in the last 300 years. He talks about his own uses of repetition, and plays recorded examples of the different ways it can function in his music (see 'Postscript 3', ii).

By the end of the lecture, Braxton has lost half of his audience (but the six who remain all come to the concert). Tony has discovered that the lecture had originally been arranged for groups of local sixth-formers, but at the last moment their teachers had refused to authorize the outing (as part of the NUT's work-to-rule campaign for better pay and working conditions). There had been no time to publicize the lecture elsewhere, hence the low turn-out.

'Teachers are badly paid here?' Braxton asks.

'Teachers and nurses particularly,' I say. 'Thatcher's running down the education system like she's run down the National Health Service. She's just destroying the Welfare State. We're back to the days when education and health-care were privileges for the rich, and the poor just got shafted.'

'It's the same in America,' Braxton sighs. 'When Ronald Reagan was elected, white America thought he was gonna *get those niggers* – and, of course, he got 'em! But they didn't realize he was gonna get them too, if they weren't born with a lot of money. I think America now could be moving towards the Dark Ages.'

'What did Charlie Parker say? *Civilization's a good idea; somebody should try it.*'

We return to the hotel, where I interview Braxton for an hour, then it's back to the Leadmill for the soundcheck and concert. The group play through a couple of tunes again, including *Half Nelson*. The acoustics of the place seem murky, the sound flying everywhere; plus there's a problem with the heating system, a huge grid-like contraption, suspended from the ceiling, that hums loudly and keeps switching itself on and off with a noise like a donkey coughing. Tony insists that it's disconnected for the concert. 'We'll just have to hope the punters' bums don't freeze to their chairs,' he mutters.

SHEFFIELD CONCERT, THE LEADMILL

First Set (Primary Territories)
Composition 69B
Composition 60 (+ 108C)
Composition 110A (+ 108B)
Composition 34

Second Set (Primary Territories)
Composition 105A
Composition 69N
Composition 40M
Bass solo (from *Composition 96*)

(This is the first concert in which all the compositions have already been played before on the tour: during the first three concerts, Braxton didn't repeat a single piece – twenty-four consecutive different compositions. The quartet will play thirty-five different pieces altogether during the tour, plus the four separate pulse tracks – *108A–D* – and extracts from *96* and five solo piano compositions: *1* and *30–33*. During tonight's interval, Braxton decides to add to the second set: 'Maybe we should have a notated bass solo. You wanna try one, Mark?' Mark nods: 'Sure. Where do you want it?' Braxton: 'Oh . . . how about at the end? You can take us out tonight.')

Because of the troublesome acoustics the group agree to stay relatively restrained; yet their energy is fierce and finely honed. The long, complex *105A* remains tight, gripping throughout; as does the delicate ensemble tiptoe of *69N* and the flying tempo of *40M*, where they scorch along on a cresting torrent of sound.

Braxton's ideal for small-group dynamics has stayed consistent over the years. On his first LP he was quoted in the sleevenotes as saying, 'Our emphasis is on the idea of total music, with each individual contributing towards it totally . . . We're working towards a feeling of *one* – the complete freedom of individuals in tune with each other, complementing each other.' Twelve years later, in his notes to *Performance 9/1/79*, he was writing:

> There is no section of the music where any member of the group is not depended on by either another musician or the music itself . . . the 'responsibility ratio' of extended creative music demands the complete involvement of every participating musician: that is, the musicians of the quartet are expected both to 'play the silences' as well as the 'sounds'. There is no point in the music where any member of the group can 'dis-connect' his or her vibrational link with the composite ensemble.

If this need for vibrational unity is most obvious in the racing, hair-pin lines of a *40M*, it is no less vital for the complex interactions of, say, *34*, built around a repeating pattern of variations, or for holding together the slower, more spacious environs of a *69N*. In fact, the 'vibrational link' is even more necessary now that Braxton has introduced pulse tracks and collage forms into the quartet music; in the way, for instance, that the rhythm section bend *108B* into the 'curved sound dynamics' of *110A*; the way that two separate pieces like *60* and *108C* can occupy the same space and be made to fit together. Complete attunement, complete freedom, complete involvement, complete responsibility. Then you *still* have to deal with dodgy acoustics! It's as well this quartet seem to thrive on challenges.

'I had a ball tonight,' Mark enthuses afterwards. He's really been hitting his stride since Birmingham, singing – and swearing – with gusto in a rich purring tone. I suspect his being given the closing solo tonight was in the nature of a vote of confidence.

'You're feeling more at home in the music now?' I ask him.

He shakes his head. 'I'd like to live with it a couple of years before I could say that.'

'How you doing, Graham?' Braxton asks, as the group wind down in the dressing-room. 'I think you'll crack soon. The second week is when it happens. You'll be saying (*piteous whine*): "Do we have to start so early? Can't we have two hours' more sleep? Do we have to play every day?" '

'Yeah, it's starting already,' I sigh.

Braxton laughs. 'I can't believe we did two months last year. Two months! It was horrible!'

Marilyn looks up. 'At the end of that tour we were ready to kill each other. I thought, that's it, I quit, I'll go into the restaurant business.'

'We did well just to survive that tour,' Braxton says. 'Like, we're tired, our nerves are shot, and at the end you still have no money! I told Nickie, well dear, it is *free* jazz.'

Marilyn sighs. 'All those nights without sleep, day after day of trying to make impossible connections . . . I think all agents should go on a tour as part of their training.'

'Especially Ulli Blobel,' Braxton adds through gritted teeth.

'We took him with us to Yugoslavia for a gig,' Gerry grins. 'That practically killed him.'

'That was one night! We did it for two months,' repeats Braxton with a disbelieving sigh. 'And still no coins.'

I remember Archie Shepp's famous description of the American nightclub scene as 'crude stables where black men are run until they bleed, or else are hacked up outright for Lepage's glue'.* It seems the European tour circuit is not a lot better; racism is presumably less acute, but the dictates of capitalism mean the artists still get 'run until they bleed'.

I ask Braxton how he rates this tour.

'Oh, this is wonderful. Nice hotels, nice venues, not too much travelling every day – this is how a tour should be.† I just wish I didn't have to do those lectures.'

---

*Quoted in Kofsky, 1970, p. 145

†I should point out that the Contemporary Music Network manage to treat their artists with

I feel a guilty pang. If I wasn't interviewing him every day, I dare say he'd handle even a morale-sapper like this afternoon's lecture fiasco with relative ease. This hiccup aside, everyone in the group seems very content with the tour organization; and Tony, besides being 100 per cent efficient, shepherds us around with the requisite blend of firmness and concern, plus an inexhaustible supply of Billy Connolly jokes.

After a few games of pool in the Leadmill bar (Braxton, shooting hard and fast, Hurricane Higgins style, remarks that he used to do a little pool hustling too when he lived with Ornette. *The Illinois Kid?*) we drive back to the hotel, situated on a hill towards the outskirts of town. Braxton climbs out of the van and, stretching, gazes up at the stars and then at the city lights spread out before him.

'Boy!' he exclaims. 'I'm really glad to be here in . . . huh, where are we?'

We all giggle. Road rot is setting in.

---

due consideration *and* present a wide range of modern musics within the confines of an extremely small budget. In 1985–6, the CMN's allocation of £240,000 represented less than a quarter of one per cent of the Arts Council's total budget of £105 million. Despite audience increases of fourteen per cent in the 1983–4 season, and eighteen per cent in the 1984–5 season, there has been no corresponding rise in the CMN's funding

METAROAD

FOREGROUND MUSIC 3

'THE HISTORY OF MUSIC EVOLUTION IS
NOT THE HISTORY OF NICE GUYS'

L: Can we talk today about Stockhausen and Cage?
B: Stockhausen is awesome. He's such a master visionary that I even buy records of his that I *hate*; that's how much I respect him. In every period of his work he's demonstrated excellence and a unique understanding of form. Experiencing his music and his visions would help me try to function to my complete potential; reading his analysis books would inspire me to systematize and calibrate every aspect of my music. It was Stockhausen who showed me the beauty and excitement of every aspect of music science. In my dark periods, in those times where I was wondering how I could get through, his music would inspire me to keep doing my work.

I've never tried to be close to Stockhausen personally. I have, like everyone else, heard the stories about what kind of person he is; but I did not let the stories delude me into not taking his music seriously, because the history of music evolution is not the history of nice guys, it's the history of human beings who have their frailties, their strong and weak points. It's true that both Stockhausen and Cage have exhibited, in my opinion, profound racist tendencies; but as I get older I find myself very much aware that I know a lot of racists, but I know of very few racists who have been able to contribute the kind of information to humanity that Cage and Stockhausen have.

As far as John Cage is concerned, the philosophical dynamics of his music would help me, as an African-American intellectual, to look into my own lineage and develop my own perspective.

Experiencing the musics of Cage and Stockhausen would be the final part of my own equation, in terms of understanding what I wanted to do with my life.

L: You became aware of their music in the mid-sixties, late in terms of your own development?

B: Yes. What it was – I discovered Schoenberg in the army: his music would be just as important to me. Schoenberg was a dynamic restructuralist: he established forces that set into motion evolution for Europe in that cycle. The significance of extended functionalism, based on trans-European information dynamics, has to do with what the post-Schoenberg, post-Webern music brought to structural, vibrational and conceptual dynamics – I'm thinking of the possibility of writing solo, chamber contexts, orchestral contexts, the electronic music that was developing. The decisions which established that music have been very important in my own evolution.

L: You've said in the past: 'You are your music'; now you're saying: 'The history of music evolution is not the history of nice guys.' What *is* the relationship between personality and music?

B: I do believe a person's personality has an effect on his or her music, but it's a complex question. The creativity of a pleasant person (whatever that is) is not necessarily more beautiful than that of someone less pleasant. But there's really no way to interpret what a particular aspect of somebody's personality means. How are we to know? To say any more would risk violating that person, so I don't think it's a question we can deal with. Except to say that nine-tenths, no, *all*, of the masters have demonstrated a unique way of affirming their personalities in the music; what I call self-realization.

'I SEE MY MUSIC AS A THREE-DIMENSIONAL PAINTING'

L: You've said that *Gruppen* and *Carré* inspired your multi-orchestral works, and *Klavierstücke IV*, *VI* and *X* inspired your solo music. I was wondering, Stockhausen dreamed compositions – *Musik Im Bauch*, for example – and Coltrane dreamed music too: has anything like that happened to you? Dreaming compositions?

B: I've had those experiences, but in fact I'm only now starting to take them seriously. I've dreamed several compositions only to wake up and not be able to notate them or not remember them. I would hope in the next cycle, as my intuition is developing and changing, that that area will open more to me. But I visually see my music anyway, I see the music as if it were a three-dimensional painting.

This is why I have encoded my music, because now that I've formalized my devices on several different levels, I can isolate various disciplines or sets of premises and begin an internal expansion based on my own ingredients. Hopefully, in the coming years, I won't have to deal with many of the problems that surround musicians who have not documented their work. You can say what you want about Braxton, but *Composition 25*, say, worked with such-and-such processes, it breaks down like this: and you can like it or not like it – you can say, 'Even with your explanations, Braxton, I still hate your music' and that's valid – but how I saw what I was doing will be documented. I've learned that from Cage and Stockhausen, who learned it from their masters, who learned it from their masters: Europeans are not the only people to establish a forward-information complex, they learned from the Egyptians. Yet I did learn from Cage and Stockhausen: it was their music that finally made me go into a room and spend ten years to complete my foundation writings. I thank them for that.

'OF COURSE I'M CRAZY' –
GO TO THE ANCIENTS

L: The other day, when we were talking about Jonathan Cott's book on Stockhausen,* you said you thought it proved Stockhausen was mad. What did you mean by that?

B: Oh, of course I said that. We will talk, and have been talking, on many different levels, Graham. Of course Stockhausen is crazy, of course I'm crazy, of course Sun Ra is crazy, of course Bach is crazy – it's the only way to be! I think everything about Stockhausen is totally insane; it's the insanity of a genius. I'd hope that everybody would be as crazy as Stockhausen. Of course he's a human being with frailties, because human beings are not perfect. But I believe that he's produced a body of works that will *help* humanity.

L: OK. Perhaps we could move on to Sun Ra and Harry Partch?

B: Let me take Harry Partch first. Harry Partch has profoundly

---

Stockhausen: Conversations with the Composer (1974)

affected me, but I've not been able to demonstrate what I've learned from this man. For instance, I've always wanted to put out my own records, like Mr Partch did, but I've never had the money. His book* would also be very inspirational, and my move to build instruments would come from Mr Partch's example. I think he's a great composer too; he's so underrated in this period it's a damned shame. It's an indictment of America that there's no understanding of, or respect for, this man's music.

The fact that he would look back to the ancients to understand better what music is, and then build a system based on the fundamentals – this is what connects me to Harry Partch because that's exactly what I've been doing. And if I'm allowed to do my work in the future that's exactly what I'll continue to do: go to the ancients and to the scientists to understand better the route of a given information line and the transformational potential of music. Harry Partch short-circuited the whole post-Webern continuum and established a whole other area for investigation. The dynamic implications of his music, as well as its actual beauty, affected me and helped me develop the mind-set to begin looking at my own evolution.

L: By ancients, are you referring again to the early Egyptians?

B: The early cultures in Egypt, Sumeria, the early cultures of Greece – Pythagoras, Plato, Socrates.

SUN RA – THE WORLD OF
ABSTRACT CONSCIOUSNESS

L: Which, to a degree, is also where Sun Ra is coming from?

B: Sun Ra can be talked of in many of the same contexts as Harry Partch, although there are also real differences. But he put out his own records too, so the record companies couldn't tamper with his evolution. Of course, this is impossible, but I would like to have every record the man's ever made! Mr Ra has demonstrated, in the last thirty years, a glorious commitment to music. He's a profound

Genesis of a Music (1974). Partch (1901–74) devised his own forty-three-note-to-the-octave scale, designed and built his own instruments to play this music, and released his first records on his own Gate 5 label. He followed the ancient belief that music was part of a composite culture that also included poetry, dance and theatre; and many of his own works are music-dramas that attempt to re-create elements like magic and ritual now generally vanished from Western art music

scholar, I might add, and is greatly respected all around the world, with the exception of America. He's able to go to Egypt and read the hieroglyphics; his understanding of Egyptian history is second to no one's.

L: Although he left Chicago before the AACM came into being, do you think Sun Ra had a particular influence on the Chicago music of the mid-sixties?

B: His use of theatre was very important. The Art Ensemble can be looked on as an extension of what Sun Ra had established in that context. His use of open improvisation led to the gains that Coltrane and Cecil Taylor generated, so he's like a bridge figure from the bebop period of the music to the extended forms, in which of course he's also a dominant force.

It's funny. When you establish a consistent body of work it makes its own reality, and there's no way it can be put down or put up: it becomes something that exists for human beings, a body of musics that will help people on the planet. I'm attracted to that, I always have been – as opposed to the concept of 'the great night'. Like, wow, this guy had a great night – one great night in twelve years! (*Laughs.*) That doesn't excite me. I'm interested in looking at the continuity of a person's involvement, and I draw strength from that; from people like Sun Ra or Warne Marsh or Evan Parker or Muhal Richard Abrams, because it really is about a life's commitment.

L: How do you see Sun Ra's mystical side? A lot of people seem to laugh it off.

B: Sun Ra is not a joke! Everybody would like to think of him as a joke, but he has understood something, something very serious, and . . . boy, I mean, how much more could he have accomplished in his life if he had been given some form of financial assistance? So that he would not have had to deal with the strain of poverty? Because he's already demonstrated a viewpoint that could take into account the whole planet and the galactic perspective of things. This is a man who understands the world of abstract consciousness and the mystical dynamics of music. What could he have done, what could he do now, if the government or some rich person were to help him? These are the kind of people who could make a difference to the future of the planet.

Thanks to Sun Ra I would begin to understand different levels of responsibility, and not be afraid to move towards the visionary or to think of Earth culture.

L: What do you mean by levels of responsibility?

B: I'm talking about . . . it's not enough simply to be involved in restructuralism, you have to have some fundamental idea of what you're dealing with. People like to think that music is just dealing with sound logic, as if the phenomenon of music is separate from not only the forces it generates but from the forces that allowed it to become manifested. To examine the work of Sun Ra is to see his attempts to uncover the information that was lost in the last 3,000 years and to transmit that information to the public, whether or not they understand it.

L: You mentioned the world of abstract consciousness just now. Could you explain what you mean by that?

B: Well . . . again, I'm talking about what sound logic really is and what is set into motion when people really hear; the phenomenon of unifying sound. To have that experience involves many different levels of logic and of attraction. John Cage likes to talk of 'let a sound be a sound' etc, but to study the meta-reality dynamics of creativity as it's viewed in world culture terms is to understand that music is not just a sound, the experience of listening to music is not just listening to sound. For those who are able to enter into abstract music, that phenomenon involves unifying what is being transmitted; and to enter the upper partials of music is to gain insight into the wonder of music, the wonder of existence. Really to enter the world of sound is to understand what a given function affirms in terms of a primary force – I'll say it like that. The world of abstract consciousness involves those areas of unity – mental or conceptual – that are the last partial before entering another level of consciousness.

WHY MUSIC IS SERIOUS – ON
AND OFF THE PLANET

One of the problems my music has had is that it's an abstract music, and people are not being educated to deal with abstract music or abstract thought. The abstract plane involves many levels, the first being self-realization or having some fundamental understanding of what you think about things. Abstract consciousness is not necessarily relevant to being a great Republican or Democrat . . . you know, it's like, this is why music is serious, it can even be dangerous politically because the upper partials of music-making or involvement in the world of sound . . . it becomes spiritual, we're moving towards the world of spirituality.

The upper partials of music are not separate from those fundamentals which are related to how this experience is sustained. What we call physicality – why does everybody think this is so normal? Of course, we can only imagine this experience, so-called, but why –

L: Hold on, I'm getting lost. Which experience do you mean, that we can only imagine?

B: Being in the body, walking around on the planet, the concept of thinking. You can only imagine what your mind will allow you to imagine; and for our purposes we're only dealing with physical universe experiences . . . and so we've come to think of this experience as *it*, when at the same time all the information tells us that before you were born you didn't exist as Graham and when you die you're not going to be on the planet any more, as we understand that experience. So we're dealing with a little, a short period, sixty, seventy, ninety years, whatever – then you're off the planet. So, if this planet is *it*, what happens when you're not here? You're *not-it*?

L: Er . . . I suppose so, yeah.

B: Well, OK. So whatever *not-it* is, that would be more is than *it*, since you're only gonna be here for ninety years.

L: It's longer, yeah.

B: It would be much longer than ninety years, can we say that? Taking into account the spectrum of options, you may think the *it* is just one experience – some people may say it's the only experience, that's fine by me. I'm just saying that whatever allowed this experience to happen, there are fundamental laws which can be observed. Or at least all of the masters, all of the lineages, talk of this experience in such a way where there are fundamentals we can look at to understand better how it works. And at that point I'll stop. But I'll say this much again: everything that you think about, there is information for it. For any level that you want to think on, for any thought that you can think, there's information that can help you with that thought.

ROAD

WEDNESDAY 20, LEICESTER

Heavy, swirling rain. Visibility is terrible: mist and headlight beams are all we can see through the van windows. We've barely left Sheffield before Braxton is chortling. 'Heard the latest about the pine scandal? *Pinegate!* Paul Sparrow told me those were deciduous pines we saw yesterday, Hemingway.'

'Yeah? Deciduous, huh?' Gerry looks bemused.

'Yes sir, they really exist. Oh no, you said, those are *dead* trees. I thought, My God and I thought they were beautiful – I must be in love with death! What's wrong with me? But you know what that alien phenomenon is really called? It's not death, it's not acid rain, it's called *winter*. Ever hear of that, Hemingway? I mean, you spoke like you *knew* about acid rain.'

'Like, I've taken acid,' Mark joins in.

'Like, my best friend is a tree,' Marilyn likewise.

Gerry groans. 'Aw, come on you guys . . .'

But Braxton is in full flight now. 'Why do you think they're called evergreens, you said. Hmm, that sounds reasonable, I thought – so what's happening to my soul, falling in love with *dead* things? But all this will be documented in Lock's book. People're gonna be coming up to you for years and asking, "Hemingway, is it true about Pinegate?"'

When we reach Leicester I interview Braxton at the hotel while the others explore the town. Marilyn returns with a fluffy, turquoise sweater that she's just bought.

'Hey, that's real nice,' says Gerry. 'You should try to keep that one awhile.'

Marilyn, it seems, has a strange habit of giving away her sweaters just a few months after she's bought them.

157

'I just can't help it,' she says with a dreamy smile. 'It's like I'm searching for something, I guess.'

Hmm, I think, Freud could have had a field day with this group's wardrobe foibles: Marilyn gives away sweaters, Braxton forgets his coat, even Gerry wears his beret back-to-front.

Later we all drive out to the polytechnic for the soundcheck. Braxton brings out *Composition 69C*, one of the two quartet pieces he's rewriting for piano, and the group run through the notated parts several times. Braxton seems pleased, telling Marilyn, 'You jumped on that music so quick.'

She smiles. 'It was jump or die.'

One of the student organizers informs us that the concert is sold out. It's almost time for the pre-concert talk, she adds. The *what*? Tony checks the itinerary: no pre-concert talk. 'But we've sold tickets,' pleads the student. With a sigh, Braxton agrees to talk. Gerry, Marilyn and Mark creep into the audience to listen.

Braxton explains that tonight's concert will deal with structured improvisation, that in general his quartet music tries to establish parameters or platforms for different types of improvisation. He talks briefly about pulse tracks and collage forms, then suggests that if people have problems getting into the music, they could look at its visual aspects, look at how the visual elements unify the space of the music. 'As we play, visualize the exchanges taking place, look at the shapes. That's a point of entry. Yet we're not so far out as to be outside anything you've experienced in your lives.'

He talks about trans-African functionalism and its relationship to creative music; the history of how form can be used to determine the nature of the interchange. Dixieland is a good example. 'Look at the music as a kind of alternative Dixieland, if you like; look for the ensemble interchanges.'

Someone asks if he's still interested in bebop. 'Oh yes. We have to remember the importance of fundamentals. But I also think bebop should not be used as a noose on African intellectual dynamics, which is what the media try to do.'

Q: 'Do you still use harmony as a basis for improvisation?'

B: 'We work with various structures – material, thematic, repetitive structures – so the kind of improvisation depends on the context. Sometimes we're operating in the same zones as bebop, sometimes not.'

'What is bebop?' a voice at the back asks. There are a couple of sniggers.

'No, that's an important question,' Braxton insists. 'In my opinion, there is no real difference between bebop, swing, Dixieland, in terms of their metaphysical dynamics. But the bebop projection – and I use that word rather than "style" because "projection" includes intellectual and political dynamics as well as the surface characteristics of the music – bebop was the name given to the vibrational and conceptual solutions that musicians like Charlie Parker evolved in response to the existential problems faced by black people in the early to mid-1940s.'

A few more questions, then Braxton calls a halt. 'Let me just say this: human beings are all alike, our spectrum of feelings, tensions, dreams are the same and these things are in the music like they're in our lives. I hope tonight's concert is a positive experience for you, but if not – I hope it's a real negative experience.'

The rest of the group, who've not heard Braxton lecture before, seem impressed. 'Yeah,' Mark nods. 'It was like the first solo of the evening.'

LEICESTER CONCERT, THE GREAT HALL, LEICESTER
POLYTECHNIC

First Set (Primary Territories)
Composition 85 (+ 108D)
Composition 69F
Composition 122 (+ 108A)

Second Set (Primary Territories)
Composition 69C
Composition 69O
Composition 116
Composition 40N

The polytechnic's 'Great Hall' is simply a very large room, so the space is very like the Birmingham gig, although the ambience the group create tonight is new to me. Everything is still tight, but rather than Birmingham's fierce dynamic the feeling here is relaxed, almost mellow; as if the group had settled into the music and were delighting in its nooks and crannies, relishing the nuances. Or maybe it's I who am just becoming aware of the nuances, now that I'm more attuned to the music? *85* is given a less frantic, more thoughtful performance, and the spaces of *69F* and

69O are explored with tender care. The energy still flies on *69C*, as a forceful rhythm section motif kick-starts the second set, Braxton adding eerie clarinet harmonics; and later, after another of Gerry's startling solos (flicking the cymbals with a towel, scratching them with his fingernails), the group scorch through *116*, ideas richocheting between them like pinballs at the speed of light, Marilyn's hands a blur of motion on her solo yet the notes clear and true, each in its own space. *40N* concludes, elegiac cadences over a serene bass drone; a gentle finale.

Backstage I introduce Braxton to Jan Kopinski, saxophonist/ leader of the highly-acclaimed Nottingham band Pinski Zoo, and they're soon exchanging recollections of Poland. Like Braxton, Pinski Zoo played in Poland in 1984, when Jan won the prize for best individual musician at the Jazz Nad Odra festival. They've released several LPs on their own Dug-Out label, to good reviews, but they still find it hard to get gigs, especially in London. Jan reckons it's chiefly because they take their inspiration from Ornette Coleman's harmolodic music rather than from bebop, currently the capital's most fashionable style (the 'noose' of bebop?); but I wonder if there's not also a deeper English philistinism at work here. Even eminent figures like John Surman and Mike Westbrook make a living only through frequent tours abroad.

Later, when we get a few moments alone, I ask Jan if he liked the concert.

'Oh yeah. It's great to see someone like Braxton who's such a powerful player yet really controls his music. I got the feeling he could be a bit impish, that he understands more than he gives out – a deep player. Marilyn too. She plays with such ferocity and style. I didn't realize the group read so much in concert, but the feeling was good – like everybody had their place.'

Back at the hotel, Braxton – who has, as per usual, grabbed a hamburger *en route* – heads for his room for a few hours' composition and flute practice, plus the daily phone call to his wife in Oakland. Gerry and Mark aren't hungry, but Marilyn and I decide to go in search of a takeaway.

'I'm sure I saw a Wimpy around here this afternoon,' she tells me, as we wander through the town centre. 'But I'm hopeless at names and places. There's a lot of Pisces in my chart.'

Finally we come across a chippie. 'Pisces and chips OK?' I ask.

As we walk back she tells me she has no more work lined up until spring: it looks like being a long, hard winter. In fact, working prospects generally are so bad she's been thinking about playing in a rock band. Playing or singing.

'You sing too?' I'm surprised. Marilyn speaks so quietly, it's hard to imagine her singing rock'n'roll.

'I used to sing folk, folk rock. It helped keep me together when my marriage broke up.' She says that after seeing *Stop Making Sense*, she decided she'd like to be in a group like Talking Heads. 'Or maybe play African pop. I called my cat Sunny, after Sunny Ade.'

'Do the Band still live in Woodstock?' I ask.

'Yeah. I jammed with Richard Manuel and a couple of other people once.'

'Yeah?' My eyes widen. The Band are one of my favourite rock groups; and Richard Manuel's such a tender, soulful singer. 'You've really played with Richard Manuel?' My admiration for Marilyn hits new heights. I offer to carry her chips.

We return to the hotel and step out of the lift to find Gerry stalking the corridor, his face knotted with anguish. When he sees us, he falls to the floor and starts biting the carpet. 'I fucked up,' he wails. 'Man, I really fucked up!'

Marilyn and I laugh, we think it's an act. 'OK, you fucked up. Pinegate's no big deal.'

'No, not that.' Gerry is tearing at his hair. 'I left my money belt in Sheffield. I hid it under the mattress in the hotel room and then forgot about it. Five hundred pounds. Waaahhhhhh!!!'

METAROAD

SOUND LOGIC, SOUND MAGIC 1: MUSICAL EVOLUTION

RESTRUCTURALISM, STYLISM, TRADITIONALISM

L: Can we begin by talking about your philosophical overview of music? You have three primary categories: restructuralism, stylism and traditionalism?

B: Three is the primary number of my generating system. Tri-partial perception dynamics permeate how I've tried to deal with my music, whether we're talking of restructuralism, stylism, traditionalism; or mental, physical, spiritual divisions; or past, present, future.*

L: Could you explain the characteristics of each category?

B: By restructuralism, I'm referring to . . . at a certain point in any information continuum, for evolution to occur, the structural properties or the whole mentality surrounding that information undergoes a change. Restructuralism is my word for that phenomenon. In fact, it's taking place all the time, natural change, change cycles – and the significance of a given form derives from the position it has in its cycle and from the forces that it activates. For instance, after Charlie Parker played his music, the language dynamics of that music would create a whole reality that could help human beings. That's what we see when we talk of the post-bebop continuum; they're the people who have been able to make a reality out of Charlie Parker's solutions.

*In view of Braxton's references to the ancients, including Pythagoras, it may be worth noting that in Pythagorean numerology, three is the number of knowledge – of music, geometry and astronomy

This is true for many different levels. If we talk about Einstein and his theories, or any restructuralist theories, we can see how humanity has absorbed that information. Sometimes given information will be used with respect to its negative partials as in, say, the dropping of the atomic bomb – that was not what Mr Einstein envisioned for his theories – or, in the case of the post-Ayler continuum, many musicians would use the concept of free jazz as an excuse for not practising, not trying to evolve. There's a big distinction between a given restructuralist cycle, or the information that manifests itself in that cycle, and how human beings decide to use it.

L: And stylism?

B: Well, once something has been set into motion by the restructuralists, people usually take that information and use it for whatever. Those are the stylists. There are master stylists too, but the masters are the ones who did not simply take without giving, who didn't just play Charlie Parker's language and do nothing to it.

It's in the stylist juncture where a given initiation usually gets to the public, the zone where television and the media will allow a given information line to get through. Stylists are usually able to become more successful than restructuralists because their music is not perceived as threatening the cultural order. This is why Phil Woods, say, wins so many polls. His playing doesn't really challenge any law, it just reaffirms what has been current, in the air, in the last thirty years; that being the dynamic implications of Charlie Parker's music. Whereas the greater public have not really had the possibility to examine the music of John Cage, Albert Ayler, the Art Ensemble of Chicago – those musics don't seem to filter through. But, in fact, before Charlie Parker demonstrated his music, *nobody* played like him; so if the value systems that surround Phil Woods are allowed to dominate, there will be no forward motion, and no future Phil Woods because he would have no one to take a music from.

L: You say restructuralists threaten the cultural order – does your music do that? Is it a dangerous music?

B: (*laughs*) You could say that! My music, my life's work, will ultimately challenge the very foundations of Western value systems, that's what's dangerous about it.

But the significance of the stylist has its merits too. People can relate to it. If it wasn't for Paul Desmond and Ahmad Jamal, I could never have heard Charlie Parker. So there are degrees of evolution and the individual has to deal with them all.

L: Is there a scientific example of stylism, like Einstein and restructuralism?

B: Well, technocrats are like stylists. Many of the problems we're dealing with in this time period, in terms of Western science, have to do with people utilizing information lines without respect to their composite implications. What we're doing to the planet, to the environment, is incredible. Gerry Hemingway may have been wrong about those pine trees, but he's right to see acid rain as a serious phenomenon. We're destroying the planet and leaving a mess for our children; although I don't mean to blame this solely on the technocrats.*

L: OK. How about traditionalism?

B: The traditionalist vibration dynamic involves forward motion with respect to having better understanding of the fundamentals and of the route a given lineage has travelled. Evolution in this context would mean a better understanding of what has gone before, and the use of that information to help people comprehend their time and their place. Without an awareness of the past, you can't avoid making the mistakes that previous cycles made.

L: What are the musical examples of traditionalism?

B: Marion Anderson, her work as a virtuoso singer, she's a traditionalist. In fact, the world of opera, with its current emphasis on the early European masters, is a traditionalist bastion right now. It's not healthy because they don't allow enough performances of new works. But to discover that music or the music played by the original Dixieland jazz bands – not the commercial groups, but the old-timers – is to have another dynamic in terms of understanding what music is.

*The links between stylists and Western scientists are perhaps clearer if both are seen as people involved with questions of process – the *how* at the expense of the *what*. In *Tri-axium Writings 3*, Braxton observes: 'Applied science is not concerned about the aesthetic or vibrational implications of a given information line, but instead with whether or not it can be of service.' This is a dangerous approach, he says, because 'while the functional dynamics of a given information line might work, this does not mean it is true. Another way of saying this is – the dynamic implications of a given information line are true on many levels that one might not want them to be true; which is to say, there is information and there is information' (p. 62). He cites the development of nuclear energy, and official belittling of attendant risks, as an example of this attitude. In *Tri-axium Writings 2*, he also attacks the technocratic basis of Western culture for its neglect of environmental issues: 'By the time Western culture makes the decision really to deal with the realness of ecological dynamics we will be living on as asteroid' (p. 523). See also pp. 317 below

It's partly because of my respect for what I call the tri-vibrational dynamics that I try to function in bebop and demonstrate some musics from the traditional continuum. I think that's important. It's just that we have to teach people to deal with the future too.

BALANCING THE TRI-VIBRATIONAL DYNAMICS

L: The implication being that traditionalism on its own is not a good thing?

B: Oh, neither is restructuralism on its own. I think the concept of a healthy culture rests in balancing the tri-vibrational tendencies of the culture. If restructuralism were the only aspect of the music that was respected, there could never be cultural solidification because restructuralism, by definition, implies change and change cannot be the basis for establishing cultural order because you have to have some context to change from, or evolve in. Stylism on its own would mean no forward motion, you'd just be trying to re-create what's already been created.

L: The music seems to be in that phase now.

B: Yes, I'd say we were in a stylistic period: I'm thinking of, say, Wynton Marsalis, Chico Freeman . . . The universities are programming young people for stylistic value systems. The problem is they're trying to separate the music from its meta-reality implications.

L: An undue emphasis on traditionalism would mean trying to use old solutions on new problems?

B: Yes. The traditional vibration dynamic gives us a wonderful sense of the past, but we can't move backwards as we've been trying to do in America, going back to 'the good old days' as a basis for dealing with the future.

L: Like Margaret Thatcher's talk of 'Victorian values'? She forgets the backstreet abortions, the child prostitution, half the population hungry, badly housed, no medical care . . .

B: Right, that's not going to work. We have to find solutions that are relevant to what's been developed. Tri-vibrational dynamics is my term to express the balance of these phenomena, the forces as manifested in this context. And I respect what that balance really means, although my own tendencies are restructuralist.

'I'VE ALWAYS PLAYED THE BLUES'

L: Does each musical continuum go through cycles of restructural-
ism, stylism and traditionalism?
B: That's right.
L: The blues, for instance, would now be in a traditionalist phase?
B: No sir! Everything goes forward – there's a restructured blues.
People say I don't play the blues – I've always played the blues, but
I never argue about those kinds of things. What we call the blues is
not just notes, it's a vibrational understanding that's been
transmitted and encoded, and it's manifested in various forms of
music in various different ways. Still, there is a science to different
periods of blues playing and that information is important. It just
depends on how you want to look at it: there's the blues as
manifested in one particular style or projection and then there's
what the blues is really affirming, and that's manifested on many
different levels.
L: How long do these cycles last?
B: Oh, that's complex, Graham. Normally the mystics talk in terms
of seven-year cycles, but it's complex: I don't know exactly when a
given information focus becomes stylistic or traditional information. We can look at the lineages of, say, the last 2,000 years, the
routes –
L: Whoa, let's not take that long!
B: (*laughs*) OK, let's look at the bebop cycles. We can look at
Charlie Parker solidifying bebop – though, of course, many people
were a part of that – we can look at the post-Parker period and see
hard bop, see the expansion of vertical harmony in the same sense
as, say, from Beethoven to Wagner; we can see the expansion of the
rhythmic dynamic from Beethoven to Stravinsky or Charlie Parker
to Albert Ayler. We can say that what we call bebop constitutes a
projection of music, and we can look at the restructural dynamics of
the music and at the stylistic and traditionalist tendencies of the
projection; and look at how it set the stage for the post-AACM
period of exploration.
L: To generalize, could you say that bebop was restructuralist in the
forties and early fifties, became stylist later in the fifties and while
some aspects of it have since become traditionalist, Ornette
Coleman also began a new restructuralist cycle by taking up certain
aspects of it and rejecting others? Is that how it works, different

branches going through different cycles?
B: That's it exactly.

CONCEPTUAL GRAFTING

L: To turn to your own evolution: we've already talked about the language music, how you established that by breaking down sound into its smallest particles and then rebuilding these in new combinations, new models. Is that the process you call conceptual grafting?
B: Well, conceptual grafting began as a means to avoid serialism. I was not interested in setting everything to an empirical system on that level; I found myself moving, or vibrating, towards the world of shape and colour. It was, like, how to create a language that respected the musics that were calling: I was very excited by the concept, the reality, of pointillistic musics, for example. I began to break down phrase construction variables with regard to material properties, functional properties, language properties; to use this as a basis to create improvised music and then rechannel that into the compositional process. I would tape my concerts, go home and dissect the music, find out what fascinated me about a particular area; what did I call good, what bad; what sustained my interest, what didn't. Conceptual grafting was the process of dissecting sound by which I would build up my language music, cataloguing over 100 different kinds of sound relationships: the ones on the sheet I give out at the lectures are just ten examples.
L: So conceptual grafting was a criterion that sidestepped harmonic or thematic approaches? More a case of deconstruct to reconstruct?
B: In my notes to the *Alto Saxophone Solos 1979* record I use the analogy of painting a picture with only one colour or mostly one colour, say blue, with just touches of red and brown; or having just the circle as your primary shape, and just the square as a secondary shape. See, I was interested in finding, first, my value systems; then, I began to understand that my value systems involved establishing some kind of criteria where I could measure my development and some kind of criteria where I could postulate different strategies and paths of evolution. The tool I used was separation: I began to separate sound elements so that I could find my own vocabulary.

CODING, CO-ORDINATE AND
SCHEMATIC MUSICS

L: You've talked in the past about various types of music – coding
musics, co-ordinate musics, schematic musics. Were these the next
steps in your musical evolution?
B: The next step up from the language music would be the coding
musics, which involved factoring friends' initials, chess moves, etc,
into the music and the titles. Co-ordinate music is the name I've
given to the structures that utilize different forms of improvisation:
it refers to the fact that I link two, three, four different
compositions together in a given performance. A performance, in
this context, comprises a series of different structural and
conceptual territories, each of which establishes its own operatives.
The co-ordinate music series would move to apply the new
vocabulary languages I had been putting together, and to forward
these languages into a structural context.
   Then the next cycle of my music was the schematic musics. By
schematic, I'm talking of total infrastructure design, where a given
composition is not just an operative here, an operative there, but a
whole sound environment that has a skeleton of different types of
structural variables which are supposed to happen in the music.
The difference between the schematic and the co-ordinate musics
would be that the schematic musics section off principles, they're
like time/space partitionings with respect to one unit of music, as
opposed to putting together different compositions.
L: The quartet music is predominantly co-ordinate?
B: Yes. We're talking about independent compositions that can be
put together like different blocks; red, blue, yellow – you can put
them together in any order, as you've seen at the concerts. We have
sixty to seventy pieces that we can integrate into our various
performances. The schematic structures are not necessarily interchangeable in terms of infrastructure dictates. A schematic
composition would be complete inside of itself; it's not a
composition I'd put inside something else, it's totally mapped out
from beginning to end – a single block with its own infrastructure
design. The piece for four saxophones, *Composition 37*, and the
over-dubbed soprano saxes piece, *Composition 22*, are both examples of the schematic musics.

RITUAL & CEREMONIAL MUSICS

L: You began to develop these musics in the late sixties, early seventies. Since then there have been other categories – dimensional musics, image musics, ritual musics?

B: The dimensional drawing musics – these are works which started to factor in intent; motivation and spiritual intent. Then the hieroglyphic structures would solidify certain inter-relationships in my music – between colour, numerology, intention, etc.

L: The hieroglyphic structures are not the image musics?

B: No. By image music I'm talking about the use of image or story as a factor in the process of the music; images, drawings, as part of the score . . . this is in the last year or two. *Composition 113*, for example, is about the image of Ojuwain that night on the train.*

L: I'm confused now. I thought *113* and the *Trillium* operas were part of the ritual musics. Isn't Ojuwain a character in *Trillium* as well as in *113*?

B: *113* is really dealing with the world of images; but it also uses some of the twelve principal characters who will be in the ritual & ceremonial musics, one of whom is Ojuwain. The *Trillium* operas will express my aesthetics as manifested through the integration schematics in the *Tri-axium Writings*† and will discuss my philosophical and mystical beliefs. The image music will be used to portray dreams and stories, that area of my intuition which is developing: this is separate from the ritual & ceremonial musics, which are all being designed for a twelve-day festival for world unification and universality, and at the end of each day there'll be one of the master operas, which will be *Trillium*. The image music will be part of that and also part of something else, but I can't talk about it because I'm still working on it.

L: But the ritual & ceremonial musics also include works prior to

---

*It is midnight and raining at a small train station in Northern Africa and finally the old locomotive has arrived. As the smoke begins to clear from around the tracks of the engine, we can see six people boarding the train – all of whom are clothed in bulky robe-like garments with long black hoods . . . When the doors of cabin twelve are opened and the six blurred figures enter into the coach it is from this point that Ojuwain (– the believer –) must make his decision.' (The opening of Braxton's notes to *Composition 113* – for one soloist, a large photograph and prepared stage. In performance, the soloist re-creates, through 'situation improvisation', the conversation on the train as each of the hooded figures, representing different 'sound attitudes and purposes', tries in turn to win the loyalty of Ojuwain.)

†See 'Postscript 2', p. 309fn, for an example of an integration schematic

Trillium, like *Composition 95*, the piece for two pianos?

B: Yes. My move towards the world of ritual and drama would begin somewhere around *Composition 76*, the *For Trio* piece; a looking for something greater . . . I mean, I've always been searching, trying to understand my relationship to this experience, but I think it would be sometime around 76 that this would become very important to me, as far as expressing it in my work. There's a difference between what you're thinking about when you're twenty and when you're forty, and time in that context only clarifies one's worldview.

The piece for two pianos, *Composition 95*, is the only example of a ritual & ceremonial composition on record. This work would attempt to establish an environment context, costumes, choreography; and begin to reflect my concern about the spiritual relationships between various world disciplines.

L: That's the composition for which the record company 'forgot' to include your sleevenotes?

B: I didn't know it until the very day I picked the record up! No one told me about it, they just gave me the records. I picked up twenty copies and got on the train to go home, I was so excited about it; I opened up the records on the train and, of course, there was no booklet. I laughed – *they got me again*! That's what I found myself thinking. But that information will be in the *Composition Notes*, and I'll include all my other liner notes that have been changed through the years.

L: Your other notes have been altered too?

B: There have been *a lot* of problems because I wanted to write my own notes, but now they'll all come out in my books.

'FROM THE ABSTRACT TO

THE CONCRETE'

L: Looking at your terms for the different musics, from the language musics to the ritual musics, there seems to be an increasing movement away from purely musical factors.

B: From the abstract to the concrete.

L: Well, isn't it more to do with additional extra-musical factors like colours, stories, dreams, affecting your structures?

B: All I can say is, from the abstract to the concrete! Go back to the early coding musics, then go to the later image musics, and you'll see the integration of forces, forms, and the evolution to portray that on a physical universe level in terms of stories and empirical dynamics that will illustrate the same information. Remember, I'm building a system of evolution, so everything is connecting to everything. It will all make sense, hopefully, in the next twenty to thirty years.

L: Oh – I was hoping it would make sense by the end of the tour (*laughs*).

B: (*laughs*) Well . . . I wish you luck, sir! But I think it's going to take *me* longer.

L: You say 'from the abstract to the concrete', yet in our last interview you talked of abstract consciousness as the goal . . .

B: (*laughs*) I started off there!

L: I thought it was, like, a higher form of consciousness?

B: Remember, we're talking of many different things. We're talking about going up – and coming down (*laughs*). We have to be careful in the upper partials because we don't want to put one dimension on this. We're going all the way up and all the way down – it's the same direction!

L: (*laughs*) Oh no, you're not a Zen master too!

STRUCTURAL CRITERIA

OK, I think we've established a kind of overview of your musical evolution. Can we look more closely at particular areas within this? You described the co-ordinate musics as a series of territories, each of which has its own operatives. By operatives, I assume you're referring to the structural criteria you've described in the lectures – principle generating structures, material structures, etc?★

B: Yes, those are the criteria within the co-ordinate music scheme.

L: How many criteria are there?

B: Thematic structures, material structures, repetitive structures . . . ah, pulse track structures are now another category of co-ordinate music, although we could also talk about those separately.

L: OK, let's do that tomorrow. How do principle generating structures fit in?

B: Well, you can have several different types of principle generating structure: repetition can be used like that, or it can be used as a

★See 'Postscript 3', i and ii

pattern structure, or . . . Just as I gave you ten languages on that
lecture list, I can give you ten types of criteria and show you how
my work integrates them in different ways.

L: I'm getting lost. We seem to be shifting levels or focuses. Is there
a hierarchical scheme of these categories?

B: I guess you could look at it in that way. Let's try and draw it.
OK, we've said that the language music is the basis of my work, so:
(*draws*)

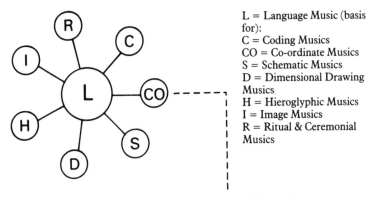

L = Language Music (basis for):
C = Coding Musics
CO = Co-ordinate Musics
S = Schematic Musics
D = Dimensional Drawing Musics
H = Hieroglyphic Musics
I = Image Musics
R = Ritual & Ceremonial Musics

Structural Criteria – Focus A: Language Music Nucleus

Now, we can take one of those categories, co-ordinate music, and
look at the operatives within that category: (*draws*)

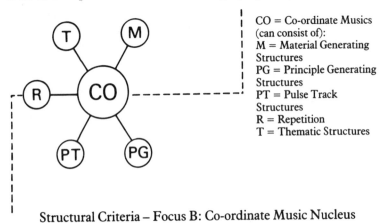

CO = Co-ordinate Musics (can consist of):
M = Material Generating Structures
PG = Principle Generating Structures
PT = Pulse Track Structures
R = Repetition
T = Thematic Structures

Structural Criteria – Focus B: Co-ordinate Music Nucleus

Then we can also take one of these operatives, say repetition, and look at the various ways it can be utilized in the music: (*draws*)

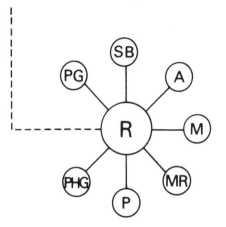

R = Repetition (can be used as):
A = Additive Structure
M = Material Generating Structure
MR = Multiple Relationship (Kaufman)
P = Pattern Structure
PHG = Phrase Generating Structure (Kelvin)
PG = Principle Generating Structure
SB = Sound Block (Colbolt)

Structural Criteria – Focus C: Repetition Nucleus

The problem with these drawings is that they're static. You have to imagine it more like particles around an atom or planetary orbits, and all these elements moving around and criss-crossing at different levels, different times.

L: In theory, you could take any one of the criteria you've mentioned, put it at the centre of its own solar system, and look at the different ways it's used in the music? Like an interlocking system of shifting focuses?

B: Yes. We're talking about a multiple layer of different inter-relationships. Repetition, for instance, can be looked at with respect to its being a co-ordinate music function, or we could look at it as a separate criterion and break down the different repetition structures. It just depends what you want to put as the nucleus, what level you want to deal with.

TERRITORIES – THE VIBRATIONAL
LIQUID OF IMPROVISATION

L: Returning to the co-ordinate musics – the sets the quartet are playing on this tour consist of specific compositions linked by improvisation?

B: That was how the co-ordinate music structural dynamics did work,* but in fact in this time period we play a composition, then I might improvise while somebody else plays another composition and somebody else plays a pulse track structure; or all four people might be playing different compositions. At this point, we can't really talk in terms of, like, notation here, improvisation there – that distinction is beginning to change in the quartet: at various points in the music, somebody could be playing structural models, notated models, language models, extended improvisation, unified structures, cross-structures, opposition structures. We're dealing now with the dynamic of collage structural formings and what that will mean for the next cycle of the music.

L: Let's talk more about that tomorrow. But, I mean, in drawing up your sets, you still specify particular compositions?

B: I name the primary territories. Then I say, well, maybe a piano solo tonight and Marilyn will pick from the material she has of mine; she has about 200 pages of my piano music, so she picks the zone she wants to play. I designate the territories of the music before each performance, but in fact that's what they are – territories. Each territory establishes a particular interaction.

L: How do you decide which territories to play on a particular night?

B: That would go back to the co-ordinate music structural dynamics; and the choices there involve, first, selecting a body of works that address different kinds of structural problems, so that the music will have diversity; and, second, based on just musical and feeling needs, to put together a set that will be interesting, that you think will work.

L: You have no breaks in your sets, so is improvisation still the means by which you move from territory to territory?

B: We have several different ways, but the most basic is we go into open improvisation. So open improvisation has become like the vibrational fabric or liquid of my music; the vibrational liquid, in between structurally defined regions, that solidifies the processes in space.

---

*A full description of co-ordinate music structural dynamics, as they stood at the end of the seventies, was included in the original issue of the *Performance 9/1/79* LP. Unfortunately, Braxton's notes, as well as his composition titles, were omitted from the reissue: an insult to composer and interested listener alike

ROAD

THURSDAY 21, BRISTOL

Rain. We haul out the luggage and Tony loads it into the van. Braxton sees me yawning and laughs. 'Look at Graham Lock. I'm taking bets that he'll crack in two or three days. The other bet is, will I crack first?'

Gerry is in good spirits; Tony rang Sheffield, the money belt was recovered intact, and we can collect it on Saturday *en route* to Leeds. Gerry celebrates by singing through rhythm exercises with Mark in the back of the van; the rest of us reach hastily for the Walkmans. We stop to look at Warwick Castle: no one wants to pay the £3.25 entrance fee for the twenty-five minutes we have spare, so we wander around the outside, huddled against the wind and drizzle, trying to get a glimpse of the grounds. Braxton starts to shiver.

'I'm going back to the van,' he mutters. 'It's too cold for me, I should've brought my coat.'

Marilyn smiles at him. 'You're wearing it, Anthony.'

'What?' He looks down in surprise: Evan Parker's tatty yellow overcoat is flapping around his torso. 'Oh. Well, I'm still cold.' He hurries off, the rest of us trailing in his wake.

We stop briefly for a pub lunch in Stratford-upon-Avon, then it's back to the van again. Gerry and Mark sing through more rhythm exercises; Braxton maintains his habitual silence beside Tony; Marilyn and I chat desultorily. I ask her if she's still writing poetry. She says, yeah, occasionally.

'They mean a lot to me when I write them because they're usually about some immediate emotional situation, but when I look at them later it just seems like a load of drivel.'

One of the few she still likes is the piece written for Cecil Taylor which appears on the sleeve of her most recent LP:

and your ivory voice
  sings,
breaking like fragile cartilage
  in the clear air,
of points, wing/ed
  and pure, beating,
colliding in subtle counterpoint . . .
  crossings . . .
birds fly between
  here and there,
singing furiously
  in delicate tongues.

It's late afternoon before we arrive in Bristol, a city which in the seventeenth and eighteenth centuries grew wealthy from its dealings in the slave trade. Selling off human beings in exchange for Virginian tobacco, Jamaican sugar and West African cocoa, Bristol became a cigarette and chocolate centre, thus disseminating cancer, bronchitis, heart disease and tooth decay to generations of English men and women. Karma? Cosmic justice? Is this what Braxton is referring to when he talks of Western materialism's failure to recognize the 'vibrational implications' of its actions?

At the soundcheck, the group play through *Four* and a few other tunes. Gerry enthuses about the Arnolfini: he likes to play solo gigs in galleries and art centres, he says – they seem to attract sympathetic audiences. Perhaps he's right: this concert too is sold out, people are being turned away at the box-office. Braxton seems pleased: when a local radio station requests an interview, he agrees to give up his interval.

BRISTOL CONCERT, ARNOLFINI

First Set (Primary Territories)
Composition 69H
Composition 88 (+ 108C)
Piano solo (from *Compositions 1, 30–33*)
Composition 23J

Second Set (Primary Territories)
Composition 6A
Percussion solo (from *Composition 96*)
Composition 115

Bass solo (from *Composition 96*)
Composition 69J

The quartet immediately hit their stride tonight. *69H* is a maze of dense textures, constant flurries of ensemble interplay that shift into a slowly spiralling swirl of agitation and calm as the group realign to *88* (played for the first time on the tour, it's the fourth of the *85–88* woodwind/bass duo series). Gerry and Marilyn play the pulse track, Mark and Braxton the primary territory: bass and C-melody sax meet at its heart, dancing together on the theme as Mark coaxes a gorgeously rich tone from his strings. The piano solo is brief, stark, dramatic: a dialectic of angularities played with Marilyn's customary power. Then Braxton's alto leads the rhythm section in like a swarm of bees and they zoom into the exhilarating rush of *23J*, given another rousing performance tonight, though the solos are less extreme than at Birmingham. The second set, punctuated by notated solos with almost ritualistic formality, becomes a play on, and with, rhythmic elasticity, the 'accordion sound space' of *115* followed by *69J*'s own accelerating and retarding patterns (including a trill motif that speeds into hilarious mania), before the final, slowing descent that Braxton conjures down beautifully on solo clarinet.

The post-gig conversations are getting bizarre. In the dressing-room, Gerry is telling me about a Japanese sound sculptor.

Braxton frowns. 'Is that the guy whose wife cut off his legs?'

'What?' Marilyn looks up, horrified.

'No, that was a jazz drummer,' says Gerry.

'She did *what*?' Marilyn demands.

'This is a real love story,' Gerry grins. 'She found out he was cheating on her, so she cut his legs off, ha-ya! Samurai style!' The edge of his hand crashes on to the table in demonstration.

Marilyn considers. 'What? While he was asleep?'

Gerry laughs. 'I guess so. But he's still playing and they're still together, apparently.'

'She cut his legs off and they're still together?' Marilyn is incredulous.

'I told you this was a real love story.'

'You sure about this, Gerry?' Mark grins. 'Remember Pinegate?'

Later, driving back to the hotel, we pass a John Lewis department store, the name shining out in green light. 'Hey, look!' Braxton's head jerks around. 'I guess he didn't do too badly with the MJQ, huh? Hmm, I like the vibe here; maybe I could move to England and start a chain of hamburger joints. Braxburgers! You can be the manager, Graham. Stick with me, I'll make you a rich man.'

Gerry laughs. 'Yay! Big Brax to go!'

QUARTET

MARILYN CRISPELL, PIANO

Before she ever played jazz Marilyn Crispell made her living by playing piano for dance classes in Boston. She remembers talking with a colleague, a jazz fan, about her playing. 'I told him, if I were going to improvise this is how I'd do it, and I improvised atonal stuff the way I do now. I said, it's really crazy, nobody would listen; he said, it's OK, you can do that, but I went no, no, no. Then, later, I heard a Cecil Taylor record and it was – YES, YES, YES! Like a door opening.'

Crispell sits in a hotel room, picking distractedly at a half-eaten salad as she tells me in her hushed voice how Cecil Taylor has been a constant source of inspiration to her. In the late seventies, when she was teaching at Karl Berger's Creative Music Studio in Woodstock, Taylor came to give some workshops: she decided she had to play for him.

'He was in the ping-pong room, so I went into the practice room next door and started playing. I played for fifteen, twenty minutes, knowing that he'd be out there listening, playing what I felt was my best, being on top every second, like you'd communicate to a true soulmate.

'When I came out he was standing there. He said, "Uh, this lady can really play," and he kissed my hand. I was in seventh heaven!' She gives a nervous laugh. 'But I was very shy, I was awestruck by him and I had a lot of trouble talking to him, so I used to write him poetry and once I gave him a rose.'

Eighth heaven came in 1984 when Taylor attended a performance of the Braxton quartet at New York's Sweet Basil. He sat by the stage with a bucket of champagne, she recalls, and after the concert gave her a big hug. 'It was such a gas playing, having him

179

sit right there in front. It didn't make me nervous, it made me
happy and excited. Like being able to talk to someone who will
finally understand.'

Cecil Taylor apart, John Coltrane was the chief reason Marilyn
Crispell began to play creative music. Born in Philadelphia (30
March 1947), she started piano lessons at seven, moved with her
family to Baltimore at age ten, and later studied piano and
composition at the New England Conservatory of Music in Boston.
In her final year there she got married and, after graduation,
practically abandoned music.

'I was interested in medicine. I was working in hospitals,
psychiatric hospitals, as a secretary. By the time I finished at the
Conservatory I was sick of music, I needed a break.'

The break lasted six years, until her marriage ended. Crispell
moved to Cape Cod and felt herself drawn to music again – not as a
pianist, but singing Bonnie Raitt songs in a rock and blues band. 'I
just wanted to sing. I felt like I was able to get into something
emotionally through singing more than I could on piano.' Then in
1975 came the moment of epiphany that changed her life. She'd
met a jazz pianist who introduced her to the work of Monk,
Coltrane, Cecil Taylor: 'One night he was out of the house and I put
on *A Love Supreme* and something, the *spirit* of it, just caught me. I
was twenty-eight years old and, ah, I said to myself, I have to learn
to play this music. I loved it so much.'

She studied improvisation and jazz harmony with a teacher
(Charlie Banacos) in Boston for two years, then attended the
Creative Music Studio, first as a student, later as a teacher, staying
until Reaganomics forced its closure. It was there that she met
Braxton, Oliver Lake, Roscoe Mitchell, Leo Smith – 'virtually
everyone I've ever played with'. Her first experience of working
with Braxton was proofreading the scores for his four-orchestra
piece, which he was scrambling to complete in time for the
recording session.

'The project went way past the deadline,' she recalls with a smile.
'Anthony had like a Santa's workshop – you know, with all the
elves. He had a million people there. These huge scores were
hanging up on posts and there were like all the little elves running
around working on them.' Prior to this, she says, Braxton had
heard her 'playing rock chords' at a George Russell workshop and,

on the strength of that, invited her to join the Creative Music Orchestra he was assembling for a European tour. That tour, in the spring of 1978, was her first 'real professional gig'.

On returning to the States, Crispell decided she'd like to make a record, but met with little record-company interest. She worked at various projects – toured with Braxton; formed her own group; played John Cage's *Piece for Six Pianos* on national radio – but still found no joy from the record industry. Then several things happened at once. First, a friend suggested she send a tape to Cadence Records; she did, they liked it, and her first LP, *Spirit Music* (with Billy Bang, John Betsch, Wes Brown) was released by Cadence in 1983. Second, while at the Creative Music Studio, she'd met two writers, Roger Riggins and Joachim Berendt, who both liked her music; Riggins wrote a piece about her in *Jazz* magazine which prompted Leo Feigin, owner of the London-based Leo label, to ask if she'd like to record a solo LP: the resulting *Rhythms Hung in Undrawn Sky* also appeared in 1983. Berendt meanwhile had recommended her to Giovanni Bonandrini, and in 1984 Black Saint duly released the *Live in Berlin* record, taken from a 1982 European tour by the Crispell quartet (Bang, Betsch and Peter Kowald). By which time another solo LP, *A Concert in Berlin*, had been issued, this one on the German FMP label, also in 1983. Since that flurry of activity, she's played with many people – Pauline Oliveros, Oliver Lake, Leo Smith, Anthony Davis (in his *X* opera); recorded with Braxton, Eric Andersen and Julie Kabat; but released only one further album of her own music, *And Your Ivory Voice Sings*, a duo LP with drummer Doug James, which came out on the Leo label in late 1985.

Listening to these LPs in sequence, you can hear Crispell transcending the early Cecil Taylor influence and developing, with increasing authority, her own distinct aesthetic: her interest in layering, in 'bouncing off', different rhythms, particularly African rhythms, results in a wonderful 'dancing in the air' feel to much of her music, though tracks like *Love* and *Early Light* show she is equally at home in more reflective modes. And, in the version of John Coltrane's *After the Rain* which closes *And Your Ivory Voice Sings*, she brilliantly exemplifies Coltrane's own sense of spiritual questing, laying bare the heart of the music, hammering at its secrets and moving from delicacy through frantic turmoil to a final, accepting peace. Even so, the phenomenal technique, the sensitivity, the imagination of her playing on the Braxton tour have come as revelations to me: I guess she has finally found *her* ivory voice and on song she must now be one of the most exciting improvisers in creative music, lyrical proof of William Blake's dictum that '*Energy is eternal delight*'.

Though none of the records really does justice to the power and beauty of her live performances, I tell Marilyn I like the solo and duo LPs for their strong playing, their clear-sighted marriage of form and intensity; the earlier group records, though, I find a little unfocused.

'I think I could criticize myself for not having enough structure,' she murmurs. 'In my work with Anthony, and in my own improvisations, I am moving much more into structure.'

Does that mean you're composing more? I ask.

'No, my composing is minimal. It's really spontaneous composition . . . I might write down a small segment to use as a basis for improvisation, but I won't write out a whole piece. I feel like I went through that for years, I'm just not interested any more.'

I'm curious about Marilyn's notions of music and spirituality: there's the title *Spirit Music*, there's a quote of hers that 'music to me is a spiritual expression and has a healing and transcending power'. Could you explain this a little? I ask her. What does 'spiritual' mean to you?

'Oh!' An embarrassed laugh. 'It's not something I can really put into words. It's . . . like an energy field, with waves of feeling that rise and fall, a feeling of going higher, to a non-mundane state. Hmm . . . when you're really hooked into the music, you reach another level of energy that goes beyond the mechanics of it. I think it comes through getting in touch with your energy or with the primal energy that exists in the universe. That's the level I'm interested in reaching.'

Crispell's work with Braxton has continued at irregular intervals since the late seventies. After Creative Music Orchestra tours in 1978 and 1979, she was in the Braxton quintet that played a week's residency in Montreal in 1980; then in 1981, she, Ray Anderson and trumpeter Hugh Ragin comprised the Braxton quartet that toured Europe with *Composition 98* – a fifty-minute, fifty-two-page score which uses extended notation (although the notation includes shapes, around which the players improvise).

'That was fun,' Marilyn enthuses. 'I think it was an attempt on

Anthony's part to merge completely the written and improvised musics.'

How did you play the shapes? I ask.

'Everyone tended to play them very fast. They were very squiggly; none of them lasted for longer than a few seconds.'

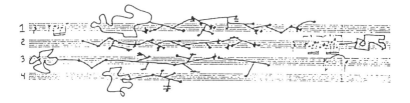

Notation and Improvisation Shapes from *Composition 98*

Following that tour, Crispell played occasional duo concerts with Braxton, but it wasn't until 1983 that she rejoined the quartet, playing on the Black Saint *Six Compositions (Quartet) 1984* LP and touring Europe with the group in 1983, '84 and '85. It's been, she says, a valuable education.

'I've learned a lot about space from Anthony. I used to play a million notes a minute without ever stopping to breathe, now I listen more and I've got a much better sense of an orchestral thing happening, all kinds of different textures and dynamics. I also feel I'm naturally in tune with the kind of music he does, and there's a lot of room for me to express myself in the improvisations.'

Do you enjoy playing the pulse track structures?

'Usually it's the bass and drums playing the pulse track underneath us, and I like that very much, the feeling of it. I hear what they're doing and play off of it, like different rhythms bouncing off each other in space. I love to play against rhythms, to play strong rhythms of my own *against* a strong rhythm.'

How about collage form structures? I think you were already exploring collage musics before you played them with Anthony?

She nods. 'To me, one of the most happening sounds is when you walk down a street and hear people playing, the sounds coming from different windows and all merging together in the street. It's like those people are not listening to each other, they're just playing their own thing very strong – yet, on a certain level, they are listening, and playing off of that, but it's not what they're *trying* to do. Like half of you is doing your own thing, then another part of you is standing aside listening to the whole thing shape itself. I like that sound, the simultaneous things going on. Maybe to some people it's confusing or chaotic, but I just like it.'

Presumably you think your collage music works better if the players are responding to each other to a degree, so there's at least an intuitive sense of unity. Is that possible in Anthony's collage form structures too – where people are not improvising but playing separate notated solos?

'Yeah, if it merges in a certain way it works. But if you're just playing the concept, reading through a bunch of solos, the dynamic will be static – there has to be something there to make it gel. It's funny, 'cause you have less control than if you were totally improvising, but there is that element of interpretation. I do listen to what the other people are doing, and I shape the way I play the written music to the total sound that is going on.'

What's your response to the accusations that Anthony's music doesn't swing or that, like the *Times* review claimed, it leaves no room for emotion?

'I think it's ridiculous,' Marilyn's eyes widen in disbelief, 'totally ridiculous. Anthony has a lot of ideas, and his ideas change quickly, he does a lot of different things . . . his moods are very changeable. You must know from talking to him every day that he's a very emotional person. At the same time he's a chess player, a thinker, an intellectual; so all those elements are combined in his music. If you look at him when he's playing, even if he's playing something that sounds like it isn't very emotional, you can see his eyes are closed, see the emotion in his face . . . I mean, he's not coming out and going "rrraaaaaaaarrr", but he's maybe expressing an inward emotion.

'I think people are just mad that he's not playing jazz with a capital J, that's all; not blowing his guts out for two hours every night. There are periods in the music where there's a lot of space; maybe people are talking about that. But those fast, complicated compositions of his, they really swing – you have to *listen* to hear it, but there are all kinds of figures in there, jagged, accented, off-the-beat phrases, that swing like crazy.'

This may be an impossible question, I say, but for you exactly how or where does the emotion come into the music?

'Oh . . .' she slumps back into her chair with a despairing groan. 'I guess it's there all the time. The emotion comes in my own playing because a lot of the time there are written notes and it's totally up to you how you interpret them. You could play them like a sewing machine, like a lot of people play Bach, *ta-ta-ta-ta-ta-ta-ta-ta-ta-ta-ta-ta*, with no expression or phrasing or understanding of what's going on. Or you could see them and put them into a picture that means something.'

I mention Mark's hypothesis that perhaps lack of rehearsal time makes those pictures harder to see at first.

Marilyn purses her lips. 'Well . . . sometimes the first time we perform a piece will be one of the best performances, because everyone just jumps in. It's like kamikaze – OK, *do it*! So there's an edge that can make those first performances real good.'

You've worked with Anthony for seven years now. Is there any incident or anecdote about him that sticks in your mind? Something that's an insight into who he is?

She ponders for a moment. 'Well, the first time I went to his house in Woodstock, it was winter, there was a stream which had iced over, very thin ice, and this dog had fallen through into the stream and couldn't get out. Anthony walked out on to the ice and saved him, pulled him out with his own two hands. I was very impressed by that. I think he's a good person, a very private person too.'

Oh no, I groan. The guy's a genius *and* he saves drowning dogs! Who's gonna believe this?

Marilyn is less than enthusiastic when I suggest taping her thoughts on 'the feminine vibration' and men's and women's musics.

'Oh, no, no, no, no, no!' She holds her head in her hands, then heaves a great sigh. 'OK, I don't like -isms, you know, movements. I guess I could say that. Doctrines. I feel like I don't want to define myself, or say I'm a feminist, because I'm always changing. And I've never felt a *need* to adopt a position like that.'

Do you not think women in the music business have a tough time?

'All musicians do, really.'

But there are extra pressures on women, particularly the notion that they should stay at home, look after the children . . .

Marilyn shakes her head slowly. 'I know there are a lot of

screwed-up things, but . . . First of all, nobody is telling a woman that she can't go out and do whatever, no one is telling her that she has to stay at home and have a family.'

The whole culture is telling her that, I interrupt. Look at advertisements . . . not to mention factors like the lack of adequate childcare facilities.

'OK, her choice is influenced by societal pressure, by cultural background, and sometimes circumstances may be beyond one's control, but no one's *making* her, it's her choice. I mean, I've made the choice not to have a family.'

When did you make that choice?

'I think I was born with it.' She gives a quiet, tentative laugh. 'I never really wanted to raise a family . . . I love children, I love families . . . mmm . . . I don't particularly like living alone – well, I don't live alone . . . I guess there's always something in me that really wants to be free, and that's how I am, that's my choice.

'I mean, I can see fighting for equal wages, childcare, the right to vote. Those are concrete things, I have no quarrel with that. I know there are a lot of instances where women don't have the same opportunities as men, but I also know a lot of women who use that as an excuse not to go out and do what they want to do.'

Even so, I say, it's not just lack of determination which explains why there's never been a woman, or a black, US president, say. There are social forces there, which presumably operate in the music business too, and in personal relationships.

Marilyn shrugs. 'I don't know . . . maybe I'm just naïve.' She smiles and rolls her eyes heavenwards. 'I know I'm a little spacey.'

Do you feel any sympathy with those women players who are questioning the extent to which music may be a male language?

'I've never thought of music in those terms. Maybe what they're really trying to do is work out a *personal* language, and that's fine.'

You really don't mind when people tell you that you play like a man? I ask. There seem to be a lot of sexist assumptions hidden in there – that only men are powerful, intense . . .

'Yeah, but it's funny to me,' she shrugs. 'I sort of get a kick out of it, like I'm shocking people. I think you can take yourself too seriously, with a capital S.'

You don't feel as if you're being misunderstood or misinterpreted?

'Hmm . . . I have noticed that people tend to equate abstraction with negativity. Sometimes people'll say, oh I can really feel how angry you are when you play, and I look at them in amazement because I wasn't angry at all. They look at it in this very simplistic way, like you're playing something intense therefore you're expressing anger. I don't feel I'm expressing anger, I feel like I'm expressing energy, a moving energy that falls into certain patterns and rhythms, and all your life experiences are in there – pain, anger, joy . . .'

I think Anthony's notion of masculine and feminine vibrations probably refers to this more abstract level, I suggest. Like levels of energy that are now out of balance.

'I think, in the universe, there's masculine energy and feminine energy and, yeah, it definitely seems off balance, like it's spearheading towards something terrible.' Marilyn pauses, frowns. 'I'm trying to remember the things I've read about space and form. Feminine energy is like spatial energy, masculine energy is a formative energy, and the combination produces life.' She looks up with one of her inscrutable stares. 'Which is the way it is, if you think about it.'

I dare say we could have argued about that too, how *the way it is* depends on the language we use to perceive and describe, and how that language is shaped by the values of its users; but I suspect I've harped on enough about the feminine vibration. Though I smile to myself at the irony of a pro-feminist man trying to unravel this concept with a non-feminist woman, it's not a situation I feel comfortable with; especially as the result seems to be that I'm edging Marilyn into a stance which perhaps distorts her deeper, more ambivalent feelings.

So just shut up, I tell myself.

We end up talking work and money, musicians' lack of.

Were you serious about working in a rock band? I ask.

'I'd definitely try it,' she nods. 'But I'm in a period of my life where I feel like I'm going more inwards than outwards. I don't know if I have the impetus to go out and make it happen like I did with the jazz thing, because I was totally inspired by that, it seemed to be my purpose in life at the time. I can't say I feel that about rock, I enjoy it but I guess if it happens it's gonna be an act of fate.'

You say jazz *seemed* to be your purpose: it's not any longer?

She stares into space for several seconds. 'No . . . not in the same sense that I felt it before. That night when I heard *A Love Supreme* I felt like something really opened up inside me, a spiritual feeling, and that's what I related to in the music. And I've gotten other things together in my life since that have become more of a focus than the actual music.'

Such as?

'Meditation. I guess that's what I'm really talking about, going inside myself. The music is like a manifestation, it isn't the purpose any more.'

Can you foresee a time when you might stop playing?

She lets out a long, slow sigh. 'Hmm-mmmm. I love to play. I can also not play. Like, months go by when I have no work and usually if I don't have work I don't tend to practise very much or be involved with music.'

She tells me about her home in Woodstock: a rented room in a large, shared house. 'It's a very simple house, there's hardly any furniture, it's got a lot of shells, branches, stones, stuff like that. An old upright piano. Books. I live on the third floor, in the attic; there's a blue rug on the floor, and I have a bed on the floor, a few books and clothes, a little table, a lamp. It's very cosy, very simple. I've got to buy a chair when I get home, when I have some money.'

You don't have a *chair*? (I'm dumbfounded: even I own a chair.)

Marilyn laughs. 'The last house I lived in, we were too poor to afford a table for the kitchen. We'd sit on cushions on the floor, eating out of bowls.'

No chair? No table? I hear Braxton's catchphrase echoing through my head: 'That's the jazz world for you, Graham.' The unfairness of it all leaves me angry, gloomy, lost for words.

Do you listen to music at home? I ask, struck by a terrible thought. You can afford a record player?

Marilyn shakes her head. 'I've got a cassette recorder, a few tapes, but I don't listen to much music.' The ghost of a smile. 'I like silence.'

ROAD

FRIDAY 22, SOUTHAMPTON

The road is getting to me: I go to bed exhausted and wake up tired. Mark gives me a packet of vitamin pills and I gulp them down gratefully.

It's a grey, bitter morning. In the van, nothing is happening: Gerry and Mark are in the back, headphones on; the rest of us sit cocooned in coats, scarves and soporific silence. I try to start up a discussion on the feminine vibration in music, dragging in Braxton and a reluctant Marilyn. It's a mistake; we talk in circles until Marilyn slumps back, eyes closed, and says she's suffering from 'Dresser syndrome'.

'Huh?' Mark's ears prick up.

'I feel sick,' she mutters.

'That's Dresser syndrome? Nausea?' Mark is aghast. 'Gee, thanks a lot, Marilyn.'

We pull into a petrol station and Marilyn gets out for some fresh air. I go with her, chastened by guilt: *I should never have started that bloody argument.* We sit on a wall in silence, huddled against a biting wind; after a while she says she's feeling better.

'I'm sorry if I . . . you know, if the arguing made you ill,' I say.

'Oh, I feel OK now,' she smiles. 'Still, it was a good way to end the conversation.'

Half an hour later, the big moment: Stonehenge! In the car park we rendezvous with photographer Nick White, who's taking pictures for the book, then we head for the stones. As we approach it, the stone circle looks insignificant against the expanse of plain and sky; but once we're in among them the stones are massive, with a desolate grandeur that shrinks the soul. Braxton says he's waited twenty years to see Stonehenge; he gazes around, wide-eyed, muttering 'Oh boy' under his breath. I wonder about his desire to rediscover the ancient wisdom; here, looking at its silent wreckage, the gulf feels too utter to bridge.

We're all shivering: an icy, razor-sharp wind is raking Salisbury Plain, giving Nick no end of trouble with the photos. His fingers are so numb he can't feel the shutter-button; plus, the group can't keep still, but grimace and hunch their bodies against the cold. Braxton, flapping his arms like an agitated penguin, suddenly rugby-tackles Gerry and they roll over the frozen earth, laughing like schoolboys. Nick looks on, mystified.

'Road rot,' I murmur knowingly. 'It can do strange things to a man.' (Eight days' travelling, and already I'm Marco Polo.)

We buy our postcards, our cups of hot soup, and hurry back to the van. Marilyn tells me about the nearby Woodhenge which, she says (quoting John Michell),* was laid out – like the Great Pyramid – by a system derived from the numbers in Mercury's magic square,† and which possibly functioned as a giant stringed instrument, on which the wind played a microcosmic music of the spheres. (I later discover that for her composition *Rounds*, Marilyn used the numbers of Mercury's magic square 'in determining the placement of the notes'.)‡

After we check into the hotel at Southampton, I interview Braxton; then Nick takes some portrait photos while Braxton reminisces about his chess-playing days. He tells of the time he played a young woman who had shot to prominence among the Washington Square cognoscenti: the buzz said her game was *out*, but Braxton ('with the arrogance of a young man') fancied he could put this upstart in her place. 'We played one game and she wiped the board with me. I couldn't believe it, I'd been *trounced*. We played a second game, she trounced me again! I was bowled over, *awed*. At the end of the match I asked her to marry me – she just

---

*Michell, 1975, pp. 109–12

†'The cabalists say that each planet has a magic square which can be used to attract the planet's influence . . . In a properly constructed square each number from one to the highest number used must appear once. Whether the numbers are added vertically or horizontally, each column must add to the same total' (Cavendish, 1984, p. 138). The square of Mercury, containing the numbers one to sixty-four, thus comprises eight rows, each of eight figures

‡Crispell, 1986, no page number. (In Thomas Mann's novel *Doctor Faustus*, the composer Leverkühn has a magic square pinned to the wall above his piano, and this inspires his later discovery of serialist composition techniques. Mann's novel offers a fascinating discourse on the relationship between mysticism and creativity, but from within a very Euro-centric framework – particularly in its use of dualistic Christian mythology)

laughed! Boy, did I feel crushed that day.' He chortles at the memory.

'Do you miss the chess life?' Nick asks.

'Well, yes and no. I love the game, but I've got a family to support, and . . . it's like, you cannot play chess every day and be a nice human being.' He shakes his head, smiling ruefully. 'You think musicians are weird? I tell you, chess masters are *insane!*'

At the soundcheck, the group play through the new *124* a couple of times. The venue, the Solent Suite, in the Guildhall, is really a large bar, its ambience distinguished only by a garish orange-yellow carpet, less jazzy than 'snazzy': in fact, it's lucky Tony's not wearing his green suit or I'd fear a mass outbreak of Dresser syndrome.

Marilyn wraps an elastoplast around a finger she'd cut during the Bristol concert. 'My hands are breaking up,' she grimaces, looking at her collection of cuts, blisters and calluses. They don't hurt, she says, 'they just feel kinda numb'.

In the dressing-room we all sit around, yawning profusely.

'Cheer up, only three more concerts after this,' Tony jokes.

'I'm dreading the end of this tour,' Marilyn murmurs.

'Yeah, who knows when we'll see each other again,' Braxton sighs. 'Dresser's moving east, everyone's gonna be on the East Coast except me. Next time you see me, I'll be playing with Shorty Rogers.'

Gerry grins. 'Yeah, on your next LP sleeve you'll be riding on a surfboard.'

SOUTHAMPTON CONCERT, GUILDHALL, SOLENT SUITE

First Set (Primary Territories)
Composition 105B
Composition 40(O)
Composition 124
Composition 86

Second Set (Primary Territories)
Composition 52
Collage Form Structure
Composition 40F
Composition 108A

(Braxton tries several experiments tonight: *86*, originally a woodwind/bass duo and usually played in the quartet context with the pulse track *108C*, is played here as three consecutive notated duets – piano/percussion, clarinet/bass, clarinet/percussion – with the remaining two instruments improvising; the collage form structure is also played without a pulse track, Marilyn playing from the solo piano pieces, the others from different parts of *96*, the particulars chosen 'in the moment' by each player; and the concert ends with the pulse track *108A*, but played – for the first time ever – by Braxton and Marilyn, while Gerry and Mark play open improvisation. '*You're* gonna do the pulse track? Hey,' Gerry grins evilly, 'I'm just gonna lay back and *listen* to that.')

105B begins the concert with a flurry of sounds, leads into the thicket of a bass/drums dialogue, and is then stretched into low curlicues of C-melody sax. Marilyn improvises a solo, as Braxton switches to alto and speeds into *40(O)*'s repetition lines; then a brief bass solo, before Braxton moves to sopranino for the wavering, playful trills that signal *124*, here generating intense solos by Braxton, Marilyn and Mark. The kinetics are refocused, heralding *86*'s duo interchanges; ribbons of sound criss-cross the silence, taut and spacious. The second set hits an immediate high with *52*, a post-bop cauldron that has Braxton screeching in all registers and Marilyn unzipping great splatters of notes along the keyboard. A percussion solo cannily transforms the energy in preparation for the collage form section, the players linking the separate scores with flashes of intuitive synchronicity. Suddenly we're into a wonderful version of *40F*, which Braxton calls his 'half-step piece', the one reminiscent of the *Batman* theme because of its up-and-down *na-na na-na na-na na-na* figure. Braxton's visual designation of the piece suggests its rising/falling dialogues very well:

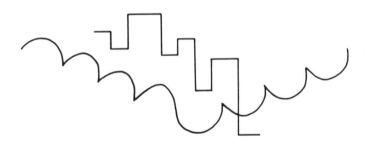

The group dig into the theme, tossing snippets of it to and fro like flickers of lightning, threading their improvisations around the car-chase tempo with whooping bravura. Then Braxton sidesteps into the pulse track, alto and piano dance a tightrope of strobe-flash changes – notes/free/notes/free – Marilyn breaking into a delighted grin as the music leaps and feints along helter-skelter curves until it halts, abruptly, impossibly, in mid-air. These sudden endings still take my breath, yet immediately they happen they're as *right* as the gentler landings of a *40N* or *69J*.

This is the third consecutive concert where the quartet have played at a superlative peak; the fourth, if you could get behind the Leadmill's dodgy acoustics to the actual music. 'Whew!' Gerry grins afterwards: 'I think some of the recent performances have been *strong*.' Marilyn agrees, citing the second set at Bristol as her favourite since Birmingham. I ask her how she liked playing the pulse track with Braxton.

'Great, *great*! That was the first time Anthony and I played a pulse track together. I had a great time with it.'

'I saw you suddenly laughing in the middle – was that relief at getting on top of it?'

'Not really,' she smiles. 'It was just such fun to play, such a great sound. You know,' she starts to hum *108A*, laughing, eyes alight, still high on the music.

After the gig, Braxton hurries off to bed, Nick goes to stay with friends (he'll rejoin us for the last two concerts), and the rest of us head for a nearby restaurant. As we eat, Tony regales us with the trials and torments of a tour manager's life: the knife fights in the band bus; the groups who smuggle pornography in their flight cases; the promoter who provided a piano but no stool, 'because "it wasn't specified in the contract" – the bloody moron'. Mark wants to know how he manages rowdy groups. You have to out-psyche them, he says; like the time he shaved his head overnight then came down to breakfast wearing a woolly hat which he casually discarded during the meal – the dropped jaws and stunned silence told him he was back in control.

'That's why you wear that green suit, right?' Mark laughs. 'To intimidate us.'

'It can help,' Tony nods. 'But you're a quiet bunch, I haven't worn it for nearly a week.'

The talk turns to Braxton. Tony says he can't make him out. 'I mean, is he a genius or is he a fruitcake? What is all that pan-African functionalism stuff?' He's particularly puzzled by Braxton's lack of interest in socializing. 'He never chats in the van, he never comes out for a drink or a meal – is he really that absorbed in the music?'

Gerry points out that Braxton's been playing music for over twenty years. 'I guess he's been through all that party party scene. He's realized that it's the music which really matters to him, so he's cut out all the other shit and he just concentrates on that.'

'I think he has a lot of Ellingtonian qualities,' Mark adds. 'That band had year after year of one-night stands, yet Duke still found time to write and arrange new pieces. Anthony has that kind of dedication. He doesn't hang out, he works his ass off.'

'Well, obviously he's a clever guy,' Tony concedes. 'But I wish he'd talk to me a bit in the van. The way he just stares through the windscreen, mile after mile – it's so bloody unnerving.'

METAROAD

SOUND LOGIC, SOUND MAGIC 2: PULSE TRACKS, COLLAGE FORMS, MULTI-ORCHESTRALISM

23G, 'SOUND ATTACKS', VERTICAL AND HORIZONTAL FORMINGS

L: What was the origin of pulse track structures?

B: The composition which really triggered the concept of pulse track structures was *23G*. But let me back up a moment.

One of the things about vertical harmony that has made it so fascinating, especially the extended vertical harmony of, say, the last 300 years since Bach and figured bass harmony, has been how it establishes particular requirements in its given time parameters – specifications to do with harmonic progression – and how that serves as a general framework for invention dynamics. Pulse track structures were an attempt to begin integrating *horizontal* structural formings into the forward space of the music.

In the beginning, when I wrote *23G*, I wasn't aware of the extended implications of the process. In *23G* the rhythm section play sound attacks, and this principle would provide definition; it would serve as a principle generating structure, which is how I originally approached it.

L: Sound attacks being a series of notated moments or points in the music when the bass and drums would suddenly come together?

B: Yes. *23G* would establish sound point attacks as a criterion that defines the space of the music, and refocuses the beat. What this would mean wasn't so apparent in the theoretical forming of the idea, but playing *23G* when the quartet toured I became aware that every time I called *23G* something was happening which could

195

really be extended. I knew I'd have to come back to it.

L: And when you did? How would you describe the later stage of pulse tracks?

B: Well, as I said, the term pulse track refers to the horizontal placement of given factors in the forward space of the music, horizontal variables that define how the space is conceived in the same sense as vertical harmony does, except here we're dealing with conceptual areas that I've generated in my own music, areas that in this context have to do with the nature of event-forming and construction dynamics. And these horizontal variables establish a dialogue, on the first level between the individual and the process; then the individual and the other players; and later the individual and the composite group consciousness.

L: Is it possible to be specific? To compare, say, bebop's vertical harmony with *23G*, and *23G* with later pulse tracks?

B: In *23G*, the use of sound attacks would be a simple example of pulse tracking. Imagine a continuum, a sound space, OK: the vertical axis is pitch, the horizontal axis is time or duration. What Bach did, what bebop would later do – a given song would be based on figured bass harmonic progressions and that would serve as the vibrational definition of the space; so improvisation in that context is defined by what Western culture calls tertial harmonic perception dynamics, that being the chord and its harmonic foundation. In bebop, you might have the theme (A), variations (A2), improvisations (B), then back to the theme (A): and the nature of the dialogue would be, like, for the upper voices, notated music to improvisation to notated music; and for the lower voices, it's a question of 'walking in the track' for the various progressions from (A) to (A). (*Draws. See 'Bebop Sound Space', p. 197.*) So the given nature of the dialogue as far as bass and drums are concerned is to have different parts of the chord they can 'walk on' in the progression: invention dynamics for that music involves what choices you take inside the chord. In pulse track structures, we're changing the nature of how the space is defined and that changes the nature of the bass/drums dialogue. For example, in *23G*: (*Draws. See 'Sound Attack Sound Space', p. 197.*)*

L: In later pulse tracks, the principle is that the rhythm section improvise until they reach a notated point or section, they both play

---

*E.g. of notation for rhythm section sound attacks in *23G* (see p. 198 fn)

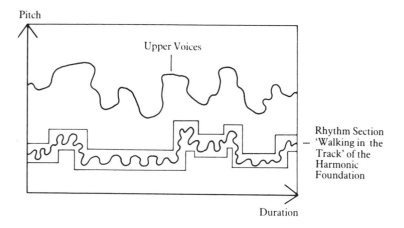

Bebop Sound Space

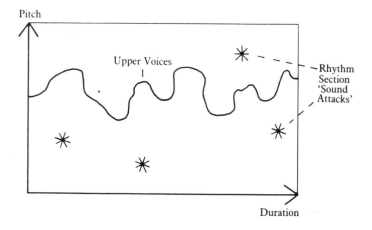

Sound Attack Sound Space

that section, then improvise independently until they reach the next notated section?

B: That's right. They're dealing with controlled, or positioned, improvisational spaces that last for seven, ten beats – the time-space between structured events changes. As I said, they're dealing with several different dialogues; there's also the dialogue between the open improvisation and the fixed point to be executed, which implies that they have to count while they improvise. So improvisation in pulse track dynamics has to do with the ensemble rather than extended improvisation for the individual. Pulse tracking requires, say, the bassist to count metric time, invent within short positioned time-spaces, and then execute notated material that is interlocked with the percussionist. And the nature of that relationship establishes its own reality.

116, A SYNCHRONIST PULSE

TRACK STRUCTURE

That's one layer of the sound space. More recent pulse track structures, say *Composition 116*, would establish a multiple system. The second layer would be extended notation with the use of short, positioned improvisation spaces for the piano. So the two continuums – the rhythm section pulse track and the piano pulse track – synchronize to establish a composite image imprint based on pulse, construction dynamics and the simultaneous clash, or overlay, of formings. On top of this you can add extended improvisation, or in *116* a third pulse track, for the saxophone; so there would be three series of events taking place in the music that I ask the listener to take note of. Check the three operational realities of the music: only then can you begin to *hear* what's taking place.

L: Let me get this absolutely clear: *116* actually comprises three different pulse tracks; that's what it is?

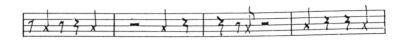

Example of Notation for Rhythm Section Sound Attacks in *Composition 23G*

B: Yes. For instance, I've told you that I often play *96* under Marilyn's solos; but in *116* when she's taking her solo, I'm playing *116*. The piece comes with its own pulse track for me.

L: Are these layered pulse tracks independent, or how are they aligned?

B: There are several possibilities: some pulse tracks are completely aligned, some are completely independent. *Composition 116* I call a synchronist structure because the notated sections in each of the pulse tracks are vertically aligned – that is, they occur at the same times for each instrumentalist – and it's also synchronist because all of the extended notated material, in all of the parts, is working from the same set of construction variables, though it's positioned in different ways (*draws; see p. 200*).

ACCORDION SOUND SPACE –

DIAMOND SOUND SPACE

Composition 115 is different again. I call this an accordion sound space, and by accordion I mean that one of the primary construction variables involves slowing the tempo and accelerating the tempo, and that establishes the dialogue between the bass and drums. The piano has a pulse track that is put inside of that – it's synchronized with the rhythm section so Marilyn has to get slower when Gerry and Mark get slower, go faster when they go faster. So that's a kind of synchronist composition too, except I put an open solo on top for the saxophone. *Composition 116* establishes that third level, the saxophone pulse track, so it's a multi-layered music: there's a whole continuum of events and formings coming together. And the reality of *116*, in terms of understanding what takes place in that music, involves how that information – the nature of the variables, the rate of formings – sets up parameters, like a prism or a diamond, a sound diamond: that's how I visualize it, a diamond that defines how the space is perceived.

I'm saying that to experience *116* is to experience a multi-dynamic sound space that for all practical purposes is as free as anything you can imagine in terms of vibrational and rhythm dynamics, etc; but it establishes a flow of events in the space that supplies the same kind of definition as vertical harmony. Once we enter into the extended space of the music, it's as defined as *Body and Soul*.

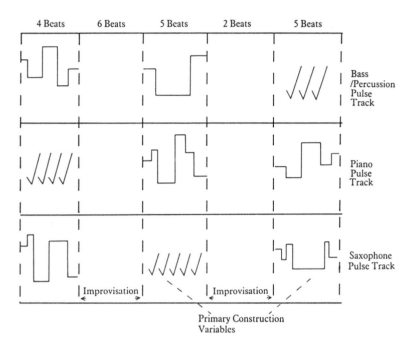

NB: The vertical alignment is not necessarily as strict as it appears, since the tempo or pulse can be different in each of the three strata

Synchronist Pulse Track Structure⋆

⋆C.f. example of actual rhythm section notation from *116*; see p. 201 fn

L: You said the other day that your work wasn't a rejection of vertical harmony, yet pulse track structures sound like an attempt to establish an alternative structural framework to vertical harmony – one that perhaps gives you more choices within the defined space?
B: Ah . . . Let me back up a little. One of the reasons I took this route was because of the misconception, on the part of many people, that collective improvisation on its own is the optimum state for the transformational musician, or transformational pedagogy. I've never agreed with that; I've always felt that the significance of collective improvisation and of restructural cycles – which is what the sixties and seventies were – is their potential to help us find relevant criteria or relevant structures. The secrets of the musics that were generated by the post-Ayler and post-AACM continuums will in this next time cycle be realized and formularized on some level, so the music can permeate into the greater culture and also, through understanding itself, go to the next partial.

The extended use of pulse track layer construction or multiple construction devices, in my opinion, will be related to the form types or the new structural models that will be used in the future. I think we've arrived at a point where we need new structural models, built on a broader perception of harmonic and rhythmic dynamics. Models which will allow for things to be put together in different orders.

THE SOLAR SYSTEM OF PULSE TRACKS —
MULTIPLE LOGIC MUSICS

L: How long are pulse tracks? Are they repeated within a composition?

B: The length of the pulse track depends on which structure we're talking about. Some are short, some are very long. For instance, on a recording date, if we're doing a seven- or eight-minute version of a piece, a given pulse track might not be played from beginning to end because there isn't enough time.

L: A composition that includes two or three pulse tracks . . . could you compare them to tape loops of different lengths playing simultaneously?

B: You could, but I prefer to think of them in terms of solar systems.

L: What!?

B: I'm serious. Solar systems as far as – shorter systems to greater systems: shorter systems being like the orbit of the planet Mercury, greater systems being like the orbit of the planet Jupiter. And talk of it in terms of the real solar system, because the orbits of the planets are not on the same plane and the sun too is moving through space; so we're talking of a complex system.

L: Presumably what you're doing in the quartet music now is putting pulse tracks to parts from older works, and also switching things around so the saxophone and piano play the pulse track while the rhythm section improvise, as last night.

B: Oh, we've gone past that. I have, in the last year, begun to throw all my structures into the quartet, to think in terms of creating giant solar systems or galaxies, and layered sound spaces, many different simultaneous events. For instance, *Composition 96* is the piece for orchestra and four slide projectors, but Mark is playing the bass part from that piece in the quartet music, I'm playing the flute part; Marilyn is playing early piano music from about 1973, the *30–33* series. The quartet music is becoming a platform for all the work I've been doing in the last twenty years; I'm starting to integrate those processes into the music at an accelerating rate. Some of the things we're doing now are like a collage of several different works all mashed together to create a dynamic sound space.

L: Are there any kinds of criteria you use to decide which pieces will fit together and which won't?

B: At this point I'm trying to place ingredients in the space based on my visual perception of what should work – how they look visually. I can't deal with your question yet, though I know I will have to deal with it: right now I'm not so much interested in what won't work as in putting together pieces I think will work. Later, I might just throw everything in there.

I'm looking for multiple logic musics. All of the early works have been designed with respect to their own internal logic, but in the new environments that we've been exploring with the quartet we're dealing with more than one logic system. By positioning *Composition 33* for solo piano inside, say, *40B* or *40F*, some of the material generating works or even the principle generating works, you arrive at a music of multiple logics. (By logic in this context I'm talking about the primary structural ingredients and vibrational identity that make a composition a composition.) For example, *Composition 33* is an extended piece that consists of eighty-plus pages and was composed with respect to region focus and also specific variations of its principles: that particular composition was based on attacks and angular formings, as well as opposition, so to put that in the sound space puts that logic in. All of the 100-plus languages that I've been working in, I'm now starting to put them all into the sound space and see what each of them will mean outside of its own logic, in a greater logic.

OPPOSITION AND COLLAGE FORMS –

VIBRATIONAL CLASH

L: You could have a quartet concert where all four players were simultaneously playing completely independent works?
B: That's exactly where it's going.
L: Isn't it very difficult to play like that?
B: Well, in terms of quartet music evolution, by 1970, say, I had begun to think in terms of opposition improvisation. Then later we got into college improvisation, thinking in terms of collage – not working from someone else's idea to form an alignment or duo or trio intention, but establishing opposition as part of the nature of the music. In fact Leo Smith and I were talking about opposition in Chicago.

Later, moving into the collage musics would help me open up my hearing. For instance, when Marilyn first played with me, I was talking about – think in terms of a practice room, like going into a music college and walking through all the practice rooms; everybody's playing something different in each room. That's what I wanted the group to think of while we were playing the music: you play what you want and I'll play what I want, you leave me alone and I'll leave you alone. Collage improvisation was simply . . . I just wanted the musicians to think in terms of *independence*. Roscoe Mitchell has often talked of how important it is to . . . like, he would say, if the music's gonna fall, let it fall – don't be frightened for nothing to happen, just stay with what you're doing.

L: You've said before that you don't consider anarchy to be an evolutionary state, yet collage improvisation sounds very like anarchy. Presumably, as with total improvisation, you see it more as a context from which to further structural evolution?

B: I was never interested in collage improvisation as the *sole* basis for anything, only in terms of what that discipline could give us in helping each person to understand their own nature. Basically, what I wanted to do in that period was establish a much broader mind-set about the space of the music and establish a thought-criterion that would help each individual in the band to develop their own sense of logic, as far as being able to understand how the music can vibrate in the space.

That period of collage improvisation was very important to me. We wouldn't be able to play the music we're playing right now if we weren't used to this kind of independence. And that independence would also set the stage for me to think in terms of broader structural models – these didn't just come about from a theoretical decision, but from participating in the music and dealing with the emotional and vibrational dynamics that collage improvisation opened up for me.

L: In theory, could you extend that principle into orchestral music and have, say, 100 people each playing separate pulse tracks or collage forms?

B: Oh yes, that will be one of the areas I intend to move into in the next cycle. We could talk about 100 people playing different pulse track structures, or 1,000 people. How many people makes no difference any more: it could be a million.

L: Surely the listener will be totally overwhelmed – it's hard enough to follow three or four musicians playing separate parts.

B: It's hard enough in this time period. Remember, the human species is evolving – that's the hope, anyway. Some of the information that's uncovered in this time period may be perceived as not relevant, but we're in a period of dynamic technological breakthroughs and there's the promise of dynamic vibrational and mystical breakthroughs.

L: And pulse track structures will be a part of this?

B: Pulse track structures are only the next degree of my structural system and, for instance, by integrating musics from the orchestral compositions into the quartet, we're not talking about pulse track systems any more, we're talking about environment systems. Where pulse tracks could be talked of as like a solar system, the environment structures could be talked of as like a galaxy – where, inside of that particular time-space, there are many different structural organisms whose logics are at work and whose aspirations fulfil, on some level, cosmic matters about which we know nothing.

L: You've said each composition has its own logic and vibrational identity; surely the more you throw together, the more risk there is of vibrational clash.

B: Oh, there's always danger of a clash, even playing tonics or the C-major scale. In my opinion, the clash involves the nature of the time period we're dealing with, its existential dynamics. Anything we can talk about we can also talk about and prove its opposite – as a Gemini you must be aware of that! All of these matters are relative. So, yes, there's a clash, but the clash is less to do with the music system than with what values are brought to it; whether the system will be used to promote understanding and unification or whether it will be used against different aspects of humanity, for whatever reasons. The reality implications of a given structural form have to do with understanding how best to use its particulars without harming anybody.

L: Was John Cage an influence on your collage forms at all? I'm thinking particularly of his *HPSCHD* piece in which several different compositions are played simultaneously.

B: No, I haven't heard this piece. How is it structured?

L: I think he has a huge number of electronic tapes, plus seven solo compositions for harpsichord, which are all played simultaneously. And the harpsichord compositions comprise both Cage's own work and extracts from Beethoven, Chopin, Mozart. There's a very simplified version on record.

B: Oh, I know nothing about this piece. I'd like to find out about it.

L: Would you consider using other composers' pieces in your collage forms?

B: Hmm, it's an interesting idea. If I go to do it, I'll have to say Graham Lock suggested this idea (*laughs*).
L: (*laughs*) Oh, don't blame me! I'm still struggling with pulse tracks!

SOUND MASS PARTICLES –
ENVIRONMENTS

Is there a link between pulse track structures and your multi-orchestral works? For example, both are to do with many different processes happening simultaneously.
B: In terms of multiple events taking place in the space, yes. But *Composition 82*, for four orchestras, deals with sound mass movement in the space, so the strategy or conceptual challenge of that piece is very different from the pulse tracks, which I perceived in their original phase – from *23G* to, say, *105A* – as rates of material in the sound space, rates of architecture.

The new environment structures will be like a cross between the multi-orchestral works and the recent pulse track music we've been performing in the last two or three years. That is, a double sound state context that will have materials moving through space and repeating in the cycle, like a solar system, and also have sound mass particle energies in the space (which is the influence of the four orchestras piece), to create a multiple sound universe of varying principles – fixed principles, as in fixed fundamental laws, and open principles, as in various kinds of improvisation taking place in the space.
L: Are there examples of sound mass particles in the music the quartet are currently playing?
B: Yes. For instance, when there's a pulse track structure going down in the rhythm section and then, say, Marilyn is playing a notated piece and I'm improvising or playing an extended notated piece from *96*, but from the real complex sections which use more mass sound materials and *whorl* more sound into the space.

The juxtaposition of extended notated material with a pulse track structure would constitute my definition of environment structure; and for those areas of the extended piece which are very complex in terms of notating large masses of material, that would be an example of real environment possibility or the kernel of what I would like to be involved with in the next cycle.

L: You've also talked about your multi-orchestral works as 'environment music'; but that would be a separate use of the word 'environment'?

B: I'm referring to different principles, yes. I don't mean to confuse you, but we're talking about an area which is not completely labelled in my own terminology. I have not dissected this area to the degree where I have all the terms.*

82: 'LIKE A CITY' – PLANET

LEVEL MUSICS

L: Can we go on to talk more about multi-orchestralism? You were inspired to explore that area by Stockhausen, Xenakis, Sun Ra?†

B: That's right. And don't forget John Philip Sousa, he's a master

---

*On the later sleevenotes to his *Five Compositions (Quartet) 1986* LP, Braxton uses the term 'universe forms' to describe the quartet 'environment' music. But he says he is unhappy with this description and may change the terminology again

†See Braxton's notes to *Composition 82* for more information on his multi-orchestral influences, which also include Charles Ives's music and his own early love of parade musics. He writes: 'There has always been something special about the reality of different ensembles making music in the same physical universe space that has excited my imagination. It is as if the whole of the universe were swallowed up – leaving us in a sea of music and colour.' In a *Cadence* (March, 1984) interview, he relates the following incident: 'When I was a young man, oh I must have been about ten years old, maybe eleven, I remember cutting school to go to this parade and I'm listening to the music, which was just really wonderful, and suddenly I looked down about two blocks or something and I saw a figure, someone I knew and he was digging the parade as much as me. And they had wonderful floats and marching bands and I started moving towards this guy and as I got closer to him I began to understand a lot about my own life, about what was happening with me, especially with parade music, because this man who was digging the music as much as me was my father, who hadn't gone to work. He missed work to check out this parade.'

African precedents for multi-orchestral music are mentioned by Eileen Southern, who quotes (p. 8) this 1817 account of a festival in Ashanti (now in Ghana): 'The sun was reflected, with a glare scarcely more supportable than the heat, from the massy gold ornaments, which glistened in every direction. More than a hundred bands burst at once on our arrival, [all playing] the peculiar airs of their several chiefs; the horns flourished their defiances [i.e. fanfare melodies], with the beating of innumerable drums and metal instruments, and then yielded for a while to the soft breathings of their long flutes, which were truly harmonious; and a pleasing instrument, like a bagpipe without the drone, was happily blended. At least a hundred large umbrellas, or canopies, which could shelter thirty persons, were sprung up and down by the bearers with brilliant effect, being made of scarlet, yellow, and the most shewy cloths and silks . . .'

Braxton would certainly be aware of this, since his *Composition 82* is dedicated to 'the historian-writer-educator Eileen Southern'. For more on *82*, see also 'Postscript 3', iii

composer, he's not respected: they only think of him in terms of his marches, but the man wrote operas, many different kinds of music. His marches are restructuralist marches! I mention him because the concept of multi-orchestralism we have somehow neglects those marching musics that Sousa and Scott Joplin composed: there was a great march tradition in America, in the Mid-West, and that's part of my multi-orchestral lineage as well. There's the Canadian composer Henry Brant, he experimented in directional music before it was popular.* And don't forget Monteverdi; in his early operas the orchestra wasn't in the pit but in different parts of the auditorium. He was far ahead of his time.

L: Could you explain what you mean by 'environment' in the multi-orchestral context?

B: The multi-orchestral works, the first being *Composition 82*, for four orchestras, would be an attempt to create a directional music. In the liner notes for *82* I talk about the different ways to channel information – information moving from orchestra to orchestra, the spread or directional change of a given idea, moving multiple information in different directions – and the different kinds of trajectorial activities that arise, like trajectorial activity with mass or trajectorial activity against opposition, and so on. Basically, I'm talking about the ability to channel information along exact 'sound paths'. This means the performance itself would have to be in a specified environment; in *82* the musicians are on different levels, just like a city, pointing in different directions with chairs that swivel.

After the piece for ten orchestras, moving to the larger orchestra pieces, I envisioned TV systems, telecommunications, becoming part of the process of the music, to help transfer information from regions of the planet and create an alternative event context.

L: Where would the audience be? In a room watching TV screens, with each orchestra on a different screen?

B: No, no – people would just be walking down the street, living their normal lives. By the time we get to planet level musics I'm not talking about going to the auditorium to hear music, I'm talking

---

*Henry Brant was born in Montreal in 1913 and has been composing 'spatial' music since 1951. His works include *Galaxies*, *Ceremonies*, *Hieroglyphics* and *Orbits*, titles which would have an obvious attraction for Braxton; as would Brant's use of heterophony and his unusual instrumental ensembles – *Orbits*, for example, is scored for eighty trombones and organ, *Fire on the Amstel* for four boatloads of twenty-five flutes each, four jazz drummers, four church carillons, three brass bands, three choruses and four street organs!

about sound being generated as part of the whole life experience.
L: So you'd just walk down the street and there it would be!
B: Yeah, kinda like how it is right now (*laughs*).
L: Suppose you don't want to hear it? What do you do?
B: Then you'd have to get out of the concert.
L: But how? (*Laughs.*) Where's the exit?
B: Well, go to a planet where this is not happening (*laughs*). I mean, we're talking about projects which won't be realized tomorrow. By the time the information is developed to deal with that level, I'm sure there'll be, you know (*sings*) '*A planet for you, a planet for me*'. I imagine, when we start talking about star systems linking to perform a piece . . . I'm sure the people who are the inhabitants will have to be in agreement or there'll be no concert.

   Let me put this into perspective. What we're really talking about is the reality of forces and how given forces in space can create a context for existence. When we get to the galactic formings, etc, we're really talking about the concept of existence.

A MUSIC TO HEAL DESERTS

L: How can you even begin to plan these compositions? Surely the technology needed to perform them is almost unimaginable?
B: In this period, yes. But, for instance, look at what human beings are doing on the planet right now: obviously we're not helping the state of the planet, in terms of the more adverse effects of present-day technological dynamics. What's wrong with the idea of establishing a universal composite information base that can help us better to sustain and appreciate physicality? With this information it might be possible to heal the planet – a music to heal deserts, say – because the planet is alive too. What about having a music that can help to prevent earthquakes, a music that can help establish physicality, a –
L: Help *what*?
B: You know, music as a practical tool to help create planets and states of being, so, since we've made this planet unhealthy, we can go to another planet. Or, if we can heal this planet, we might still want to go to another planet just because it exists.
L: Are you researching these areas? Checking out what particular sounds can do?
B: Right now, I'm just trying to get through this tour! As far as

staying abreast of real state-of-the-art changes in technology, I'm very far behind. Poverty has not helped me to get access to the information needed. I'm happy to be at Mills College now where I can finally study electronic music, because I've never had the money to buy a synthesizer or that kind of equipment. But I need information about physics, about science; I need to meet people who have specialized in those areas and work with them in larger projects, because some of what we're talking about – some being, like, ninety-nine per cent – might be too much for one human being to think about doing by him- or herself. There is a need for groups who are concerned about the planet and the planet experience, what it could really be for human beings, and what a higher state of existence or evolution means in a practical sense.

These ideas might sound far-fetched, but they shouldn't. The inter-relationship of music to science has long been an understood fact in world culture; it's only in the West, where we've become so existential, so specialist, that we've forgotten about the whole.

FALLING BEHIND SCHEDULE

L: How far have you progressed with your multi-orchestral series?
B: I've about finished the piece for five orchestras, which was originally listed as four orchestras and tape. I decided as I was writing it, I already have a piece for four orchestras, why write another one? (*Laughs.*) If you've got four, you might as well have five!
L: You're a little behind schedule. That piece was due for completion in 1979; you said you'd have the piece for 100 orchestras written by 1985, and the one for three planets by 1988.
B: Graham, I can tell you honestly, falling behind schedule doesn't begin to touch how far behind I am. In the last fifteen years we've been dealing with . . . not just poverty, the struggle has been so intense, I'm happy I still know how to play a C-major scale. Yes, I am *way* behind schedule. But I'm happy still to be on the planet to have a schedule (*laughs*).
L: It might be thought a little impractical to talk about plans for compositions that link star systems.
B: No, I don't think it's impractical. It's impractical maybe to give the actual year (*laughs*). That's what I've learned.
L: So you still think it could happen?

B: Oh, it's not a question of it *could* happen.
L: You're going to write those pieces?
B: Of course I'm going to write the pieces. There are much bigger ideas than that!
L: Huh!?
B: Are you kidding?
L: Such as?
B: Oh no! (*Laughs.*)
L: Come on, let's hear one.
B: I've said enough (*laughs*).

HIGHER THOUGHTS — A

MUSIC TO PLAY GOD

The challenge of creativity, as far as I'm concerned, is to move towards the greatest thought that you can think of.
L: You could have a music that played transformation or world unity? A music that played God?
B: I'll say it again – the highest thought that you can think of. And even that can be regenerated. Remember, there's the law of material generation. That means it's not about *not*-generation.
L: So the highest thought could be restructured? A music that played a restructured God? That played a new concept of love?
B: I'm saying that whatever you think can be manifested. And whatever that is can be regenerated. I imagine. Or I don't imagine. Whatever that is. I'm only dealing with, as a human being, what you can think about on this planet.
L: What is your highest thought? What would that be for you?
B: (*laughs*) I say, first do the first book, Graham. After that we'll talk about higher thoughts.

ROAD

SATURDAY 23, LEEDS

Our second rest day. As we sit in the hotel lobby waiting for Marilyn, Braxton tells Gerry and Mark about the Warne Marsh photo on the *Blues for a Reason* LP sleeve; how he looks old, drawn, his hair turning white.

'He looks like a man whose life has been a struggle. Sometimes I fear Mr Marsh won't be with us much longer, but I get scared even thinking like that. I only hope he gets some reward soon, some recognition of the genius his music demonstrates.'

Gerry, draped over an armchair, nods in agreement. 'I did a gig with Warne Marsh in New York. Man, he played a *Body and Soul* that was so beautiful. I practically stopped playing, he knocked me out so much.'

'You should hear the *How Deep, How High* LP,' Braxton enthuses. 'Warne, Sal Mosca, Roy Haynes, Sam Jones. That's a great album! Listen to Sal Mosca on that – boy, his sense of time is *out*! I'd like to record with Mr Mosca; I'd love to do a double album of Lennie Tristano tunes with him.'

Gerry grunts. 'What gets me is how those Tristano-school cats just play the same tunes all the time. They've been playing the same twenty or so tunes for the last thirty-five years.'

Braxton laughs. 'Yeah, but how!'

Marilyn arrives breathless, apologizing for her lateness. 'It keeps happening to me on this tour, I don't understand it.'

'Crispell syndrome,' Mark declares triumphantly. 'Chronic Crispell syndrome.'

The drive to Leeds is a nightmare. We get stuck in a huge traffic jam at Newbury (it's race day) and it takes an hour to get through the town. The daylight fades in early afternoon and a succession of thunderstorms lash the van as we spray along endless gloomy motorways. Gerry plays me a gospel track with the lyrics, '*If religion was a thing that money could buy, then the rich would live and the poor would die*'.

'That's a joke,' I mutter darkly. 'The rich do live and the poor do die. Capitalism's replaced God with private health insurance.'

Gerry points out that the fundamentalists go for capitalism in a big way. 'Those guys really coin it in, playing on people's fears and confusion.'

'Yeah, I can't wait till they start burning the libraries.' I heave a sigh, thinking of Braxton's belief that America is heading for the Dark Ages and Sun Ra's forebodings that righteousness will lay waste the earth. I'm in a deathly mood where a handful of wiggy musicians who believe in the mystic power of sound and the necessity of beauty for survival seem as reassuring as a straw hat in a hurricane. Huge raindrops like nails batter against the van, the sky resembles an angry bruise. I try to imagine the landscape outside after a nuclear war. Fire? Ash? Darkness? Nothing.

Gerry cheers me up by playing me tapes of his recent projects. *Fallside* is a duo with guitarist Allan Jaffe based on Nigerian juju music and full of shimmering rhythmic nuance; *Totem*, a tape work of glass sounds, is a mysterious collage of harmonic flows, drones, undulating sound masses; and *Waterways*, my favourite, superimposes marimba, vibraphone, tympani and steel drums over a tape of water sounds recorded at a brook then spliced and edited into a strikingly beautiful 'rainfall of pitches'. He also plays me a solo drum LP, *Tubworks*, and a quintet LP, *Outerbridge Crossing*, both of which he's recorded himself. 'I can't find a record company who're interested,' he grimaces. 'I may have to resurrect my own label, but all that administrative crap takes up so much time and effort.'

We retrieve Gerry's money-belt from Sheffield, then drive on to Leeds, arriving late, tired and haggard: so much for our 'rest' day. Braxton announces he'll spend the evening at the hotel, composing; the rest of us go in search of a curry house that, Tony tells us, comes highly recommended on the tour managers' grapevine. After the hours cooped up in the van, Leeds feels too big, too loud, too wild. The streets and buildings dwarf us as we slip through the shadows: groups of youths run through the city centre, shouting and shoving. It's Saturday night in the north of England, and the pubs are full of unemployed teenagers drinking to forget.

Tony and Mark stride ahead, Gerry, Marilyn and I dawdle behind, talking politics. Marilyn asks why Gerry and I support feminism.

'Because it made things clearer,' I say vaguely; 'because it's just.'

Luckily, Gerry is more forthcoming. 'I think that seventies' wave of feminism affected my whole generation, made us rethink our relationships, our role models, our sexuality. I think it's been a wholly positive change. The old ideas weren't working any longer. I think it's also made it easier for people to bring out, like, the opposite sides of their personalities – men are less afraid to be sensitive, women are more involved in physical things, in their careers, or whatever. I think it's great, I'm right behind it.'

'You don't think it gets a bit extreme?' asks Marilyn. 'The hate men part of it?'

'Every movement of power has its extremist element,' Gerry shrugs. 'Personally, I don't think hating men is a very helpful position. We're all stuck on the planet and our only hope is that we'll be able to deal with each other.'

'After 3,000 years or whatever of male oppression, I'm not very hopeful,' I grumble. 'The karmic backlash could blow us all away.'

'Hey Graham, you're in a real fun mood today,' Gerry laughs.

Just as we reach the curry house, a woman stumbles out and vomits copiously into the gutter in front of us. I freeze in horror, but Gerry is unperturbed. 'Hmm,' he drawls, heading for the door, 'looks like my kind of place.'

It's midnight when we arrive back at the hotel: the late-night bar is just opening, the lounge almost empty save for a few couples smooching in the outer shadows. Gerry sits at the hotel grand piano and begins a hilarious 'drunken pianist' impression – Tom Waits meets Chico Marx, all sheets to the wind. Scurrying out of nowhere comes an officious little man, fiftyish, sky-blue jacket, maroon bow-tie, who shoos Gerry away: *he's* the hotel pianist, thank you very much, and he does *not* appreciate piss artists. He starts to lock up the piano, but we plead with him to let Marilyn play a tune first. He looks her over, dubious, acidic: 'Well, if your feet can reach the pedals, dear.'

She chooses Coltrane's *After the Rain*, treating it as a delicate, bluesy ballad. She plays straighter than I've heard her play before, slow, spacious, and it's beautiful, hushing the whole room: a magical night flower that suddenly blooms and then is gone. The little man is nonplussed. 'Ah . . . my dear, yes . . . very nice, very

. . . er . . . lyrical.' He tells us his name is Bert and his friend, a chubby, smiling man with a purple, crinkly face like a currant bun, is Alf, an organist.

When Bert discovers we're a jazz group, our fate is sealed. Why, he's a *big* jazz TV star in Yorkshire, *The Great Bert* no less; plus he's a *personal friend* of Jacques Loussier. In fact, Jacques called in to jam with him only last week. ('Fuck Jacques Loussier,' Tony snorts after the umpteenth name-drop, 'I met Jacques Cousteau last week, playing in a dive.') Bert is not to be fazed. First he tries to inveigle us into a Name-that-Song quiz, playing show tunes in a banal, jaunty style; then he drags the hotel receptionist over ('pretty little thing, isn't she?') and makes her sing *Brown Eyes Blue*; then he suggests, 'I know, let's all have a sing-song.' Without a hint of irony he begins to play *Show Me the Way to Go Home*.

It's too much for Gerry. 'I'll drink to that,' he splutters; helpless with laughter, he slides off his chair and disappears under the table.

Bert carries on regardless. 'Altogether now! Come on, don't Americans know how to sing? Ohhhhh – *Show me the way . . .*' We look at each other in amazement: *huh? Is this guy for real?* Only Alf, waving his arm to the beat and beaming proudly at his friend, is partaking of the sing-song.

''E's a great player, is Bert,' he announces. ''E can play eight, ten hours, non-stop . . .'

'God help us,' groans Tony.

'. . . *and* read book at same time,' Alf concludes triumphantly. 'Ay, 'e's what tha'd call a real musicians' musician.'

METAROAD

SOUND LOGIC, SOUND MAGIC 3: TITLES, COLOURS, SHAPES

LET 'A' EQUAL CURVE LINE

L: I know you've used different titling systems that correspond to the various musical categories we've talked of, so there are formula titles for the coding musics, schematic titles, image titles etc. Could you take one example of each and explain how they work?

B: I can't do that without the *Composition Notes*. I can't give you a specific breakdown of 230 compositions without the scores or my notes on them. Let me tell you what I can. The formula titles, the formula music group – basically I encoded the processes, what languages I used, what velocity, what structure, etc; and I also left open variables in terms of the pieces' mystical designations.

L: Which means what?

B: I . . . There are two areas to my titles. The first would be – basically, the titles of the compositions are representative of the categories you just mentioned. But the titles also have another purpose, which is to encode . . . how can I say it? . . . the mystical inter-relationships of my music, the mystical calibrations, which I cannot talk about because this is simply not the time: there's still more work to do.

L: Work for whom?

B: Me.

L: But you're already using the titles.

B: That's why I've said I can talk about the structural context, the structural decisions relating to the titling process. All of the ingredients for any composition that I've ever written are calibrated and labelled from A to Z and are then arranged with respect to the integration of the sound or the nature of the sound logic. It was not apparent to me at the beginning, but in fact what I've been doing is designing a system that will later serve my purposes for encoding its mystical implications. For now I can only say that the titles, the formula music group titles, have to do with the integration of compositional elements and how these elements are designated with letters and put into a mix. I can't be more specific; if I had my notes here, I could say, OK, *6A* is made from this and this, these letters and these properties, and the title is an affirmation of the mix.

L: If we take a recent composition like *113*, could you remember the specifics in any more detail?

B: Not without the analysis books. Ah, it would be like 'A' equals curve line, 'B' equals fast velocity, 'C' equals whatever. When I go to compose, I'm always factoring and the information from these factors might also be integrated into the title. Sometimes I'll compose a piece in a day, but the title might take two weeks.

L: How about the shapes on *113*?

B: The shapes are only a part of it.

L: The part I don't understand! (*Laughs.*)

B: Well . . . the titles have changed. Whereas in the beginning the formula titles factored sound type, velocity, etc, there are no numbers on *113* at all, simply categories. For image compositions we're talking about a factoring system very different from the one of twenty years ago. I didn't know then what I know now, and hopefully in the next twenty years I'll know more again. This is a whole other series . . . we can't talk about this until I'm able to get the next criterion of axium writings finished, the *Quod-axium Writings*. That'll take some years, though.

In the beginning, I didn't realize the titles would cause such a storm. But it's irrelevant. I've always been, as they say, inflexible.

L: I don't know about a storm. It's just that they're unique and people are naturally intrigued.

B: I know, I know. Just look at the titles like you'd look at Mr Coltrane's titles.

L: But, Anthony, you can't!

B: (*laughs*) Or when Albert says *Witches and Devils, Spiritual Unity* – I'm saying the same thing. See, all of the masters even name their records and their compositions in a special way. Albert Ayler had these spiritual titles, yet they were very different from Coltrane's, which were also very spiritual-sounding compositions. Everybody found their space. But John Coltrane documented a music whose titles set into motion his thoughts, his motivation, his worldview. I've tried to do the same, only my nature's different from Mr Coltrane's, plus I was born in a time where I had the benefit of his music to help me in my life.

ENCODING – 'THE TITLE WILL DO ITS OWN JOB'

L: Why do you need to encode information in the title?
B: There's information . . . and there's information. How can I say it? Every partial that you want to enter is possible, but everything has to do with your intentions. We're living at a time where the misuse of information is not only rampant, it's part of our way of life. There's a reason why the mystical teachings are written in a way where, you know, you don't just pick them up and understand the universe in five minutes, and then go out and tell people how to live. I have never taken any kind of position where I could be perceived of as trying to be the mystical guru and telling people how to live.

Whatever my titles are – and for that group of people who say, oh his titles are just b. nonsense, that viewpoint is fine with me. But my opinion about what I've been trying to do is: I've been interested in designing a music and a context to establish evolution with respect to sound logic, with respect to abstract consciousness, to philosophy, to world perception, to information integration, to affinity dynamics – and my titles are an affirmation of my work as much as my music is.

I'll say this – and I hope you'll put it in your book – *anybody who puts out a record of mine without the correct title or who omits the title on my record is doing me a profound disservice: that person is no friend of mine.* It's a violent, flagrant misuse of what my music is all about. I have worked to the best of my ability in my craft to create a music that respected what I was thinking about and offer that to humanity – and the titling system is part of that. It's *very important* to me that the titles are . . . well, they don't have to be respected, but if someone's going to put out a record of my music I ask that they put out the right titles next to the compositions. The title will do its own job, just like the music will.

A REALITY OF FUNDAMENTALS

L: Leaving aside the misusers of information, I'm sure there are many well-intentioned people who are seriously interested in how your titles work. Is there nothing you can say to them?

B: I would say that the information that allowed me to create my music structures and titling systems is not just available to me, it's available to anybody who's interested in it. Go to the sources I've gone to.

L: Which are?

B: *The Egyptian Book of the Dead*, *The Tibetan Book of the Dead*. Read the mystery systems teachings, go back and understand what took place in Luxor, in the libraries in that period. Read the mystics like Alice Bailey . . .

I think it's important for us not to make this a joke or something. I'm saying that my titles are related to my mystical and composite world purpose, my life's purpose, my concept of everything; and this is not the kind of information that should be played with. I talked before about the composite knowledge that's been lost in the West; there's a whole reality of fundamentals related to every area of information and I've tried to tie my music into that. What does it mean in terms of its mystical sense? Hmm . . . that's a question I'm not even prepared to deal with. I might not even deal with that in twenty years from now, because I don't want to hurt anybody. I've gone back and put opus numbers on all the compositions so they can be easily referred to; all I ask from future historians and musicologists or people that will put out records 100 years from now – if they want to deal with my music, also put in the title. My intent is to create a positive music that will be helpful to humanity; I'm not involved in any negative kind of so-called occult informations that would hurt anybody.

L: That's twice you've talked about not hurting people. I don't understand: where's the danger?

B: Well, for instance . . . how can I say this? How much reading have you done about upper partial information, Graham? Are you familiar with, say, the Rosicrucians?*

L: No.

B: OK, there are a lot of different groups all over the planet, people who believe in spirituality, the spiritual reality of this experience,

---

*For information on the Rosicrucians (and Luxor), see 'Postscript 1'

and there are many different levels of information about this. I'll
say it again – for anything you can think of, there is information on
it. My titles are about everything I can think of.

'THINK A THOUGHT THAT
WILL AFFECT THE PLANET'

L: You say people can understand your titles by going to your
sources, but surely you've put your own imprint on that information.
B: Yes, of course. But . . . there are some things you simply can't
talk about like you'd talk about throwing the baseball to the left, or
. . . I can say, let me have a sweetroll Graham, and you say, OK
what kind do you want, Danish or whatever. I can say, Graham
let's think a thought that will affect the planet, and you'll say,
what?! And then I'll say, yeah, what?! I mean, neither of us would
understand that. So it's like we can only talk about those kinds of
things that we can talk about. You might, for instance, be of the
persuasion that the concept of mysticism is nonsense, and if you say
that, I'll say I completely agree. Then, if you say, no, I think the
concept of mysticism is valid, I'll say I completely agree. And then
you might say . . . well, whatever you say, I would agree with you
(*laughs*).
L: Suppose I say, I'm not sure about this – what do *you* think?
B: I'm not sure either (*laughs*). But as far as the ancients are
concerned, there are things about this experience that can be
understood and there are some things that cannot be understood.
But for the things that can be understood, you cannot understand
them by standing on a box. Or by putting two bricks together and
saying, yup, that's it (*laughs*). To enter the world of my titles, so far
as – what *is* that? We can't even deal with that right now, believe
me. Let's say it's nonsense that Braxton has developed.
L: That's being disingenuous, Anthony. It's not nonsense. You've
already said you've organized a system.
B: Yeah, it's a system – half of which is understood.
L: (*laughs*) I think you must understand more than half.
B: (*laughs*) I hope you're right!
L: Oh, come on . . .
B: Graham, I just can't. There is a lot of misuse of some of the
upper partial information, and that misuse is happening because

whatever the forces are that are misusing it, those forces are fulfilling their destinies. The important thing for me is that this is not the time to talk about the mystery system implications of my music, and if we talk too much about the titles we would in fact be talking about my mystical feelings and beliefs with respect to forces and forms, etc. This information is not even something I can *begin* to talk about. Fortunately I don't even *know* it.

L: (*laughs*) Well, I don't believe that for a second.

B: (*falsetto*) I'm telling the truth, sir (*laughs*).

OPUS NUMBERS

L: Can we talk about the opus numbers? What system did you use for those?

B: I just tried to sequence the works in chronological order. For the most part, the music is in its correct order, but I have lost maybe fifty compositions I wrote as a young man. I've tried to remember the sequence, it's probably not completely accurate, but it's the best I could do. The only exception is the quartet books, where I took the quartet music and lumped it together in four books – the *6*, *23*, *40* and *69* series.*

L: Are the works within each series linked in any way?

B: The only link is that those pieces were all conceived for the quartet. But otherwise I've given them regular opus numbers; so the *40* series was composed before the *69* series, the *6* series was written in Chicago, the *23* series was the music that Circle and some of the early quartets played. Basically, I just went back and assigned everything with chronological opus numbers.

THE EMOTIONAL ZONE OF RED

L: Can we move on to your use of colour and shape notation? Is this a learned language that you teach your musicians, or is it more of an intuitive thing?

B: It's more of an intuitive relationship. But first of all the inter-relationship between music and colour is not my discovery, it goes back to the early information as to how the ancients looked at music. Originally music was not perceived or practised as separate

---

*The other exception is the solo music, which has also been collected into separate books – the *8*, *26*, *77*, *99*, *106*, *118* and *119* series

from dance, sculpture, painting, the reality of a living, breathing culture. Like I've told you, the sound that rules Gemini is F-sharp, the colour that rules F-sharp is orange, there's a gesture, a movement, that corresponds to those same variables – F-sharp also rules the neck and shoulders. Sooner or later the thrust of Western technology will move to reintegrate some of these things.

I've used colour as a subjective interpretation device in improvisation and some of the notated structures; and colour in that context can be equated to velocity or feeling or the perceived emotional dynamics of the music. In fact, I've had many different compositions that attempt to integrate various factors, colours and shapes, that kind of information, which is strictly scientific information; and in the analysis books each piece is broken down in terms of how it works. But there's no one piece that characterizes how I use integration; each has its own laws. For instance, *Composition 76*, for trio, the modular notation for that piece uses colour as an emotional consideration, whereas *Composition 82*, for four orchestras, was actually written in colour. I've tried to integrate colour in various ways in my music, usually with respect to emotional possibilities, or loud and soft, volume possibilities.

L: So if I was playing 76 and I came to red, could I just play what I felt red to be?

B: No, no. In the score I describe red and say which is the emotional characteristic zone I was thinking of for red. Then each person would subjectively, after reading the score, make a decision on how to treat it.*

L: And red might mean play more intensely or play louder – that kind of criterion?

B: Yes. Or the lighter the colour the faster you play. And the shapes in 76 . . . one might mean long improvisation, one might mean this can either be played or sung. I can't be more specific about the symbols without my notes. In the last twenty years I've written 220, 230 compositions, each with their own little logic, and I can't keep them all in my head otherwise I'd be completely insane.

---

*The colour code to *Composition 76* is actually based on astrological correspondences. That is, Braxton selected a set of the emotional characteristics attributed to various signs of the zodiac and then designated them in the score by using the colours associated with the same signs. The code is: blue = sombre or moody (Sagittarius); red = explosive or intense (Aries); green = calm, restrained or contained (Taurus); violet = vibrant or pulsing or energetic or vigorous (Pisces); brown = complementary or harmonious or balancing (Libra); yellow = strong, lyrical or bright (Leo). For more on *Composition 76*, see 'Postscript 3', iii

L: It seems your symbolic notation, like your structured improvisation, is a method of defining the space yet leaving the performers free to make their own choices within that space.

B: Well, I try to, in the various processes, create musics that give more control or less control to the performer – again it depends on the composition. Remember, the people who influenced me most were restructuralists and what I learned from them was not to write the same piece 500 times over, but each time to try something different so each structure would be a little bit unique. For instance, in *Composition 123*, for solo flute, I've included a seven-page story as part of the score.

THE LOST SIGN OF THE ZODIAC
– NEGATIVE ENERGIES

L: You've also used astrological factors in your music. Can you talk about these?

B: One of the earlier pieces – I think it's *Composition 2* – used astrological devices in terms of, if you were a Gemini you'd have to play your note in given places. But, again, it depends on the composition we're discussing. Stockhausen's *Tierkreis* is based on characters from the zodiac, I think; I haven't used astrology like that . . . hmm, it's an interesting idea for the future (*laughs*).

L: Have you heard about Arachne, the lost sign of the zodiac?

B: No! Tell me.

L: It seems some early calendars and zodiacs, which were lunar rather than solar based, divided the year into thirteen zones; and one theory is that the thirteenth sign was Arachne, the spider, whose characteristics are to do with communication, spiritual healing, integration, synthesis, holding things together – the sign of the web. Supposedly the sign was suppressed with the rise of patriarchal cultures because it was associated with various powerful spider-goddesses and so was a potent image of female strength. I mentioned it because the Arachne sign is thought to have fallen in late May/early June, so if the theory's right you and I wouldn't be Geminis, we'd be Arachnes.

B: Wow! My publishing company is called Synthesis (*laughs*). I'd like to find out more about this. I know one thing: either human beings are going to establish some understanding of unification or . . . well, if we blow up the planet, it would be a tragedy for sure, and it seems we're moving towards that. World unification must be, on some level, world tolerance. That must be the objective – understanding, forgiveness, the concept of love; these are not just words. I've been fortunate to travel around the planet and see how other people live and think; I've come to see the beauty in all the differences, and I've also come to see that there are no differences.

L: To love humanity is rather an abstract concept. I don't mean to sound facetious, but how is it possible to love a person like, say, Ronald Reagan?

B: By love . . . because I love the fact that somebody invented the automobile doesn't mean I'll just lie down in the road and let the automobile run over me (*laughs*). People like Ronald Reagan – it's like, I've come to see that it's nothing personal, you know; there's nothing personal for the guy who takes that knife and cuts off your head, he's only dealing with the information he's been given, plus he's probably ill. Of course, we try to keep out of the way of illness, though in fact we generally try to avoid overt negative physical energies even as we run in to caress negative vibrational energies, so it's complex. I can understand the ritual sense of good and evil forces, their portrayal on a ritual level; but it's more complex on the physical universe level, in actual life, to partition in the same way. I have no negative feelings about Ronald Reagan. I just want to do my work, I have no need or time for the luxury of hate.

THE DIFFERENCE BETWEEN
TALK AND TALK

L: OK, shall we call it a day?

B: I hope I haven't disappointed you as far as the titles are concerned, because I haven't meant to. There are simply areas I cannot talk about at this point; it would be ridiculous to even try. I say the listener should look at the titles and enjoy them or not enjoy them, but I don't think you need to understand them in order to listen to the music.

L: Do you talk to the musicians about these mystical factors?

B: Leo Smith and I were students in many of these areas; but if you mean the musicians who play my music, I tell them what they need to know to play the music, which is the scientific information, how to play it. If the attitude or treatment of a piece is not right I would explain how it's supposed to work, but generally for the musicians

I've worked with in this period I give them just enough information to play the music. In the future my hope would be to have musicians who have studied my music system, who understand what it's really about, because that will be needed to take the music to the next stage.

L: So you'll have to talk then!

B: Graham, the areas you're interested in, you can't talk to people about that! If you have to talk about it, it means you're not at a point where you should be talking about it! (*Laughs.*) I mean, there's talk and there's talk.

L: Oh no, you're not retreating into Taoism! '*Those who know do not speak, those who speak do not know.*'

B: I'd like to help you in whatever way I can, but those areas I can't tell you about, I can't tell you about. Those areas I can tell you about, I'll tell you about (*laughs*). I'm a reasonable man, Graham!

L: (*laughs*) Yeah, reasonably inflexible.

ROAD

Braxton has another lecture this afternoon. On the way there, he mentions that his *Trillium* operas have word, as well as diagram, titles. Like what?

'*Trillium A* is called "After a Period of Change, Zackko Returns to His Place of Birth", *Trillium M* is called "Joreo's Vision of Forward Motion", *Trillium BK* is "Because of Non-belief, Ojuwain is no Longer with Us", *Trillium R* is "Shala Fears for the Poor".'

(They remind me a little of Harry Partch's 'dance-satire' *The Bewitched*, the scene titles for which include the wonderful 'The Cognoscenti are Plunged into a Demonic Descent while at Cocktails'.)

Braxton's lecture, on repetition as a process generating factor (see 'Postscript 3', ii), covers essentially the same ground as at Sheffield; today though there's an audience of thirty to forty people and, despite Braxton's evident tiredness, it turns out to be a lively afternoon. In his notes to *Composition 98*, Braxton drew up a list of 'reception dynamics' that charted audiences' responses to the work:

1. Where is dee jazz?
2. Boredum
3. Humer
4. Anger
5. What is it?

A similar list of 'reception dynamics' to the lectures might go:

1. Huh?
2. But what about dee jazz?
3. This guy is crazee!
4. Hmmm . . .?
5. Tell us more!

I guess some people never make it past 2 or 3, but judging by the questions at the end, a lot make it through to 4 and 5. Today is no exception.

Q: 'Can you play painting or paint music? I think Schoenberg and Klee experimented with this?'

B: 'Yes, Kandinsky too. He was very interested in the correspondences between music and painting. He's very special to me, he created his own system of colour and shape dynamics, he was very involved in the spiritual dimensions of art. Scriabin was also very concerned with music, colour, spirituality – composite world culture.* I certainly think there's an inter-relationship between painting and music, theatre and music, physics and music. It's only in the West in the last 300 years that the knowledge of these relationships has been lost.'

Q: 'How do you choose the people for your quartet?'

B: 'I try to pick people in the same vibrational zone, with the same sensibility, though I'm also interested in music that expresses particular co-ordinates, in a form that sets into motion various forces irrespective of the player. My hope is to move towards people who totally understand the systems I'm building – music, science, philosophy, ritual. What I envisage is different schools of scientists, musicians, spiritual people all working together to help each other.'

Q: 'How long do people stay in the quartet? Presumably, it takes some time to learn your music?'

B: 'Well, I'd say the first six months, I'm teaching a player the

---

*Wassily Kandinsky (1866–1944) was a pioneer of modern abstract art. He wrote that, 'Just as sounds and rhythms combine in music, so must forms and colours be united in painting by the play of their manifold relationships.' His oeuvre includes several paintings entitled either 'Composition' or 'Improvisation'; his *Black Relationship* was reproduced on the sleeve of Braxton's *Six Compositions: Quartet* LP. Kandinsky's book, *Concerning the Spiritual in Art*, discusses the relationship between music and painting, as well as the metaphysical dimensions of colour, form and movement.

The Russian composer Alexander Scriabin (1872–1915) had chromesthetic perception, that is he literally 'saw' colours in relation to sounds; and he tried to express these correspondences in his work. For *Prometheus: the Poem of Fire* he had a colleague build a 'keyboard of light' which played the colours of the music; for his *Prefatory Action* he wished to include coloured lights, processions, scents and tastes in the score. His work, harmonically complex, intensely symbolic and mystical (he was a student of Theosophy), culminated in his plans for a meta-composition, *Mysterium*, which would incorporate all the arts, re-create the history of the universe from his mystical perspective, and take the form of a seven-day festival in the Himalayas to climax in the actual destruction of our physical plane of existence, as his music dissolved the world in an abyss of flame, and the return of all being to its spiritual state on the 'plane of unity'. (See Bowers, 1974, pp. 43–100, 124–6)

music; the next six months they're getting into it; the third six months I'm learning from them. Generally, I'd try to keep a quartet line-up together for two years, at least, to give it time to fulfil its collective identity; but that's not always possible.'

Q: 'Do the people in your groups have to agree with your theories?'

B: 'Not necessarily. But the ensemble is the next degree of family: we have to trust each other, care for each other, look out for each other. If there was someone in the group who didn't respect what I was doing, I would respect *them* by firing them immediately.'

As at the Guildhall, there are a crowd of people who stay at the end for autographs and/or personal queries. Braxton, though drained by his two-hour talk, deals with them all patiently, inviting would-be composers to send him tapes and asking of each one, 'Are you serious about dedicating your life to music?'

At the soundcheck the group play through *23G* several times; last night, Braxton finished transposing it for piano. He seems happy with the run-through, but then leaves *23G* off the set lists.

LEEDS CONCERT, CIVIC THEATRE

First Set (Primary Territories)
Composition 122 (+ *108A*)
Composition 69N
Composition 69Q
Piano solo (from *Piano Piece 1*)
Composition 69M

Second Set (Primary Territories)
Composition 69H
Bass solo (from *Composition 96*)
Composition 69(O)
Composition 116

(The theatre's acoustics are troublesome; the sound seems muffled and erratic. Also, it's an old-fashioned proscenium-arch theatre, golden stars decorating a dark-blue ceiling, and a high stage that emphatically separates the group from the audience. To me it feels uncomfortable, at odds with the spirit of the music, which I've found at its most effective in the more intimate settings at Birmingham, Leicester, Southampton and Bristol – in fact, I'd love to sit right in the middle of the players and bathe in the sounds as they flowed around me. My God, what an egoist! Still, the group are highly energized tonight and, soupy sound apart, it's another excellent concert.)

122 opens with smooth clarinet phrases that become increasingly choppy, as the quartet simmer through a tangled improvisation and into *69N*, a tense see-saw bass figure beneath a theme that prowls, lopes, then flares into a dreamy sopranino solo before the group hit the jaunty line that signals *69Q*: a quick, ferocious rendition gives way to *Piano Piece 1*, Braxton's debut composition, a work of sudden intervallic leaps, unexpected pauses, abrupt spurts of sound within a slowly turning space; Braxton listens, eyes closed, swaying slightly, as Marilyn brings the notes to life, occasionally glancing towards him. Next, a duet of bows – the bass's subterranean rumbles mesh with whooshing harmonics as Gerry bows the cymbal rim; then the sopranino leads into the joyful dash of *69M*, one of Braxton's most ebullient themes and embellished here by a superbly percussive piano solo and Gerry's inspired flailing, before a typically heart-stopping unison halt.

The second set begins musingly on *69H*, then quickly settles into a long section of frenetic improvisation that I can't get into at all. Mark's solo re-earths the quartet, Gerry follows with a passage of 'little sounds' – twangs, scratches, rattles – and piano/clarinet intertwine for a lovely reading of *69(O)*, its gently rolling theme lapped by a wash of cymbals and humming bass. A new space opens up – cool, fresh, dawnlike – and across the silence float clarinet trills, ghostly yelps, piano ripples; bass lines uncoil like strands of fog. Braxton takes a brief *a cappella* alto solo, slivers and tiny whorls of sound so quiet you can hear the keys click against the metal of his horn. A slight swing of the alto and everyone leaps into *116*, an extensive version fired first by Braxton's squealing sopranino then a Crispell solo that starts like light dancing on water and ends with clusters of notes coursing through the pulse track as if shooting rapids. The final sprint along the synchronized pulse tracks is like four champion hurdlers racing neck-and-neck for the line – and freeze-frame on a perfect dead-heat!

Back in the dressing-room, Marilyn suddenly cocks her head towards the PA speaker on the wall. 'What record is that?' We listen, mystified, to this weird, dissonant torch song on solo piano. 'It's not a record,' says Gerry, coming in. 'It's Anthony upstairs.'

We dash back up to the stage. Braxton, the scraggly collar of Evan Parker's overcoat upturned, is hunched over the piano picking a slow, perverse blues out of *What's New*. He looks up with an abashed grin. 'I love those torchy songs – Jerome Kern, George Gershwin . . .'

He plays on in his quirky style (edgy, like his alto can be, but less deft, more crabbed). It's like a film scene: the empty auditorium, a stage strewn with cables and wires, and, half-hidden in the shadows, Braxton doodling a lonesome blues.

I smile. 'They should make a movie of this tour.'

'Hey, yeah!' Braxton's face lights up. 'Who'll be me? Can we get Sammy Davis Jr?'

Later, driving back to the hotel, we make our usual stop-over at McDonalds for Braxton to get his late-night burger. Waiting in the van, I feel a sudden pang of hunger. Oh no! I know there'll be nothing to eat back at the hotel. My conscience wrestles with my stomach for a full twenty seconds; but it's no contest.

As I join him in the queue, Braxton chortles with glee. 'He's cracked! Lock has cracked! A Big Mac for Graham Lock!'

'Just a fishburger,' I snap testily. 'I still have *some* integrity.'

But a few moments later Braxton is irrepressible: Marilyn and Mark sheepishly join us in the queue. 'Yay, they're all cracking now!' he whoops. 'We better rename this group the Braxburger Four.'

METAROAD

SOUND LOGIC, SOUND MAGIC 4: THE METAPHYSICS OF STRUCTURE

(This interview was, to a large degree, an attempt to clarify and amplify some of the statements on structure that Braxton had made during our meeting in 1984. The first three sections below are the relevant extracts from that earlier conversation.)

AFFINITY INSIGHT – WHAT STRUCTURE IS

L: Your liner notes talk about the formal and structural aspects of the music, but never its emotional dimension. Why is that?

B: Hmm . . . I don't know how to deal with that . . . It seems to me that the significance of improvisation, as it's been practised through the trans-African continuum, has to do with its relation to affinity dynamics and affinity insight; and every period of the music has established the same relationships between process and the dynamics of 'doing'. So I haven't talked about feeling, or tried to discuss the emotional aspects of the music, because it seemed to me that the significance of improvisation is for each person to find his or her own relationship with 'doing'; to be as true as you can be to yourself, the concept to self-realization.

L: You've talked before of the three degrees of affinity postulation and insight – could you explain what these are?

B: Well, the underlying basis of music has to do with affinity insight: on the third degree, for the individual with respect to self-realization; on the second degree, for the individual with respect to the ensemble and the larger community group; on the first degree, for the individual with respect to establishing a relationship with God or whatever the higher forces would be for the person reading this. In this context, affinity postulation is the term I use for the thoughts and information that go *out* with the sound, while affinity insight refers to the same information as it comes back to the player in the playing, a process of self-realization.*

To return to your original question, my fascination, up until 1981, '82, had been with the concept of structure, the concept of form: not as a dry, theoretical exercise but rather to look into the reality of structure and what it poses to the dynamics of the music – the understanding being that given structures will make certain things happen. That's what structure *is*; it doesn't have anything to do with me telling somebody what to feel, but with creating a structural situation or a language situation that has particular variables which will allow certain things to happen, and each individual will be able to establish their own relationship with it.

Structure on that level can be seen as an extension of the concept of chord changes; writing down a path of harmonic progressions and creating a language inside of that, which is what we're dealing with in the concept of vertical harmony. I was looking for a horizontal continuity; the reality of structural ingredients as a basis for setting up given vibrational properties – and each individual participating in that act will discover their own dynamics in terms of feeling or the emotional weight of the music.

BOPBE

I've always respected the science in the music, though I haven't respected some of the related value systems: for instance, the concept of notation – I don't think notation is the problem, it's the concepts that surround notation. Bach, Beethoven, Mozart, all of the master Europeans who solidified Western art music were instrumentalists and improvisers as well as composers. Notation wasn't used then as a choking device to stop the blood, the dynamic, of the culture; it was later, when the technocrats made the process more important than the results, that we got the so-called crisis of Western art music, which is still with us. In fact, we can see

---

*The three degrees of affinity insight should not be confused with the affinity insight principles (1) and (2), which represent a completely separate concept; see pp. 312–13fn

the same mind-set entering the bebop continuum: now they're making bebop so 'correct', it will be bopbe or something – it won't be the same music that Charlie Parker and John Coltrane played.

INVENTING THE WHEEL 500 TIMES

L: The link between Bach and Charlie Parker being that each evolved a new musical language using improvisation as a major resource?

B: Yes. What it is, I'm interested in individuals who develop a *body* of music. In the sixties and seventies there was so much disrespect for composition: I felt that could not be correct, as everything that has been demonstrated in the last 1,000 years seems to have a relationship to preconceived variables as well as to spontaneity. I thought it a mistake to put down notation simply because of its misuse by the technocrats.

If you look at Bach, Mozart, Harry Partch, Fletcher Henderson, Duke Ellington – all of those people, though on the surface they seem very different, there's an awful lot in common there. I see similarities on every level. Bach . . . the first thing I have to deal with is the actual music, that's powerful music, it's . . . I don't want to say it's beautiful because that's one-dimensional and doesn't capture what I really feel about it. All I can say is, it's *real*; and that kind of music attracts me. There was a law, an order, about the music, and improvisation was used to establish the nature of that law system. It's the same for Duke Ellington's music, or any restructuralist who's trying to establish a body of work.

I'm interested in structure because the concept of structure can be transmitted on several different levels; the understanding being that there *are* things to be transmitted, to be forwarded. Without the concept of structure each generation would have to rediscover the same things, learn the same lessons: like, we'd have to invent the wheel 500 times. The significance of form is that information can be carried forward; a given form can make given variables come into play.

The concept of music science has to do with establishing the restructural dynamics of the time zone, establishing devices so people will later be able to participate – the concept of ritual. Of course, we're riddled with entertainment in the West, which is not my idea of the highest use of creativity: but form as ritual could serve as the basis to involve participation with meaning, to establish a context to be able to deal with what we call God or the higher forces. I think that is the proper role of creativity, and it's certainly in accordance with the dictates of African dynamics and with those of early Europe, before the technocrats came.

GOING TO SEE THE CHICKEN FIGHT

L: Today I'd like to try and talk about structure on the abstract level; maybe uncover a little more of its significance for you.
B: Oh, I'm not that interested in structure (*laughs*).
L: When we talked last year you told me one of your fascinations with structure was that given structures make certain things happen.
B: That's right.
L: Exactly what kind of things do you mean?
B: I'm saying that the reality of a given set of variables in the space sets into motion many different variables – *vibrational* variables. The problem with the nature of present-day Western expansionalism has been that, in many cases, we've tapped into various areas of fundamentals but we've forgotten the primary information that made a given area what it is. We're working with a lot of areas of information whose spiritual function we don't really understand, so we're dealing only with the empirical function or with what happens when a given set of empirical operatives are put into the space. I'm saying that there's no real function without its meta-function and significance.

In *Tri-axium Writings 1* I talk about Indian music, the fact that they designed a music where, if a given scale is played, they'll tell you what that scale is for. When people die, there's a music for dying; when people are born, there's a music: different musics for different ceremonies. That's why I say the concept of ritual is the highest possible function, because the ritual is an affirmation of our existence. We've lost that since the onslaught of the European technocrat and instead we have whatever empirical logics are set into motion based on empirical criteria. OK, that's . . . interesting. I'm as grateful as everyone for the wonderful discoveries we have, whether it's frozen TV dinners or going to see the chicken fight (*laughs*). I mean, I'm constantly amazed at the wonder of Western culture (*laughs*).

But, in the process, I believe there are other variables which have been sacrificed in this time period, variables based on value systems; and, you know, the lack of some of these fundamentals has certainly made life in black America complex. Has made life for the creative woman (and the non-creative woman) complex. Has made life for the European mystic complex. Not to mention the so-called Third World.

I'd like to be part of some new realignment, although I have no illusions that my music or my thoughts are going to change anything, as far as the reality of present-day 'influences'. But I can still think about these matters and function in my music with respect to my beliefs.

THE THEORY OF THE ISOLATED
PAWN — SAVED BY UNLOGIC!

L: You're saying that each of the language types you've compiled, for example, has a particular function separate from its musical function?

B: I'm saying that every force sets something into motion. If you say, what? I'd say that's part of what I'm learning.

L: The question would be more how do you find out which forces you set in motion?

B: I'll let you know by your book ten (*laughs*).

L: After twenty years of study, you must have *some* idea!

B: I can only talk about aspects of this. In terms of what I'm really dealing with in this time period, I can't talk about that because I would be disrespecting you and disrespecting me.

L: Well, tell me what you can tell me (*laughs*).

B: But I've just told you! (*Laughs*.) OK, I don't want to play with you in this area . . . play is not the right way of saying it, but I don't want to disrespect you by talking about something that I have not thought out, or that I have thought out but am not ready to talk about. Remember the isolated pawn theory!

L: The *what*?

B: The isolated pawn theory. Is it justified to kill an innocent pawn just because your opponent has made a mistake and left that pawn unprotected? I was very concerned about this question as a young man and later in Paris I met Bruce Carrington, who is a very special friend of mine, and he talked to me about a woman who had told him that she had just destroyed a man, destroyed him vibrationally, and this man was hurt. He asked her, why did you do it? And she said, well, he came into my path. That's what she said; so we had to deal with that – she destroyed him because he was there. OK, I can relate to that. Now, on the chess board, if a person puts out a pawn that is not protected, you have to destroy that pawn – like, how dare they do that! It's *just* to kill a pawn that is not protected, as long as it doesn't disturb your position on the board and it further enhances your objectives. To destroy that pawn would be part of the lesson that has to be learned: destruction in that context becomes even respectable. That was the isolated pawn theory.

L: This is a justice without mercy . . .

B: No, wait, that's not the end of the story. I suddenly discovered something – you don't *want* to destroy anybody! If you can help it. Don't kill the pawn. Why? Because of *unlogic*. OK, back to the question: I can't answer it because of the isolated pawn theory.

DEVELOP INTO A ROCK

L: Anthony, that's as clear as mud (*laughs*). But I don't want to be destroyed, so let's move on. You also said that structure is coded information: can we talk about this?

B: We could maybe deal a little bit with that question (*laughs*). Structure is coded information: the American Indian certainly understood that, the early Europeans understood, before and after the Dark Ages; Africans have always known it. So what's the question?

L: Er . . .

B: You're talking about calibrations, is that it?

L: I've no idea *what* I'm talking about (*laughs*). How is structure coded information?

B: What about African rhythms? Each rhythm activates something, each rhythm is played for a function, a purpose. I'm saying there's a relationship between that rhythm and what is.

L: These facets of structure, are they the chief reason why you're not interested in total improvisation *per se*?

B: Yes and no. Let me explore that. I'm not interested in only total improvisation because I don't believe existential anarchy is the highest context. Of course, this wasn't apparent in the early sixties, but what became apparent was that no evolution was taking place (in terms of what my interests were) in collective improvisation, except for affinity insight on the third degree. In other words, as an individual participating in collective improvisation, I would have the opportunity to understand myself better; as I've said, the significance of improvisation resides in the fact that it helps you to develop your nature. *But* the concept of development is very existential. You can *develop* into a mass murderer. You can *develop* into a rock! (*Laughs.*) And without structural criteria, there can be no unity for the ensemble: or, at least, evolution for the individual is one reality, evolution for the group involves another reality. Structure is part of how evolution is arrived at; but I don't mean any disrespect for collective improvisation. I am an improviser.

WHERE THINKING IS A DIRTY WORD

L: Last year we also talked about the relationship between structure and emotion, and the reasons why you don't discuss the emotional dimensions of the music in your notes. Your position is that emotion is brought to the music by the player, it's a subjective element that can't be composed – is that right?
B: Let me clarify that. Every member of the quartet, of course, has the possibility to take solos, extended improvisation; I try to get out of their way and make sure everybody has a chance to express themselves. That's part of what the family is; and inside that, each person brings their own emotions to the moment.

I didn't talk about emotion so much as a young man because of what I was dealing with then as a young African-American: everywhere I looked I was seeing a profound disrespect in how the music was written about. I reacted against that; I didn't want my music to be perceived as having no thought. I mean, only in jazz is thinking a dirty word! It's incredible, the value systems and political forces that surround and manipulate the music every day.

In this time period my work is perceived as being very cold and Braxton doesn't swing – that's only because those same forces are dictating and defining what feeling is. I don't think I'm the only one who suffers from this mind-set: the reality implications of the white improviser are not separate from the notion that white people can think great but they can't feel, while black people have all this feeling but no real thoughts. You know, the real experts on black people are white people. The experts on *elbows* are white people, the experts on *ankles* are white people. The experts on Charlie Parker are white people. Well, that's fine, but it doesn't really express all of what's happening. (Let me also add this: if African-American and trans-African intellectuals are content to let the Europeans do all the defining, then it serves them right for us to be in the mess that we're in now.)

EMOTIONAL ZONES — 'I NEVER MEANT
BECOME AN ANDROID'

L: I'd like to talk more about this, but can we leave it for tomorrow? Just now, let's carry on with structure and emotion.
B: What more can I say about emotion? I mean, there's no one kind of emotion. If a given piece of music is written with particular dynamics, in terms of interpretation, I want it executed like it's written; but when we get into the actual improvisation, there are other laws at work. What I've tried to do is design a music whose *science* would establish certain variables, and the improvisation will take care of itself. I don't *worry* so much about emotion, but that doesn't mean I have no respect for it. I'm interested in establishing contexts where we can fulfil ourselves and approach creativity on whatever level of emotion we can bring to it. So, the people in the quartet, I don't talk to them about what to play, I just establish a structural framework which will set into motion its own operatives. Improvisation in that context is improvisation in a controlled space or an understood space, a *perceived* space. And the structure will help define the nature of the thoughts which will take place in the music. As far as the emotion is concerned, we never know exactly what the emotions are going to be: our intentions are positive, though, just as my structural intentions are positive.
L: You've talked about music for different functions – music to heal, etc: presumably there is also a music for sadness, a music for anger?
B: Yes, and my hope is, as I learn more about my work and as I'm able to work harder and evolve the music, that I might be able to create a music that would establish precise emotional zones – even further than that, let's say precise vibrational zones. But we'll come back to that in book ten (*laughs*).
L: Does the blues not already do this? I know blues is a versatile music, but on one level there are archetypal blues structures and

there are specific emotional zones associated with the blues. I mean, I always seem to end up drowning my sorrows with Bobby Bland and Smokey Robinson records (*laughs*).

B: Well then, you have very good taste, sir! (*Laughs.*)

L: Have you found that particular structures fit particular emotional states?

B: Yes, but I can't really go into it any further, it's a current area of research.

L: Can you say if you think such a relationship is an inherent potential of the musical form or is it also to do with cultural influences, a learned response?

B: I think that information dynamics have a lot to do with the time period, with the part of the planet that a given group of people have migrated to – and also with what cosmic decisions have been made. I think that for every primary information strain there is a meta-reality dynamic that is manifested in different ways, but which establishes the same forces in motion in every time period.

L: So structure can be a manifestation of cosmic forces and/or a form of personal expression?

B: Structure is a thought process. As human beings evolve we will have to develop forms that are relevant to whatever planes people are thinking on. But the concept of sound logic is not that separate from the concept of just waking up and getting through the day. It's all part of the same phenomenon as far as I'm concerned.

L: Yes, without music, just waking up would be too much to deal with! (*Laughs.*) I also wanted to ask you about something referred to in your *Cadence* interview,* that at one time you had tried to exclude personality from your music. I assume you were really talking about ego.

B: There's more to it than that. I was actually trying to approach something else and that's been greatly misunderstood. I wanted, as a young man, for myself and for the people I played with not to think *only* about the dynamics that had been opened up by John Coltrane, the whole world of extended solos. Everybody was playing for five hours! I was looking for alternatives and I thought then in terms of not putting so much emphasis on your emotion at the expense of potential event-forming possibilities in the music. I kind of wanted to approach it from a Zen-like attitude – I was very influenced by John Cage in that period – but I found that that would not work for me.

*Carey, 1984, p. 9

I haven't changed my emotional relationship to the music in any real way. Even when I was trying to approach it from the other side, I never meant become an android, I just meant, you know, let's also look at the other responsibilities that take place in the space.

FREEDOM – 'NOW I CAN KILL YOU'

It's like, everybody wanted to use freedom as a context to *freak out*, and that was not what I was talking about. One of the problems with collective improvisation, as far as I'm concerned, is that people who use anarchy or collective improvisation will interpret that to mean 'Now I can kill you'; and I'm saying, wait a minute! OK, it's true that in a free-thought zone, you can think of anything you want to think, but that was not the optimum state of what I had in mind when I said, let's have freedom. I thought any transformational understanding of so-called freedom would imply that you would be free to find those disciplines that suited you, free to understand your own value systems; but not that you would just freak out because 'the teacher's not there'. *The teacher is still there!*

It's one thing to talk about the post-Ayler cycle with respect to the events which took place in the first year, the second year . . . but if you look back at the last twenty years, what has freedom meant? For a great many people, so-called freedom music is more limiting than bebop, because in bebop you can play a ballad or change the tempo or the key. So-called freedom has not helped us as a family, as a collective, to understand responsibility better. Only the master musicians, the ones who really understood what they were doing and who did their homework, have been able to generate forward motion. So the notion of freedom that was being perpetrated in the sixties might not have been the healthiest notion. I say 'healthiest notion' because I'm not opposed to the *state* of freedom; I believe that with correct information and an understanding of respect for humanity, human beings can rise to their potential. But fixed and open variables, with the fixed variables functioning from fundamental value systems – that's what freedom means to me.*

---

*C.f. Stockhausen's comments on a free jazz concert he attended in 1971: 'Everyone played as loud and as fast as possible, and everyone at once . . . But that's what always happens when people say "Let's be free": it produces chaos and destruction, because they have never learnt to use freedom as a means of restricting oneself, so that others can also be free.' Quoted in Maconie, 1981, p. 244

TRANSFORMATION AND RITUAL

L: You've talked about transformational understanding, transformational culture. Could you explain more precisely the relationship between music and transformation?

B: Let me go back to how I see music. I've explained that for me the concept of form, in its optimum state, establishes some fundamental line about the workings of this experience, what we call physicality. I think the concept of form is also not separate from the forces it sets into motion.

L: You're talking about vibrational forces?

B: Yes, a hierarchy of vibrations which have to do with spiritual matters. Now, the degree you're talking about, the degree of transformation, there are several levels to that: *the vibrational function* would be that information transmitted to the individual based on self-realization and life experience – in the context of music, the vibrational function would have to do with what is set into motion in sound; *the living function* would have to do with establishing the scientific and spiritual inter-relationships of a given sound and how that would serve on a higher plane for the community; *the scientific function* would be calibrating the materials and understanding the order and inter-relationship and expansion of those materials in terms of how they express their laws, and the inter-relationship of that information to fundamentals; *the composite function* would be what that body of information would mean to humanity and how people would be able to use that information to live and, we hope, evolve; and the *ritual function* would be a ritualization of that information – the ritual function is the highest function that I will deal with in terms of establishing materials and establishing a meta-reality context for these materials.

L: Why is ritual the highest function? I'm sorry, I'm not clear about this.

B: Ah . . . rather than disrespect myself by thinking I could understand more than I could understand, I go to the significance of ritual as a way of establishing a platform for my spiritual beliefs, and to portray a methodological and fantasy projection of my worldview and spiritual view as a platform to state my beliefs.

L: Is it like an enactment of the vibrational function?

B: No, no. It would be an affirmation of all the degrees, coupled with the consideration of ethics, spirituality – all that ritual really

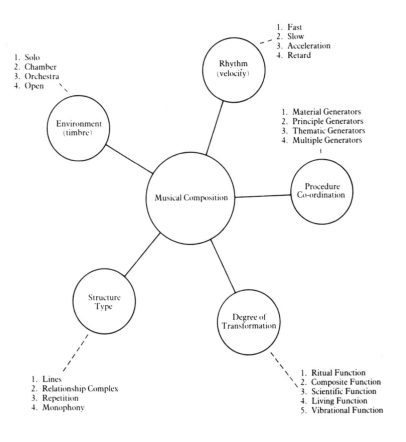

1. Fast
2. Slow
3. Acceleration
4. Retard

Rhythm
(velocity)

1. Solo
2. Chamber
3. Orchestra
4. Open

Environment
(timbre)

1. Material Generators
2. Principle Generators
3. Thematic Generators
4. Multiple Generators

Musical Composition

Procedure
Co-ordination

Structure
Type

Degree of
Transformation

1. Lines
2. Relationship Complex
3. Repetition
4. Monophony

1. Ritual Function
2. Composite Function
3. Scientific Function
4. Living Function
5. Vibrational Function

Elements of Musical Composition

means: to erect an *experience* that reflects my beliefs about the cosmos, about physicality, about life, intention, purpose, motivation, etc. I want every aspect of my music, every function, at some point to be able to be viewed from all of these contexts.

L: And the degrees of transformation can be seen as aspects of musical form in the way that, say, structural criteria can?

B: Well, for instance, if we draw, on the abstract level, the ingredients of musical composition, using the same format that we did before: *(draws; see p. 242)*.

ENDGAME

L: One last point: you mentioned last year that sometimes when you get stuck with a musical problem, you go and read Plato or Aristotle. Could you expand on that?

B: All I can say is that I'll be reading much more of their work in the future too. I'm interested in the ancient literature; Plato and Aristotle are not that long ago, but I include them as part of the early information. I'm interested in the world of thought, hopefully better to understand – or not understand – this experience.

L: I thought there might be a more specific purpose.

B: Well, there is, but I can't talk about it *(laughs)*.

L: Aaaarrrggghhhh!!!

B: Graham, I can't talk about what has not been demonstrated. But I think we've got a lot done today. Or have we? *(Laughs.)*

L: The fact that you refuse to talk about so much kind of speeds it along.

B: You're a hard man, sir. *Hard!* You must be from the old school *(laughs)*. Do you play chess, Graham?

L: No. I haven't played since I left school.

B: Is that so? I bet you're really a grandmaster *(laughs)*.

L: *(laughs)* Well, I thought I was winning today, but you still managed a stalemate.

ROAD

MONDAY 25, HUDDERSFIELD

I wake up and realize the tour is almost over; only two gigs to go. Tomorrow night I'll be home. I feel like crying.

'You're finally cracking, huh, Graham?' Braxton notes my glum face.

'I think I may crack after the tour,' I tell him. 'Getting back to everyday life is gonna be hard.'

He nods. 'I know what you mean, but I'm tired. I'll be glad to get home.' He asks if anyone saw the in-house movie on TV last night: no one did. 'It was pornography,' he says with a surprised grimace. 'I got so embarrassed at myself for watching it, I turned it off after twenty minutes. Boy, if that's sex, I'm against it! I mean, I must've been doing something else for the last twenty years.'

As we head towards Huddersfield I muse on the fact that in-house pornographic films seem to be a common feature in hotels nowadays: Braxton's criticism of 'freedom' in sixties music, the *now I can kill you* syndrome, seems equally applicable to current debates about pornography and censorship (debates also rooted in sixties notions of 'freedom'). Not only are snuff movies a literal example of *now I can kill you;** but the liberal argument that freedom of

---

*And, perhaps, of *now you can be killed*. C.f. Tracey A. Gardner, writing on how white lynchings of black men dramatically increased *after* the abolition of slavery: 'I believe that this obscene, inhuman treatment of Black men by white men, has a direct correlation to white men's increasingly obscene and inhuman treatment of women, particularly white women, in pornography and real life. White women, working towards their own strength and identity, their own sexuality, have in a sense become uppity niggers' ('Racism in Pornography and the Women's Movement', in Lederer (ed), 1980, p. 111). Braxton made a similar point, talking about 'black exotica', see p. 66 above; and he also notes some parallels between sexism and racism in the chapter on 'The Reality of the Creative Woman' in *Tri-axium Writings 3*

expression is an absolute has hardly helped us to 'understand responsibility better'. Can any freedom be absolute? As soon as you use your freedom to violate someone else, isn't that oppression? Perhaps freedom has to be, as it is in the quartet music, a kind of social contract, a dialogue of give and take. Plus, you have to respect the Otherness of – everything!

What's also curious are the very partial perspectives used in debates about censorship. So that, whereas attempts to curtail pornography are decried as attacks on freedom of expression (though it expresses nothing but misogynist fantasy and the publisher's desire for profits), the record industry's refusal to release music by Braxton or Cecil Taylor or Ornette Coleman or Marilyn Crispell is not seen as censorship or a block on freedom of expression, but simply as sound commercial logic. In capitalistic society, it seems, whatever sells is permissible, while anything that implies an alternative value system can be suppressed by being deemed 'non-commercial'. Capitalism has finally reduced all values to commodity value; freedom to a choice of exploit or be exploited, kill or be killed.

Driving through the outskirts of Huddersfield, I notice there are plumes of yellow and purple smoke curling malevolently from factory chimneys. *Now I can kill you* say the industrialists (and the drug companies, the junk-food companies, the tobacco companies, the breweries, the nuclear-power industry, the arms manufacturers, all the wonderful representatives of our wonderful Free World). I think of Cecil Taylor saying 'Freedom in America is the freedom of having poison in the air';* and Albert Ayler, taking that last solo flight into the cold, grey waters as the ferry passed by the Statue of Liberty.† *Free at last, free at last.*

We check in to the hotel, rendezvous with Nick White, who's rejoined us for the final phase of the tour, then head back into the town centre, to St Paul's Hall, where a group of students from Huddersfield Polytechnic are to perform a public rehearsal of Braxton's *Composition 100* as part of the city's annual Contemporary Music Festival. (Tonight's concert is also part of the festival.) Braxton is anxious to be reassured that he's not expected to lecture on *Composition 100*.

'No,' says Tony, 'I think you're just supposed to make a few

*Buholzer, 1984, p. 5
†See Hames, 1984, p. 27

introductory remarks, then afterwards make a few comments on the performance.'

'OK,' says Braxton, 'but I'm too tired to give a lecture.' (He's been looking deathly tired since the long drive to Leeds, so much so that I haven't dared to interview him in the last few days: the best thing, I decide, is to leave him alone and hope he'll get some rest. Except we're running out of time and there's still so much to talk about!)

Composition 100, originally composed for thirteen wind instruments and two percussion, had its British première in June 1985 at Islington's Almeida Theatre in a specially arranged version that included strings;* for today's performance there are seventeen players and the instrumentation is different again, the line-up being two trumpets, French horn, trombone, tenor sax, tuba, two percussionists (including xylophones), four clarinets, bass clarinet, bassoon, oboe, flute and piccolo. Braxton makes a few prefatory remarks, describing the work as 'an environment structure of fixed and open occurrences', the fixed elements being traditional notation, the open being 'open improvisation in controlled space'. What controls this space is language music vocabulary plus visual shape improvisation (as in *Composition 98*): the language music vocabulary being designated in the score by the numbers 1–17, each of which refers to a specific language music component.† If they wish, explains Braxton, the musicians can reshuffle the number/vocabulary correspondences for any given performance, and that either independently (so everyone has a different correspondence list) or together (so everyone will be playing the same number/vocabulary correspondence): options which, he says, allow 'the vibrational quality of each performance to be different'. The challenge, he concludes, was 'to establish a platform that would utilize different strategies'.

---

*If anyone has a tape of this performance, I'd be very grateful if they would contact me
†There are actually three kinds of improvisation indicated in the score for *Composition 100*: 1) improvisation based on language music variables, designated in the score by the numbers 1–17 (e.g. 3 = trills, 10 = instrument sounds); 2) shape improvisations, in which the player traces in sound the outline of the shape (see below); 3) open collective improvisation, controlled by specified categories of improvisation, designated in the score by initials (e.g. OP = opposition improvisation, K(M) = match the dynamics of the sound space, K(L) = increase the dynamics, i.e. play louder). For example, see p. 247.

In his notes to the work, Braxton likens the composition to an 'empty glass' to be filled by improvisation; and also to the human skeletal structure and vibrational system, which is fleshed out differently by every individual human being

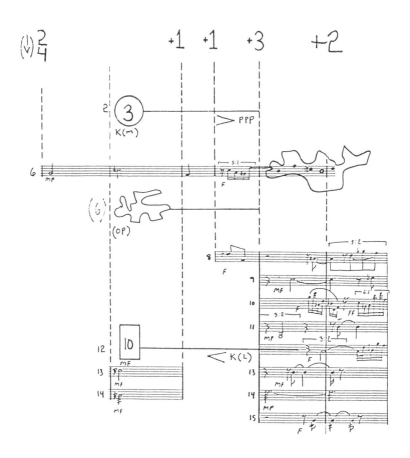

Example from Score of *Composition 100*

Turning to the students, he offers a last few words of advice. 'If the performance is too correct, it means you've made a mistake. When you're improvising, take a chance, have fun.'

The students play. *Composition 100* is a relatively short piece, about twenty minutes long, a slow flux of bright, pointillistic colours through which the reeds and brass seem to bounce wavy lines to and fro. Braxton, who's never heard the piece before from the audience,* is visibly moved. The conductor, lecturer Barrie Webb, asks him if he'd like to talk the students through parts of the score, so Braxton gets them to practise a few of the improvisations, urging 'use more power, put yourselves on the line more, don't be too comfortable about what you're going to play'. The students are keen to play the whole piece through again and Barrie Webb invites Braxton to conduct them; this he does in firm, emphatic fashion.

We still have a few hours free before the soundcheck. I decide it would be too cruel to exhaust Braxton further with another interview, besides which I suspect I'd only end up banging my head again on the wall of mysticism that seems to lie around the core of his music. (I respect his silence, but I'm determined to research this whole area when I get home; after all, if there's one thing that I've learned it's that for anything you can think of, there is information on it!)

Braxton, Nick and I wander around the town's art gallery, where the sound-sculpture exhibition *A Noise in Your Eye* is running for the duration of the music festival. We find Gerry here, plus composer/instrument-inventor Hugh Davies, taking a screwdriver to his own macro-process organ. 'It doesn't travel very well,' he explains, 'bloody bits keep falling off.'

The macro-process organ is a fantastical instrument that takes up a room on its own. A tangle of wires, small instruments and household objects dangles from all parts of the ceiling; the control panel stands in the centre of the floor – a small keyboard of twenty-one switches which activate tiny electric motors and buzzers. Flick one switch and a toothbrush in a far corner of the ceiling starts to jerk around and bang against a finger-cymbal; throw a second switch and a tiny propeller whirs into motion, or a plastic bottle jostles into a set of chimes. Press the same switch

---

*He conducted the world première performance at the Hartford Center for the Arts in Connecticut, at a concert organized by Leo Smith

twice and something different happens; throw all the switches at once and the room comes alive with a multitude of tiny noises that ring and buzz in the air around you.

Perhaps the best-known piece on show is Alvin Lucier's *Music on a Long Thin Wire*. 'A fifty-foot-long taut wire passes through the poles of a large magnet and is driven by an oscillator. The vibrations of the wire are miked at either end, amplified and broadcast in stereo.' The vibrations are affected by the environment, by changes in temperature, the number of people in the room, etc: so that what you hear, what the piece is about, says Lucier, is 'the phenomenology of the wire'.*

My own favourite (Gerry's too) is more directly participatory: the ballaststrings, by sculptor/composer Paul Fuchs of the German group Anima Music, comprises bronze or steel weights suspended by wire from drumskin-membranes that are mounted on a large wooden frame, a little like a gallows. It's an amazing thing to play; you can pluck the wire, beat the weights, sing into it, even swing the whole apparatus so, as Fuchs says, 'the sounds seem to laugh'. I hit the metal weight and at once a web of harmonics ripples around me, the sound beautifully rich and powerful. We have a lovely, rowdy time with the ballaststrings; Nick takes some pictures, and Braxton, looking considerably cheered-up, declares the exhibition 'very inspiring'. By one of those rare happy quirks of fate, when we return to St Paul's Hall we find Marilyn chatting to – Anima Music! (Paul Fuchs, Limpe Fuchs and Zoro Babel.) It transpires that they're old friends of hers from the Creative Music Studio, where they taught in 1981 and '82. They invite us all to a concert they'll be giving at the London Musicians' Collective on Wednesday evening.

The quartet go through their soundcheck, playing *All the Things You are, After the Rain* (at Marilyn's instigation), *23G* and *69C*. 'Boy, what a sound,' Braxton mutters, looking up dubiously at the high roof. St Paul's Hall is a converted church and the acoustics are trebly and crystal clear, so sharp that the notes seem to freeze and sparkle in mid-air.

'Too much echo,' Gerry frowns. 'Getting the dynamics right will be a real hassle.'

---

*The Alvin Lucier quotes are from Laycock (ed), 1985, p. 50

HUDDERSFIELD CONCERT, ST PAUL'S HALL

First Set (Primary Territories)
Composition 23G
Composition 87 (+ 108C)
Composition 121
Composition 69G

Second Set (Primary Territories)
Composition 69C
Composition 69F
Composition 124
Composition 40N

The first set begins and ends in a surging flash of energy; Braxton's mercurial alto feinting through the rhythm section's sound attacks in *23G*, then flying above *69G*'s racing tempo. In between comes the complex, fifty-page *121* (hypnotic if it catches you at the start, otherwise it may just seem difficult) and *87*, one of the bass/woodwind duos, here revolving around Braxton (on clarinet, then sopranino) dueting with Mark on a reflective theme that leads into some marvellous, helter-skelter ensemble play, slippery cascades of sounds followed by an improvised piano solo of vicious power.

If Braxton was fired up in the first set, in the second he's white hot. Bass and drums stab out the *'vroosh vroosh'* propulsive figure which is the germ of *69C* and soon Braxton's sopranino is snarling quicksilver, the intensity pushed by sudden rhythm-section accelerations into lines of whiplash ferocity. Piano, percussion and bass solos follow before Mark takes up the stately, stepping motif of *69F*: the ensemble weave around the theme then fall silent as Braxton, on alto, slips into his only long *a cappella* solo of the tour. Working thematic quotes into fragments of plaintive melody, he gradually increases the velocity, the phrases getting faster, more complex, as he rises into the upper registers then soars free along shrieking coils of sound: finally he reins in with a sequence of looping, split-pitch gulps, their slurry urgency trailing away into a last, peaceful ribbon of whistles. The audience burst into spontaneous applause, and the group begin a long improvised prelude to *124*, marked tonight by more fierce sopranino and counterbalanced by a poised, spacey piano solo which then whooshes up its own energy spiral just as the rest of the group descend towards the bass drone that leads into *40N*'s lovely theme, though the feeling tonight is unlike Leicester's elegant grace, the space stretched by a tension that dissolves only as the clarinet's tiny rinds of sound fade into silence.

The couple behind me can't make up their minds about the concert. 'I don't think I really understood it,' a male voice complains.

'Oh, I didn't *understand* it,' replies a female voice, 'but I thought it had an incredible sense of beauty.'

Backstage, Mark is in no doubt. 'Man, it was happening tonight! I think we went through every possible duo and trio combination. And Anthony's solo in the second set was fantastic! Something like that really fires you – everyone was so up after that!'

Braxton, meanwhile, is still enthusing about the students' performance of *Composition 100*. 'They wanted to play it again,' he tells Marilyn with a delighted smile. 'Boy, I'm not used to musicians who *like* my music.'

QUARTET

GERRY HEMINGWAY, PERCUSSION

Gerry Hemingway lolls in a hotel-room armchair late at night, a crooked grin on his face. I've just asked my stock quartet question: what's his response to the criticisms that Braxton's music is cold, doesn't swing, lacks emotion?

'Clearly they're right,' he chuckles. 'The shit doesn't swing and furthermore it's the coldest, no, the iciest music I've ever run into. Arctic!' He shakes his head slowly, giving me an exasperated glare. 'Nooooo . . . you should know what I feel about that. If people think that, their problem is that *they* are cold or they don't hear for some reason, they want to block it out. I mean, immediately they see notation up there they make the assumption the music couldn't possibly come out of somewhere soulful and warm. I think that's what they're really saying; it's a cultural judgement.

'All I can tell you is that after playing the music for a couple of years now, my experience is of such a high level of emotion on stage that sometimes I've been frightened by what I hear. It's exploding with such intensity and feeling that *cold* is the last word . . .'

What is all this emotion on stage? I ask.

'The feeling that's driving you through all the music is . . . there's a kind of love behind it. If you can get inside the music, and you care about what you're playing, you're not only trying to do your best but also trying to bring yourself into the music. So, on that level, everything we play has a certain emotional warmth: it can get very intense, or very quiet and sensitive, or almost carefree.'

He leans forward, a fast, confident talker. 'I think the issue is honesty. The players in this band are pretty honest, they don't go out and bullshit or do any sort of half-assed job. We're genuinely trying to play the music each time, we care about Anthony and his

252

music, we care about supporting each other onstage. We *believe* in the music, I guess that's the issue.'

You said the emotion onstage could be frightening?

'Yeah! It gets so powerful it seems we're going to blast off!' He gives a soft, appreciative chuckle. 'It's frightening in that it has a lot of power. I'm not a manic type person, I don't get real excited or real depressed, but this moves me; at times it's damn exciting. We've had moments onstage . . . it really felt as if we had lift off. It usually happens in a more rhythmical context, but not necessarily. There's a feeling of intense power, where everything physically unifies and, like, the excitement reaches a crescendo, almost orgasmic, a *phwoooosh*! Just exploding. I remember when we played at the Nicklesdorf Festival in Austria, there were points in the music where I felt it was like a stick of dynamite ready to blow. It was great, great! Everything lifting all the time, a feeling of suspension – and once you're inside it . . . there's nothing that can describe it, an amazing feeling. It has to do with connection, where all four of you are really unified.

'It can also happen in very quiet dynamics, where the tension is just right, the space is just right, everybody is restraining it to that particular point where the shit really *pops*, just falls into place, and all those independent parts that have no logical relationship suddenly all relate.' He leans back, a distracted smile on his face. 'It's like a total mystery, I guess. There's a real mystical quality to it.'

I smile back. Yes, that's it; that's how I feel it too. The group display such intense, delighted absorption that the listener is absorbed too. Everything connects. We all become the music.

Gerry Hemingway was born on 23 March 1955 and grew up in New Haven, Connecticut. His father had wanted to be a composer (and had studied with Hindemith) but he had been drawn into the family banking business by *his* father, who had earlier cut short his own wife's career as a concert pianist, demanding that she stay at home to fulfil the role of wife and mother.

The young Hemingway, attracted 'from the first' to the drums, attended numerous classical concerts at nearby Yale, but the first live music he remembers was played by Jimi Hendrix: 'I must have been eleven, twelve, it was just after *Electric Ladyland* came out. Oh man, I was in heaven, the guy really had something special.' By the late sixties, he was buying psychedelic and proto-heavy-metal records: 'I was a hippy, had long hair, took drugs.'

Sent to high school in New Jersey, he seized the chance to drive into New York for the rock shows at the Filmore East and his first taste of live jazz at Slug's: Sun Ra, Weather Report, Larry Coryell. That was *it*. When he returned to New Haven he placed an ad in *Rolling Stone* for a pianist and a bassist to play jazz; through the ad he met pianist Anthony Davis, who was then living in New Haven and studying at Yale, and soon after he met trombonist George Lewis, also studying at Yale, and Leo Smith, who had moved to the area following the break-up of the Creative Construction Company. Then, just as Bobby Bradford and Stanley Crouch had tutored Mark Dresser in the history of black music, so Anthony Davis and Leo Smith turned Gerry Hemingway on to John Coltrane, Charles Mingus, Fletcher Henderson, Louis Armstrong, Duke Ellington.

'Tony Davis was very excited by Mingus, so I listened to *Mingus Ah Um*, all the Atlantic records, *Charles Mingus Presents Charles Mingus* – amazing! I got interested in his extended pieces too, like *Meditations on Integration*, and, of course, from that to Ellington, *Black, Brown and Beige*, all the suites. Leo really got me inside Duke Ellington and all the earlier stages of the music.'

Inspired to study music more formally, Hemingway attended the Berklee College of Music in Boston; but after one semester he left. Like Mark Dresser, he found the academic approach to music rubbed the wrong way with him: 'They had figured out a system which employed all the harmonic and rhythmic developments in the music, they had pasteurized all the elements into a system which taught you correct harmonies, correct voicings, a whole bunch of rules about chords and playing everything correctly. Well, you know, *bullshit!*'

Instead, he listened: to all the records he could find, to all the concerts in the area – Cannonball Adderley, Cecil Taylor, a whole week of Ornette Coleman: 'I didn't miss a single rimshot from Mr Blackwell.' He was listening not only to learn the history of the music's evolution, but also to find out 'what it was in the music that was making me want to play'. Because you have to *know*. 'Like, you realize as a career it's a joke, you can't make any money, so you need to realize what it is that's making you crazy to do this stuff.'

Hemingway returned to New Haven and, together with Anthony Davis, George Lewis, Hal Lewis and Wes Brown, formed a group, Advent, which later became the Anthony Davis Quartet with

Marilyn and trilithon

The quartet at Stonehenge

The tour party: *L-R* Crispell, Dresser, Hemingway, Cresswell, Braxton, Lock

Braxton talking to students at the Royal Academy of Music

Gerry playing Paul Fuchs's ballaststrings at the 'A Noise in Your Eye' exhibition in Huddersfield

Above and opposite: Lock and Braxton play the sound sculptures

'I'm a reasonable man, Graham!'

Davis, Hemingway, bassist Mark Helias and vibraphonist Jay Hoggard. He also put together a 'home-made' college curriculum, unofficially attending classes at Yale and Wesleyan universities where he studied composition, Karnatic (Southern Indian) music, particularly Mridangam (double-headed drum) music, and West African drumming. In the meantime, he also drove to Boston once a fortnight for two years to study trap drums with Alan Dawson; and, inspired by a series of Leo Smith solo concerts, began to develop his own solo music – between 1974 and 1977, he constructed a series of four solo concerts, each dedicated to an innovative trap drummer (Chick Webb, Max Roach, Sunny Murray, Tony Williams). He also taught, promoted concerts, played frequent duos with Leo Smith (with whom he and Bobby Naughton founded the Creative Musicians Improvisors Forum – the CMIF – in the mid-seventies), and began gigging with trombonist Ray Anderson, whom Mark Dresser, in his brief New Haven sojourn, had introduced to the local scene.

'I was working my ass off,' Gerry recalls. 'I got married too; it was a really happy period of my life.' Before the decade ended, Hemingway had set up his own Auricle Records label, released a debut LP *Kwambe*, featuring most of the musicians mentioned above, and started to work with Anderson and Helias in a regular trio called Oahspe ('a word that means earth, sky and spirit – later we dropped it because it was too difficult for everybody to pronounce!'). In 1979 Oahspe too released their debut LP on Auricle Records.

Then things began to go wrong. Many of his associates had moved to New York and although Hemingway followed in 1979, it was too late – regular colleagues like Davis, Anderson and Helias were already involved in other projects. Gerry formed a large, floating group called the Improvisors Ensemble, but work was hard to come by. In 1980 he did a European tour with Anderson, Dresser and guitarist Allan Jaffe, during which they recorded the *Harrisburg Half Life* LP (dedicated, says the sleeve, 'to all people working to prevent nuclear disaster'); but once back in New York the scene was impossible. 'I spent $1,500 sending out brochures, making phone calls – got no gigs, nothing. This was one of the worst periods in my life; I had no work, no money, I broke up with my wife . . . Oh, man.'

It was around this time, however, that he met saxophonist/ composer/electronic music expert Earl Howard, and found himself making a transition from 'the so-called jazz scene' towards an involvement with tape, experimental musics, composition – 'a context I would call new music'. He began to extend his solo repertoire: Leo Smith and Mark Helias had already composed pieces for him, now Earl Howard did the same; and, with Howard's help, he started to categorize and document all his sound techniques, building up a personal language for solo trap drum music.

'The concern was *sound*; to create a variety of sounds that have a certain fluency in their communication so they become tools or vocabulary for composition. The thing about drums is that there is no familiar sense of harmony, melody, to help draw people into an awareness of linear structure, so the challenge was to make linear statements that hung together, particularly for the longer forms which I was keen to try.'

The first fruit of this exploration was the *Solo Works* LP, released on Auricle in 1981: but work remained scarce and Hemingway paid the rent by 'doing construction work, building houses' as well as the occasional pit job for musicals. Then in 1983 he joined the Braxton Quartet (of which more below), touring Europe in '83, '84 and '85 and playing on the group's first two Black Saint LPs; through these trips he began to find work in Europe, playing particularly with Dutch cellist Ernst Reijseger and indomitable improviser Derek Bailey. Back in New York, he had also reactivated his relationship with Anthony Davis, joining the latter's Episteme group and performing (with Marilyn Crispell) in Davis's opera *X*, about the life of Malcolm X. The trio with Ray Anderson and Mark Helias revived too, and they recorded the *Right Down Your Alley* LP for Black Saint (one track being *Portrait of Mark Dresser*) plus the *You Be* LP for Minor Music. Meanwhile, Hemingway continued to compile his own projects, including the solo, quintet and tape musics he had played me on the drive to Leeds.

Tell me more about *Waterways*, I ask. How did that come about?

'*Waterways* is part of a set of pieces I call *Sound Dreams*; it's for tape and percussion and originally involved slide projection and a lighting system too. The piece is inspired by a brook near where I grew up. I went back a couple of years ago to photograph it, trying to capture the cellophane textures you get when light hits water that's running very fast over rocks. I did a lot of double, triple exposures so I got very dense textures which I then sequenced and showed in a dissolve format, one slide fading out as the next comes in, so you get a very smooth, almost watery, flowing texture. To complement this, I recorded the water at the brook, putting the microphone half an inch from the surface, trying to capture specific areas of sound inside the water which I further extended by electronic filtering so I could isolate particular pitches that were coming by very rapidly. Then I used tape manipulation, splicing, mostly slowing it all down so the pitches were at a level where the rhythms that were occurring became very discernible.

'I was also interested in taping a single drop of water as it hit a stone, a nice resonant *plop* which I heightened as much as I could, then sped it up, slowed it down, to hundreds of different pitches, so I had a wall of sounds, like a rainfall of pitches, that really complements the marimba, vibraphone, tympani and steel drums I play with that piece.'

Gerry Hemingway first met Anthony Braxton through their mutual friendship with Leo Smith: this was in 1974 when Braxton, just back from Paris, visited New Haven to perform in a large ensemble piece by Smith. They continued to 'bump into one another' frequently, not least because George Lewis, Ray Anderson and Mark Helias were all, at different times, in Braxton's quartet; but it wasn't until 1983, at a 'CMIF meets AACM' festival in New Haven (where Braxton was then living) that Hemingway was finally invited to join the quartet. It was, he says, something of a dream come true.

'I was excited by the creativity in the quartet, by the fact that the language Anthony was talking about encompassed so many different things. I was attracted to Anthony as a player too, I think he's a wonderful player and I'd loved his solo music, right from *For Alto*. He was clearly a person who was serious about what he was doing, and he did not do what other people seemed to do after a period of time, which is get swept away by issues like having to make a living. I've always admired how Anthony's stuck to his guns, I still do.'

I ask him what he's found to be the particular challenges and rewards of playing Braxton's music. One thing, he replies, is simply the number of different challenges, particularly the various technical demands involved in executing the notated material.

'What that's done for me . . . it gives a very keen sense of focus, the reward being that the level of concentration, of thinking, required to play the music makes the music *happen* much more consistently. The material helps transport you into a zone where you get past whatever it is that holds you back or distracts you. I like that very much.'

Presumably you still find room in the music to be yourself?

'Oh sure,' Gerry nods. 'Anthony's very good about giving his players space; he allows us to explore, to improvise solos, duos, all kinds of things, and that's bringing out aspects of my playing I haven't found before. He allows that to happen, though the music – the writing, the structure – is entirely his. Plus, I *like* the guy's music too. So the playing experience is wonderful. Also, I'm behind many of the things he's trying to do.'

By which you mean what exactly?

He shrugs. 'Like I said, that essentially he's stuck to his guns. He's said, "I've got a body of music that I'm developing – languages, ideas, structures – and I'm not going to give that up for some more attractive financial situation, because . . ." well, I guess he has the sense that he'd be selling his soul. He's been damned consistent about that. I've witnessed the fact that he's gone through some pretty hard times, the guy's been very poor, for different reasons maybe, and maybe he could've controlled some of that better, but he lives first for the music and worries second about the business side of it. That takes a lot of guts.

'He's certainly inspired me because, like, he's out there fighting for certain ideals, and what else is there except to fight for the ideals you believe in? That's just so positive. Like, fuck all the other crap, you know, all those games that go on to get record contracts or a foot in the door. The music business really sucks like that; it forces a lot of good artists to break down. You have to admire Anthony for staying with it as long as he has; he's never flinched, he's always remained positive about the field in general, and he treats everybody with real respect. Those are all qualities I like a lot.'

Do you know very much about Anthony's mystical beliefs or the spiritual side of his musical theory? I ask.

Gerry shakes his head. 'I'm aware of it only in that I know the guy well, but I've never heard him go on about it particularly.'

How about his idea that there are identifiable male and female vibrations in music, and that the latter have been suppressed? Would you agree?

'Hmm . . . I think it depends too much on the individual. I

mean, I'd listen to Marilyn as an individual before I'd listen to her as a woman, though she is a woman and she does bring so-called feminine characteristics to her music –'

Such as? I interrupt.

'You would say that,' Gerry smiles. 'Ah . . . it's hard for me to say . . . I just feel, what she has inside her as a person, something about it has a feminine quality – but this gets into what's feminine, what's masculine . . . No, I can't wriggle out of this, you've got me in a corner here.' He laughs and leans forward, stroking his chin thoughtfully.

'Well, Marilyn is an exceptional person, she's so extremely gifted as a musician, as a craftsperson, and she has such powerful command of the instrument that . . . hmm . . . she kind of defies everything that she looks. One of the things about her that's so wonderful is that she has this shy, very quiet and gentle characteristic to her as a person, yet when she plays there is such ferocity, such power, such . . . what sounds like very male-ish, profound, intense angst and energy coming out . . . it's not really male, but . . .' he tails off.

Angst? I say. I don't think Marilyn would agree with that. I'm not sure that I do either; I think there's a lot of joy and celebration in her music.

'Yeah, but a lot of anger, violence, power too,' Gerry insists. 'I hear that in her playing, violence particularly. None of those characteristics can you see in her as a person, especially on the surface level, yet they're all in the music so clearly she has them in her as well. I mean, to play music you have to have all of those elements going for you. Violence in music is a complex issue. I do incredibly violent things in music, things I would never do as a person.'

He frowns, then shakes his head. 'You'll have to give me more time on this, Graham. I haven't really thought about these things before. Tomorrow morning I'll probably disagree with everything I've just said.'

How about the hypothesis that because, historically, men have dominated musical traditions, they've inevitably created music as a male language?

Gerry remains sceptical. 'Well, maybe, but that doesn't mean that they *own* it. I don't know, I'm not sure you can define musical language in terms of gender anyway.' He shifts in his chair, mulling the issues, still intrigued.

'I'm gonna try another angle on this,' he grins, 'which is to say that music, for me, actually has many so-called feminine character-istics to it, inherently, within its form . . . I just don't think that it's a male form. You could say a male musician has chosen a *sensitive* route, one that has many "feminine" qualities to it, so he's already up against what the male tradition is all about, yeah?'

There's certainly a great ballad tradition in jazz which allows men to express extreme tenderness and vulnerability; but, at the same time, there's also a very macho streak – in cutting contests, in some hard bop, in some free music where it's like all the sax studs are queueing up to out-climax each other.

Gerry sighs. 'Yeah, a lot of players are into that, and I think they have a problem because that's just not what it's all about.'

We move on to the equally thorny matter of music and race. Gerry, like Mark, had encountered problems in being a white player of what, historically, in all of its significant aspects, has been a black music tradition. 'When I first entered the music, the term Black Music was popular and it had a militant angle to it, so if you were white you felt excluded.'

He admits with a rueful grin that there were times early on when he changed his dialect, spoke more in jive, 'so I could be *cool* and hang out with the *cats*'. But that, he says, was his own insecurity talking and, besides, it was a superficial thing compared to the fact that 'the musicians I met, most of whom were black, had no problem with the race issue, that wasn't their viewpoint, so I was always in a cultural mix and it felt natural to me'. Such a cultural mix is, he suggests, a politically desirable goal and one which he admires both Anthonys – Braxton and Davis – for pursuing.

Do they make it a deliberate policy? I ask.

'They're conscious of it, I think it affects their decisions sometimes, though ultimately I guess they're left with the fact that, you know, they have to make decisions about players based on what they can play. Well, that's *me* speaking – for me, the problem is that only a handful of people can play my music,' he laughs. 'I think it can be deliberate policy up to a point, but people are too diverse to be considered as categories. Still, I mean, here we have a group – one African-American, one woman, one Jew, and one WASP: so, it's happening!'

It's 2 a.m. We break for a pot of tea, then get down to the

nitty-gritty of Braxton's music. Gerry says he hasn't played any of the colour or shape scores, only the occasional idiosyncrasies of the quartet compositions.

'There are some pieces that use graphic notation, and some pieces use diagrams that go inside the notated materials. *105A* has, in its middle section, a round . . . it's like seven, eight notes, then there's a shape, then four, five notes, then a shape. As to the shape, Anthony's not so particular how you play it as he is about how many beats that shape goes for; the shape does suggest a contrast to what you're playing, but he wasn't specific that you really adhered to the shape, like you do in *98*.

Example from the Score of *Composition 105A*

'Then there's *110A* where Mark and I play a pulse track, *108B*, that is nothing but numbers and lines that go up and down, with circular, wavy motions to them that suggest glissandos, dynamics, but could be anything – Anthony didn't specify, he allowed us to make our own interpretation of what the shapes are. They're interesting in that they do hold you together, though Mark and I as well as John Lindberg and I developed various ways of interpreting that score.'

I ask Gerry to draw an example and talk me through it. He draws (from memory)*

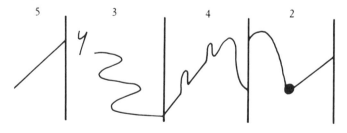

*C.f. example from the score of *Composition 108B*; see p. 262fn

'OK. So, for approximately five given beats we might do a glissando up, which is what happens on the record, the *Six Compositions (Quartet) 1984* LP. John Lindberg and I tended to lean towards glissando, we would follow the shapes fairly literally and we'd try to adhere to the time lapses that were happening: we'd be deliberate, but not too much, so we'd stretch them out and open them up in certain ways. More recently Mark and I do a number of other things within this diagram system – sometimes I use it as a velocity diagram, so as the line goes up I increase the velocity of whatever I'm doing; sometimes it gets faster, sometimes faster and louder, speed and dynamic; or I'll do inverse things, so when the line goes up I slow down. I try to keep changing the relationship.

'The other thing is that these dots also keep appearing in the score. We usually hit them, but sometimes we mime them, just to keep ourselves connected. I use them sometimes as accents; other times I use the dots as points of change; where I'm doing one sound that leads me down to the dot (like in the example I've drawn), then, from the dot, I'll change to a whole other texture or from glissando to velocity. Mark and I have actually gone further with this and figured out more things to do, but it's very open-ended, you can do a lot with it. The kick of it is we're usually figuring out how to do these things right on stage. We talked about it when we first played it, but since then we don't articulate to each other directly, we're doing it right there in the moment, being quick with each other, each understanding what the other is doing.'

So, although you're both with the same shape at the same time, you're not necessarily playing it the same way: it's like a multi-choice method of interpretation?

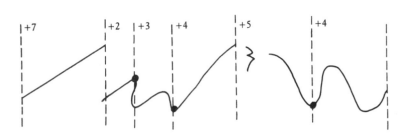

Example from the Score of *Composition 108B*

'Sort of. Anthony had some kind of feeling about what he wanted, but he wasn't specific, just threw out a couple of possibilities and said don't only go for the obvious, which is the glissando, go for other things too. It takes time to figure these things out because you have to keep together, which isn't easy when you're following weird shapes and all the other things are going on too; but I think it's really developed into something now.'

Is Anthony usually that unspecific about how to play the pulse tracks?

Gerry sips his tea thoughtfully. 'I guess there's always been a slightly open-ended aspect to all the pulse tracks because essentially it was something that John and I developed in the course of playing them over and over. The first one we ever did was *105A*, which has . . . after the melody's been played for the second time, we repeat the accompaniment to that melody as a pulse track and what John and I did right away was to extend the dynamics of the time, stretch it a little longer than was actually written: in other words, we slowed the whole pulse down or we extended various parts of it, and that allowed us time to develop more sound, so instead of just playing the pitch we'd turn the pitch into a sound, an event.

'John and I tended to fall into the same pattern of slowing the thing down, elongating it; but since Mark and I got into it, we've tried different approaches – we've sped it up terrifically faster than it's supposed to go and just kept rushing through it, very accurately but real quick; or we change the tempo constantly, speeding up and slowing down in the course of doing it. Mmm . . . we also do event-type things, like playing the notes as accents: that's something I do particularly – I like playing a wash of sound, where I'm hitting the accents. Anthony's given no special instructions, he just tells us he likes what he hears, so because we're improvisers we open up the possibilities. But we're true to it, too: I mean, it's holding you into a pattern that you have to play and you've got to stay together. There are little pizzicato figures through *105A*, for instance, which are almost the same every time.'

I didn't realize you could vary the tempo at will. Is that true of other pulse tracks too?

'Not necessarily, it depends on the pulse track.' Gerry leans back wearily in his chair. 'It's not a given parameter but it's a factor that Mark and I particularly go for – we share an interest in the concept of changing the tempo all the time, so you don't get locked into one tempo. Especially in a situation like the quartet where the dynamics are so various, and the amount of things going on is so complex, it seems to suggest a *shifting* – like, we're shifting between pitches, why not shift tempo, why not shift dynamic too?'

He smiles, as if at some recollected quartet concert playing in his head. 'Dynamic is a wonderful thing in this quartet; when everything is very loud and suddenly we'll be playing a whole set of pitches very quietly, as a contrast. Generally, there's a real musical *flow* going on between Mark and myself, but we're also listening to what else is going on and reacting to that. A clear-cut instance would be if Anthony is high in the upper register, really screaming, then that's either going to bring out more dynamic in us, a more intense interpretation to help complement what he's doing, or maybe we'll choose to contrast that, so, like, he's going crazy and we stay cool. Or we'll go crazy and he'll just stay, like, down there.

'All the dynamics are always happening and they're very, very quick: the way they work out, it's different every time we play. That's nice,' he declares, with a tired smile; 'that's the way it should be.'

ROAD

1983, BELGRADE/VENICE

(At the end of my interview with Gerry I asked him if there was any incident or anecdote about playing with Braxton that he'd like to relate. The following story, from the quartet's late-1983 European tour – the line-up is Braxton, Crispell, Hemingway, Lindberg – is, he says, 'the most wonderful anecdote I could tell about how crazy the road can get'.)

The story begins in Yugoslavia. The quartet have played at a jazz festival and been paid in Yugoslavian currency – dinars – which they've arranged to take to their tour promoter in Switzerland and exchange for dollars. There are two minor problems: one, they have first to travel from Belgrade to Milan to Venice for their next gig, taking their dinars with them; two, because of arcane currency regulations, the larger, 1,000-dinar notes are almost impossible to exchange and, therefore, practically worthless outside Yugoslavia. Consequently, the group have been paid mostly in the smaller, 100-dinar notes, which they're carrying around in five bulging plastic carrier-bags; plus they have one plastic bagful of 1,000-dinar notes which they have to change for 100-dinar notes before they leave Yugoslavia.

The next morning they get up early and go to a local bank. But it's too early – the bank doesn't have enough small change in its vaults! They try a second bank, a third, a fourth; none of them can change the 1,000-dinar notes. Time is beginning to slip away. Finally, their guide takes them to a large State Bank; they're in luck, the bank can change the notes if they'll just wait a few minutes.

'So we're sitting in the bank and I notice there's a group of peasant women sitting on a bench in front and to the side of me –

265

behind me are Braxton and his wife, Nickie. OK, I'm checking out
the scene and I have my camera with me, and like this scene
captures the whole feeling I have about Yugoslavia: a kind of
greenish-grey light, the women talking, the mood on their faces
. . . I pick up my camera, trying to be cool, not wanting to make
them uptight, just working out the logistics on the camera so I can
bring it up and quickly click the shot.'

What Gerry doesn't know is that a bank guard has walked up
behind him, drawn a revolver, and has it pointed at his head.
Braxton sees the gun, sees the camera and almost flips.

'Anthony leans forward and hisses at me, "Gerry, Gerry, don't
do that. Whaddya think this is, Coney Island?" Immediately I get
the vibe I'm doing something wrong, though I still have no idea
about the guard. I put the camera back in my bag, try to act cool,
like, hmm, what's happening?'

The guard walks off. The group are given their 100-dinar notes
and make for the doors; but the doors are locked. No one can leave
the bank. People outside are hammering to get in, people inside are
hammering to get out. Nobody knows what's going on. The bank
vestibule is milling with uptight, angry citizens. 'It's a weird scene,
and all eyes are turning to Anthony, the one black person in the
crowd, so he's like a clear target, *he* must be the culprit. Meanwhile
I have a terrible feeling that maybe *I*'m the culprit.'

Gerry's right. Taking photographs in a State Bank is highly
illegal and the bank guard has called the police. Finally they arrive
and usher the group into a back office for a spot of third degree.
'These police officers are rapping high-speed Yugoslavian at us,
yelling . . . Luckily we're with a guide 'cause we don't have a clue
what's going on, but our passports are coming out, it's getting real
intense.' Braxton and Nickie are looking daggers at Gerry, who's
feeling 'an inch high' because he knows they have to be back at the
hotel within twenty minutes to take a van to catch a plane to Milan
to catch another plane to Venice: 'only it doesn't look like we're
going anywhere in a hurry'.

Gradually the mood lightens. The police officers realize they're
not dealing with a bunch of CIA spies. 'They decide we're cool, like
"oh jazz musicians, ha ha ha"; they give us our passports back,
don't even take the film from the camera, just shake our hands and
say "come back to Yugoslavia", like everything is hunky-dory.'

The group run back to their hotel, only to find their transport
hasn't arrived. The van is late. Braxton turns to Gerry: 'You know

why the van is late? They're checking us out now. You think we're gonna get out of here? This is the East, Hemingway, things get heavy!' At last, the van turns up, but everyone is beginning to feel a little paranoid and, sure enough, a few miles down the highway they run into a road block. The police pull the van over and begin to scrutinize the driver's papers.

'I'm sitting in the van saying, "Why don't I just give them the film? I'll give them the camera!" And everybody is looking at me, like, Hemingway you really fucked up, man, you *really* fucked up.'

But it's just a routine check, the van is allowed through and speeds out into the countryside, heading for the airport. 'We're travelling really fast, the brakes are squeaking, like this van is *funky*, and we're whizzing past these hayricks, right out into the country where it's really crazy – so crazy that we come to this river we have to cross and we can't cross it because the bridge has disappeared! They've taken the bridge down to work on it. So we find a detour . . . Oh man, the clock is running, the plane leaves in half an hour, it's totally insane. The detour road is bumpy, the van is shaking, I'm thinking the brakes can't hold out much longer – we're all gonna die in this van!'

They arrive at the airport one minute before the plane is scheduled to leave, and it's held for them while they check in their baggage and go through a stringent security search. They keep their instruments with them (plus their innumerable bags of 100-dinar notes) because they suspect it'll be a mad scramble to change planes at Milan. But, for now, they're on the plane, they're on schedule; everyone breathes a sigh of relief.

Thirty minutes later, they're in trouble. The plane has landed unexpectedly (they think) at Zagreb, where they discover they have to switch planes – a connection that hadn't been listed on their tickets. What's worse, the plane for Milan is late. They wait one hour, two hours . . . it's getting desperate. 'If we'd been perfectly on time we'd have had only thirty minutes between planes at Milan, which is a pretty stupid connection at the best of times. Now our only hope is that Italy will be so *out*, the plane to Venice will be late too.'

And Italy *is* out. When they finally arrive in Milan, they learn the plane for Venice was two hours late – it left just five minutes ago! But no sweat – the group have a back-up plan; the promoter, realizing it was a dodgy connection, has reserved them seats on the train. All they have to do is get to the railway station. Without any

Italian money. Panic! There's a desperate rush to change some 100-dinar notes, a dash to the station, instruments and dinars flying: but it's too late, the train has gone. Luckily, they've changed enough money to be able to buy tickets for the next train, which is already standing in the station. And is full up.

'We walk all along the platform and there is *no* room on this train. It's rush hour, the train is packed, and you haven't got a prayer of getting on the damned thing. We walk to the first-class cars – we thought this might happen so we bought first-class tickets – but they're the same, loaded up like cattle trucks. The platform by now is teeming with people who can't get on the train, so they connect some new cars to the train but somehow these are filled with people too. It's bedlam. In the end we get standing-space in a first-class car; we can't sit down, we gotta stand in the aisle with our instruments and all our bags of dinars, but at least we *are* going to Venice.'

The train journey from Milan to Venice takes three hours: the train leaves at 6 p.m., the concert is at 9 p.m.; they should just make it. 'Sure enough we arrive in Venice five minutes before the concert is supposed to start and stuff some sandwiches and cappuccino down our throats; by now we're starving and we're road-weary like crazy.' Their next problem is getting to the gig; the problem is they have to go by boat. 'We climb into this boat, which is a wonderful moment; I've never been to Venice before and I'm like, huh? We have to get a *boat* to the gig? But it's cool.'

The venue is right beside a dock. The boat drops them off, the local promoter rushes over to greet them and leads them into a jampacked auditorium. 'The audience rises to its feet, cheering us like we're soldiers back from war – which is *exactly* how it feels.' They fight their way through the crowd on to the stage – and find it's a disaster. 'The drum kit is a joke, there're no music stands, we have to set our music out on crates, tape it up . . . Oh, man!'

The group rush around, getting themselves organized; Gerry whips the kit into playable shape. They're about ready to go on when they realize there's a violent argument in progress just offstage between the tour agent Renzo and the local promoter. 'Renzo turns around and says to us, I dunno, this isn't working out so well, the promoter says there are too many people in the auditorium, it's against the fire regulations, we're gonna have to cancel. Can you play the concert tomorrow night?'

Stunned silence. Then the group begin to giggle uncontrollably.

'Man, is this for real? It's not happening!' Renzo thinks they've gone hysterical, but they sober up and tell him, *no*, they can't play tomorrow – it's tonight or never. OK, says Renzo, and resumes his argument with the promoter, who eventually gives in, marches out on stage and makes an impassioned speech to the audience. 'He says, like, "We may all go to gaol, but it's for the music!" He's thumping his chest like crazy – boy, we're in Italy now.'

At last the band can play. And they play a fantastic set. 'After all that hassle you've got so much shit to say, like – *AAAAARRRRRGGGGGHHHHH!!!!!* So the music is happening, it's wonderful.' They play a marathon set, which Gerry assumes is the whole concert – but there's still a second set to come. 'I'm ready to die now, hungry, exhausted, feeling uuuuhhhh. But nope, we've gotta play another set. OK, fuck it, let's play.'

The second set gets under way. They've just started into *105A* when Gerry notices a plume of smoke wafting from behind the stage. Something is definitely burning. He looks around: they're playing in an old church, which is made entirely of . . . '*Wood!* Oh no! John and I can see the smoke, Marilyn and Anthony can't see it, but John and I are staring at it – and it's getting thicker. I'm thinking, oh man, this is insane, there's a fucking *fire* back there.' He looks around again: the church is made of wood, it's packed with people, and the only exits are at the back of the auditorium. 'So we're gonna be the last people to leave. In fact, we're the ones who're gonna get *burnt!*'

Marilyn and Anthony, meanwhile, are flying blithely through *105A*, but the pulse track is getting a little raggedy, John and Gerry struggling to hold it together as they watch the smoke get denser and denser . . . Oh God! The bags of dinars are back there! John Lindberg has an extra worry buzzing in his head: his jacket, with his passport and his wallet in the pocket, is backstage . . . exactly where the smoke is coming from.

'What happens . . . there's a guy who goes off to deal with the fire and he waves to me that it's OK, under control, but John doesn't see him, so he's really freaking, 'cause for a time there's more and more smoke.' Somehow the group get through the set, get backstage – and find it was John Lindberg's jacket on fire. He'd draped it over a light which, switched on after the intermission, had set his coat ablaze. Luckily, his passport and wallet had survived, as had the carrier-bags full of 100-dinar notes. Braxton seizes a bag and starts to pull out wad after wad of notes, scattering them in the air like confetti.

'Look at all these notes, Lindberg,' he cackles, dancing around the room. 'I'm a rich man, I'm a millionaire. Now I'll have power. Power! Wheeee!'

The story is nearly over, but for Gerry the best part of the night is still to come. Bewitched by the beauty and silence of Venice, he throws his kit into his room then goes out for a wander. 'I walked around Venice all night, didn't go to bed at all, just walked through the city from end to end. I didn't see another soul for hours, nobody. I had the whole city to myself, a wonderful experience.'

The day which had begun with him nearly getting his head blown off in a Yugoslav bank and then climaxed with the nightmare of a mid-concert fire, finally closes with a touch of Venetian magic.

METAROAD

CODA

THE QUARTET

L: This is our last interview so perhaps you'd like to say something about the people in the quartet.

B: Let me say this first – we're at the point where this particular quartet has just about come to an end. I'm thinking that we've completed a cycle and it's time for a change.

L: But . . . I mean, I can't believe it . . . what makes you think the quartet is at an end?

B: For one, I'm on the West Coast and everybody else is gonna be on the East Coast; it's impossible to hold the group together with that much space between us. But then there's another problem – there's simply not enough work, and in the future I'd like to concentrate on the world of opera and on having a creative music orchestra, fifteen to twenty people. I'd like to function in what I call my traditional quartet music medium for say two or three weeks a year, but I'll be lucky if I can do that now I have a job, so it's unrealistic to think about holding this group together. Not to mention, I'm feeling the need for change again.

L: It seems so sad . . .

B: Well, I hope we can get some of the tapes of the tour released on record. And I'm sure we're all gonna play together again. But, you know, there are so many areas . . .

OK, now I'll talk about the quartet. Gerry has been in the group for maybe the last three years, I found out about his work from George Lewis and Ray Anderson. One of the reasons his music has been so valuable to me is that he's a total percussionist, he can function in every area. I needed musicians who were knowledgeable about world musics, musicians who could function in bebop, who could execute notated music no matter how complex, people who can technically take care of business. For instance, *Composition 121*, the fifty-page piece – I had a day off in New York so I went to the library and wrote *121* and spent half the day getting it xeroxed. We had a fifteen-, twenty-minute rehearsal, we sang the parts, then we went to the club and played it that night. So I have to have people who can understand a concept quickly and execute notated material with the minimum amount of rehearsal, so there's time to talk about other problems.

The thing about Hemingway that I find fascinating is that he has real sensitivity. In the beginning I used to complain to him that for the stronger sections he wasn't forceful enough, but he quickly got that together and he can now execute that kind of mass;* but he still has this very subtle edge in his music. He's a really sensitive percussionist, and because he's so knowledgeable about world music he's able to bring a very broad perspective to the music.

Marilyn – as far as I'm concerned, after Cecil Taylor, she's the strongest pianist that I know of. She's at a point where, if she had or took the opportunity to form her own ensembles and began to compose more of her own music, she would become a master in the full sense of the word. She's technically a virtuoso, she can read materials that I don't think many pianists of her generation can comfortably take care of; she has the kind of facility that's really awesome. She's a *real* musician on the piano, she has a very keen intellect, and she can also respond quickly in the moment. The first time I heard Marilyn she was playing in Woodstock, seven, eight years ago, and I saw then she was very gifted, even though her music was still in the transition from student to finding her own voice. In fact, in the last two years or so I've watched her shake her Cecil Taylor influence, move past that to the point now where she's playing her own music, starting to tell her own story. I'd like to hope in the next cycle she will continue to write and evolve into whatever areas she'd like to evolve into. It's been a pleasure to work with Marilyn.

Mark Dresser has been with us three or four months; this is the second tour where we've had the possibility to play together night after night and, based on our brief experiences at this point, I have to say I enjoy working with the man. He came into the quartet in

---

*The group still joke about one of the phrases Braxton used when urging Gerry to make more noise: 'Give me garbage cans, *clouds of garbage cans*!'

the middle of a tour, when John Lindberg and I split up, and tackled the music . . . the quartet book is not easy music – I mean, the compositions run the gamut from simple pieces to pieces that are technically very demanding, and Mark just jumped on it. And on this tour Mark has really contributed, he has a beautiful sound on his instrument, perfect time: so I'm feeling that we'll be working together more in the future, that's my hope anyway. I think we're only beginning to scratch the surface, Mark and I.

GEORGE LEWIS – MR RZEWSKI

& MR TEITELBAUM

L: Would you like to say anything about past members of the quartet: Ray Anderson, John Lindberg, Hugh Ragin, George Lewis –?
B: I'll talk about George Lewis. I think George Lewis is a super-genius. He came to me as a young man – Muhal Richard Abrams recommended him to me – and I could not believe him, he was such an incredible musician. I was in a period of change in my life and I asked him to join the quartet: his first concert with me was at the Jazz Workshop in Boston in 1976 – I gave him impossible music to play and maybe half a rehearsal, and of course he played it impeccably.

I've come to admire this man so . . . Where in the beginning he was my student, now, if I can only work hard enough in electronic music, I'm thinking maybe in three or four years I can take lessons from George. He's a brilliant musician, a man of total dedication – and, of course, he would have to get out of America to do his work! George would be the first of the musicians from the post-AACM juncture really to establish himself and also to move into the world of electronic and computer musics, in which he's now an acknowledged master. I can't say enough about George Lewis, it's been inspirational knowing the man.
L: You don't want to talk about the others?
B: No, but I don't mean anything negative. I've played with five billion people in my life and we're not gonna talk about them all. Let's just say I have a great deal of respect for those other guys; I'm grateful that I've had the chance to play with them. I mention George Lewis because I *have* to, because of what he's demonstrated.

I'll tell you who else I'd like to mention – Richard Teitelbaum. We've played duo concerts for over fifteen years now, and I've never had a moment of playing with this man where he wasn't amazing me. I think the whole thrust of electronic music has benefited from Mr Teitelbaum, and my hope is that he will begin to get some of the credit he so rightfully deserves. I'd also like to mention Frederic Rzewski: this is another master who has been demonstrating excellence for thirty years in every sphere, whether we're talking about his work in notated music or in improvisation or his work in political dynamics or as a master composer. His work has been very inspirational to me. I'm grateful to count Mr Rzewski and Mr Teitelbaum among my real friends.

THE POLITICAL OPTION

DYNAMICS FOR WOMEN

L: I'd like to spend the rest of today clarifying a few of the philosophical and political points that have come up during the interviews. For instance, your interest in feminism and what you call in *Tri-axium Writings 3*, 'the reality of the creative woman': when and how did this come about?

B: I'm not sure when I first became aware of the feminist movement, or even if I am aware of it now. Slowly but surely I found myself aware of the arguments which were in the air in the late sixties and seventies, women talking about the situations they were dealing with; and looking at my own life, my own experiences, I began to realize that there was something strange happening in the sense that I was not very much aware of the great women masters. In fact, I had not even been aware that I wasn't aware of them!

It's been a slow process of looking at my own life and trying to understand what areas of information I have to learn about, talking with friends . . . After a while, you find yourself suddenly aware that what was being discussed on the theoretical level is directly relevant to physical universe reality; and as that awareness comes in, you try to deal with it.

Let me be clear, though. I don't consider myself a feminist, I don't even know if I support three-fourths of the ideas I hear about feminists and the feminist movement. But I can't agree with any view of humanity that doesn't give the same rights to every sector of humanity; so there is no way I can ignore the fact that women are dealing with a very different set of political option dynamics to men, or that by examining history we can see that what women are dealing with in this time period doesn't seem to be very different from what they've been dealing with for the last three or four thousand years. So what *is* this?

It's not for me, as a man, to establish any criteria to measure whether or not there's a feminist movement or feminist value systems – I don't quite understand that subject any more – but just based on my own expectations for myself, I've had to look at the subject and try to understand what it means. In *Tri-axium Writings* I write about the particulars of the black composer, the particulars of the white improviser; I felt I would be ignoring a very serious subject if I didn't try to deal with the situation in which creative women find themselves in this time period.

L: Do you think there are now more women breaking through the male constraints on creativity?

B: Ojuwain, when he takes a stroll in *Trillium A*, scene two, says, *'there is nothing happening now that wasn't happening before'*. I kind of agree with Ojuwain. I find myself thinking that the surge of creative women we're seeing in this period, the dynamic women who are functioning and trying to contribute to humanity, are not separate from women in every time period; and that there has always been a sector of men *and* women who have been concerned about human evolution and how to live. I believe that in every period there have been master composers, masters of all kinds, and we need to understand better their contributions, their viewpoints, in any attempt to forge a transformational aesthetic.

'MASTERS' – THE SEXIST
BIAS OF LANGUAGE

L: I wanted to ask about your use of the word 'master'. I mean, one of the problems I've found in writing about women musicians is the sexist bias of language, the way so many words to do with praise or power have a masculine slant, like 'master'. My response has been to try and avoid those words, but you seem to be doing the opposite – trying to force new meanings into old words.

B: Well, my definition of 'master' is anyone who's done their homework, who's demonstrated either the information in terms of wisdom and insight or some understanding of fundamentals:

mastership is fulfilling potential and establishing and being a part of evolution.

The fact that we have not had a real understanding of the great African masters, the great Asian masters, the great women masters, or that many of the great European white men masters too have not been understood (I'm thinking of Paul Desmond, Lennie Tristano, Warne Marsh), is to do with the way everything is defined in this time period. The notion that the Europeans are the superior races and that every philosophical and scientific idea which has helped the cause of human evolution is related only to the European male is a profound misuse of thinking. Yet this is what young children have to grow up under – the weight of misdefinitions, the weight of gradualism,* of racism, of sexism . . .

So I simply define a master as someone who has demonstrated some area of expertise.

L: But just by having a personal definition of the word – do you think that outweighs the fact that its commonplace use is so loaded towards the male?

B: *Everything* is loaded towards the male, because men are defining all the terms right now; white men, that is, of a particular political and vibrational stratum. This is part of why the planet is not healthy. But it's complex, you know . . . There are African-American intellectuals who, if they read this section, would say, 'yes, Braxton's right, he's really telling 'em'; but they wouldn't want me to take a look at African-American intellectuals and the fact that they haven't been functioning on the level one would've thought.

AFRICAN-AMERICAN INTELLECTUALS

– THE LEFT

Here we are, you and I, sitting in this room because you're interested enough in my music to do the book. So OK, that's great. For those African-American intellectuals who look at this book and say, 'Well, Graham Lock is white' . . . Ted Joans, for instance, put down Ross Russell for *Bird Lives* – that was ten years ago, we're still waiting for Mr Joans's book! I can name – I won't do it, but I could – fifteen African-American intellectuals, so-called, who would

---

*For more on gradualism, see 'Postscript 2', p. 313 below

protest to the heights if they see an article or a book on Benny Carter, say, written by a white American intellectual. They would cry out – and rightfully – that a black guy could have written this too. OK, but where are these people? I see only a handful of African-Americans at my concerts – well, Braxton's the so-called White Negro, I'm not a good example – but I don't see many at the Art Ensemble's concerts, I don't see many at Dexter Gordon's concerts. Are we gonna blame this on white people too?

The African-American intellectual is great at being able to point out how the Europeans have fooled us and suppressed us, but they're not so good at explaining why they haven't documented some area of expertise themselves. I would love to judge Mr Russell's book on Charlie Parker against some of those African-American writers Charlie Parker hung out with, to look at the differences and see what there is to learn. But it's the age-old problem that it's better to talk about it than to do it.

L: Well, I'm talking only as an outsider, but surely there are some African-American writers who are functioning?

B: Oh yes! For instance, Dr Yosef ben-Jochannan: this is an African-American intellectual who is like a shining tower in an ocean of despair, an ocean of negligence.* There are a handful of African-American scholars who are functioning on Dr ben-Jochannan's level, but why is it that in 1985 there is so much ignorance in black communities across America with respect to history, to documentation, to understanding the political machinery that's been set into motion? The rivalries and separations that happened in the sixties between the Garvey and DuBois vibrational sectors of the community – why did they occur? Why is it that African-Americans have not only not supported my music, but all of the musics after Charlie Parker? No one wants to say this, but the turn-out of the black community for the music is a sign of real danger; and this is not only true for music, but for theatre, dance . . .

What has happened, in my opinion, is that African-Americans have been profoundly shaped and manipulated by the media, by the

---

*Dr Yosef ben-Jochannan, writer, historian, Egyptologist, was a student of George G.M. James and has since done extensive research into James's theses that ancient Egypt was a) a black African civilization, and b) the primary source of much supposedly Greek classical philosophy. Dr ben-Jochannan has also written about the black roots of both Christianity and Freemasonry; his numerous books include *Black Man of the Nile and His Family* and *Africa: Mother of "Western Civilization"*. (See also 'Postscript 1')

Top Ten mentality, *and* by a persuasion of nationalism that seeks to
establish Europe as the only source of the illness we're dealing with,
as if we have had no part in creating the sadness that's taking place
in this time period.

Why have African-Americans not been able to mobilize? Of
course, we are dealing with overwhelming forces, very sophisticated forces, in so far as how our suppression is maintained *still*; but
the fact is that there is no jazz magazine from African-American
intellectuals, no jazz record company, no art music record company
. . . Yes, we can blame it on Europe, blame it on white America,
that's fine with me, blame it on white America for the next 5,000
years – but the only way something's gonna get done is for someone
to do it.

L: How do you relate this malaise to the hope and promise of the
sixties? I know a lot of black leaders were assassinated or
imprisoned, but – what's happened, say, to the notion of Black
Power?

B: If we look at the young nationalists, the concept of Black Power,
in the last fifteen years we've seen a robust, dynamic movement,
full of hope – young people thinking about world consciousness and
change – be reduced to rubble, where all that's left is a twelve-hour
handshake that isn't even used any more.

L: But how did it happen?

B: Oh, it's complex, Graham . . . I believe there were many levels
of dishonesty associated with the left. Historically, the left have
constantly run to the black community when any kind of . . . mmm
. . . diversion is needed, but they've never dealt with the music
with respect to its own definitions. The reason I indict the left is
that, at every point of the way, the left could have tried to teach
people about what was happening, but they chose only to take those
areas of information that were conducive to their own interests. It
was very fashionable to talk about black power, black rage, the
music as screaming, etc, etc – a concept of nationalism that made it
impossible to talk about fundamentals; but, in fact, everybody
knows that at some point fundamentals, the concepts of information and evolution, are laws which are manifested in every period.
There *are* universal fundamentals, and to respect them does not
imply no commitment to Africa.

The Black Power movement came to a stop because it was based
on unhealthy premises, one of those being that all the problems
African-Americans are facing can be reduced to European-

Americans. It's more complex than that: African-Americans are dealing with divisions between themselves – particularly the dichotomy between the Marcus Garvey and the W.E.B. DuBois intellectual forces – just as Europeans are dealing with the war between the technocrat and the European mystic. If we look too at what's happened to the feminist movement, we can see that it's gotten bogged down in the same *distortions of essence* that the black community fell to. I see all of these things as being part of the central problem – not having the power to define your own terms.*

'PUT THE MYSTICS IN CHARGE'

L: You said in 1967 that you thought we were on the eve of the fall of Western values: do you still believe that?

B: Well, as a young man I might have overstated it (*laughs*). Looking back at what took place in the sixties and seventies, especially in the black community, I've had to come to terms with that and integrate it into my understanding. I might not make the same statement today, although I wouldn't disagree with it either – I just wouldn't be the person to say it (*laughs*).

L: Isn't there a contradiction between your critique of Western values and the sophisticated level of technology that, say, your projected multi-orchestral works will require?

B: Where's the contradiction?

L: Well, in current Western value systems, technology has a high priority and is allocated enormous funds. The change we would both like to see involves reshuffling those priorities so that first everyone is fed, clothed, housed – which would mean less funds available for technological research.

B: Oh, I don't agree. I think there's enough money to do whatever we want to do. The US military budget alone is so outlandish that

---

*Braxton examines the relationship between music, culture and politics in much greater detail in *Tri-axium Writings*, particularly in volume two, chapters one ('Social Reality and Trans Information') and four ('Music and Politics'). These pages include his critiques of both mainstream Western culture and of Marxism (as a Western European philosophy, it is, he argues, inapplicable to the situation of African-Americans), as well as his analysis of how, for various reasons, the black radical movement of the sixties became fragmented. His own 'internationalist' philosophy, which appears to draw heavily on the spiritual message of both John Coltrane and Martin Luther King, is perhaps indicated by the quote: 'The seeds underlying positive world change can only be based on a profound love of "all that is" – and as such, world change involves the hope of a better "state of being" for all peoples – and "things" (because "it" is not necessarily about people either).' (*T-a W2*, pp. 460–1)

we could not imagine what the figures mean in real money: just the budget for the army bands, the money to buy those guys saxophones and stuff, is greater than the *entire* National Endowment of the Arts in America. The money's there, but the value systems are not, nor the awareness of the people.

The divisions in present-day American society are tragic. The fragmented left, you know . . . It's like everybody broke up into little factions and sat in front of the television. Now we're all wondering how we ever got to this point in time. I say, give the musicians a shot! They can't make the planet any worse (*laughs*). Put the mystics in charge! You know, *do something*.

The Pentagon has shown that they are not morally capable of dealing with the consideration of war, let alone that of peace. Hmm, I like that idea – put the creative people in charge . . . I don't know though, let me stop and think about this. I wouldn't want some of the musicians I've known to be in charge (*laughs*). No, take the creative people out! (*Laughs.*)

HOW TO LIVE?

L: Could you say a little more about the ancients, how you became aware of that information?
B: I'll say it *again* – for every thought you think, there is information related to that thought. What do I mean by that? I'm only saying that all of us are dealing with the wonderful experience of living and no one knows what this is – but then maybe someone knows what this is. OK, from there I'll go to here. I believe very much in God; and in the last ten years, which have brought me and my family to our knees because of the intensity of our struggle and the poverty that we've been dealing with, this has only increased my convictions about the oneness of . . . wonder, and how fortunate it is to exist. And when I say I believe in God, by that I'm only saying that I believe in God. OK, from that I'll go to this. I'm very interested in trying to understand for myself how to live, how to be the best person that I can possibly be – whatever that means. And I'm trying to understand what it does mean.

This kind of information can be obtained in many different directions (though it seems to me that they all go back to the Negative Confessions),* and, of course, whatever level of

---

*The Negative Confessions were an ancient Egyptian code of ethics which Dr ben-Jochannan has traced as the likely source of the Ten Commandments

understanding you want from that information depends upon what you're walking with, what your thoughts are, and how serious you are in applying your forces to understanding better what it is you say you're interested in.

L: And encoding this information in music will set forces for good, or for change, into motion? You've said that you hope your music will help to bring about world change.

B: By that I just mean . . . My hope is to establish a body of music that will represent my potential, my aspirations, in terms of how I see music and sound logic. I stated before that a force sets its operatives into motion; by that I was talking of the power of music to set given forces and values into motion. I can say for a fact, based on my own life, that John Coltrane's music has helped me to be a better person, that Arnold Schoenberg's and Karlheinz Stockhausen's music has made me work harder and want to be a better person. I could also say that the body of musics I've been trying to deal with . . . the thoughts it brings me are not in the zone of trying to hurt anyone, I don't walk around in a perceived·negative space.

I believe music has much more power than we generally associate with it, but at the same time I don't mean to say, 'listen to my music and you're gonna be a better person' or that my work is going to change the world. Even though, of course, I think it has its place: I think everything has its place. You do the best work you can do and it will set into motion what it sets into motion.

L: You said earlier that, on one level, it didn't matter if your music wasn't performed so long as you were free to compose it: but, surely, if music has this power, it's vital that it be played.

B: Oh yes, but I don't want to confuse *me* with music; I'm just one person on the planet. I think it's important so I'm dedicating my life to my work, but whether Anthony Braxton succeeds or not is not even the question. Music is important and we have to find a way to bring people back to true information, real information, that can really help in this experience; but it's not dependent on any one person. A lot of creative people have gone down the tubes, down the drain into poverty: if that's my fate, I'm not unique. Many jazz musicians, as you know . . . Coltrane never got to fifty years old, Booker Little – so I'm fortunate to be on the planet.

EVERYTHING IS A VIBRATION
– FORCES AT WORK!

L: So can you say – and I know this is an impossible question – what music really is? What it's for? Does it have an inherent purpose or is it a neutral force that people can use for good or bad?

B: I think what we call music is a limitation, but I think the world of vibrations is what this experience is part of, and I think there are many things happening and I wouldn't have it any other way. I also think I don't have the *slightest idea* what is happening.

L: You haven't answered the question (*laughs*).

B: Because your question is so complex.

L: Yeah, it's a big one (*laughs*).

B: (*laughs*) OK. I think what we call music is part of the forces which are available on the planet. I mean, everything is a vibration, isn't it? We could just talk about different degrees of density. I think that music is what can happen through sound, through vibration. Music has a lot to do with intention and a lot to do with the upper partials, as much to do with that as anything. That's not to say you can't have a great dance, there are times when only a great dance will do.

There are so many other areas related to music. Like I've said, music does not exist separate from its meta-reality and vibrational functions and implications. It has not only a scientific degree, but a vibrational and mystical degree.

L: Do you make any distinction between words like spiritual, mystical and vibrational, or do they all mean approximately the same thing?

B: I make distinctions. By spiritual, I'm talking with respect to God; but for the person who'd say, 'Wait a minute, I don't believe in God,' then it's OK to say vibrational – it serves the same purpose (*laughs*). What was the other word?

L: Mystical.

B: Well, mystical would have to do with the same area, but by mystical I'd be talking more in terms of forces, spiritual forces at work, when .you're asleep (*laughs*). And when you're awake! (*Laughs.*)

MULTI-DIMENSIONAL LANGUAGE
– CHOO CHOO TRAINS

L: I guess this brings us to my final question – it's another big one (*laughs*) – language! I have a quote of yours here: 'One of the most sophisticated weapons that white people have come up with would be language – words – a mono-dimensional language used to evaluate and distort a multi-dimensional music.' I assume your own writings, your insistence on evolving your own definitions and terminology, is basically your attempt to create a multi-dimensional language in opposition to the one-dimensional white monopoly.
B: Not really. To say it was in opposition would have too much of a negative connotation. I was looking for a way to express how I really felt, to solidify a worldview that respected what I was experiencing.

Everybody looks at the media in this time period as if their political positions, their dynamics, their focuses, are normal and natural. I even had a student, a young lady, who was completely shocked that I was interested in what I call trans-feminist progressionalism: her understanding was that it couldn't be important because it wasn't in the history books! She was wondering whether I was trying to pull some wool over her eyes, to fool her. In fact, nothing is separate from how it's interpreted; there's no such thing as an existential event. As soon as you interpret something, you're interpreting it with respect to your values and, as you know, everyone is walking around with different values. But this is not manifested on the TV news or in the university system, where so many sectors are denied access: we're just getting one value system from those places, and it's not healthy – for Africans, Asians *and* Europeans, for women *and* men. How can I say it? I just want to be part of the world.
L: But if everybody adopts your strategy, which is – to a degree – to create a personal language, isn't that going to make communication harder?
B: But everyone will not do what I'm doing because I'm only fulfilling my mission and my tendencies. If I could have chosen a life, as a young man, I'd have wanted it to be as easy as possible; I'd have wanted to be successful and do the least amount to achieve it (*laughs*). I don't know if I'd have *said* that . . . but probably the

tendency is not to be involved in any extra struggle if you can help it.

It gave me no pleasure to have to spend ten years working out my terms so I could do the philosophical writings. I just wanted to be involved in music, I had not planned to write *at all*. I thought the job of writing was supposed to be left to the writers and journalists. It was only after reading 500,000 dumb reviews that I found myself thinking, hmmm . . . I disagree with the critics who even *like* my music! So it was like – I don't have any choice, I don't see my viewpoint out there, so here I come! I had to write a book that established my right to have an opinion, and to do that I had to design a philosophical system that would allow me to – from that point – postulate what I wanted to do.

But I would have preferred to . . . work on my model railroad trains and have fun.

L: Ah, you have a model railway?

B: Yes sir. My children and I are very involved in choo choo trains (*laughs*).

ROAD

The last day. I wake up feeling tired and bleak. At breakfast I spill the muesli and pour tea over myself, nerves about to snap. Gratefully I gulp down another packet of Mark's vitamin pills. We take a leisurely route to Coventry, stopping off for lunch at a country pub called, irresistibly, the Rag and Louse.

During the meal Braxton reminisces about the music business, telling us about his meeting with Sid Bernstein, the rock impresario who, for a time, was Ornette Coleman's manager.

'Boy, you should've seen his office, walls covered in gold discs, thick carpets, this enormous sofa that I *sank* into. And you know how these guys talk: "Anthony, I want you to know I respect your work, truly, but you gotta forget everything you've done in the past. No, hear me out: I can guarantee I'll make you half a million dollars in the next nine months, that's *half-a-mill-i-on dollars*, but there's one condition – you have to do everything I tell you. OK, OK, I know you have your ideals, believe me I can relate to that, but ideals aren't gonna feed your family, are they? Anthony, let's be realistic, huh? We think you should record with Johnny Chicken-shit – no, no, let me finish – Johnny's also on our books, he's a very good musician – well, the critics think so – and *he's* popular, I mean, we think this will be a viable commercial project. Of course, you may have to be a bit more flexible about your music . . . OK, I appreciate you have your dreams, but c'mon, are you gonna let your children starve for the sake of a *few dreams*? Anthony, just sign the contract, huh? Don't you owe your children that much? Is a little flexibility such an unreasonable thing to ask in return for all the money you ever wanted?" '

Braxton shakes his head, eyes wide in disbelief. 'I'm sitting there, *still* sinking into the danged sofa, thinking, "Uh? What is this?" I told him thank you very much sir, but when it comes to my music, my flexibility is minus twelve point eight degrees.'

'Ornette signed with him?' I ask.

'Ornette signed. He said, OK, I'd like to be a millionaire. What Sid Bernstein didn't realize was that you can't tell Ornette what to do. Ornette is *out there*.' He swallows a mouthful of fish and chips, then shakes his head ruefully.

'I'm always turning down people who're gonna make me a millionaire. That happened with Circle too. The Scientology people told us that if we stayed together and altered our music a bit – you know, played something *a little more commercial* – they could make us millionaires. They did it too for Chick: after we split, he formed Return to Forever and made a lot of money.'

'They just let you leave Scientology?' Mark asks. 'I heard those guys really pressurize people to stay.'

'We were just small fry, besides they still had Chick . . .' Braxton shrugs. 'They tried to persuade us to stay, yeah. I remember one of the high-up officials called me into his office in New York, he took me to the window, high over Central Park, and pointed to all the people walking around below. He said, "Look! Do you want to be one of *them* or one of us?" I looked down and I thought, that's not *them*, that's *people*. I told him, sir, I want out.'

'What would you do if you did have a lot of money?' Nick asks.

'Oh –' Braxton considers. 'Maybe build a rest home for ageing musicians. Somewhere nice they could retire to, where they could write, stroll around the countryside . . .'

'I see,' Nick laughs. 'Composing and decomposing.'

'Don't laugh,' protests Braxton. 'Boy, that's what I'm doing now.'

We arrive in Coventry in mid-afternoon. Because we'll be driving back to London after the gig we have no hotel here, so we go straight to tonight's venue – the Warwick University Arts Centre. Nick and I find an empty room backstage for the final interview with Braxton: it's a bare, hostile space, no heating, huge cell-like breeze-block walls, glaring lights, hard chairs. Braxton is looking dead on his feet, grey with exhaustion. We sit in a corner, Braxton hunched up in Evan Parker's ever-grubbier overcoat, me scrabbling through my notes, trying to tie up 5,000 loose ends. When Braxton reveals he's going to break up the quartet, I stare at him in horror: how does this fit in with talk of the ensemble as family? But he's clearly in no mood to argue and, anyway, I guess it's none of my business.

There's a quick soundcheck, a perfunctory run through *All the Things You are* that suggests everyone is saving their energy for later; then we adjourn to the snack bar. Braxton tells us about his workroom at home, a 'laboratory' with four drawing-boards in constant use and various coloured lights that he employs as composition aids (he won't say how). 'I wear a special coat too,' he chuckles, 'a white doctor's coat that my brother-in-law gave me. It's even got *Dr Braxton* printed across the pocket.' We talk about our favourite soul singers. 'Marvin Gaye was my man,' Braxton declares. 'When he brought out *What's Going On* I thought he was really gonna get into spiritual music. Then what happened! His next record was *Let's Get It On*, that old "I love you baby, woh woh" boogaloo.'

Back in the dressing-room, Braxton asks for my notes of the set lists. Michael Gerzon, the sound engineer, has turned up to record tonight's concert and Braxton's anxious not to repeat any composition played either at Birmingham (which Michael also recorded) or at London (which the BBC recorded). 'That way we can bring out all three concerts on record,' Braxton enthuses.

'That would take six or seven LPs,' I point out.

'We could have a boxed set,' he says excitedly, 'show the complete spectrum of what this quartet is capable of. Yeah! I'll call it, let's see . . . *Quartet (England) 1985*, that's it! Maybe you'd like to write the liner notes as you were here; it'd be nice to get it released on an English label too.'

Braxton's spiralling energy takes me aback. Ever-cautious, I mention it might be more practical to release each concert separately as a double album or even as a cassette, but Braxton's high on his dream: it's a boxed set or nothing. I begin to realize that 'minus twelve point eight degrees' of flexibility can be a double-edged sword, especially if the result is that the tour concerts are never released. Still, *be realistic – demand the impossible.*★

★The story of the various attempts to get these tapes released could make a chapter in itself. Briefly, both Impetus and Leo Records were keen to release the music, but unable to raise the money for a six-LP boxed set. Then Ulli Blobel offered to release the tapes on his new ITM label, but that project foundered almost immediately when Braxton and Blobel had a disagreement about tour monies, and Michael Gerzon felt it would be unethical to release the tapes to Blobel while he was in dispute with Braxton. The BBC, meanwhile, were refusing to make their tape available until the concert had been broadcast – a fair enough stipulation,

COVENTRY CONCERT, WARWICK UNIVERSITY
ARTS CENTRE STUDIO

First Set (Primary Territories)
Composition 124 (+ *96*)
Composition 88 (+ *108C*)
Piano solo (from *Compositions 30–33*)
Composition 23G
Composition 40N

Second Set (Primary Territories)
Composition 69C
Percussion solo (from *Composition 96*)
Composition 69F
Composition 69B
Bass solo (from *Composition 96*)
Composition 6A

(The Arts Centre Studio, an intimate space with good acoustics, is ideally suited to the quartet music. Braxton's set lists provide a fortuitous history of his quartet composition, beginning with the latest quartet piece, closing with the first, and drawing in between on each of the major quartet series: *23*, *40*, *69*. The set also includes, in *23G* and *124*, the original and most recent examples of pulse tracking. This 'historic' quality is enhanced by my awareness that this could be the last time this particular quartet line-up will play together. The group themselves, knowing only that it's the last concert of the tour, are in almost solemn mood, intent on a final fusing of their talents. One step into the music, and you're *somewhere else*. The four players are so attuned now that every tone, every silence, is alive; their interplay a dancing web of energies, particles, shooting stars. Forces in motion.)

The group rush into *124* as if it's an old friend, Braxton's sopranino a darting tongue that loops around the pulse track; Marilyn lets loose torrential runs while Braxton blows plaintively from *96*, then a brief bass solo prefaces the winding clarinet lines

---

except that *eighteen months* after the event the concert had still not been broadcast.

When I related this latter to Braxton over the telephone, he replied gloomily, 'Oh great. The speed those guys are moving, they'll be able to call it *The Braxton Memorial Album*.'

(The concert was finally broadcast on 7 September 1987.)

that lead into *88*'s ebb and flow, the basic motif handed to and fro between C-melody sax and piano until it vanishes in a short free passage, the ensemble 'playing the silence' as much as the sounds. A spiralling alto swirls into the notated piano solo – leaping intervals, abrupt halts, loud/soft attacks – then splutters back to signal the realignment to *23G*, sax and piano breezing over the rhythm section's sound attacks. Braxton's solo twists and glides like a swift, Marilyn follows with cascades of notes; then Gerry, slapping the kit with open palms. Mark sets up a low drone, and the group move into *40N*, a sombre, elegiac version, the clarinet shadowed by beautiful bass harmonics until it falls, a dying breath, to silence.

The second set begins with *69C*, sopranino chirping crazy figures around the rhythm section's staccato beat, the interactions becoming more tangled until Marilyn's solo sprints clear, flying free. Gerry's notated solo sets flurries, patters, and the drama of a sudden, solitary *thwack* into pools of silence; then a quiet alto whistle leads into *69F*, here taking on a dreamlike quality via a floating interplay of call and response that switches, with a burst of thundery percussion, into *69B*'s skittering rhythms. Braxton unleashes an eerie howling, Gerry throws in 'clouds of garbage cans' and Marilyn hammers the keys at impossible speeds. Bass and drums groan and pop, chasing each other in circles until Mark's notated solo – his growling tone loping through ruminative landscapes. A breathy alto re-enters, the bass adds creaking harmonics, then piano and percussion flounces lead into *6A*, a bass arco-march around which the other instruments hover and scurry, like tiny spirals of wind that drop, finally, into stillness; peace.

WEDNESDAY 27, LONDON

We arrive back in London at 2 a.m. Attempts to strike up a party mood on the journey back (by playing Screamin' Jay Hawkins tapes *loud*) are scuppered by Braxton's weary plea for quiet: 'Take pity on an old man.' It's true; he looks as if he's aged five years in the last two weeks.

The following lunchtime, when I meet him at the hotel, he's still tired and chafing against the six hours' teaching which the afternoon has in store. 'Do we really have to go? Can't I just sneak away someplace and die?'

He's lecturing today at the Royal Academy of Music: a three-hour talk then, after a fifteen-minute (!) break, a three-hour workshop, both part of a weekly series of big-band projects organized at the RA by composer Graham Collier. Braxton's lecture is on 'spatial distancing and alternative structural models in my music', with particular reference to *Composition 82* (for four orchestras) and *Composition 76* (for trio).*

As usual, there are numerous questions from the audience at the end.

Q: 'Your intention is to create a universe in miniature in the music?'

B: (*Nods.*)

Q: 'And you've talked about the forces the music sets into motion, which are presumably also the forces generally operating in the universe. I'd like to know if you see these forces as human, super-human, sub-human or what?'

B: 'Well, the human realm exists on Earth only, so we can only speculate about other kinds of forces. I think we're part of, and at the mercy of, those forces.'

Q: 'But how exactly do you see these forces?'

B: 'You mean my metaphysics, how I see the universe? Ah . . . nowadays I find myself thinking in terms of various energies and intentions, but I have no understanding of them in terms of how we talk about empirical truths. The energies in *82*, with regard to their spiritual significance – this is part of what I'm learning about. When I wrote *82* I was only aware then of the nature of processes, I didn't understand the meta-reality of forces. I still don't. I'm dealing with existential investigations like everyone else. Until humanity can come together and solidify the spiritual context, we all go our separate ways.'

Q: 'Some of the processes and terms you've talked about are reminiscent of ceremonial magic.'

B: 'Hmm, is that so? Well, I'm just at the beginning of learning all kinds of information. As I've told Graham Lock these last two weeks, whatever path you're on, some spirit has probably travelled before and left some information for you.'

Q: 'Do you find that in seeking to establish new structural models, the composer runs the risk of becoming too intellectual?'

B: 'What is *too* intellectual? If you mean *only* intellectual, then the

*See 'Postscript 3', iii

answer is no. I'm as *excited* by computer music as I am by Dixieland; I approached my multi-orchestral work with *enthusiasm* for that context. I know I'm perceived in the jazz world as the Iceman Cometh, but I get satisfaction from both the scientific *and* vibrational aspects of music, and I see no contradiction between them. At all.'

Q: 'So do you think there's an emotional content to serial music?'

B: 'Yes. The intention of forces and pressures is an exciting area, though of course it depends on what you bring to it. But it's all part of the spectrum of forces we're dealing with, and each force must be respected.'

We break for a quick cup of tea in the student canteen, then it's back for the workshop. Braxton begins by handing out his sheet of ten language types and runs through a few structural improvisations based on the different languages. Then he hands out scores of *Composition 100*, explaining the various terms and numbers he uses. A couple of trial runs through the opening pages end in complete disarray as people either get lost, get their numbers mixed up, or forget them altogether. The students are struggling to take in the flood of information they need to play the piece. Braxton, looking utterly exhausted, tries to rally them with tidbits of advice: 'What you don't play is as important as what you do play. If you're improvising, try to fit the music into the space. Think in terms of the whole, think in terms of your life, then don't think. Use the music to take a look at your own nature.'

Another run-through peters out in confusion. A couple of students have no idea what he's talking about and obviously think he's crazy, sniggering together over their mistakes; most, though, are intrigued and interested enough to persevere through the initial shambles and attain the beginnings of coherence.

I slip out before the end and grab a taxi to the London Musicians' Collective in Camden, where Anima Music are to play their debut London concert. The first person I meet there is Michael Gerzon, who's come to record the gig for his archives: he's still in raptures about last night's Coventry concert. 'It was so different from the other concerts, almost like chamber music in its degree of intensity. It's the most moving music I've heard Braxton play.'

LMC concerts take place in a large, draughty room beneath which the underground trains regularly rumble. Tonight it's freezing, but a couple of electric fires have taken the chill from the air and Anima Music have created a special atmosphere by turning off the lights and illuminating the space with nine candles placed in line on a strip of white paper that divides performers from audience. Their array of home-built instruments and sound sculptures lurks, half-hidden, in the shadows except for a gigantic set of ballaststrings that looms up, like a medieval siege machine, to dominate the room.

The concert itself is a magical affair, filled with the strange, wondrous noises that the trio coax from their unique instruments: the curling Fuchshorn, the electric lyre-like Fuchsharp, a xylophone of slates. The ballaststrings remains their most extraordinary and versatile invention: one minute it resonates so deeply you're at the bottom of a well, the next it's wailing like a mountain wind.

I talk briefly to Paul Fuchs after the concert. He gives me a leaflet about a festival in Heidelberg at which the group will play the following week – a festival whose theme is the number three. Anima, he says, take their name from Jung's notion of the feminine archetype; and their aim is a 'music for growing'.

'In Germany, the trees are dying, all of our forests are dying from acid rain. We hope the music will help. We don't know if it will, or even if it can, but we hope.'

For a moment, I feel panic, as if reality were playing tricks on me. The significance of the number three, the feminine archetype, acid rain, the invisible powers of music: haven't I heard all this before? My God, the crazies are everywhere!

A wild optimism stirs inside me. A music to heal forests? Why not? If enough people care, who knows what forces may be set into motion?

THURSDAY 28, LONDON

The group return to America today, except for Gerry who first flies to Holland to play a couple of gigs. Nick and I call in to say our farewells. We find Braxton in his hotel room, surrounded by piles of bags and boxes. Realizing he'd never be able to carry all of these separately, his solution has been to go out and buy one enormous suitcase, into which he's now trying to stuff all his smaller luggage. The problem is that, crammed full, the meta-case is too heavy to lift.

'Ah, maybe you guys could help me take my cases downstairs,' he says casually.

Uh huh. I'd offer to carry his horns but I can guess what's coming.

'I think I can manage the instrument cases,' he suggests, 'if you could just take care of that big case between you.'

Nick and I heave at the case and stagger out into the corridor, barely able to hold it off the ground; Braxton follows with his instruments. It's not very mythic, I reflect; I should be carrying the saxophones in homage, not grappling sweatily with two weeks' accumulated laundry, books, records, scores and miscellaneous odds and sods. Still, I suppose it is kind of appropriate: the critic struggling with the extraneous meta-baggage while the musician takes care of the music.

The rest of the group are in the lobby. A fervent round of hugs, then they pile into the van for Heathrow. Braxton is about to slam the door when a last query occurs to me. His glasses!

'Anthony, are you long- or short-sighted?'

Seventeen days, nine interviews and I had to ask?

POSTSCRIPT 1

CELESTIAL HARMONIES: A NOTE ON MUSIC, MYSTICISM, ANCIENT EGYPT AND WORLD CULTURE

As above, so below.

– Hermes Trismegistus

I hope the below data will shed light on Braxton's contention that, particularly in ancient societies, music was integrated into a composite, spiritually-centred culture and sound accorded a mystical significance that is currently denied in the materialistic West. This 'Postscript' is by no means a comprehensive survey of the topic, but I think it is sufficient to indicate the historical and philosophical lineages to which Braxton's own metaphysics of music are aligned.

Much of the information comes from standard reference sources: *The Encyclopaedia Britannica*, *The New Grove Dictionary of Music and Musicians* and *The New Oxford History of Music*. Other major reference sources include: for details about the esoteric aspects of music history and structure, Gorman, Hamel and Rudhyar; for information about ancient Egypt, James, ben-Jochannan and Sertima; for African musics, Bebey; and for Renaissance Hermeticism and Rosicrucianism, Yates (see Bibliography for details).

I am also indebted to Jill Purce for taking the time and trouble to share with me her knowledge about music and mysticism. Ms Purce worked with Stockhausen in the early seventies, collaborating with him on the *Alphabet für Liège*;* later studied Tibetan and

---

Alphabet für Liège, first performed in 1972, is described by Stockhausen as 'thirteen

294

Mongolian sacred musics; and currently runs voice workshops in Europe and America with the aim of promoting spiritual health and transformation. She is the author of *The Mystic Spiral: Journey of the Soul* and was general editor of the Thames and Hudson 'Art and Imagination' series of books on sacred traditions, art and cosmology.

In many early creation myths sound is of primary importance, the universe (or aspects of it) coming into being through some kind of divine utterance or similar vibratory event: this notion occurs, for example, in ancient Egyptian and Vedic creation myths, and is given especially poetic expression in Cree native American mythology: 'The Great Spirit hid and divided up into niece and nephew. Together they sang the creation song. Everything vibrates with this voice – the universe, the galaxies, the sun and the earth. Light and darkness and all things are but a song of the Great Spirit.'* The idea is perhaps best-known in the West in its incarnation at the opening of St John's Gospel: 'In the beginning was the Word, and the Word was with God, and the Word was God.' Beliefs about 'names of power', the sacred origins of mantra, the potency of magical incantations, etc, are all related to this perception of sound as a medium that connects divine and human realms.†

The vital role that music played in ancient cultures is well illustrated by the example of China, where music lay at the very

---

situations in which acoustical vibrations modulate matter (also living things)'. Jill Purce explained that its purpose was to 'demonstrate the effect of sound on matter in different ways . . . [Stockhausen] listed a number of tasks, and it was open to the musicians to decide which task to choose and how they wanted to illustrate it. There were various tasks: to demonstrate the effect of sound in water, to demonstrate the effect of sound in flame, to show the effect of rhythm on the metabolism, to show the effect of mantra on the body, to eliminate sound with sound, to decompose matter with sound, to make love with sound, to show the effect of prayer on matter . . . I can't remember them all' (from unpublished interview with author). One of these 'thirteen situations', based on native American chants, has been released separately on the record '*Am Himmel Wandre ich . . .*'
*Agnes Whistling Elk, quoted in Andrews, 1983, p. 96
†In his introduction to *The Egyptian Book of the Dead*, E.A. Wallis Budge comments on 'the great importance attached by the Egyptians to the knowledge of the names of gods, supernatural beings etc' and cites numerous instances from the text where the deceased is required to speak these names (p. dxxxix). Similar beliefs were widespread in the ancient world and can be found, for example, in Hebrew and Cabalistic traditions about the 'secret name' of God. (See Cavendish, 1984, pp. 81–141)

centre of the entire cosmology. The Chinese believed that the
acoustical laws manifest in music reflected the laws of cosmic order,
and tried to organize their lives in accordance with musical precepts
so that their whole society would be in harmony with the heavens.
Hence Confucius's comment that, 'If one should desire to know
whether a kingdom is well-governed, if its morals are good or bad,
the quality of its music will furnish the answer.'*

The Chinese musical system was based on twelve *lü*, or notes,
each of which corresponded to one of the twelve zodiacal regions of
the sky, to one of the twelve moons of the Chinese year, and to one
of the twelve hours in the Chinese day; one consequence of these
correspondences being, for example, that the key-note of a piece of
music would change according to the time of year and day at which
it was being played. The foundation note, or *huang chung* (literally
'yellow bell'), of the Chinese musical system was also the basis for
the Chinese systems of weights and measurements: since only a
pipe of specific length and volume could sound the *huang chung*,
that length became the standard unit of measurement and that
volume the standard unit of capacity.

In practice, Chinese music appears to have centred on a
pentatonic scale, each of whose notes – *Kung, Shang, Chiao, Chi*
and *Yu* – was integrated into a network of symbolic correspondences which encompassed politics, the seasons, the elements,
colours, directions, planets and domestic animals. The note *Chi*,
for example, was associated with public works, summer, fire, red,
the South, Mars and the pig; the note *Shang* with ministers,
autumn, metal, white, the West, Venus and sheep. Similarly,
Chinese instruments were traditionally divided into five categories,
each of which had its set of correspondences: for instance, the
panpipes were linked with bamboo, the East, spring, thunder and
the symbol ☳ (Chên).

As well as providing precedents for astrological, colour and
directional associations in music, the Chinese were exponents of
large orchestras and of ritual and ceremonial musics. In the Hann
Dynasty (202BC–AD270) the Imperial orchestra comprised over 800
musicians, while by the time of the T'ang Dynasty (618–907AD) the
royal family maintained at least ten orchestras, and important

*More than 2,000 years later, the South African pianist Abdullah Ibrahim told me the same
thing: 'See, you don't have to read about people – just listen to their music and eat their food.
Let the racists play their music and we'll play ours, and you can be the judge.' (Lock, *Wire*
10/84)

outdoor ceremonies could involve ensembles of 1,000 or more musicians. A variety of factors regulated the numbers and deployment of these orchestras, particularly the type of music to be played – itself determined by considerations like the occasion of the performance and the social class of the audience. For instance, there were four versions of the court ensemble music known as *Yueh-hsuan*, depending on whether emperors, lords, ministers or lower officials comprised the audience: each type of *Yueh-hsuan* required a different number of musicians and a different directional deployment of the ensemble. The dances, and number of dancers, that accompanied these performances also varied accordingly.

The reason for this highly detailed particularity, namely that the Chinese believed music to be imbued with great spiritual and ethical significance, is attested by a variety of texts and musical treatises which date back as early as the fourth century BC. *The Historical Memoirs of Su-Ma-Tsien* (*c*.100BC) remarks: 'Correct teachings find all their principles in musical tones. When the tones are correct, men's conduct is correct. Sounds and music are what agitates and stirs arteries and veins; what circulates through the life essences and gives to the heart harmony and rectitude.'* Su-Ma-Tsien then lists the correspondences between the five notes, the bodily organs and various virtues: *Shang*, for example, is linked with the lungs and with perfect justice. Later he claims that 'music is what unifies . . . By means of the unifying process, mutual respect is born', and gives this account of how forces are set into motion: 'Music is the harmony of Sky and Earth; the rites are the hierarchy produced by Sky and Earth. By means of harmony, the various beings come into existence; by means of hierarchy, the various beings are distinguished.'†

The Spring and Autumn of Lu Bu Ve, another well-known Chinese treatise, underscores music's central role in the cosmology of ancient China: 'When desires and emotions do not follow false paths, then music can be perfected. Perfected music has its causes. It arises out of balance. Balance arises from justice. Justice arises from the true purpose of the world. Therefore one can speak of music only with one who has recognized the true purpose of the world.'‡

---

*Quoted in Rudhyar, 1982, p. 169
†Quoted in Rudhyar, p. 171
‡Quoted in Hamel, 1978, p. 210

Though music's significance in Chinese thought and social order was not always replicated to the same degree in other cultures, similar webs of correspondence were and are associated with music in many traditions, including those of India, Islam, early Greece, the European Renaissance and numerous contemporary African societies. In the Indian tradition, for example, ragas are associated with particular times of day and year and with particular moods, and each interval of the scale corresponds to a colour; while mantras are widely believed to possess an extraordinary range of capabilities, from the power to kill to the power to heal, in what is obviously a complex and subtly differentiated system of musical metaphysics.

In many African cultures too music still retains its social, ritual and magical functions: Bebey lists various categories of purpose to which music is put in everyday life, including birth songs, lullabies, initiation songs, love songs, laments, praise songs, work songs, satirical songs, court music, war songs, healing songs, magical songs, death and funeral songs. He stresses the symbolic and ritual nature of much African music, as well as its close association with magic, and observes that 'each sound has a particular meaning'. Many instruments too carry specific meanings: the structure of the *Deza Sanza* ('little African piano') of the Lemba tribe of the Transvaal is a symbolic representation of both their creation myth and, consequently, the laws and structures of their society:

> Every single component of the *Deza* is symbolic: the calabash resonator is the womb, the sound . . . is the child that is born; the string that is tied around the calabash represents the python skin that encircles the village; the keys are the people who are seated inside the python – eight men (the high notes), seven old women represented by copper keys (copper being the metal of the womenfolk – the Lemba consider red to be a feminine colour); the hole in the rectangular sound-box is the deflowered maiden, and so on.*

Western musical history has its mythical hero in Orpheus, whose music was so powerful it made the rocks and trees dance, and its first theorist in Pythagoras (born 569BC) who set out the relationship between music and number in the intervallic ratios he demonstrated on the monochord.† Pythagoras too believed that

*Bebey, 1975, p. 84
†Curiously, the ghostly figure of Pythagoras and his monochord flitted through the *A Noise*

music was a reflection of cosmic order, symbolically and actually expressed in 'the music of the spheres' – a notion that Plato later developed in the concluding passages of *The Republic* (Book Ten). Pythagoras's beliefs that 'there is geometry in the humming of the strings, there is music in the spacings of the spheres' and that 'all meaning is number' have been taken as the starting-points for many strands of Western scientific and mystical investigation. He was also reputed to use music to cure both physical and mental illnesses, and his emphasis on health as a harmony of bodily constituents anticipated the theoretic basis of Hippocratic medicine. Later Greek music retained strong philosophical and ethical connotations: particular scales were associated with particular characteristics and feelings, the Mixed Lydian and Extreme Lydian, for example, being rejected from Plato's Republic as suitable only for dirges and laments (Book Three). The Greeks also used music in their architecture; designs for buildings such as temples being translated into music and then played to ensure that their proportions were 'sound'.

Yet while classical Greek thought is generally regarded as the origin of Western civilization, there is considerable evidence that the Greek philosophers drew heavily on the teachings of other cultures. In particular, a growing number of African and African-American scholars point to the influence of ancient Egypt, a black, African civilization, on the early Greek thinkers – an influence which many classical authorities (but rather fewer contemporary Western commentators) readily acknowledge.* It is certainly true

---

in Your Eye exhibition. Paul Fuchs wrote in the catalogue that one inspiration for his ballaststrings was the information that 'Pythagoras used the principle of a weight attached to his monochord to reduce the effects of changes in temperature and humidity' (Laycock [ed], 1985, p. 18): conversely, Alvin Lucier's *Long Thin Wire* – almost a post-modernist monochord – was specifically designed to 'play' such changes

*Bernal argues that it was not until the eighteenth and nineteenth centuries that the idea of an autonomous, classical Greece as the root of European culture became commonplace. He links this with a racism that developed hand-in-hand with the growth of the slave-trade. 'Racism based on skin colour had developed in late-seventeenth-century England, alongside the increasing importance of the American colonies – with their twin policies of extermination of the native Americans and the enslavement of African blacks' (quoted in the *Guardian*, 2/3/87). Bernal also points out that the idea of an advanced, ancient, black civilization as a major influence on Europe was anathema to both the Judaeo-Christian tradition and to the Victorian belief in 'Progress': the European response was racial stereotyping and the rewriting of Egyptian history. Braxton makes many similar points, including his concepts of 'gradualism' and 'the grand trade off' in *Tri-axium Writings 3*. (See 'Postscript 2', p. 313 below)

that Pythagoras and many other Greek philosophers travelled to
Egypt and studied at the Egyptian mystery schools, whose chief
study centre was at Luxor; it is certainly true that many aspects of
the mathematical and mystical teachings attributed to Pythagoras
were already known to Egyptian and Babylonian cultures. James
and ben-Jochannan further suggest that many of the writings
ascribed to Aristotle were actually stolen by him during the
ransacking of the libraries which followed Alexander's conquest of
Egypt; and James advances a persuasive argument that practically
all 'Greek' philosophy can be traced back to Egyptian sources.
There is separate evidence too (cited by various contributors to
Sertima) of Egyptian precedents for 'Greek' science, medicine,
geometry and mathematics.*

Unfortunately, little is known of early Egyptian music systems
and no Egyptian texts on the subject have survived; though the
second-century Roman historian Dio Cassius reported that ancient
Egyptian music was inter-related with astrology and suggested that
the names of the days of the week were derived from a series of
fourths and their planetary equivalents – the sequence going from E
(Saturn) to A (the Sun) to D (the Moon) to G (Mars) to C (Mercury)
to F (Jupiter) to B (Venus). That music played a prominent role in
Egyptian society is evident from tomb decorations and other
existent depictions of musicians and musical events. Texts of songs
have also survived, complete with lyrics and lists of instruments
used, but with no indication of notation; and theories that the
Egyptians knew and practised harmony are inconclusive. Both
music and chanting seem to have played a significant part in
Egyptian religious ceremonies, one likelihood being that vowel
sounds were chanted to invoke the deities,† while songs and charms
were used for healing and magical rites.

African and African-American scholars also point to the fact that,
for several centuries, between Alexander's invasion of Egypt in

*See, for example, the essays of Lumpkin, Newsome and Pappademos. It's worth noting that
Braxton's emphasis on music as a tool for self-realization (the third degree of affinity insight)
is, of course, a variation of the Socratic precept 'Know thyself'; except that, as James points
out, long before Socrates was born those words were being carved on the outside of Egyptian
temples

†Coincidentally, Hildegard von Bingen closed several of her chants with a kind of mantra of
vowel sounds, while Stockhausen's *Stimmung* is based on the *a cappella* vocal sounding of
different series of overtones. (Jill Purce told me that one of the inspirations behind *Stimmung*
was Stockhausen's reflecting on the fact that the hum of his electric razor sounded different
harmonics as he moved it over different parts of his face)

332BC and the Arab invasion of 640AD, the Egyptian city of Alexandria grew into a thriving metropolis that replaced Athens as the major centre for 'Greek' philosophy and science: Euclid, Heron, Ptolemy and Hypatia all lived and studied in Alexandria and may well have been native Africans. The third-century writer Athenaeus, himself Egyptian, observed that Alexandrians were reputed to be the most musical people in history; he also reported that, during the reign of Philadelphius (285–246BC), there existed a choir of 600 singers and 300 harpists – possibly the earliest surviving reference to an Egyptian creative orchestra tradition! However, Alexandria's influence began to decline after the murder of the mathematician Hypatia by fanatical Christian monks in 415AD; and, with the spread of Christianity as the dominant ideology in Europe and North Africa – often enforced by the barbaric destruction of teachings and teachers who opposed Church dogma – the Graeco-Egyptian traditions of mathematics, science and philosophy were suppressed.* The knowledge accrued by these traditions was dispersed throughout Turkey, the Middle East and the southern and western nations of Africa; while in Europe it was forced underground and preserved in various gnostic and mystical texts. A thousand years later it was resurrected in Europe, partly through the work of Moorish and Arabic scholars, and played a vital role in sparking off the Renaissance.

Neo-Platonic and neo-Pythagorean ideals were among the dominant forces in early Renaissance thought, as was the cult of 'Egyptianism' that lay behind a remarkable flowering of Hermetic philosophy. A primary source of this new Hermeticism was the *Corpus Hermeticum*, a Greek manuscript first translated into Latin by Marsilio Ficino in 1464 and widely distributed throughout Europe shortly after. Thought to be the authentic writings of Hermes Trismegistus, supposedly an Egyptian priest/god of great antiquity,† the *Corpus* mixed religious mysticism with elements of

---

*Ironically, ben-Jochannan points out that many tenets of Christian ideology derive from Egyptian philosophical sources; including the idea of monotheism, the notion of a resurrected god, the concepts of heaven and hell, and a code of conduct (the Negative Confessions) that became the Ten Commandments

†In mythological terms, Hermes was the Greek equivalent of the Egyptian god Thoth. In historical terms, Isaac Casaubon proved in 1614 that the *Corpus Hermeticum* collection was not written in Egyptian antiquity but in the first to third centuries AD – a discovery that spelt

magic; and, together with a contemporaneous upsurge of interest in both Christian Cabala and Paracelsian alchemy, helped to form what was almost a 'third force' in a Europe torn by the religious wars of the Reformation and Counter-Reformation. Characterized by its pacifism, its religious tolerance, its advocacy of 'good' (or 'natural') magic and its belief in the imminence of a new age of wonder through intellectual advance, this 'third force' flourished in the sixteenth century and peaked, during the early years of the seventeenth, in the 'Rosicrucian Enlightenment' described by Frances Yates.*

Astrology and numerology were vital components of this 'Magia–Cabala–Alchymia' trinity, and the Pythagorean belief that 'all meaning is number' underlay both the practical mathematics on which Keplerian and Copernican astronomy were based and the mystical uses of mathematics found in thinkers like Robert Fludd and John Dee, the latter of whom not only wrote a preface to an English translation of Euclid's *Elements of Geometry* (in which he surveyed the current state of scientific mathematics), but also evolved his own magical mathematics with which he believed he could summon angelic spirits. Most orthodox thinkers, of both Catholic and Protestant hue, viewed such magic and all its accoutrements with suspicion, even dread: in 1550, for example, during an anti-Catholic purge of Oxford University libraries, any books 'wherein appeared Angles or Mathematical Diagrams were thought sufficient to be destroyed because accounted Papish or diabolical, or both'.† And in 1600 one of the foremost Hermetic thinkers, Giordano Bruno, was burnt at the stake as a heretic.

In this strange world of numerological and astrological magic, music – as one of the principal mathematical sciences – played an important role. Pythagorean and Platonic notions of universal

---

the beginning of the end for Renaissance Hermeticism (though modern historians still disagree on the extent to which the *Corpus* derived from genuine ancient Egyptian sources). See Yates, 1978

*See Yates, 1986. The Rosicrucians were a (possibly non-existent) secret society of mystical intellectuals whose beliefs were set out in two anonymous manifestos (in 1614 and 1615), which created a furore in European society. Ms Yates's brilliant work of historical detection traces the roots of Rosicrucianism in the Hermetic (i.e. 'Egyptian') tradition – particularly the philosophy of John Dee – and places the appearance of the mysterious manifestos into the context of Protestant and Catholic political rivalry. Various Hermetic philosophers, including Robert Fludd and Michael Maier (see below), were supposedly associated with the Rosicrucians, though no one at the time ever admitted to belonging to the group

†Quoted in Yates, 1978, p. 167. The original commentator was one Anthony à Wood

harmony and the music of the spheres, duly translated into
Christian cosmology, became an accepted part of Renaissance
thought;* but to them, in the words of Frances Yates, 'Hermeticism and Cabalism added immense richness and complexity,
swelling out the universal harmonies into a new symphony'. The
same Marsilio Ficino who translated the *Corpus Hermeticum* also
initiated an esoteric use of Renaissance musical magic – the
chanting of what were thought to be original Orphic hymns

> set to some kind of simple monodic music which Ficino believed echoed the
> musical notes emitted by the planetary spheres, to form that music of the
> spheres of which Pythagoras spoke. Thus one could sing Sun hymns, or Jupiter
> hymns, or Venus hymns attuned to those planets and this, being reinforced by
> the invocation of their names and powers, was a way of drawing down their
> influence.†

Such practices, developed by Hermeticists and Magi like Pico Della
Mirandola, Francesco Giorgio and Cornelius Agrippa, engendered
a complex network of musical-magical associations which could
involve names, numbers, planets, plants, colours, talismans,
instruments, times of day, etc, etc. This process perhaps reached its
apotheosis in Michael Maier's *Atalanta Fugiens* (1618), a book of
highly detailed and enigmatic emblems, each of which illustrated
various esoteric philosophical-alchemical teachings and each of
which 'had a musical, as well as a pictorial, mode of expression'.‡
  During the first half of the seventeenth century there were
curious overlaps between the fading Hermetic tradition and the
dawning Age of Reason: Kepler believed in the harmony of the
spheres, Descartes was accused of being a Rosicrucian,‡ and even

---

*See, for example, Lorenzo's famous speech in *The Merchant of Venice* (V.i.):
  'There's not the smallest orb which thou behold'st
  But in his motion like an angel sings,
  Still quiring to the young-eyed Cherubims;
  Such harmony is in immortal souls,
  But whilst this muddy vesture of decay
  Doth grossly close it in, we cannot hear it.'
And in *Henry VIII* the dying Katherine refers to '*that celestial harmony I go to*'
†Yates, 1978, p. 78
‡Yates, 1986, p. 82. A footnote refers the reader to a fuller discussion of the music in
Atalanta Fugiens in John Read's *Prelude to Chemistry* (London, 1936), pp. 213–54, 281–9
‡The Rosicrucians were popularly believed to be invisible. Descartes pointed out that since
he was visible *ergo* he wasn't a Rosicrucian: an argument that was necessary as well as logical
since there was a witch-hunt against Rosicrucians at the time. See Yates, 1986, pp. 115–16

Isaac Newton, the arch-mechanist, was deeply involved in alchemy
(particularly Maier's writings) and apparently believed 'he had
found his system of the universe shadowed forth in Apollo's lyre,
with its seven strings'.* But, gradually, a combination of religious
persecution, materialist philosophy and mechanistic science drove
Hermeticism and its associated disciplines like numerology and
alchemy out of mainstream culture and into a plethora of obscure
occult groups, many of which still survive and still claim Egyptian
origins.†

With the advent of Newtonian physics, the widespread use of the
printing-press and numerous other social, technological and
philosophical changes, the nature of Western music changed too.‡
An emphasis on notation and the adoption of the tempered scale
(which led to a unique exploration of tonality) separated Western
music from both its own past and the musics of other cultures.
Participation became an increasingly specialized activity, impro-

*Yates, 1986, pp. 204–5
†The Freemasons, for example, seem to have come out of the Hermetic tradition (see Yates,
1986, pp. 206–19). Bernal notes: 'The Masons, who included almost every significant figure
in the Enlightenment, saw their religion as Egyptian; their signs as hieroglyphs; their lodges
as Egyptian temples; and themselves as an Egyptian priesthood' (quoted in the *Guardian*
2/3/87). Bernal remarks that the Masons of the late sixteenth and early seventeenth centuries
almost certainly thought of the ancient Egyptians as being white. Both James and
ben-Jochannan argue that the ancient Egyptian mystery schools really were the origins of the
Masonic lodges, and that Freemasonry was thus a black movement at root. There is certainly
a long tradition of African-American Freemasonry, the first black lodge, called African
Lodge Number One, being established in Boston in 1787 (Southern, 1983, p. 71).
Rosicrucianism also survives in African-America: in the sleevenotes to his *Musique D'Afrique
Nouvelle Orleans* LP, clarinettist Alvin Batiste reports that the music on the album originated
in the early 1970s when 'I was studying with the Rosicrucian order (AMORC) and beginning
to apply the Rosicrucian Principles to music'
‡Though tangential to the scope of this 'Postscript', there have been some interesting
sociological studies that attempt to situate musical language in the social, intellectual and
economic structures of its time. See, for example, Durant and, particularly, John Shepherd's
essay 'The Musical Coding of Ideologies' in Shepherd *et alia*. Shepherd argues that the
pentatonicism of European medieval music articulated the ideal feudal social structure, while
the later language of tonality was inherent in the structures and worldview of Western
industrial society. Moreover: 'Tonal music is, above all, the music of explicitly sequential
cause and effect – a cause and effect, that is, which depends, in the fashion of materialism,
upon the reduction of a phenomenon undergoing explanation into "indivisible" and discrete,
but contiguous constituents that are then viewed as affecting one another in a mono-causal
and linear manner.' (pp. 106–7)

visation died out, and the music itself was divested of its mystical and ethical resonances. The crisis that Western art music faced in the early twentieth century can perhaps be seen as a result not only of the intellectual exhaustion of its internal processes, but also of their loss of meaning, since the kind of composite, spiritually-centred culture in which such meaning resides no longer existed in the West. This may also explain why many modern composers, trying to reintroduce a spiritual dimension to their music, have turned to esoteric or non-Western traditions (for example, Scriabin's interest in Theosophy, Satie's in Rosicrucianism, Cage's in ancient Chinese philosophy); and why various mystical elements have been reappearing in music, like the colour correspondences of Scriabin and Messiaen or Stockhausen's statement that the four soloists in *Sirius* are 'the musical embodiments of the four cardinal points, elements, sexes, times of day, stages of growth and seasons of the year'. In such a context it is impossible to overestimate the significance of African-American creative music, which has not only reintroduced improvisation into Western music on a wide scale but also, through the contributions of Duke Ellington, Albert Ayler, John Coltrane, Sun Ra, Muhal Richard Abrams, Anthony Braxton, Leo Smith, Horace Tapscott, Cecil Taylor and many, many more, re-emphasized both music's spiritual aspects and its unifying role in the impulse towards a composite world culture.

Ironically, just as modern science is now describing the universe in terms analogous to those of the ancient mystics,* so it is also beginning to accord sound the same potency as they did. The work of Ernst Chladin, Hans Jenny and, more recently, Ralph Abrahams at the University of California, has demonstrated the effects that different sounds can have on different types of matter; often the sounds creating beautiful patterns that resemble both natural forms and ancient mystical symbols. The effects of sound on human beings has also been studied and music is known to influence pulse

---

*See, for example, Capra, 1983. Language may be a factor too: see Steiner's discussion of the 'metalinguistics' of Benjamin Lee Whorf: 'Whorf finds the paradox that the "semantic field" of numerous so-called primitive communities segments experience into a phenomenology which is closer than that of the Indo-European language family to the data of twentieth-century physics and *Gestalt* psychology' (p. 92). Steiner particularly compares Whorf's analysis of Hopi language, which has no concepts of sequential time or motion in our senses of the words, with the perceptions of contemporary astrophysics and wave-particle theory. It seems Braxton has a point about the West's 'mono-dimensional' language

rate, blood pressure, brain waves and heart rhythm;* music therapy, perhaps not entirely dissimilar to that practised by Pythagoras, is now an established area of medicine and scientific research.

Hamel cites two contemporary scientific authors who are trying to reintegrate music into a composite cosmic design: 'In his books *Der horende Mensch, Akroasis, Harmonia Planetarum* and above all in *Orphikon*, Hans Kayser demonstrates. in rigorous scientific and mathematical terms that, in chemistry, atomic physics, crystallography, astronomy, architecture, spectroanalysis, botany etc, there exists an underlying framework of whole-number ratios such as we hear in notes – as octave, third, fifth, fourth.'† He also mentions Wilfred Krüger, whose writings examine, among other things, the relationship between musical ratios and the internal structures of different atoms: 'One of the deepest secrets of Pythagorean secret teachings, the sacred *Tetraktys*, is traced in Krüger's work to the prime elements of organic life, the nucleic acids.'‡ In the more mystical realm, Rudhyar has explored the numerological and metaphysical connotations of the harmonic series and the septenary tone cycle, drawing extensively on Hindu, ancient Greek and Gnostic mythology.‡

To end on a less controversial note, many New Physicists have come to see the universe in terms of levels of vibration, a flow and flux of various energy waves differentiated by frequency (or number), such as the waves of the electro-magnetic spectrum. It is these kinds of considerations which have led a modern scientist like Donald Hatch Andrews to declare that 'the universe is more like music than matter'; though in so doing he is merely echoing the voices of the ancients, whose wisdom regarding the forces that

---

*In *Tri-axium Writings 1*, Braxton mentions that Richard Teitelbaum was a pioneer of Brain Wave music (p. 333)

†Hamel, 1978, pp. 105–6

‡Hamel, p. 107. Such correspondences are carried into even more speculative realms by Lamy, 1981, who tries to equate the significance of number in Egyptian creation myths with the internal structures of both the hydrogen atom and the male spermatozoan (pp. 8–18). The idea is also anticipated by James (chapter VIII). If this all seems beyond belief, consider that the Dogon people of Mali have had, for at least several hundred years, a complex knowledge of the Sirius star system that still seems to be, in some respects, in advance of current Western astronomy. See Adams, in Sertima (ed), 1985

‡Rudhyar, 1982, pp. 55–88

music set into motion was admirably summarized by the sixth-century encyclopaedist Isidore of Seville in his *Etymologiae*:

'Nothing exists without music, for the universe itself is said to have been formed by a kind of harmony of sounds, and the heaven itself revolves under the tones of that harmony.'

POSTSCRIPT 2

'IN THE LIGHT OF THE GREATER FORCES': A
NOTE ON *TRI-AXIUM WRITINGS*

> But we do not merely protest; we make renewed demand for freedom in that
> vast kingdom of the human spirit where freedom has ever had the right to dwell:
> the expressing of thought to unstuffed ears; the dreaming of dreams by
> untwisted souls.
>
>   – W.E.B. DuBois, *The Notion of Intellectual Freedom*

In view of the limited availability of *Tri-axium Writings* it seemed
essential to make some attempt here to discuss their central theses.
However, given their size (three volumes, 1,600+ pages), their
complexity and my own limited space, neither a detailed critique
nor even a comprehensive survey of their contents has proved
feasible. So I must emphasize that what follows is by no means a
complete account of *Tri-axium Writings*: for instance, I make no
reference to their structure (in which Braxton employs three 'levels'
of investigation) nor to the 'integration schematics' which occur
throughout the text (these being diagrammatic representations of
the very abstract relationships that Braxton discusses).* Nor do I
cover every area of Braxton's concerns: for instance, I omit mention
of his sections on specific musical genres (the post-Cage continuum,
jazz-rock etc, etc), on music in various European and Asian
countries, and on the radical US political movements of the 1960s.
Rather, what I have done is to extricate what seem to me to be the
central concepts of Braxton's worldview and briefly outline these,

*See p. 309fn for the example that Braxton uses in his 'Introduction' to all three volumes.

using *Tri-axium Writings* as a reference source, though losing inevitably much of the subtlety and detail of argument. Until funds are provided to make the complete writings available to the greater public, I'm afraid we're still working in the context of 'you take what you can get'.

Tri-axium Writings 1 begins with a chapter entitled 'Underlying Philosophical Bases' in which Braxton discusses the nature of creativity with respect to three particular contexts: world music, Western art music and trans-African music. Creativity, he argues,

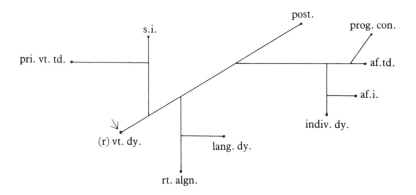

Integration Schematic

The arrow indicates the subject of the schematic, here (r) vt. dy. (the reality of vibrational dynamics), as it relates to post. (postulation), in the contexts of 1) s.i. (source initiation), involving pri. vt. td. (primary vibrational tendencies); 2) rt. algn. (reality alignment), involving lang. dy. (language dynamics); 3) af. td. (affinity tendencies), involving indiv. dy. (individual dynamics) as related to af. i. (affinity insight), and involving prog. con. (progressional continuance).

Obviously the schematics are extremely complex and require close familiarity with Braxton's terminology (or an extensive glossary, as in the *Tri-axium Writings* themselves), so it is not possible to deal with them in this 'Postscript'. However, the reader should bear in mind that they constitute an 'extended information platform' which provides an extra dimension to the arguments of the text. I'm indebted to George Lewis for the observation that whereas most philosophies comprise a static hierarchy of concepts, Braxton's schematics allow him to develop a dynamic approach and to express, graphically and precisely, the changing levels and degrees of significance his concepts have in relation to each other.

'has to do with "doing" as a means to celebrate and "affirm" the vibrational forces that dictate "living" '. Thus music is not *about* music: 'rather music, sculpture, dance and painting are connected to "cosmic zones" and have to do with "cosmic matters"', and so form and the elements of form, such as harmony and rhythm, are linked to cosmic correspondences and the transmission of forces: 'Creativity can be viewed as a manifestation of a given cosmic, social and vibrational (cultural) alignment and the science which determined how a given form is actualized is related to spiritual, mystical and functional considerations with regard to what I will call higher forces.'*

This understanding of creativity, says Braxton, has long been implicit in what he calls world group cultures, where creative disciplines like music and drama are not seen as separate or professional activities, but are integrated into a composite, spiritually-based culture which affirms, in ritual, 'the essence foundation of its culture group's meta-reality position' and thus helps to unify society. He talks about the 'multi-implicational realness of creativity', citing both the Indian mantra (as a form which 'dealt not only with the science of a given sound in functional terms but also with the meta-reality of that sound') and the Nile Valley Mystery System. (as an early example of 'a composite information and spiritual system for culture dynamics') and stressing the need to explore all facets of creativity, including its relationship to disciplines, like astrology, currently neglected and undervalued in Western culture.

He also examines the role of improvisation in world musics, suggesting it is the means by which individual self-expression (including the feeling of the moment) can take place within a disciplined and ritual culture:

Improvisation – as it is 'ised' in the world group aesthetic – has to do with the ability to function in a given context in accordance with each individual's own vibrational flow. In the functional context of African creativity where form is ritual – each individual, while utilizing the language content of the occasion, is in the position of interpreting the nature of what that given reality means subjectively, objectively (or bi-jectively). The totalness of this relationship can be viewed as individuals creating in 'actual time' from a composite essence alignment that also affirms the meta-reality of the culture in the 'doing'

T-a W1, pp. 141

(creating). The realness of this condition thus affects the individual, communal and spiritual well-being of the culture.*

However, the de-spiritualization of Western society and the gradual collapse of its traditional cultural verities during the last 2–300 years has meant that Western art music became separate from world music and developed according to intellectual, or existential, criteria – such as the expansion of its own inner logic systems – rather than with regard to spiritual values or essence factors. This empiricism (which goes hand-in-glove with materialism and mechanistic science and is part of the overall direction of Western civilization) has resulted in separation and specialization, in the elevation of the composer over the player, and in an emphasis on technique and 'correct' playing at the expense of improvisation. It is the playing out of these processes which, Braxton suggests, led to the crisis of Western art music in the first half of the twentieth century.

The third factor in this Braxtonian musical equation is trans-African music. One consequence of slavery was that African cultures were transplanted to the Americas, and in the US an African-American music tradition grew up which found itself in the anomalous position of being a spiritually-based music, aligned to the world group, yet forced to exist within the confines of a materialist Western society. It is this unique situation from which African-American music both derives its great potential (as a force to respiritualize Western culture and end the unjust global dominance of current Western values) and faces its greatest danger – because, says Braxton, the music is a) misdocumented by the Western media, who misjudge and misdefine it using inappropriate Western aesthetic standards; and b) misunderstood by the commercial sectors of Western society, who ignore its spiritual essence, distort its reality by appropriating its surface features as 'style' or 'spectacle', and try to make it conform to mainstream (i.e. white) cultural values – a process Braxton refers to as 'source transfer'.†

In *Tri-axium Writings 2* Braxton focuses more closely on the relationship between creative music and what he calls 'the spectacle

T-a W1, p. 36
†See Ibid, pp. 97–103

diversion syndrome', or 'what America has rather than culture'. He argues that because of various historical factors, including slavery and the virtual annihilation of the native American, America has developed a mainstream culture that is not only racist but also peculiarly hostile to alternative value systems; especially those from within its own world culture group minority populations.* Thus, mainstream culture values spectacle (what is of *interest*) rather than substance (what is of *use* for living); that is, entertainment rather than creativity.

> For if the highest understanding of creativity in world culture terms has to do with activity that reaffirms the vibrational alignment of its culture group (as a means to establish both how to live and the composite dynamics of its spiritual intent); what we have instead in America when we talk of entertainment is activity that moves to take our minds off of reality.†

The spectacle diversion syndrome is, he says, an integral part of American culture's vibrational lining; it is the chief means by which alternative or protest movements (like the beatniks and the hippies) are turned into fads and so absorbed into mainstream culture; it creates the illusion of change (fashion) so as to prevent real, fundamental change taking place. It represents the constant movement of 'nothing to nothing'.

One serious effect of the spectacle diversion syndrome is its interference with what Braxton calls 'affinity dynamics';‡ that is,

---

*Braxton suggests that the mistreatment of the native American and the widespread use of slavery, at the outset of modern American society, 'has produced a profound vibrational karma' for that society which has yet to be worked through. If this is true, it must also be true for modern Europe, which began with the massacres of thousands (perhaps millions) of women as witches, followed this with over two centuries of colonialist murder and exploitation, and climaxed, in the current century, with two world wars that brought with them the Holocaust and the atom bombs on Hiroshima and Nagasaki. History, it seems, substantiates Alice Walker's claim that 'under the white man every star would become a South Africa, every planet a Vietnam'. ('Only Justice Can Stop a Curse', in Walker, 1984, p. 341)

†*T-a W2*, p. 16

‡Ibid, pp. 52–95. With regard to music, Braxton earlier identifies two principles – affinity insight (1) and affinity insight (2) – from which creative music in all cultures functions. The latter, (2), establishes creativity 'as a social factor' that promotes both 'functional unification' and 'social interchange and harmony'; it then becomes 'the vibrational flow that moves towards "composite knowingness" on the physical plane'. The other principle, affinity insight (1), works as 'a vibrational factor which moves to solidify the correct spiritual and vibrational alignment of the culture': this helps to determine 'how the intellectual and

the way in which particular people and culture groups are aligned, or vibrate, to different 'information lines' (loosely translatable as ways of living and the knowledge encoded therein). Because Western culture views itself as superior to, or more advanced than, other world cultures (past and present), and because of its currently dominant position in global politics, it distorts and suppresses world group information lines, subjecting them to the spectacle diversion syndrome and trying to realign their affinity dynamics. And since Western society is basically controlled by a small group of very rich, white men, who define everything in terms of their own affinity alignment, this is bad news for everybody else. It's particularly bad news for African-Americans because their affinity dynamics are already under threat from what Braxton calls 'gradualism' and 'the grand trade-off'. Gradualism refers to the redefining of information in the interests of the redefiners (he gives as examples the way Egypt has been written out of classical Greek history, and the white 'takeovers' of both big-band swing and rock'n'roll);* the grand trade-off refers to the belief prevalent in post-slavery Western society that black people are, for instance, 'great tap dancers' while white people are 'great thinkers'† – that is, black people are allowed to be creative only within specific 'low culture' zones in order that Western society can avoid facing the full implications of slavery and the pillage of Africa.

> Europeans have historically been interested in keeping black people in the 'exotic zone' as a means not to deal with the significance of Africa. It is important to understand that the mantle of 'black exotica' is not separate from the notion that black people are not thinking human beings and, as such, the raping of Africa was not a negative act towards a civilized people.‡

---

spiritual affinity relationship within the culture is to be "affirmed"'. In fact, (1) can be seen in terms of affirmation, of moving towards transformation; (2) in terms of 'celebration', of moving towards stabilization. For instance, says Braxton, Charlie Parker's activity 'documented the emergence of the affinity insight (1) principle after the Second World War (which represented a transformation period to black Americans)' (*T-a W1*, pp. 121–4). In the glossary to *Tri-axium Writings* Braxton gives the two principles a slightly different emphasis: affinity insight (1) is to do with the relationship between self-realization and spiritual understanding; affinity insight (2) is to do with the relationship between self-realization and 'one's own "life realness"'

*T-a W1, pp. 292–4. For a detailed account of the prevalence of this kind of ethnocentrism, see Preiswerk and Perrot, 1978

†Ibid, pp. 301–8

‡*T-a W3*, p. 288. Perhaps it's worth reminding readers what the 'raping' of Africa actually

As a result of all these factors, says Braxton, the affinity dynamics and 'vibrational options' of African-Americans have been redefined (and internalized) in narrower and narrower terms, so that nowadays 'few black people can perceive of themselves in an extended context without feeling as if they have violated the proper vibrational reality of black culture'. In fact, *all* people outside the principal affinity alignment of Western culture are not only forced to think of themselves as being less than they are (or could be), they also face the real threat of vibrational oblivion. Such people (who may include groupings like non-whites, women, poor people, white mystics, etc etc) are constantly forced to struggle to define their own reality; a struggle which in turn often serves to fragment these alternative forces, since each group becomes entrenched around its own 'reality base' and insists *this* is the essence (rather than an aspect) of what has to change.* Yet meaningful change can only take place if it is seen in terms of composite, not isolated, functionalism.

> There can be no real change unless the composite dynamics of planet injustices are corrected – and this involves the particular reality dynamics of black people, women's liberation, the American Indian, human rights all over the planet, ecology, new politics, new spiritualism, etc etc. The significance of any particular focus of activism has not only to do with what it poses for its isolated reality base but must include what it poses for the greater dynamics of composite change (this is true even though 'one must start at one place at a time').†

Thus, the protest movements of the sixties, as they became more separate and extreme, sacrificed the chance of long-term composite change to the needs of short-term isolated activism, and so failed to deliver the promise of their original ideals. In fact, within the context of US politics, and with particular reference to the welfare of black people, Braxton notes that 'nothing has changed, unless in many cases for the worse'.

---

entailed. Oliver reports that, 'Over 300 years it has been estimated that anything between ten and thirty million African slaves were shipped from their homelands. J.C. Furnas estimates that between fifteen and twenty million arrived in the New World and that some three to four million died on the passage' (p. 67). Dr ben-Jochannan estimates the total number of Africans killed through slavery and colonialization between 1503 and 1865 as more than 100 million: the word he uses is 'genocide'

*T-a W2, pp. 96–131
†Ibid, p. 122

In a chapter called 'Reality Aspect of Creative Music',* Braxton examines some of the means by which Western values are enforced on the composite society, and the dynamics of change thus negated. In particular, he looks at the institutions through which creative music is filtered (television, radio, record companies, promotional agencies, newspapers, colleges) and in which it is likely 'to be utilized as a diversion factor by pseudo-intellectual groups and definers' who 'exoticize alternative functionalism with many of the concepts of "hipness" that surround the music'. (Braxton allows elsewhere that Western culture's distortions of alternative creativity may not be a goal, so much as a consequence of the fact that 'in many cases, the realness of alternative definitions are simply outside of Western culture's affinity relationship with information'.)† Whatever the case, the outcome is still that alternative creativity is denied media coverage until it can be redefined in accordance with 'what these people feel they already know' or decide is desirable to know: that is, until the real potential of (for example) the music is disguised within 'sanctioned definitions' which do not threaten an established order that is founded on the values of capitalism. Basically, says Braxton, 'there is no real appreciation of any kind of creativity not viewed as commercial' and so 'Western culture is slowly bringing the dynamics of creativity down to its lowest possible level because of limited economic interest and gain'.

He is particularly scathing about the role of journalism within Western society, remarking at one point that 'this culture has come to the juncture where whether or not a given area of information is true is beside the point . . . We call this syndrome "freedom of the press"'.‡ In *Tri-axium Writings 3* he devotes a section to 'jazz criticism' and the false ideology it espouses.‡ The history of this journalism is, he suggests, the history of white failure to understand black music, in the main because 'the secrets that surround the vibrational thrust of black music' fall outside of Western terms of reference. To begin with, Western commentary has never recognized that 'vibrational reality' rather than 'methodological diversity' is what determines 'the realness of world creativity'; nor has it

*T-a W2, pp. 313–427
†T-a W3, p. 199
‡T-a W2 pp. 367–8
‡T-a W3, pp. 235–308

realized the importance of affinity dynamics, but rather assumed that creative music has the same affinity alignment as Western culture. The result of these misconceptions is that Western journalism has mistakenly focused on isolated aspects of music functionalism – the mechanics of harmony, rhythm etc – as 'a measuring tool for the composite reality of the projection'; yet 'the science of a given form in black creativity has always followed the vibrational necessity of the invention' and not vice versa.

This misunderstanding of African-American music's vibrational level is paralleled by a failure to appreciate its extended functional dynamics: in particular, improvisation, as 'a vibrational continuum that differs from moment to moment/from person to person', has consistently flummoxed Western critics' reliance on 'empirical information degrees (this means this, and this means that)'. Thus, commentators 'completely overlook the meta-implications' of the music and instead assess each player according to whether he/she executes the science of the music 'correctly' (notions of correctness being derived from Western art music and/or 'rules' which critics have extrapolated from the particulars of previous 'great solos' and tried to turn into 'universal laws'). Yet:

> The fact is, improvisation as practised in the working arena of black creativity is related to many other factors that are outside the actual 'doing' in the music. I am writing of a functional area that utilizes both a fixed and open operational scheme – whose ultimate significance has nothing to do with the execution of its co-ordinates but is instead concerned with how a given participation is able vibrationally to affirm what is being dealt with.*

Braxton goes on to examine jazz journalists' use of gradualism and the grand trade-off, explaining his notions of 'the across-the-tracks syndrome', 'the reality of the sweating brow' and 'the concept of the good night' (which I've already discussed, see pp. 114–16 above). He also points out that:

> Western culture has long utilized black creativity as a lever to invoke some

*T-a W3, p. 248. C.f. Cecil Taylor's statement: 'Most people don't have any idea of what improvisation is . . . It means the magical lifting of one's spirits to a state of trance. It means the most heightened perception of one's self, but one's self in relation to other forms of life . . . It has to do with religious forces . . .' (Quoted on the sleeve to the *Live in the Black Forest* LP)

aspect of its own desires – either with respect to spiritualism, sexuality, rebellion, or to get individually or collectively rich. But in every case, there has been no attempt by the Western establishment to view black creativity and/or its related information on its own terms.*

Here too, it's still 'business as usual'.

The section on 'Black Notated Music'† argues that the same Western misconceptions which have dogged black improvised music also dog African-American composition. For one, black people are not even supposed to enter such a 'high culture' zone – despite the facts that a) the earliest known use of notation has been traced to ancient Egypt, and b) European classical music itself was partly rooted in Spanish Moorish sources. For two, Western critics have never understood that black notated music, especially when used within the context of creative music, has a completely different role from notation as used in Western art music.

> Notation as practised in black improvised creativity is not viewed as a factor that only involves the duplication of a given piece of music – and as such an end in itself. Rather, this consideration has been utilized as both a recall factor as well as a generating factor to establish improvisational co-ordinates. In this context notation is utilized as a ritual consideration and this difference is important for what it signifies about extended functionalism. For in this position notation can be viewed as a factor for establishing the reality platform of the music – dictating the harmonic and rhythmic sound-path of activity and also as a centre factor . . . Notation in this context invariably becomes a stabilizing factor that functions with the total scheme of the music rather than a dominant factor at the expense of the music.‡

Braxton traces the evolution of particular 'projections' within the continuum of black creative music: blues, boogie, ragtime, the creative orchestra tradition. Each one, he stresses, 'has functioned with respect to both its functional dynamics and its vibrational identity'. Only in Western culture are these aspects separated.

In the section on 'Science and Creativity'‡ he further claims that the existential perspectives which characterize Western views of creativity similarly shape its notions of science; although,

---

*T-a *W3*, pp. 289–90
†Ibid, pp. 1–50. The modern African-American composers to whom Braxton gives special mention are Talib Rasul Hakim, Wendell Logan, Alvin Singleton and Olly Wilson
‡Ibid, pp. 35–6
‡Ibid, pp. 51–87

paradoxically, Western culture sees the two disciplines as being entirely separate. This is a fundamental error, since both are functionalisms whose basic purpose is:

> to understand better the reality of things, as it pertains to either the laws sustaining 'this region' or as it pertains to the greater cosmic realness of being. The reality of science is the same as all creativity – that being 'doing in the light of the greater forces' and 'doing as a means to uncover what is to be uncovered' – and nothing more.*

Braxton differentiates between three levels of science: 1) vibrational, 2) theoretical, 3) applied. The first, comprising studies like astrology, magic, parapsychology and philosophy, is currently ignored by a Western science that considers the 'truth' of a phenomenon to be solely to do with how it works, not with its 'meta-reality implications'. The result is a scientific establishment that suffers from an 'inability to recognize the total context of actual life – and life sensitivity', as is shown by the history of the nuclear industry and the proliferating man-made hazards to the environment. Science needs to reintegrate intuition and spiritual awareness into its functionalism because 'the fact is, dynamic functionalism without a spiritual basis means nothing . . . contemporary technology without a feeling for humanity is not impressive . . . dynamic productivity while half the world is starving is not just'. Or, as he later asks, 'what good is technical brilliance and political domination if there is no reason for living?'

At the heart of transformation, says Braxton, lies cosmic justice. This is why the position of women is so important, and why the chapter on transformation which concludes *Tri-axium Writings 3* begins with a section on 'The Reality of the Creative Woman'.†
Women have contributed to all cultures at all times, but their efforts have often been overlooked or undervalued. Braxton admits that 'the present planet situation' makes it almost impossible for women to commit their lives to creativity, and acknowledges that many male musicians are suspicious of women players and unable to deal with them: thus, few efforts have been made to include

*T-a W3, p. 52
†Ibid, pp. 428–68

women in creative music, which means that 'the meta-reality of the music might not be perceived of as relevant to where women want to go'. In this situation we all lose, because:

> Unless sexism is eradicated, I see no immediate chance to gain insight into our potential – as earth people. Moreso, the realness of both sexism and racism stands as a major blockage to real transformation. It is not just a question of women having the right to be creative – obviously this is what is needed – but it is also necessary for men to understand that without the participation of women in creative music, an important factor is missing from the music. In other words the fact that half of the population is denied the opportunity to be creative is also reflected in the actual music . . . the resulting creativity we are left with has to be looked at as being less than what it should (and could) be.*

Braxton goes on to explain his belief that African-American music is essentially 'bi-aitional' (that is, it incorporates both the masculine and the feminine vibrational principles within its vibrational lining and is thus open to both male and female participation) because it was rooted in a Church whose main concern was the wellbeing of the entire black community, men and women.† However, because of the particular socio-political context in which bebop was forced to evolve, and because it was seen as disreputable by the black middle class, a masculine slant was accentuated that has remained in the music through succeeding projections. (This is not to say that sexism did not exist in African-American music before bebop, nor to deny that there has been a long lineage of women 'masters' throughout all periods of the music, including the bebop and post-bebop eras, whose work has often been neglected or undervalued by male critics.‡ What we need, Braxton suggests, is not only more research into these areas,

---

*T-a W3, p. 437

†I later queried this point with Braxton on the grounds that *all* varieties of the Christian Church tended to be extremely patriarchal in both ideology and social structure. He agreed that this was so, but emphasized that women had always played a particularly active role in the African-American Church and that it would be a mistake to overlook that activity because of the 'apparent identity' of the institution. There were many such institutions and organizations, he added, which 'if the women stopped working, would fall immediately'. He also cited the virtual exclusion of women from the black radical movements of the 1960s as a major reason for their collapse

‡For information on the history of women musicians, see Cavin, Dahl, and Placksin. Cavin suggests that jazz has specifically female origins and is derived from the ritual musics practised by the voodoo queens of New Orleans

but research guided by new, non-masculine value systems in which musicians are not graded in terms of 'better' and 'best'.)

In the final sections of *Tri-axium Writings 3* Braxton turns to the concept of transformation itself: it is, he says, 'the word I use to speak of vibrational-cosmic and physical universe cycles that take place on the chemical and vibrational universe level'. This transformation happens whether we want it to or not and whether we're ready or not (indeed, it may involve tragic events like war, plague and violent destruction): but our activity here and now may affect whether the changes turn out to be positive or negative. In this perspective, everything we do can be seen in terms of 'the responsibility of the position'; that is, each form of participation, from political activism to playing or writing about creative music, comes with its 'implication degrees', which are to do with what participation means to '(1) the individual, (2) to the greater collective or movement that generates the dictates of that individual and finally (3) to the greater country or planet space'. Each of these degrees can have positive effects, but Western society tends to affirm the importance of the individual degree at the expense of the others; and it is the third degree which represents 'the highest degree for the greater good of humanity'.

The breakdown of Western culture's composite centre and the rapidly growing planet-wide rejection of Western values suggest that a new transformation may be in the offing; so the aim, suggests Braxton, must be for 'the unification of human beings on the planet' and for 'the solidification of an alternative composite spiritual and cosmic stance'. This means a new understanding of spirituality, a fresh appreciation of 'essence' and purpose, the relearning of ritual, perhaps even the recognition of 'new gods': plus, there is an immediate and urgent need for 'the redistribution of land, wealth, food and information dynamics (knowledge and availability of knowledge)'. Such changes will inevitably mean the downfall of Western civilization; and while 'the collected forces now dictating earth order' will not relinquish their power willingly: 'there is also the realness that people are struggling to understand one another – and there is also sufficient evidence outlining dynamic positive activity throughout the culture and planet'.

Beyond the shadow of the coming transformation lies the great dream of synthesis, and making that dream a reality may be our best, perhaps even our only, hope of a future in which our children will be free to follow their own dreams and visions of change.

POSTSCRIPT 3

LECTURE NOTES

i) LANGUAGE MUSIC

Braxton's lecture at the Guildhall is to do with the ways in which the pool of 'language types' that he has built up over the years can be employed in the compositional process. He takes one example of his 'language types', staccato line formings, and demonstrates (on record) its various functions as a generating form: these are (a) as a language generating form (in the solo context); (b) as a material generating form (as notated material inserted into the co-ordinate music); (c) as a principle generating form (as a given variable used to determine the nature of the music); (d) as a multiple generating form (inserted into a larger context). Most of the 100+ language types, or various combinations of them, can be used in these same ways.

As an example of (a) he plays *Composition 26B* (*Solo: Live at Moers Festival*, side A track 1). There are no notated sequences in this first example; this type of variable is simply the combination of various sound components, primary and secondary formings, as 'routes for exploration dynamics'. There is, says Braxton, 'no development here at all, because we are not dealing with development or preconceived objectives'. Think of the music in terms of lights or shapes; or think of it like baking a cake – the basic ingredient is the staccato line forming, but there are others, maybe ten to fifteen working ingredients, and the challenge of each interpretation is to integrate all these variables – so it's a very open music.

As an example of (b) he plays *Composition 40B* (*Six Compositions: Quartet*, A–1). Basically this is an ABBA structure in which A is

notated material and B is improvised. The staccato line formings
here are part of the notated material.

As an example of (c) he plays *Composition 23A* (*New York Fall
1974*, B–3). This is a cell structure shape which integrates staccato
line formings 'as a basis to establish territories for improvisation'. It
consists of notated and language music variables, and has different
focuses in each of its sections. The staccato line formings can be
established in several different ways; the musicians are given this
variable (and others) as a principle at different points in the music
and are free to actualize it however they think best serves the
context and the needs of the moment. Here, the language types
'help define the nature of the space and provide a context for its
investigation'. Another example of (c) is *Composition 23P* (*Four
Compositions* (*1973*, A–2), where the staccato line formings establish
a basis for open-ended collective improvisation. On this track the
staccato line is played by the bassist, who can refer to it at any time,
even though once it has been established the ensemble move into
'open space'.

As an example of (d) he plays an extract of *Composition 25*
(*Creative Music Orchestra*). Here each instrumentalist has a part to
be played in his or her own time, a type of 'indeterminate structure
which can also be found in John Cage, Duke Ellington and some
African musics too'. Each musician has twenty balloons to
manipulate, the staccato line formings here being part of 'a multiple
sound/fabric environment'.

ii) REPETITION AND STRUCTURAL GENERATION

This is an amalgam of Braxton's lectures at Newcastle, Sheffield
and Leeds, all of which were concerned with the various uses of
repetition in his music.

To begin with, there are three separate categories of composition
that focus specifically on repetition: Kelvin, Colbolt and Kaufman
(the names derived from the initials of friends). In the Kelvin
series, the musician is given a particular rhythmic shape or pattern
which can be used in various (sometimes specified) ways; in
Kaufman, this practice is extended into a 'multiple context', where
repetition is only one of various components employed (a modified
use of Kaufman on record is *Composition 55* on *Creative Orchestra
Music 1976*, B–2); the Colbolt series is concerned with 'sound

blocks', a static use of repetition where, for example, an orchestra may keep repeating one chord but with a tiny variation each time. 'It's like watching fireflies,' says Braxton – little flickers of light in an unchanging space: 'Some of these compositions can go on for eight hours or more. I don't have any on record yet.'

He returns to Kelvin, describing it in terms of 'additive and subtractive variables as a basis for repetition' and talking of 'phrase generating structures as material for ensemble improvisation'; for instance – (he sings a phrase) – 'that particular phrase, very complex rhythmically, serves in Kelvin as the centre of the improvisation, which is based on that shape, going in and out of that shape, almost like phasing, but I don't want to use that word because Steve Reich's co-opted it. But the Kelvin generation structures establish phrase grouping contours as a platform for collective improvisation.'

To begin with, though, he plays two versions of a solo example of Kelvin (*Composition 26F*, *Alto Saxophone Solos 1979*, B–3 and *Solo: Live at Moers Festival*, B–2). He says that *26F* is based on the concept of a repetition continuum in which the music changes via the gradual change of events, either through adding to or subtracting from or modulating the basic elements of the music. The material here can consist of simple configurations (ideas built from one or two notes) or multiple configurations, in which ideas are built from several different figures or shapes that act as generators for repetition.

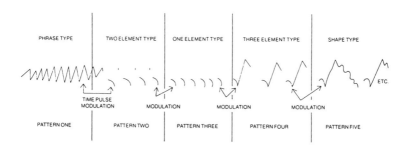

Repetition Continuum (e.g. *26F*)

PATTERN VARIATIONS

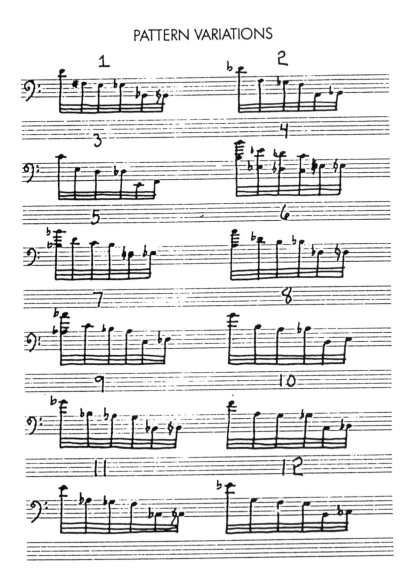

Pattern Variations in *Composition 34*

He also plays two ensemble uses of Kelvin, *Compositions 40(O)* and *6F* (*Montreux/Berlin Concerts*, B–1 and C–1 respectively), examples in turn of repetition as a phrase generating structure and repetition as a factor for group improvisation.

He then moves to the other, more general, uses of repetition in his work. These comprise (a) as a pattern operative, (b) as a principle structure operative, (c) as an additive factor, (d) as a material generator.

As an example of (a) he plays *Composition 34* (*Six Compositions: Quartet*, A–3). This shows the use of pattern as a unifier (in a different sense to Kelvin); here each instrumentalist is given twelve permutations of a six-note pattern that can be put into open space in any order, and used in various ways (as a 'centre' between improvisations, as a focus for solo improvisation, as a platform for opposition improvisation, etc). See p. 324.

As an example of (b) he plays *Composition 40A* (*Six Compositions: Quartet*, B–1). Here a sixteen-note scale system, which is the basis for all the notated material in the composition, is also played by the bassist (in a variety of ways) to establish the principle for improvisation in the extended solo section of the piece (this too can take a number of options: for example, on the record the pianist plays an opposition solo to the bass).

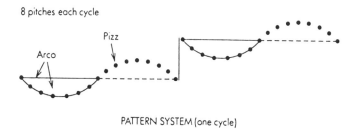

Pattern System from *Composition 40A*

The ways in which the bassist can vary this pattern include 1) to raise the pattern an octave when repeated; 2) to play it twice, then raise it; 3) to intermix it with short open improvisations and re-establish it at different time intervals; 4) to isolate given aspects of the notated material for particular elaboration.

Another example of (b) is *Composition 59* (*Creative Orchestra*

Music 1976 B–3), where repetition is used as a principle generating factor in the context of a large ensemble. Here sound attacks and pulse repetitions are used as principle generators under the solos, the sound attacks setting into motion different language variables. The two extended improvisations, played on the record by Roscoe Mitchell and Braxton respectively, occur 'in the same sound field environment, but the variables change'; each change being cued by the repeating sound attacks. (Braxton adds that twenty different language variables are available to the soloist, who can choose which to play: thus, each performance will be different.)

As an example of (c) he plays *Composition 23C* (*New York Fall 1974*, A–2), explaining that, in terms of the quartet music, this category also functions as a material structure. 'It's like Kelvin, except we're talking here of *fixed* notated structures.' He says this piece came about when he was practising the flute and 'I just stumbled on to something'. The use of additive structures happened here through 'notating the form spread dynamics' of the original idea.

As an example of (d) he plays *Composition 38A* (*New York Fall 1974*, B–1), remarking that repetition here is not so much a material generating factor as a means to define *vibrationally* the space of the music. The repetition is part of a notated section inserted into the space, and improvisation here need not necessarily refer to it at all (as would be required in a genuine example of a material generator). Braxton mentions that material structures were the first use of structure in his music: they originally comprised notated material, set into open space, that required no extra response from the musicians (i.e. they improvised from whatever vibrational presence the notation had established rather than from its particular co-ordinates). Another example of (d) is *Composition 69N* (*Six Compositions: Quartet*, A–2).

(A diagram of these uses of repetition has already appeared on p. 173 above. Braxton pointed out that pulse track structures represented a further category of repetition use in his work, but he barely mentioned them in the lectures since they constitute a special and complex use of repetition: see pp. 195–206 above for a full discussion of this.)

iii) SPATIAL DISTANCE AND ALTERNATIVE
STRUCTURAL MODELS

Braxton's lecture at the Royal Academy of Music is based almost entirely on his *Compositions 76* (for trio) and *82* (for four orchestras).

He begins with *82*, describing his multi-orchestral work as to do with 'the factoring of distance' in music. The primary elements of *82* include sound lines, sound mass clusters, and several of the language types: the construction variables include (1) multiple formings, (2) mass formings, (3) directional forming logics, (4) synchronist forming logics (i.e. orchestras in tempos independent of each other, using other zones of alignment), (5) independent line formings, (6) tracking, (7) solo events. The aim, he says, 'was to create a sound environment like star systems'. The four orchestras are each placed near a corner of the auditorium, with the audience in the middle: both audience and musicians are on swivel chairs, and the musicians are also on different levels so 'vertical sound energies' can be created. There are twelve specified playing-directions in the score, each designated by a colour and each having astrological and numerological significance.* The conductors, one

*In his notes to the work, Braxton elaborates thus: 'All of the multi-orchestral compositions in Series A & B will be drawn from a pool of master co-ordinates (i.e. time and density sound formations) as a means to establish a particular investigatory approach . . . All of the materials in these master co-ordinates are in colour and each situation has been created with the understanding that alternative (and later transformational) philosophical and spiritual degrees would be transposed on each master shape – as that shape meets the requirement for its particular cosmic law (relating to the question of information sorting and designation). Each colour can then be viewed with respect to both its astrological and numerological equivalent. Moreover, the use of this technique would also involve its directional assignment – that being each colour would signify a given area of the performing space (for the musicians to project the music to) while at the same time also provide the actual notated music (for execution).'
Concerning numerology: in *Tri-axium Writings 3*, Braxton says that transformational science will alter our understanding of the concept of numbers, which will 'expand to include its feeling degree'. One plus one does not necessarily equal two, and even 'the whole concept of one' needs to be re-examined. 'The multi-implications of numbers have to do with many facts which are not yet practised in contemporary science' (p. 80).
In view of Braxton's interest in numerology I decided to supplement the earlier astrological character reading (pp. 78–81 above) with one based on numerological principles: I did this myself, using the standard method set out in Cavendish (pp. 47–9). Basically, every person has two significant numbers – a name number and a birth number. The birth number is found simply by adding together the figures of the date of birth: in Braxton's case, 4 June

for each orchestra, are linked by television monitors (which the musicians also follow when required to play 'directionally' away from their conductor). The whole project, Braxton summarizes, was 'a fresh attempt at placing, or route-ing sound'.

He talks about the circumstances of the recording, explaining that lack of rehearsal time meant that the work on record is both incomplete and played at too slow a tempo; also, most of the directional aspects of the music are lost on a stereo hi-fi. 'I guess you only hear about forty per cent of the music on stereo speakers.'

He turns to the use of sound mass clusters in *82*, as illustrating one set of 'alternative structural models'. There are various kinds of sound mass cluster: some use different sound lines or timbral exchanges, for example, in which different groups of instruments move in synchronized directions, their inner moving sound particles travelling like energies across the space: there are also static block clusters, or sound walls, which he likens to 'giant searchlight beams moving across space, families of instruments moving across a prism, across frozen blocks of space'. He differentiates them visually (horizontal axis is duration, vertical axis is pitch, each 'line' is played by a different group of instruments):

$1945 = 4/6/1945 = 4+6+1+9+4+5 = 29 = 2+9 = 11$. To find the name number (according to modern numerological practice), you find the number equivalent of the letters in the name, using the below grid, and add them together:

1	2	3	4	5	6	7	8	9
A	B	C	D	E	F	G	H	I
J	K	L	M	N	O	P	Q	R
S	T	U	V	W	X	Y	Z	

So: A　N　T　H　O　N　Y　B　R　A　X　T　O　N
$1 + 5 + 2 + 8 + 6 + 5 + 7 + 2 + 9 + 1 + 6 + 2 + 6 + 5 = 65 = 6 + 5 = 11$

Usually any number above nine is reduced to its digital root, but numerologists often except the numbers eleven and twenty-two as having a special significance. As Braxton's birth and name numbers both add up to eleven, he is presumably one of the special cases. But what does eleven signify in numerological terms? 'Eleven and twenty-two are particularly fortunate and excellent numbers, representing a higher plane of experience than the numbers one to nine. *Eleven* is the number of revelation and martyrdom. Elevens are people who have a special message to give to the world. They may become great teachers and preachers, inspired visionaries in religion, science, politics or the arts . . . Intensely subjective, they live by the light of their own inner vision and they may not always understand the real characters and needs of the people around them . . . They are powerful personalities of great vigour, convinced of the rightness and importance of their mission and prepared to make any sacrifice for it.' (Cavendish, 1984, p. 53)

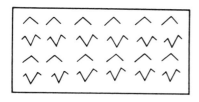

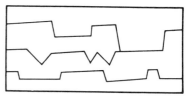

Sound Mass Cluster   Static Block Cluster
Using Sound Lines

For a second example of alternative structural models, Braxton cites the use of different line forming strategies in *82*. Plate-forming strategies, for instance:

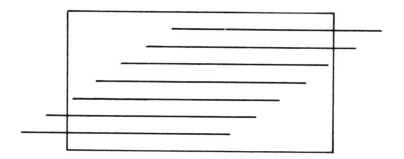

Or wave-forming logics, visually designated as:

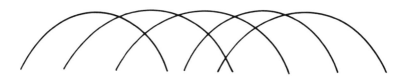

'Even if I don't focus on a visual image, it manifests itself,' Braxton remarks at one point, adding that 'only later would I begin to understand the power of images. The real implications of what they could mean escaped me as a young man, but hopefully I'm learning about them now.'

He moves on to *Composition 76*, describing it as 'an entry into the world of drama and gesture', 'a response to the advancements of the AACM' and 'a structured improvisational sound state (fifty per cent structured, fifty per cent improvised) based on visual and modular improvisational strategies'. 76 is for three instrumentalists, each of whom may function on several single-line instruments plus various percussion and sound tools and voice; its modular notation 'factors in colour and shape as emotional variables';* and it requires each player to be in costume and placed on separate platforms, 'so each postulation is a gesture, a movement'. Braxton likens the music to Japanese painting: 'very stark, no ruffles or flourishes, just the stroke of the sound, each created in four or five seconds'.

He refers to the three degrees of affinity postulation and insight, and explains that in 76 he asks the players not to think of the third degree (self-realization) but to concentrate on the second ('with respect to the ensemble'), to balance the fixed, notated formings with short, improvisational bursts: 76, he says, is 'a series of events hung in space', a series of moments with no development, a form of dialogue in which 'extended improvisation is not primary'. It is also, he adds, a context designed for the use of an arsenal of instruments. He cites as inspirations Cage's *Imaginary Landscapes*, Stockhausen's *Zyklus* and, particularly, the challenges of the AACM; namely, here, creating 'extreme vocabularies of sound', the use of 'outside sound possibilities' such as sound tools, and the use of 'vocal improvisations and manipulations'.†

*Though the use of colour and shape here is different from *82*, there is a similar underlying purpose: 'This then is a music designed with respect to multi-dimensional extension – that is: a structure designed with respect to both astrological (spiritual) and scientific information . . . At the heart of this work is my desire to create a composition that in "transformation" can function as a "ritual" activity (when the composite astral and vibrational precepts are established for rebuilding culture for the next cycle.' (From Braxton's notes to 76: see also p. 222 above)

†In view of Braxton's belief that nothing is really new, it's perhaps worth mentioning that Tibetan ritual music is 'built upon the deepest vibrations that an instrument or a human voice can produce', that it is 'not concerned with the emotions of temporal individuality' and that its musical material consists of 'a number of basic sound and note patterns that can be combined and varied at will' (see Hamel, 1978, pp. 71–3, quoting Lama Anagarika Govinda's *The Way of the White Clouds*). In his notes to 76, Braxton describes the work as 'a temple of sound' and talks of it as 'realigning a kind of ancient chant context ("as in a monastery or closed time/space") back into our consciousness'

He draws an example of 76's modular notation:

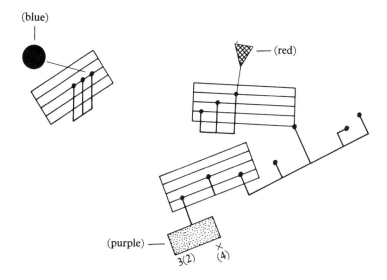

The musician can enter the module at any point, and go around it in any direction (i.e. playing the notation 'backwards' if necessary). All primary shapes (circle, triangle, oblong etc) are in colour (as is some of the notation) and designate improvisation, the different colours and shapes indicating the kinds of improvisation to be played (see p. 222 above). Braxton also gives an example of the kind of coding system used in the score for 76: '3' on the diagram above means 'play a three-phrase grouping', '2' then a two-phrase grouping, '4' then a four-phrase grouping; the brackets indicate 'change instrument'; the 'X' indicates the option of singing the phrase grouping (the players each have a megaphone in their arsenal of sound tools). The modules of notation appear on a series of cards, which can be placed in any order (so every performance is different); there are also two 'primary notated insert sections' which are placed by the composer. The piece, Braxton concludes, is 'a static sound space music' and was conceived to be 'like a slow-moving dance'.

CATALOGUE OF WORKS, 1966–86

This is a slightly abbreviated and smaller-format version of the official catalogue published by Synthesis Music.

1. **Piano Piece No. 1 (1968)**

   Six pages of notated music.

2. **L-J-74**
   C

   for four instruments (1968)

   Twenty-one pages of notated music for any four single line instruments.

3.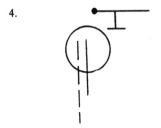

   for eleven instruments (1968)

   Twenty pages of notated music for any eight single line instruments, piano, and two percussion (one inside piano).

4.

   for five tubas (1968)

   Twenty-two pages of approximate pitched notation.

5.

   for piano (1968)

   Three pieces; six pages of notated music.

6. **SIXTEEN COMPOSITIONS (1966–72)**

   A collection of short compositions for the creative improvisational ensemble. Unless indicated, this material can be utilized by any combination of players and/or instruments. This material can be interlinked in any way desired and can also be integrated with material from *Compositions 23, 40* and *69*.

   a. **67M**
      F-12

      Arco march.

b. **GRR-P**
   AM(SGK)

c. **C-M = B05**
   │
   7
   Circus piece.

d.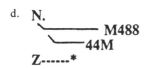

Fast pulse relationships.

e.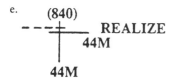

Vocal piece for trio.

f. **73° KELVIN**
   │
   │
   Series of repetition structures.

g.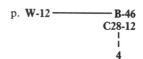

For quartet.

h. **DM-REX**
   (OPQ)

   W

   Open fast pulse structure.

i.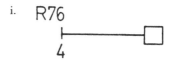

Tempo structure for quartet.

j. **J-572**
   (431)-1
   Ballad for quartet.

k. **N508-10**
   (4G)
   Line for fast pulse extension.

l. └─────────── **JNK**
   4°
   Ballad.

m. └─────────── 4-16
                 CJF
   Ballad.

n. **S-37C-67B**
   │
   F7
   Medium tempo structure.

o. **G-10⌐4ZI**
        FK=47
   Ballad structure.

p. **W-12** ─────── **B-46**
            C28-12
            │
            4

   For vocalist and ensemble.

7. **D-J-30**
N

for orchestra (1969)

Thirty-one pages of graphed notation. Instrumentation: Six woodwinds (any single-line instruments), three trumpets, three trombones, two tubas, two string basses, two percussion (instruments unspecified).

8. **SOLO MUSIC – BOOK ONE (1966–9)**

Eleven compositions for a solo instrument utilizing visual notation and co-ordinate instructions. Can be performed in any combination as well as with material from *Compositions 26* and *77*.

a.

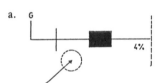

Ballad language.

b.

Medium fast pulse relationships.

c.

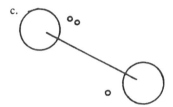

Ballad language.

d.

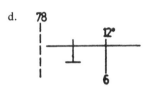

Very slow language with silence.

e.

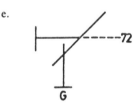

Medium fast relationships.

f.

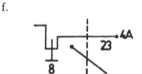

Fast pulse intensity language.

g.

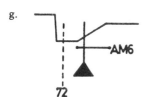

72

Multiphonics – medium pulse.

h.

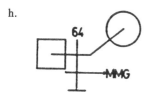

64

Trills – medium slow pulse.

i. **BWC-12**
   N-48K

Relationship series.

STAGE ONE
Medium fast pulse.

STAGE TWO
Medium fast pulse.

STAGE THREE
Medium fast pulse with silence.

STAGE FOUR
Fast pulse language.

STAGE FIVE
Medium pulse.

j. **NBH-7C**
   |
   K7

Eighth note patterns.

k. **JD-C**
   IP-(LIL)
   |
   M

Ballad.

9. **SH-G46**
   |
   (337)

for four amplified shovels (1969)

Fifteen pages of cell structure notation to be utilized with one large pile of coal – with costumes and choreography. In addition to this material, electronic modulation is also required.

10.

for solo piano (1969)

Nine pages of symbolic notation to be performed in any order or time length.

11.

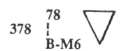

378 | 78
    | **B-M6**

for creative orchestra (1969)

Two pages of visual notation for any ten to thirty instrumentalists. (Most of piece was lost.)

12. **W-306**
    (427)

    for woodwind quintet (1969)

    Twenty-three pages of notated music for flute, oboe, clarinet, horn, bassoon.

13. **LJ-75**
    C

    for four instrumentalists (1970)

    In three sections – approximately seven pages for any four single-line instruments.

14.

$$\sum\text{]}---\overset{\text{10}}{\underset{\text{3}}{\text{M6M7}}}$$

    for solo instrumentalist (1970)

    15″ × 24″ page of schematic notation with instructions to be performed in any time length – for any instrument.

15. **RKM-B6**
    MSO ¦
        ¦
        7

    for four instruments (1970)

    Three pages of regulated symbolic notation for any four instruments.

16. **GN6**
    (X′70B) . . . K

    for four pianos (1971)

    Ten pages of schematic music and symbolic notation to be prepared by the performer – for whatever duration desired.

17. **8KN-(B-12)**
    |
    R¹⁰

    for string quartet (1971)

    Sixteen pages of visual notation to be prepared in any order or length for performance. A performance may utilize all of the material or whatever is desired or needed.

18. **8KN-(J-6)**
    |
    R¹⁰

    for string quartet (1971)

    Sixteen pages of visual notation to be prepared in any order or length for performance. Performers may use all of the material or whatever is desired or needed.

19.

    for one hundred tubas (1971)

    Twenty pages of schematic music and instructions to be prepared for four groups of marching ensembles – twenty-five musicians in each – in any order and for any length.

20. **SBN-A-12**
    66K

    for two instruments (1971)

    Four pages of single line (monophonic) notation with instructions for the preparation of one magnetic tape for accompaniment.

21. **CK7(GN)**
    437

    **for recorded tape with or
    without instruments (1971)**

    Ten pages of notated music that
    can be played or not played by
    from one to as many instruments
    as desired. Plus five pages of
    instructions for the preparation of
    one magnetic tape – or several
    magnetic tapes.

22.

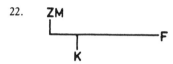

    **for four soprano saxophones
    (1971)**

    Twelve pages of schematic and
    symbolic notation to be prepared
    in any order or performance
    length.

23. **SIXTEEN COMPOSITIONS**
    (1971–4)

    Second series of short
    compositions for the creative
    ensemble (see *Composition 6*).
    This material can be interlinked
    in any combination and can also
    be integrated with material from
    Compositions 6, 40 and *69*.

a.

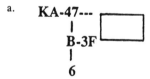

    Monophonic line – medium
    slow pulse.

b.

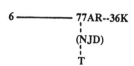

    Line fast pulse – in stop time.

c.

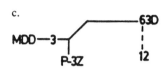

    Repetition line – additive.

d.

    Medium tempo line.

e. **489M**
   70-2--(TH-B)
   M

    Slow to very fast pulse line.

f. **H-488**
   F64

    Medium tempo line with
    broken time accents.

g.

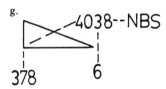

    Medium tempo line with
    accent shifts.

h. **G-647**
   (BNK)-□

Medium slow structure.

i. **RNTG**
   (NN̦SK)
   |
   M

Medium fast line – Spanish
melody.

j.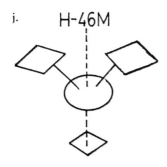

Medium fast to very fast line.

k. **60666C**
   66M

Monophonic line.

l. **H-204**
   $3 = \dfrac{HF}{3}$

Slow pulse structure.

m.

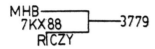

Medium fast line.

n.

Medium fast relationship
complex.

o.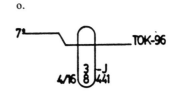

Fast pulse relationship
complex.

p. (3-F6) ——— ¦- - - ANR
   |
   674H
   (3712)
   ¦
   B

Ballad.

24. **L J-84M**
    C

for orchestra (1971)

123 pages of notated music. Instrumentation: 3(1 pic)+3+
3(b.clar.)+3(c.b. bassoon),
2+4+3+1, per (gongs, vibes,
marimba, cymbal) harp, strings:
16+12+8+6+4

25. **RBN---3°**
    K-12

    for creative orchestra (1972)

    Composition in twelve parts for creative orchestra, to be arranged in any order, that calls for the added use of 112 bells for its performance as well as 100 balloons. This work utilizes several forms of procedure, from conventional notation to open material, and is designed to create a dynamic platform for creative orchestra music – from solo to collective postulation. Instrumentation: 4 reeds (multi-instrumentalists if possible); 4 trmpt, tb, piano, 2 sb, 2 per (2 kits if possible).

26. **SOLO MUSIC – BOOK TWO**
    (1970–4)

    Second series of solo compositions for the creative instrumentalist (see *Composition 8*). Can be performed in any combination as well as with material from *Compositions 8* and *77*.

    a. **NR-12-C**
       (33M)

       Ballad.

    b. **JMK-80**
       CFN-7

       Staccato language.

    c. **MMKF-6**
       (CN-72)

       Medium tempo bebop language.

    d. **178-F4**
       312

       Ballad.

e. **AOTH**
   MBA
   H

   Phrase shifting language.

f. **104°-KELVIN**
   |
   M

   Repetition structure.

g. **RZ04M(6)**
   AHW

   Multiphonics. Medium fast pulse.

h. **NNWZ**
   48   KB
   N

   Ballad.

i. **(348-R)**
   |
   C-233

   Ballad.

j. **RFO-M°**
   |
   F(32)

   Medium pulse composition.

27. **L J-800**
    C

    for orchestra (1972)

    Eighty-one pages of notated music. Instrumentation: 3 fts (1 pic), 2+1 E. hn+2+1 b clar+2+1, contra-bassoon, 4+4+3+2 tb, 12+6+6+6+6, 4 per (gongs, b. dr., tymp, cym).

28. **LAYSA-4**

for six musicians and dancers (1973)

Ten pages of notated music with improvisation for six musicians and dancers. Duration: ca. 90 minutes. Scored for two reeds (multi-instrumentalists if possible), two brass (multi-instrumentalists if possible), synthesizer and percussion.

29. **FIVE COMPOSITIONS (1973–5)**

Set of five short compositions for piano and two wind instruments. This material can be intermixed together or played separately. Basically these works are vehicles for extended improvisation.

a. **HB-(NRR)Z**
   | **BKM**
   |
   37

   Medium pulse line for thematic extension.

b. **(SD)CLK**
      (66)-TN

   Monophonic ballad line for open improvisation.

c. **AQ(WH-M)**
   | **COH**
   |
   BN-5

   Medium fast structure with sixteenth note thematic material.

d.

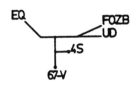

Medium fast structure with sixteenth note thematic material.

e. **DRQV-SUH**
   | **(BNV)**
   |
   TH

   Medium fast pulse structure with sustaining chords.

30. **P-JOK**
    S-D-12
    |
    |
    4

    for piano (1973)

    Eighty-three pages of phrase-sequenced notated music to be arranged by the performer in whatever order desired. This material can also be mixed with *Compositions 31, 32* and *33.*

31. **P-JOK**
    S-D-37
    |
    |
    4

    for piano (1974)

    Eighty-three pages of phrase-sequenced notated music to be arranged by the performer in whatever order desired. This material can also be mixed with *Compositions 30, 32* and *33.*

32. **P-JOK**
    S-D-31
    |
    |
    4

    for piano (1974)

    Eighty pages of phrase-sequenced
    music to be arranged by the
    performer in whatever order
    desired. This material can also be
    mixed with *Compositions 30, 31*
    and *33*.

33. **P-JOK**
    S-D-22
    |
    |
    4

    for piano (1974)

    Ten pages of phrase-sequenced
    notated music to be arranged by
    the performer in whatever order
    desired. This material can also be
    mixed with *Compositions 30, 31*
    and *32*.

34, 35, 36. **THREE
    COMPOSITIONS (1974)**

    A set of three compositions for
    synthesizer and two instruments
    to be utilized in live performance.
    Each of these works is designed to
    provide a context for structural
    improvisation.

    (34)

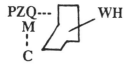

    Structure in three sections
    (medium fast) for
    synthesizer, winds (multi-
    instrumentalists if possible)
    and piano.

(35) **ARZH(N7)**
    G4D----64
    D

    Multiple structure for
    piano, winds (multi-
    instrumentalists if possible),
    and tuba.

(36) **HM-421**
    | **(RTS)**
    47

    Structure in three sections
    for synthesizer, one
    woodwind (B flat) and
    trumpet.

37.
    30
    ----------------EGM
    KBM
    |
    78

    for saxophone quartet (1974)

    Four pages of cell structure
    notation and instructions.

38. **TWO COMPOSITIONS (1974)**

    A pair of compositions for one
    single-line instrument and
    synthesizer.

    a.
    WH   70
    N----------------MMA
    ----)--R
    26

    Duo for clarinet and
    synthesizer.

b.

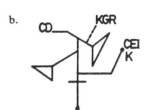

Duo for multi-instrumentalist
(any given instrument) and
synthesizer.

39. **ANZ-46
WM-2**

for creative orchestra (1974)

5 saxes (2 alto, 2 tenor, bass), 4
tpt, 4 trmb, guitar, piano, sb,
percussion. Nine pages of
regulated (adjustable) notation.

40. **SEVENTEEN
COMPOSITIONS (1974–6)**

This is the third collection of
compositions for the creative
ensemble (see *Composition 6*).
Unless indicated, this material
can be utilized by any
combination of players and/or
instruments, and can also be
interlinked in any way desired
with material from *Compositions
6, 23* and *69*.

a. **DK(RHX)T
GIL-6** |
                U

Medium pulse structure with
pattern under solos.

b.

Medium fast to fast line for
solo extension (chords are
optional).

c.

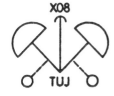

Madrigal-like slow pulse
structure.

d.

**ANNF
(GM-6)--** ▯
          |
         30

Medium fast pulse for
extension.

e. **ANSY
G-OH(RM)**
        |
        B

March structure for open
extension.

f.

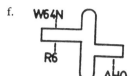

Medium fast chromatic phrase
structure.

g.

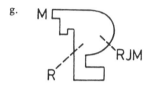

Ballad.

h.

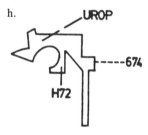

Medium tempo structure for
solo extension.

i.

F04(G)WN
OQO-26–

March with three collective
extension sections.

j.

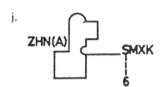

Medium pulse relationship
structure.

k.

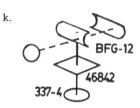

Medium to fast tempo line for
solo extension.

l.

ONZWT
(SNRU)B-4

Medium pulse relationship
structure.

m.

BOR----○ H
N-K64   S
(60)
M

Fast tempo line over bass
vamp.

n.
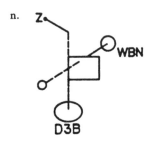

Concert A drone structure.

o. 72° KELVIN
   |
   L

Repetition structure.

p.
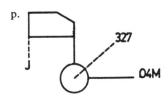

Medium tempo line for solo
extension.

q.
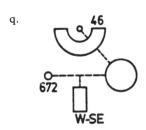

March structure for open
improvisation.

41. L-J-637
    C

for chamber orchestra (1974)

Eighty-three or sixty-two pages of

notated music (there are two
versions). Instrumentation: 1 ft,
ob, clar, bassoon, hn, tpt, trom,
b. trom, tb, per (chimes, gong, s.
gong, s.d., b. dr), strings:
4+4+3+3.

42. **INTRODUCTION TO CELL
    STRUCTURE AND
    LANGUAGE DESIGN**

for creative orchestra (1974)

Composition on four large pages
designed for the study and
practice of language
improvisation. For any
instrumentation.

43, 44. **TWO COMPOSITIONS
    FOR QUINTET (1974)**

A pair of extended compositions
for the creative quintet which can
be utilized in both a strict and
open procedural approach. Both
works are primarily designed to
establish a foundation for
improvisation – from solo to
collective. Each piece is scored for
one wind, one brass, piano, string
bass and percussion.

(43)
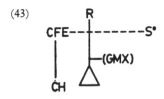

Medium fast pulse multi-
structure for extension.

(44) (FMQN)-RCM
     236-T |
                    |
                    QPB

Medium fast pulse structure
for extension.

45.

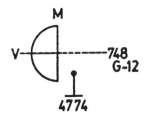

for creative orchestra (1975)

March for creative orchestra with solo and collective improvisation. Instrumentation: 3 saxes (E flat, 2 tenor), 1 b clar, 3 tpt, 3 trom (1 bs trom), tb, sb, piano, percussion (trap set).

46. **LQS-26**
   D

for ten instruments (1975)

Eighty pages of regulated notation. Instrumentation: flute, oboe, E hn, clar, b. clar, horn, tpt, trom, b. trom, tb.

47, 48. **TWO COMPOSITIONS FOR QUINTET (1975)**

A set of two compositions for the creative quintet ensemble context to be utilized in either a strict or open procedural approach. Both works are primarily designed to establish a foundation for improvisation – from solo to collective participation. Scored for 1 wind, tpt, trombone and rhythm section.

(47)

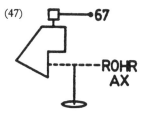

Medium fast/fast pulse structure for extended improvisation.

(48)

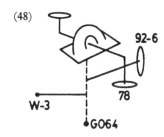

Medium/slow structure for extended improvisation.

49.

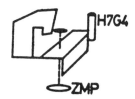

for one to twenty musicians with or without dancers (1975)

Eight pages of language notation to be prepared for performance. For any instruments, and for any duration.

50.

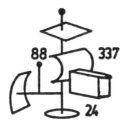

for two instrumentalists and two synthesizer players (1975)

Ten pages of sequence and visual notation.

51.

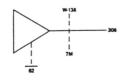

for creative orchestra (1976)

Fast tempo structure for creative orchestra. Instruments: 4 sax (2 alto, tenor, bass), 3 tpt, 2 trom, 1 bs trom, tb, piano, sb, percussion.

52, 53, 54.   **THREE COMPO-SITIONS FOR QUARTET (1976)**

A set of three compositions for the traditional creative music quartet context to be performed in any order, sequence and duration. The instrumentation is one single-line instrument, piano and rhythm section.

(52)

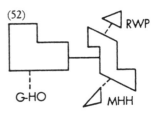

Medium/fast structure for tempo solo extension.

(53)

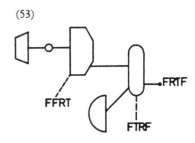

Medium fast pulse structure for open improvisation.

(54)

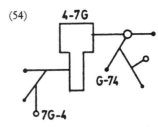

Medium pulse structure for solo and collective improvisation.

55.

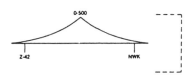

for creative orchestra (1976)

Medium tempo composition with
tempo and vamp solo bass.
Instrumentation: 4 sax (E flat,
alto, tenor, bass), 3 tpt, 2 trom, 1
b. trom, tb, vibes, piano, sb,
percussion (trap set).

56.

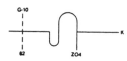

for creative orchestra (1976)
Slow pulse structure with live
electronics. Instrumentation: 2 B-
flat sax, 3 clar (1 b. clar), 4 tpt, 2
trom, 1 b. trom, tb, synth, 2
piano, sb, percussion.

57.

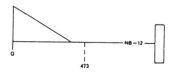

for creative orchestra (1976)

Slow pulse structure with open
improvisation. Instrumentation: 3
flts (2 doubles on B-flat sax), clar,
b clar, 4 tpt, 2 trom, 1 b. trom,
tb, 2 pianos, cello, vibes, b.
marimba, bells, and percussion.

58.

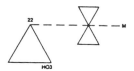

**for creative marching orchestra
(1976)**

Medium tempo march with solo
and collective postulation.
Instrumentation: 2 alto (1 doubles
on clar, 1 on flt), tenor, bari
(doubles on b. clar), 4 tpt (1
doubles on pic. tpt), 2 trom, tb,
sb, glock, 2 sn. dr. and marching
cymbals.

59.

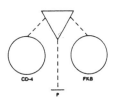

**for two soloists and thirteen
instrumentalists (1976)**

Composition for any two soloists
and chamber ensemble. The work
is constructed to utilize
completely notated sections as
well as solo and open
improvisational sections.
Instrumentation: 2 soloists, E-flat
sop sax, flt, clar, b. clar, 4 tpt, 2
trom, b. trom, tb, cello.

60, 61, 62. **THREE DUO
COMPOSITIONS (1976)**

Set of three compositions for
piano and one wind instrument.
This material can be intermixed
or performed separately.

(60)

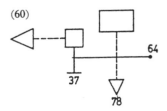

Extended composition with improvisation for clarinet and piano.

(61)

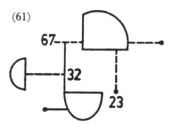

Short thematic structure for one single-line instrument and piano.

(62)

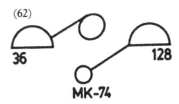

Extended composition for one multi-instrumentalist and piano.

63.

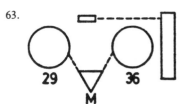

for two soloists and chamber orchestra (1976)

Composition for any two single-line instruments and chamber orchestra. This work utilizes conventional notation as well as open improvisational sections for both the soloists and orchestra.

64, 65, 66, 67, 68.   **FIVE COMPOSITIONS (1976–8)**

A collection of five compositions for the creative instrumentalist that utilize extended construction with improvisation. This material is designed for many different interpretational context possibilities. For any performance duration and instrumentation.

(64)

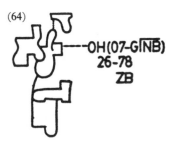

Extended structure for any two single-line wind instrumentalists or multi-instrumentalists. Medium/medium fast pulse.

(65)

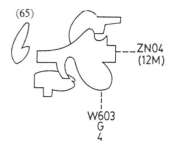

ZN04
(12M)

W603
G
4

Extended structure for E-flat soprano and trombone (or sb). Medium pulse.

(66)

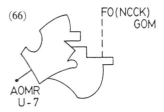

FO(NCCK)
GOM

AOMR
U-7

Composition for 1 B-flat instrument, sb and percussion to be utilized as a vehicle for extended solo postulation. Medium pulse.

(67)

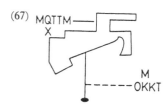

MQTTM
X

M
OKKT

Seven note repetition motif to be utilized as a pivot figure for improvisation.

(68)

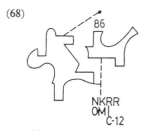

86

NKRR
OM
C-12

Medium fast structure for any saxophone, sb and percussion. For extended open improvisation.

69. **SEVENTEEN COMPOSITIONS (1976–9)**

This is the fourth collection of compositions for the creative ensemble (see *Composition 6*). Unless indicated, this material can be utilized by any combination of players and/or instruments, and can also be interlinked in any way desired with material from *Compositions 6, 23* and *40*.

a.

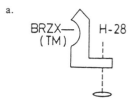

BRZX—
(TM)

H-28

Medium pulse structure for solo extension.

b.

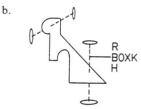

R
BOXK
H

Fast pulse structure with staccato solo support figure.

c.

Principle generating structure
for extended improvisation.

d.

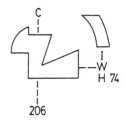

Ballad with arco bass repeating
figure.

e.

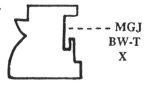

Relationship complex for
collective improvisation.

f.

Slow pulse structure for
extended collective
improvisation.

g.

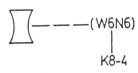

Medium/fast tempo line for
solo extension.

h.

Medium/fast pulse structure
for extended improvisation.

i.

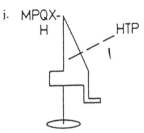

Medium tempo line for solo
extension.

j.

Fast pulse structure with
accelerating and retarding
patterns for extended
improvisation and/or solo
postulation.

k.

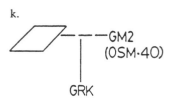

Staccato composition for
extended improvisation.

l.

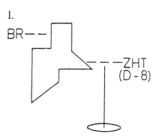

Medium fast line for solo
extension.

m.

Fast pulse structure with
triplet support pattern for solo
extension.

n.

Ballad for slow pulse open
improvisation.

o.

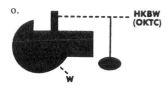

Medium slow pulse structure
for open improvisation.

p.

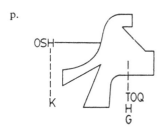

Composition in three sections
for open and collective
improvisation. Slow/medium
pulse.

q.

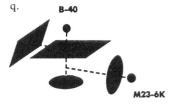

Repetition phrase pattern for
structural improvisation.

70.

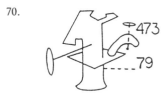

for quintet (1976)

Eight pages of composition with
improvisation for one wind, one
brass, piano, bass, percussion.

71.

for creative orchestra (1977)

Twenty-two pages of notated
music with improvisation for the
creative orchestra.
Instrumentation: 5 saxes (2 alto, 2
tenor, bass), 4 tpt, 4 trom (1 b.
trom), vibes, accordion, guitar,
piano, sb, percussion (trap set).

72. **EIGHT DUET
COMPOSITIONS (1977)**

Eight compositions for one single
line instrument and string bass.
Each composition is a vehicle for
extended improvisation and can
be utilized in whatever context
desired.

a.

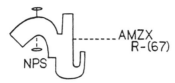

Medium pulse structure for
extended improvisation.

b. **H6OZQ-12
CKNM**
|
S

Fast pulse relationship
complex for extended solo
postulation.

c.

Medium tempo bebop line for
solo postulation.

d.

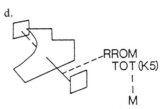

Fast pulse line for solo
extension.

e.

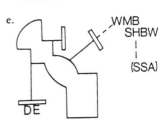

Medium pulse structure for
open improvisation.

f.

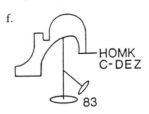

Medium fast structure with
dynamics co-ordination for
open improvisation.

g. **FFEF(GF)**
   EE-GF
    |
   EF

Monophonic ballad line for
slow pulse open improvisation.

h. **B-⌐ROQQ**
    CNC
     |
    W

Monophonic ballad line for
slow pulse open improvisation.

73.

for three instrumentalists (1977)

Fourteen pages of notated music
for three creative instrumentalists
(if possible, multi-
instrumentalists) that utilizes
extended composition and
improvisation. Can be performed
by any single-line instruments,
for any duration between ten
minutes and one hour.

74. **FIVE DUET COMPOSITIONS
(1977)**

A set of five extended
compositions for the creative duo
that is designed to establish a
particular structural context for
dynamic improvisation. All of
these works are totally scored
from beginning to end and as such
are not only 'heads' for thematic
extension.

a.

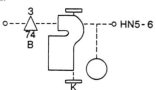

Extended structure for one B-
flat and one E-flat instrument
for collective improvisation.
Medium pulse.

b.

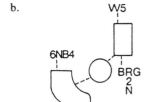

Extended composition for two
flutes. Medium pulse
collective improvisation.

c.

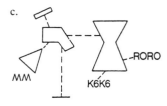

Medium pulse extended
composition for two multi-
instrumentalists (single-line
instruments). Instrument
designation must be prepared
(chosen) before use.

d.

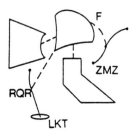

RQR
F
ZMZ
LKT

Medium pulse extended
composition for two
instruments in the same key.

e.

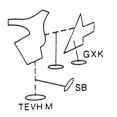

GXK
SB
TEVH M

Extended composition in three
sections for two instruments in
the same key. Medium slow
pulse.

75.

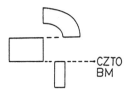

CZTO
BM

for three instrumentalists (1977)

Fifteen pages of multiple notation
in three or four sections that can
be performed together or
separately, for any three
instruments.

76.

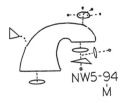

NW5-94
M

for three musicians (1977)

Twenty-seven cards of modular
notation for any three creative
instrumentalists (preferably
multi-instrumentalists) to be
performed in any order or
duration. Score in colour.

77. **SOLO MUSIC – BOOK
THREE (1977–80)**

Third series of solo compositions
for the creative instrumentalist
(see *Composition 8*). Can be
performed in any combination or
duration, as well as with material
from *Compositions 8* and *26*.

a. **GNG
B-(RN)**
|
R

Fast pulse relationship
language.

b. **RORRT
33H7T**
4

Fast pulse bebop-like phrasing
language.

c. **RKRR
(SMBA)
W**

Medium slow pulse with
diatonic triplet patterns.

d. **KSZMK**
  PQ
  EGN

Medium fast pulse language
with slap tongue technique.

e. **SOVA**
  NOUB
  V-(AO)

Five note scale language.
Medium slow pulse.

f.   **ATZ**
  GG-NOWH
  KR

Ballad with subtone techniques.

g. **VHR**
  G-(HWF)
  APQ

Medium pulse language with
whole tone scale and even
eighth note phrasing.

h. **NMMN**
  TOWR
  VK-N

Medium slow pulse language
with trills.

i. **Q**
  TOHR-W
  (IOI)

Medium pulse composition
with quarter note skips.

j. **ABZAZ**
  (BABZ)
  |
  A

Medium fast language with
harmonic minor basis.

78. **INTRODUCTION TO CELL
STRUCTURE AND
LANGUAGE DESIGN
NUMBER TWO (1977)**

See *Composition 42.*

79, 80, 81.   **THREE COMPO-
SITIONS (1977–8)**

A set of three compositions for
piano, two woodwinds (multi-
instrumentalists if possible) and
brass (multi-instrumentalists if
possible). Each of these works is
designed to establish a particular
kind of improvisation – from
thematic to open layered
structures.

(79)

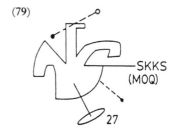

Extended medium tempo
structure for solo
postulation.

(80)

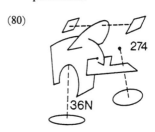

Slow pulse multi-structure
for open improvisation.

(81)

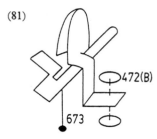

472(B)

673

Relationship structure in
three sections for extended
improvisation. Med/slow
and fast pulse.

82.

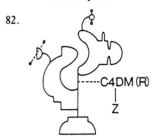

C4DM (R)

Z

for four orchestras (1978)

303 pages of notated music for
four orchestras and four
conductors. Each orchestra is
positioned to have the optimum
sonic possibilities for a three-
dimensional spatial music. All of
the musicians are seated on
rotating chairs with the addition
of television sets for regulation, as
well as specially built risers for
vertical sound possibilities. Each
orchestra has the same
instrumentation, that being 2
(pic) 1+1, 2 (sop clar) 1, 2+2+1
b trom + tb, harp, 5+5+5+4+3
and 3 per.

83.

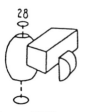

for orchestra (1978)

140 pages of notated music.
Instrumentation: 2 flts (1 pic), 1
oboe, E. horn, 3 clar (1 b clar) 1
bassoon, 1 contra-bassoon, 2+2+
b. trom, tb, harp, 6+6+6+4+3,
per (vibes, marimba, gongs, sn
dr, bs dr, cym, etc).

84.

HHH·Q
D

**for any number of instruments
(1978)**

Fourteen pages of symbolic
notation to be used in any order –
either completely or in part.

85, 86, 87, 88.   **FOUR DUET
COMPOSITIONS (1978)**

A set of four compositions for one
woodwind instrument and string
bass. Each piece is designed to
establish a particular conceptual
area for improvisation – both
thematically and structurally.
This material can also be linked
together for performance in any
combination desired.

(85)

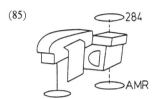

Medium tempo extended composition for solo postulation.

(86)

Extended relationship structure for collective and solo postulation. Medium/medium slow pulse.

(87)

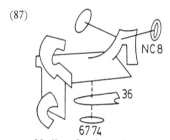

Medium fast/fast pulse extended structure for scored improvisation.

(88)

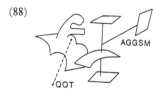

Medium slow extended structure for solo and collective improvisation.

89.

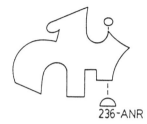

for creative orchestra (1979)

Twenty-seven pages of multiple notation. Instrumentation: 5 rds (any instr), 4 tpt, 4 trom, b. trom, tb, piano, synth, sb, 2 per (both on trap set).

90.

for any number of instruments (1979)

Eleven pages of graphed notation with additional instructions to be used in any order and for any duration.

91.

for creative orchestra (1979)

Twenty-six pages of notated music with improvisation, for the creative orchestra. Instrumentation: 4 ww (any inst), 3 tpt, 4 trom (1 b. trom), tb, piano, synth, sb, 2 per.

92.

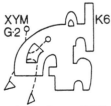

for creative orchestra (1979)

Twenty-six pages of notated music with improvisation, for the creative orchestra.
Instrumentation: 3 reeds (alto, tenor, bass), 3 tpt, 3 trom, b. trom, tb, guitar, piano, sb, per (set).

93.

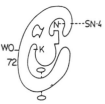

for creative orchestra (1979)

Twenty-five pages of regulated notation for the creative orchestra. Instrumentation: 4 reeds (multi-instrumentalists if possible), 2 alto, tenor, bass, 3 tpt, 3 trom, 1 b. trom, tb, synth, piano, sb, per (set).

94.

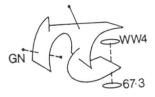

for three instrumentalists (1980)

Thirty-four pages of multiple and symbolic notation in three sections, for any three single-line instruments, that can be

performed in any order and duration. This composition is designed for the use of language improvisation, rather than as a thematic structure.

95.

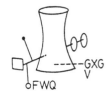

for two pianists (1980)

Forty-six pages of notated music for two pianists, each of whom also plays a melodica and a zither. To be performed with costumes (with special instructions for choreography if desired) for the purpose of 'preparation' for coming change (either vibrational or actual).

96.

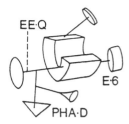

for orchestra and four slide projectors (1980)

240 pages of notated music for orchestra, four slide projectors and slides to be performed in a ceremonial concert context for positive transformation and historical re-solidification. Instrumentation: 3 flts+2+1 E. hn +3, 1 alto sax +1, 1+2+2, harp, 8+8+6+6+4, per (tymp, vibes, marimba, cym, etc).

97. **KELVIN SYSTEM STRUCTURES**

for any instrumentation (1966–84)

Ten pages of rhythmic notation for extended improvisation. Each composition can be utilized as a separate or combination platform (for creative subject material focus).

a. **206°-KELVIN R**

Staccato line grouping.

b. **303°-KELVIN H**

Quarter note grouping – platform.

c. **507°-KELVIN M**

Intervallic note grouping – platform.

d. **604°-KELVIN**

Curve line grouping – focus.

e. **689°-KELVIN K**

Trill line grouping.

f. **756°-KELVIN R**

Cluster sound grouping.

g. **800°-KELVIN W**

Pulse focus grouping.

h. **866°-KELVIN BH**

Legato contour line formings.

i. **920°-KELVIN G(N)**

Ascending contour principle formings.

j. **1008°-KELVIN MR**

Circular breathing formings.

98.

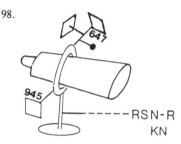

for four winds, two brass and piano (1981)

Fifty-eight pages of multiple and tracing notation for extended interpretation. This is a structural space for multiple strategies – involving notated and improvisational directives. Each part can be approached from either a single instrumental perspective or from a multiple instrumental perspective (i.e. that allows for doubling, tripling, etc.). Duration: ca. 40 min.

99. **SOLO MUSIC – BOOK FOUR (1978–83)**

Fourth series of solo compositions and vocabularies for the creative instrumentalist. Can be performed in any combination or duration, depending on the needs of the moment.

a.

Ballad region.

b.

Line complex.

c.

Metric gradient complex.

d.

Column logic (circular
breathing).

e.

'Grace note' logic (beam
columns).

f.

'Muffled sound' piece.

g.

'Dog barks' (logic).

h.

Medium pulse relationships.

i.

'Wo-wo' sound line pieces.

j.

Medium pulse pointillistic (intervallics)

k.

Square line complex.

100.

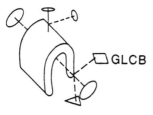

for fifteen instruments (1981)

Seventy-one pages of multiple notation for any thirteen wind and/or brass instruments with the addition of two percussion parts (tym, cym, bells, large and small drums).

101.

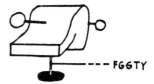

for one multi-instrumentalist (wind or brass) and piano (1981)

Twenty pages of multiple notation to be utilized for creative exploration. Duration: ca. 20 min.

102.

for orchestra and puppet theatre (1982)

271 pages of notated music for orchestra and three specially designed operating puppet figures (construction specifics are included with the score). This is a fantasy context that seeks to reawaken the wonder of imagery and ceremony. Instrumentation: 2 conductors, 3 flt, 3 ob, 3 E horn, sop clar, 2 clar, b clar, bsn, 3 tpt, 1 bari horn, b trom, tb, solo piano, 3 per (includes gg – large and small, tymp, cymbals) and strings: 8v1, 8v2, 8v3, 8vo, 6c, 4sb. A given performance of this work will also call for a crew to build and operate the puppets (plus specially designed staging directives, which are also included in the score). A performance of this work should be enjoyable for both children and adults. Duration: 90 min.

103.

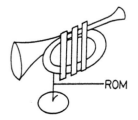

ROM

for seven trumpets (1983)

145 pages of notated music and
choreography for seven costumed
instrumentalists. A given
performance of this work calls for
the construction of specially built
risers and special lighting.
Duration: 45 min.

104. **COBALT SYSTEM
STRUCTURES
for any instrumentation (1966–
84)**

Pulse repetition system for
extended participation which uses
sound block structural materials.
These pieces can have any
duration.

a. **COBALT-AAX**
G

Sound line block.

b. **COBALT-AMS**
R

Sound point block.

c. **COBALT-MSK**
G

Mass increase block.

d. **COBALT-ZKK**
W

Trill line block.

e. **COBALT-ROH**
XK

Curve line block.

f. **COBALT-GNN**
(OX)

Intervallic line block.

g. **COBALT-ODCC**
Y

Legato line block.

h. **COBALT-TCHE**
T

Metric line block.

i. **COBALT-ZZO**
A-R

Relationship line block.

j. **COBALT-DJB**
L(R)

Beam line block.

k. **COBALT-XYZ**
(ZZ)

Mass decrease block.

l. **COBALT-NBILY**
AMF

Pulse line block.

105. THREE QUARTET STRUCTURES (1984)

a.

Ten pages of notated music for extended structural improvisation.
Instrumentation: wind, piano, sb, and per (set). Duration is relative. Structure contains pulse track material.

b.

Eight pages of notated music for extended structural improvisation.
Instrumentation: Clarinet, piano, string bass and percussion (set). Structure contains pulse track material.

c.

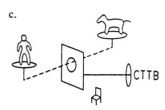

Light structure that can be used for extended improvisation, or as an isolated statement in itself.

106. SOLO MUSIC – BOOK FIVE (1982–5)

Fifth series of solo compositions and vocabularies for the creative instrumentalist. Can be performed as single or combination material (in conjunction with the complete solo materials of my music system) depending on the needs of the moment.

a.

Quarter tone pieces.

b.

Vibrato (line) pieces.

c.

Triadic spiral continuum (pattern).

d.

Relationship complex.

e.

Square line formings (fast pulse).

f.

'Phrase brick' formings (slow staccato line formings).

g.

Square phrasing lines.

h.

Ballad.

i.

Ballad.

j.

Pointillistic logic.

k.

Line logics (stages 1–4).

l.

Ballad (thematic extension).

m.

Line constructions (fast
pulse).

107.

**for two multi-instrumentalists
(wind or brass) and piano (1983)**

Seventy-nine pages of multiple
notation in five sections to be
utilized for creative exploration.
Duration: ca. 35 min.

108. **FOUR PULSE TRACK
STRUCTURES (1984)
for any instrumentation**

Each structure in this group can
be utilized as a separate or
combination structure – to be
used as a platform for extended
improvisation. This material can
be integrated with any mixture of
structures and/or strategies. Each
structure can be viewed as an

'imprint logic' that establishes its
own operational and conceptual
particulars.

a.

Eleven pages of notated music
with positioned improvisation
spaces for structural
improvisation. Duration is
open.

b.

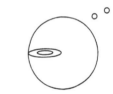

Curved line formings.

c.

Phrase grouping
constructions.

d.

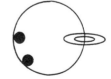

Medium tempo formings.

109. **KAUFMAN SYSTEM
STRUCTURES
for any instrumentation (1966–
84)**

Ten pages of multiple rhythmic
complex structures for extended
improvisation. Each composition
can be performed individually or
in combination.

a. **KAUFMAN-GGGGGGH**

Staccato complex.

b. **KAUFMAN-AAAAAAK**

Intervallic complex.

c. **KAUFMAN-RRRRRRT**

Curve line complex.

d. **KAUFMAN-WWWWWWX**

Intervallic line complex.

e. **KAUFMAN-RRRRRRb**

Trill line complex.

f. **KAUFMAN-bbbbMM**

Legato line complex.

g. **KAUFMAN-XXXXLLL**

Cluster forming complex.

h. **KAUFMAN-MMMM-(MZ)**

Accenting principle complex.

i. **KAUFMAN-GGGHHHMM**

Circular breathing complex.

j. **KAUFMAN-CCCC-T-CCC**

Pulse focus complex.

k. **KAUFMAN-AA-TT(XXX)A**

Metric note complex.

l. **KAUFMAN-QQQ(ZZZ)QZ**

Mass shifting complex.

110. **FOUR (SHORT) QUARTET
PIECES (1984)**

A set of four short (and relatively
easy) structures for extended
improvisation. Originally written
for my quartet, this material can
be used for any context – or
positive purpose.

a.

Thematic structure for
extended improvisation.

b.

Material structure for
extended improvisation.

c.

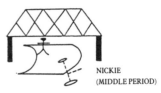

Material structure for
collective improvisation.

d.

NICKIE JOURNEYS TO THE CITY OF
CLOUDS TO MAKE A DECISION

Ballad structure for collective
improvisation.

111. **ENVIRONMENT STROLLS**
     (1970–84)

Eight pages of verbal instructions
for any instrumentation to be
used as a material and conceptual
source for extended
improvisation.

112.

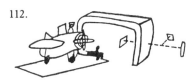

for creative orchestra (1983)

Twenty-one pages of notated
music and improvisation (solo and
collective) for the creative
orchestra. 5 wind (doubling and
tripling required), 4 tpt, 4 trom,
rhythm section (piano, bass,
percussion set), vibes, guitar.
Duration: ca. 25 min.

113.

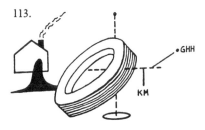

for one soloist, a large
photograph and prepared stage
(1983)

Seven pages of notated music and
'story instructions' for extended
improvisation. This is a
performance piece that utilizes
movements and special staging
dynamics. For any wind
instrument. There is also a special
version for piano, percussion and
guitar.

114.

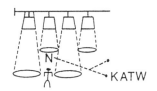

for any instrumentation (1984)

Four pages of notated material for
structural improvisation. C major
axis platform for creative
exploration. Scored for single line
instruments. Duration is open.

115.

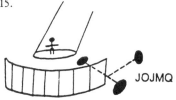

for any instrumentation (1984)

Line structure for extended
improvisation (with variable
tempo bottom and additional
pulse track materials). Open
duration.

116.

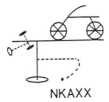

NKAXX

for four instruments (1984)

Nineteen pages of notated music
for extended structural
improvisation. Scored for
saxophone, piano, s bass, and per
(set), but can be refitted to any
instrumentation. Open duration.

17.

for any instrumentation (1984)

Principle generating structure for
extended improvisation.

**SOLO MUSIC – BOOK SIX
(1984–6)**

Sixth series of solo compositions
ınd vocabularies (strategies) for
he creative instrumentalist. Can
be performed as single or
:ombination material (in
:onjunction with the composite
iolo materials of my music
ystem), depending on the needs
ıf the moment.

a.

Intervallic logic (fast pulse).

b.

Melodic/static logic.

c.

Ballad (short).

d.

Contour logic.

e.

Squeak sound logic.

f.

Buzz sound logic.

g.

Smear sound logic.

h.

Phrase repetition

i.

Ballad (short).

j.

Intervallic formings (fast pulse).

k.

Octave/distance trill logics.

l.

Ballad.

119. **SOLO MUSIC – BOOK SEVEN (1985–6)**

Seventh series of solo compositions and vocabularies (strategies) for the creative instrumentalist. Can be performed as single or combination material (in conjunction with the composite solo material of my music system), depending on the needs of the moment.

a.

(Fast 'running' lines) parts 1 through 5.

b.

Ballad.

c.

'Bach' piece.

d.

Line forming construction.

e.

Slow pulse ballad.

f.

'Line steps' diatonic formings (bebop phrasing).

g.

Line multiphonic complex (beam).

h.

Multiphonics ('sparks').

i.

Med/dance.

TRILLIUM (1984...)

Trillium is a point of definition in my music system. The continuum of works that will make up this 'music state' represents the third solidification (layer) of my evolving materials (the first being vocabularies, the second being the form and/or system type and the third being ritual statements). When completed, *Trillium* will consist of a complex of thirty-six autonomous acts that can be refitted into any combination to total twelve three-act operas.

120.  (. . . AFTER A PERIOD OF CHANGE ZACKKO RETURNS TO HIS PLACE OF BIRTH . . .)

TRILLIUM – DIALOGUES A

Four-scene, one-act opera with two interludes for six soloists, six instrumentalists, dancers, choir of flexible size (preferably twenty sopranos, twenty altos, fifteen tenors, ten basses) and large orchestra (three flutes, three oboes, three clarinets, three bass clarinets, three bassoons, three horns, two trumpets, two trombones, bass trombone, tuba, harp, strings 20, 20, 20, 15, 10 and percussion). Vocal soloists: two sopranos, two altos, two tenors, two baritones. Solo instrumentalists: one flute, one baritone sax, one trombone, one oboe, clarinet, B-flat soprano sax. Complete with stage design and instructions for costumes and slide projections.

(120B)

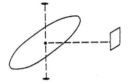

ZACKKO RING (for any instrumentation)

Scale system for 'Zackko of Trillium' and target compass system for centurian duty. Prelude, intermission and postlude structure. To be performed thirty minutes before and after *Trillium A* when put in the position of 'signature structure'. Wind instruments are preferred.

(120C)

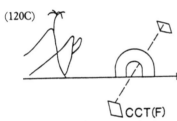

for solo baritone saxophone

Complete (and extended) solo materials extracted from *Trillium A*. To be performed as an independent statement. Three large pages.

(120D)

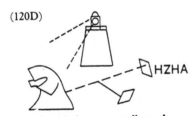

for solo instrumentalist and dancer

Scale system of 'Zackko of Trillium' and body movement position materials to be used for interconnected strategies of one wind instrumentalist and dancer. This is a story fantasy for two creative people: one wind instrumentalist and dancer representing the beginning of the 'Zackko movements'.

(120E)

for solo sousaphone or tuba

Four pages of notated music extracted from *Trillium Dialogues A*.

121.

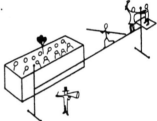

for piano, any two single-line instruments and percussion (1984)

Fifty pages of notated music for piano and upper-voice wind instrument and lower-voice wind or string instrument, with the addition of percussion doubling the lower line.

122.

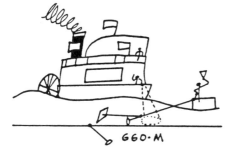

for piano, two single-line instruments and percussion (1985)

Principle generating structure for extended improvisation. Open duration.

123.

....SHALA ADDRESSES THE CONCERNS OF THE GUARDSMEN (AND REDIRECTS THEIR ENERGIES)

for solo flute, slides and constructed environment (1985)

Eighty-seven pages of notated music and choreographed movement for solo flute. This is a fantasy context that contains specified costume information, body movement positions, and staging. Instructions and design of the environment included with score.

124.

for any instrumentation (1985)

Multiple line structure (complex) for extended improvisation. Open duration.

125

**(...'heh! Don't fear this guy-
Bubba John Jack is one of us!')**

for solo tuba, light show and constructed environment (1986)

Eighty-two pages of notated music with and without choreographed
movements for solo tuba (or sousaphone). This is a fantasy context that
contains specified costume information, body movement positions and
strategy (staging). Instructions and design of environment also included in
score.

126.

**JOREO'S VISION OF
FORWARD MOTION**

TRILLIUM – DIALOGUES M (1986)

Four-scene, one-act opera with two interludes for six soloists, dancers, choir
(flexible size, preferably 20 sopranos, 20 altos, 15 tenors, 10 basses), solo
piano and large orchestra (3 flutes, 3 oboes, 3 clarinets, bass clarinet,
bassoon, French horn, 2 trumpets, 2 trombones, bass trombone, tuba, harp,
strings (20, 20, 20, 15, 10), and percussion. Complete with instructions for
stage design and costumes.

(126B)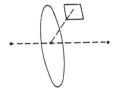

JOREO RING (for any instrumentation) (1986)

Scale system for 'Joreo of Trillium' and target compass system for centurian duty. This material is constructed as a prelude, intermission and postlude experience that is interconnected with the logic system of *Trillium M* when utilized in the position of 'signature structure'. Wind instruments are preferred, depending on what combinations of opera acts are performed, but all options are open.

127.

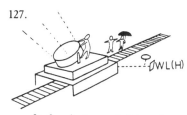

for four instrumentalists and dance ensemble (1986)

Twenty-three pages of combination and relative notation for violin, E-flat saxophone, trombone and piano. To be utilized as a sound landscape environment for extended interpretation dynamics. Can be performed with or without dancers. Duration from twenty-five to thirty-five minutes. Conductor required.

128.

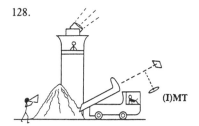

for solo wind instrument and two dancers (1986)

Twenty-two pages of schematic/block diagram notation for any single-line wind instrument and two dancers. Body movement positions included in score. Duration ca. twenty minutes.

129.

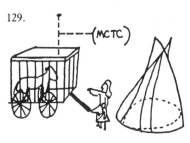

for five woodwind instrumentalists (1986)

Multiple phrase grouping structure notated in traditional notation for any five woodwind instruments. Originally written for five saxophones, the piece may now be approached by any woodwind instruments.

130.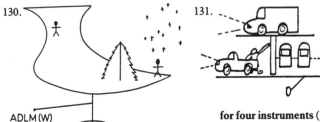

ADLM (W)

for four instruments (1986)

Corridor structure to be used as a
context for structural integration.
For any four instruments. This is
a forum for combining any four
structures from my music system
to be used as one re-composite
form. Open duration.

131.

↳ TCHOT

for four instruments (1986)

Medium/fast line for solo
extension. Originally constructed
as a sequential 'tempo structure
release platform' for my quartet
music material bank. Scored for
upper voice (any wind
instrument), piano, lower voice
(string bass or wind instrument),
and percussion (doubling the bass
line).

132.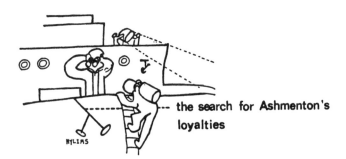

------- the search for Ashmenton's
loyalties

HYLIAS

**for two dancers, six mobile soloists, organ and two chamber orchestras
(1986)**

164 pages of notated music and instructions for a ritual presentation and
theatre. The score calls for the construction of special costumes and
choreographed movement for the six soloists and dancers. Also requires the
use of special headphone sets for each of two conductors. Scored for two
dancers (male or female), six B-flat saxophones (or six clarinets or E-flat
sopranino saxophones – the only provision being that all soloists must play
the same instrument), two conductors and two string orchestras: 16 or 8
violins, 12 or 6 violas, 8 or 4 cellos and 6 or 2 string basses, open percussion
accompaniment (of 'soft' or 'smooth' timbres to support the orchestra) and
grand organ (ideally a cathedral organ).

All compositions published by Synthesis Music.

NB: Each volume of *Tri-axium Writings* also has a diagrammatic title

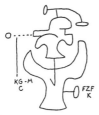

Volume One

Volume Two

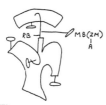

Volume Three

DISCOGRAPHY

My chief aims in the Discography have been a) to list every recorded instance of Braxton as player, composer and conductor; and b) to list the opus numbers which, in the early 1980s, he assigned to all of his earlier compositions. Lack of space has meant many limitations: no personnel listings, complete track listings only on records under Braxton's name (though I note the Braxton compositions on other records), only original issue details (wherever possible) plus the most readily available reissue, designated (RI), where I thought it would be helpful. Most of this missing information (up to 1982) is available in Wachtmeister (see Bibliography). Place and date of recording have been listed only in the Braxton section – Part One; although year of recording (not release) is also given in Part Two, which lists the records by the other members of the quartet.

Part Three lists LPs referred to in the text, plus a brief selection of records by artists mentioned in the text, up to an arbitrary maximum of seven entries. Here, where particular recordings were not cited by Braxton, I've tried to juggle considerations such as availability, relevance to various topics discussed in the book (like solo music, spatial or environment music, unusual instrumentation, the AACM, spiritual music, etc etc) as well as presenting an acceptably representative selection for the artists in question. An impossible task, but I had a wonderful time listening to the records.

(NB: The discographies for Braxton and the quartet have been updated as to late 1987, and therefore include LPs not mentioned in the interviews.)

PART ONE – ANTHONY BRAXTON

A: OWN RECORDINGS (All compositions by Braxton except where otherwise indicated.)

Three Compositions of New Jazz Delmark DS 415 (Chicago, Spring 1968)
– Side One: *6E*; Side Two: *6D, The Bell* (Smith)
For Alto Delmark DS 420/1 (Chicago, Autumn 1968)
– Side One: *8A, 8F, 8H, 8(A/B) Blues*; Side Two: *8D*; Side Three: *8C, 8G*; Side Four: *8B*
Silence Freedom FLP 40123 (Paris, July 1969)
– Side One: *Off the Top of My Head* (Jenkins); Side Two: *Silence* (Smith)

B–X°—NO/47A Byg 529 315/(RI) Affinity AFF 15 (Paris, September 1969)
– Side One: *The Lights on the Dalta* (Smith), *Simple Like* (Jenkins); Side Two: *6G*
This Time Byg 529 347/(RI) Affinity AFF 25 (Paris, January 1970)
– Side One: *6H, 8K*; Side Two: *6F* (five versions), environment improvisation,
   This Time
Recital Paris '71 Musica MUS 2004 (Paris, January 1971)
– Side One: *Come Sunday* (Ellington); Side Two: *16*
   NB: *16* is Braxton's only recorded performance as a pianist.
The Complete Braxton Freedom 400112/3/(RI) (add *1971* to title) Arista-Freedom
1902 (London, February 1971)
– Side One: *6K, 6J*; Side Two: *6A, 22*; Side Three: *6I, 4*; Side Four: *6L, 6M*
   NB: Leo Smith's sleevenotes appear only on the Arista reissue.
Donna Lee America 30 AM 6122 (Paris, February 1972)
– Side One: *Donna Lee* (Parker), *23L*; Side Two: *You Go to My Head*
   (Coots/Gillespie) – two versions, *23K*
Saxophone Improvisations Series F America 30 AM 011/2 (Paris, February 1972)
– Side One: *8I, 26A, 26J*; Side Two: *26B*; Side Three: *26D, 8J, 26C, 26I*; Side
   Four: *26F*
   NB: Sides One and Two only (RI) Inner City IC 1008.
Creative Music Orchestra Ring Records 01024/5/6 (Chatellerault, March 1972)
– Sides One through Six: *25*
Town Hall 1972 Trio Records PA 3008/9 (New York, May 1972)
– Side One: *6N, 6(O)*; Side Two: *All the Things You are* (Kern); Sides Three and
   Four: *6P*
Four Compositions (1973) Nippon Columbia NCB 8504-N/(RI)Denon YX-7506-
ND (Tokyo, January 1973)
– Side One: *23N, 23P*; Side Two: *23M, 23(O)*
In the Tradition, Volume One Steeplechase SCS-1015 (Copenhagen, May 1974)
– Side One: *Marshmallow* (Marsh), *Good Bye Pork Pie Hat* (Mingus), *Just Friends*
   (Klenner/Lewis); Side Two: *Ornithology* (Parker/Harris), *Lush Life* (Strayhorn)
In the Tradition, Volume Two Steeplechase SCS-1045 (Copenhagen, May 1974)
– Side One: *What's New* (Haggart), *Duet* (Braxton/Orsted Pedersen), *Body and
   Soul* (Green); Side Two: *Donna Lee* (Parker), *My Funny Valentine* (Rodgers),
   Half Nelson (Davis)
Solo: Live at Moers Festival Ring Records/Moers Music 01002 (Moers, June 1974)
– Side One: *26B, 26H, 77B*; Side Two: *26E, 26F, 26G*
Live at Moers Festival Ring Records 01010/11 (Moers, June 1974)
– Side One: *23B*; Side Two: *23E*; Side Three: *40(O), 40M*; Side Four: *23F, 23D*
Duo (w/DEREK BAILEY) Emanem 3313/4/(RI) *Live at Wigmor* Inner City 1041
(London, June 1974)
– Sides One through Four: improvisations
Royal, Volume One (w/DEREK BAILEY) Incus 43 (London, July 1974)
– Sides One and Two: improvisation
Trio & Duet Sackville 3007 (Toronto, September 1974)
– Side One: *36*; Side Two: *The Song is You* (Kern/Hammerstein II), *Embraceable
   You* (G. and I. Gershwin), *You Go to My Head* (Coots/Gillespie)
New York Fall 1974 Arista AL 4032 (New York, September/October 1974)
– Side One: *23B, 23C, 23D*; Side Two: *38A, 37, 23A*
Five Pieces 1975 Arista AL 4064 (New York, July 1975)

– Side One: *You Stepped out of a Dream* (Brown/Kahn), *23H*, *23G*; Side Two: *23E*, *40M*
The Montreux/Berlin Concerts Arista AL 5002 (Montreux, July 1975/Berlin, November 1976)
– Side One: *40N*, *23J*; Side Two: *40(O)*, *6C*; Side Three: *6F*, *40K*; Side Four: *63*
Creative Orchestra Music 1976 Arista 4080 (New York, February 1976)
– Side One: *51*, *56*, *58*; Side Two: *57*, *55*, *59*
Elements of Surprise (w/GEORGE LEWIS) Moers Music MOMU 01036 (Moers, June 1976)
– Side One: *64*, *Ornithology* (Parker), *65*; Side Two: *Music for Trombone and Bb Soprano* (Lewis)
Duets 1976 with Muhal Richard Abrams Arista AL 4101 (New York, August 1976)
– Side One: *Miss Ann* (Dolphy), *60*, *40P*; Side Two: *Maple Leaf Rag* (Joplin), *62*, *Nickie* (Braxton/Abrams)
For Trio Arista AB 4181 (Chicago, September 1977)
– Sides One and Two: *76* – two versions
For Four Orchestras Arista A3L 8900 (Ohio, May 1978)
– Sides One through Six: *82*
Alto Saxophone Improvisations 1979 Arista A2L 8602 (New York, November 1978/June 1979)
– Side One: *77A*, *77C*, *Red Top* (Hampton/Kynard); Side Two: *77D*, *77E*, *26F*, *77F*; Side Three: *26B*, *Along Came Betty* (Golson), *77G*; Side Four: *26E*, *Giant Steps* (Coltrane), *77H*
Performance 9/1/79 hat Hut 2R19/(RI) hat ART 2019 (Willisau, September 1979)
– Side One: *69C*, collage improvisation, *69E*, open improvisation; Side Two: open improvisation (contd), *69G*; Side Three: bass solo, *40F*, language improvisation, *69F*, open improvisation; Side Four: open improvisation (contd), *23G*, *40I*
NB: Braxton's diagram-titles and sleevenotes appear only in the original issue of this LP.
Anthony Braxton/Robert Schumann String Quartet sound aspects sas 009 (Köln, November 1979)
– Side One: *17* (version one – string quartet plus saxophone), *26E*, *26I*; Side Two: *17* (version two – string quartet only), *77D*, *77E*, *77B*, *26B*
NB: The diagram-title for *26B* which appears on the LP sleeve and label is completely erroneous.
Seven Compositions 1978 Moers Music 01066 (Paris, November 1979)
– Side One: *69G*, *40F*, *69M*; Side Two: *40D*, *40I*, *69H*, *69K*
NB: The diagram-titles for *40I* and *69H* have been transposed on the LP sleeve and label.
For Two Pianos Arista AL 9559 (Milan, September 1980)
– Sides One and Two: *95*
NB: Braxton does not play on this record.
Composition 98 hat ART 1984 (Ludwigsburg/Bern, January, 1981)
– Sides One and Two: *98* (studio version); Sides Three and Four: *98* (live version)
Six Compositions: Quartet Antilles AN 1005 (New York, October 1981)
– Side One: *40B*, *69N*, *34*; Side Two: *40A*, *40G*, *52*
NB: The diagram-titles for *34* and *40A* have been transposed in the sleevenotes.
Open Aspects '82 (featuring RICHARD TEITELBAUM) hat ART 1995/6

(Ludwigsburg, March 1982)
- Side One: *3, 1.2*; Side Two: *2, 4*; Side Three: *5, 6.1, 6.2, 6.3*; Side Four: *1.1*
(All compositions Braxton/Teitelbaum)
Six Duets (1982) (featuring JOHN LINDBERG) Cecma 1005 (Florence, July
1982)
- Side One: *69B, 69A, 23J*; Side Two: *6A, 69P, 6N*
Four Compositions (Quartet) 1983 Black Saint BSR 0066 (Milan, March 1983)
- Side One: *105A*; Side Two: *69M, 69(O), 69Q*
Composition 113 sound aspects sas 003 (Stuttgart, December 1983)
- Sides One and Two: *113*
Six Compositions (Quartet) 1984 Black Saint BSR 0086 (New York, September
1984)
- Side One: *114 (+108A), 110C, 115*; Side Two: *110A (+108B), 110D, 116*
NB: Some copies of this record were originally released with the erroneous title
Four Compositions (Quartet) 1984
Seven Standards 1985, Volume One Magenta MA 0203 (New York, January 1985)
- Side One: *Joy Spring* (Brown), *Spring is Here* (Rodgers/Hart), *I Remember You*
(Mercer/Schertzinger); Side Two: *You Go to My Head* (Coots/Gillespie), *Old
Folks* (Robeson/Hill), *Background Music* (Marsh)
Seven Standards 1985, Volume Two Magenta 0205 (New York, January 1985)
- Side One: *Moment's Notice* (Coltrane), *Ruby My Dear* (Monk), *Groovin' High*
(Gillespie); Side Two: *Yardbird Suite* (Parker), *Nica's Dream* (Silver), *Milestones*
(Davis), *Trinkle Tinkle* (Monk)
Five Compositions (Quartet) 1986 Black Saint BSR 0106 (Milan, July 1986)
- Side One: *131, 88 (+108C), 124 (+96)*; Side Two: *122 (+108A+96), 101
(+31+96+30)*
NB: There are several errors in the composition numbers listed on the LP sleeve
and label; the above opus numbers are correct.
Moment Précieux (w/DEREK BAILEY) Victo VICTO 02 (Victoriaville, October
1986)
- Sides One and Two: improvisation

B: ALSO PLAYS ON (Braxton opus numbers are indicated where

applicable; collective and co-composition credits which include Braxton are not

noted.)

Muhal Richard Abrams: *Levels and Degrees of Light* Delmark DS 413 (Chicago,
June 1967)
Jacques Coursil: *Black Suite* Byg 529 349/(RI) America 30 AM 6111 (Paris, June
1969)
Gunter Hampel: *The 8th of July 1969* Birth NJ001 (Nederhorst den Berg, July
1969)
Instant Composers Pool: (no title) ICP 007/8 (Nederhorst den Berg, July 1969)
- NB: Braxton plays only on one track.
Alan Silva: *Lunar Surface* Byg 529 312 (Paris, August 1969)
Archie Shepp/Philly Joe Jones: (no title) America 30 AM 6102 (Paris, December
1969)

Creative Construction Company: *Volume One* Muse 5071 (New York, May 1970)
Creative Construction Company: *Volume Two* Muse 5097 (New York, May 1970)
Marion Brown: *Afternoon of a Georgia Faun* ECM 1004 (New York, August 1970)
Chick Corea: *Circulus* Blue Note BN-LA882–J2 (New York, August 1970)
– NB: Braxton plays only on three of the record's four sides.
Chick Corea: *Circling in* Blue Note BN-LA472-H2 (New York, October 1970)
– NB: Braxton plays on one record of this two-record set; it includes Braxton's *Composition 6F*, called here *73°–A Kelvin*.
Circle: *Live in Germany Concert* CBS-Sony SOPL 19XJ (Isolome, November 1970)
Circle: *Paris Concert* ECM 1018/19 ST (Paris, February 1971)
– NB: LP includes Braxton's *Composition 6F*, called here *73 Kelvin (Variation 3)*.
Circle: *Gathering* CBS-Sony 20XJ (New York, March 1971)
Joseph Jarman/Anthony Braxton: *Together Alone* Delmark DS 428 (Paris, December 1971)
– NB: One side of LP comprises Braxton's *Compositions 21* and *20*.
Gunter Hampel: *Familie* Birth 008 (Paris, April 1972)
David Holland Quartet: *Conference of the Birds* ECM 1027 ST (New York, November 1972)
Dave Brubeck: *All the Things We are* Atlantic 1684 (New York, October 1974)
– NB: Braxton plays only on two tracks.
Leroy Jenkins & the Jazz Composers Orchestra: *For Players Only* JCOA/Virgin J2005 (New York, January 1975)
Gunter Hampel: *Enfant Terrible* Birth 0025 (Woodstock, September 1975)
New York Section of Composers of 70s: *New American Music, Volume 3* Folkways 33903 (New York, Autumn 1975)
– NB: Braxton plays only on two tracks.
Globe Unity Orchestra: *Jahrmarkt/Local Fair* Po Torch Records PTR JWD2 (Baden-Baden, Autumn 1975)
Frederic Rzewski: *First Recordings* Finnadar SR 9011 (New York, 1976)
– NB: Includes excerpts from Braxton's *Composition 30* and *Composition 31*: Braxton does not play on the LP.
Various: *Wildflowers 2 – the New York Loft Jazz Sessions* Douglas NBLP 7046 (New York, May 1976)
– NB: Braxton plays only on one track; this is an excerpt from his *Composition 6F*, called here *73°–S Kelvin*.
Richard Teitelbaum: *Time Zones* Arista AL 1037 (Mt Tremper, June 1976/ Woodstock, September 1976)
Evan Parker/Anthony Braxton/Derek Bailey: *Company 2* Incus 23 (London, August 1976)
Roscoe Mitchell: *Duets with Anthony Braxton* Sackville 3016 (Toronto, December 1976)
– NB: Side Two comprises Braxton's *Compositions 40Q, 74B, 74A*.
Roscoe Mitchell: *Noonah* Nessa N 9/10 (Chicago, January 1977)
– NB: Braxton plays only on one track.
Woody Shaw, w/Anthony Braxton: *The Iron Men* Muse MR 5160 (New York, April 1977)
– NB: Braxton plays only on three tracks.
Various: *Company 5* Incus 28 (London, May 1977)
Various: *Company 6* Incus 29 (London, May 1977)
– NB: Braxton plays only on two tracks.

Various: *Company 7* Incus 30 (London, May 1977)
- NB: Braxton plays only on three tracks.
Dave Holland: *Emerald Tears* ECM 1–1109 (Oslo, August 1977)
- NB: Includes solo bass version of Braxton's *Composition 69Q*; Braxton does not play on the LP.
Globe Unity Orchestra & Guests: *Pearl* Free Music Production FMP 0380 (Berlin, November 1977)
Muhal Richard Abrams: *1–0QA+19* Black Saint BSR 0017 (New York, November/December 1977)
Ran Blake: *Rapport* Arista-Novus AN 3006 (New York, April/May 1978)
- NB: Braxton plays only on one track.
Roscoe Mitchell: *LRG/The Maze/S 11 Examples* Nessa 14/15 (New York, July 1978)
- NB: Braxton plays only on *The Maze*; he plays only percussion instruments.
Max Roach, featuring Anthony Braxton: *Birth and Rebirth* Black Saint BSR 0024 (Milan, September 1978)
Three Motions: *Impressions* RAU 1010 (Krems, September 1978)
Roscoe Mitchell Creative Orchestra: *Sketches from Bamboo* Moers Music 02024 (Paris, June 1979)
Leo Smith Creative Orchestra: *Budding of a Rose* Moers Music 02026 (Paris, June 1979)
Max Roach, featuring Anthony Braxton: *One in Two – Two in One* hat Hut 2R06/(RI) as part of *The Long March* hat ART 4026 (Willisau, August 1979)
Walter Thompson: *Four Compositions* Dane 001 (Willow, 1979/80)
- NB: Braxton plays only on one track.
Neighbours: *With Anthony Braxton* GNM vol 3 120 754 (Austria, July 1980)
Roscoe Mitchell & the Sound Ensemble: *Snurdy McGurdy and Her Dancin' Shoes* Nessa N20 (Chicago, December 1980)
- NB: Includes Braxton's *Composition 42*, called here *March*; Braxton does not play on the LP.
Giorgio Gaslini/Anthony Braxton Duo: *Four Pieces* Dischi Della Quercia Q28015 (Milan, November 1981)
- NB: Side One comprises Braxton's *Composition 101*.
Marianne Schroeder: *Braxton & Stockhausen* hat ART 2030 (Ludwigsburg, April 1982)
- NB: Sides One and Two comprise Braxton's *Composition 107*; Sides Three and Four comprise Stockhausen's *Klavierstücke VI, VII, VIII*: Braxton plays only on *107*.
Vienna Art Orchestra: *From No Time to Rag Time* hat ART 1999/2000 (Rubigen, October 1982)
- NB: Includes a version of, and variations on, Braxton's *Composition 6K*; Braxton does not play on the LP.
Paul Smoker: *QB* Alvas Records AR 101 (Iowa, February 1984)
- NB: Braxton plays only on three tracks.
Gyorgy Szabados: *Szabraxtondos* Krém SLPX 17909 (Budapest, June 1984)
John Lindberg: *Trilogy of Works for Eleven Instrumentalists* Black Saint BSR 0082 (New York, September 1984)
- NB: Braxton performs only as the conductor on this LP.
Various: *Music from Mills* MC001 (Oakland, 1986)
- NB: Braxton plays only on one track; this is his *Composition 62 (+30+96)*, played as a duo with David Rosenboom, piano.

C: RELEASES PENDING

Anthony Braxton/Derek Bailey: *Royal, Volume 2* Incus 44 (London, July 1974)
- Sides One and Two: improvisation
Anthony Braxton: *Quartet (Prague) 1984* sound aspects (Prague, Summer 1984)
- Side One: *105A*; Side Two: *110A (+108B), 114 (+108A)*
Anthony Braxton: *Saxophone Improvisations 1985* Stil Editions (Paris, Summer 1985)
- Record One. Side One: *99A, 99B, 99C, 77H*; Side Two: *Four* (Davis), *99D, 77I*
- Record Two. Side One: *99E, 99F, 106A*; Side Two: *106B, 106C*
- Record Three. Side One: *118A, 118B, 118C, Tune Up* (Davis), *119H*; Side Two: *All the Things You are* (Kern/Hammerstein II), *119G, 77D, 77E*
- Record Four. Sides One and Two: *118D*
- Record Five. Side One: *118E, 26F, 118F*; Side Two: *106D, 118G*
- Record Six. Side One: *119A* (Parts 1-5), *119B, 99J* (Areas 1-3), *106J* (Sections 1 and 2), *77F, 99K* (Parts 1-3), *119C, 119D*; Side Two: *118H, 77J, 77C*
- Record Seven. Side One: *106E*; Side Two: *119E*
- Record Eight. Side One: *99G, 99H, 77G*; Side Two: *99I*
- Record Nine. Sides One and Two: *106F* (First Part)
- Record Ten. Side One: *106F* (Conclusion); Side Two: *118I, 8B, 119I, 118J*
- Record Eleven. Side One: *26B, 106K* (Stages 1-4), *106L, 106M, Round Midnite* (Monk); Side Two: *118K, 118L, 26E*
- Record Twelve. Side One: *106G, 106H, 106I*; Side Two: *119F* (First Part)
- Record Thirteen. Sides One and Two: *119F* (Middle Part)
- Record Fourteen. Sides One and Two: *119F* (Conclusion)
Anthony Braxton: *Six Thelonious Monk Compositions 1987* Black Saint (Milan, June 1987)
- Side One: *Brilliant Corners, Reflections, Played Twice*; Side Two: *Four in One, Ask Me Now, Skippy* (all compositions Monk)
Gino Robair and Anthony Braxton: *Duets 1987* Rastascan BRD 002 (Haywood, October 1987)
- NB: LP includes Braxton's *Composition 40D* (*+ 108A + 108B*), *Composition 136* (*+ 96*) and *Composition 86*

PART TWO — MARILYN CRISPELL, MARK DRESSER, GERRY HEMINGWAY

MARILYN CRISPELL —

A: OWN RECORDINGS

Spirit Music Cadence CJR 1015 (1981/2)
Live in Berlin Black Saint BSR 0069 (1982)
Rhythms Hung in Undrawn Sky Leo LR 118 (1983)
A Concert in Berlin FMP Records SAJ 46 (1983)
And Your Ivory Voice Sings (w/DOUG JAMES) Leo LR 126 (1985)
Quartet Improvisations Paris 1986 Leo LR 144 (1986)

B: ALSO PLAYS ON

Roscoe Mitchell Creative Orchestra: *Sketches from Bamboo* Moers Music 02024 (1979)
Leo Smith Creative Orchestra: *Budding of a Rose* Moers Music 02026 (1979)
Eric Andersen: *Istanbul* EMI 1A 064–11 9196 1 (1985)
Julie Kabat: *On Edge* Leonarda LP1 119 (1985)
Reggie Workman Ensemble: *Synthesis* Leo LR 131 (1986)
Ed Sanders: *Star Peace: a Musical Drama in Three Acts* New Rose ROSE 115 (1987)
– See also ANTHONY BRAXTON (A) hat ART 1984 (1981), BSR 0086 (1984)

C: RELEASES PENDING

Marilyn Crispell: *Gaia* Leo (1987)
– See also ANTHONY BRAXTON (C) (1984)

MARK DRESSER –

A: OWN RECORDINGS

Bass Excursions Dresser/Wolfe (cassette only) (1983)

B: ALSO PLAYS ON

James Newton: *Binu* Circle RK 21877/11 (1977)
Ray Anderson: *Harrisburg Half Life* Moers Music 01074 (1980)
Bobby Bradford & the Mo'Tet: *Lost in LA* Soul Note SN 1068 (1983)
Ray Anderson: *It Just So Happens* Enja 5037 (1987)
– See also ANTHONY BRAXTON (A) BSR 0106 (1986)

C: RELEASES PENDING

Gerard Siracusa: *Slumberland* Nato (1986)
Tim Berne: *Sanctified Dreams* Columbia (1987)

GERRY HEMINGWAY –

A: OWN RECORDINGS

Kwambe Auricle AUR 1 (1978)
Solo Works Auricle AUR 3 (1981)
Outerbridge Crossing sound aspects sas 017 (1985)

B: ALSO PLAYS ON

Oahspe: *Oahspe* Auricle AUR 2 (1979)
Allan Jaffe: *Soundscape* Kromel KR 1001 (1979)

Ray Anderson: *Harrisburg Half Life* Moers Music 01074 (1980)
Creative Improvisors Orchestra: *The Sky Cries the Blues* CMIF Records CMIF 1
(1982)
Ned Rothenberg: *Portal* Lumina Records L006 (1983)
Ray Anderson: *Right down Your Alley* Soul Note SN 1087 (1984)
Mark Helias: *Split Image* Enja 4086 (1985)
Anderson/Helias/Hemingway: *You Be* Minor Music 007 (1986)
Anthony Davis's Episteme: *Undine* Gramavision 18–8612–4 (1987)
– See ANTHONY BRAXTON (A) BSR 0066 (1983), BSR 0086 (1984), BSR
0106 (1986)

C: RELEASES PENDING

– See ANTHONY BRAXTON (C) (1984)

PART THREE – OTHER ARTISTS

MUHAL RICHARD ABRAMS

Young at Heart, Wise in Time Delmark DS 423
Things to Come from Those Now Gone Delmark DS 430
Lifea Blinec Arista-Novus AN 3000
Spihumonesty Black Saint BSR 0034
Afrisong Why Not/(RI) India Navigation IN 1058
Mama and Dada Black Saint BSR 0041
Rejoicing with the Light Black Saint BSR 0071
– See also ANTHONY BRAXTON (A) 1976, (B) 1967, 1977; and LEROY
JENKINS

ANIMA MUSIC

"Bruchstücke Für Ilona" Loft 1010/11

ART ENSEMBLE OF CHICAGO

People in Sorrow Nessa N 3
Message to Our Folks Byg 529 328/(RI) Affinity AFF 77
Fanfare for the Warriors Atlantic SD 1651/(RI) 90046
Urban Bushmen ECM 1211/12

ALBERT AYLER

Spirits Debut DEB 146/(RI) *Witches & Devils* Freedom FLP 41018
Ghosts Debut DEB 144/(RI) *Vibrations* Freedom FLP 40117
Spiritual Unity ESP 1002
Bells ESP 1010
Nuits de la Fondation Maeght Shandar 83503/4

DEREK BAILEY

Lot 74 Solo Improvisations Incus 12
Notes Incus 48
Compatibles (w/EVAN PARKER) Incus 50
– See also ANTHONY BRAXTON (A) 1974 × 2, 1986 (B) Parker, 1976 (C)
1974; and STEVE LACY

CHET BAKER

Blues for a Reason (featuring WARNE MARSH) Criss Cross Jazz 1010

ALVIN BATISTE

Musique D'Afrique Nouvelle Orleans India Navigation IN 1065

CAPTAIN BEEFHEART

Trout Mask Replica Reprise K64026

HILDEGARD VON BINGEN

A Feather on the Breath of God Hyperion A66039

HENRY BRANT

Angels and Devils – Concerto for Flute and Orchestra CRI SD 106
Orbits: a Spatial Symphonic Ritual CRI SD 422
Western Springs CRI SD 512
Vuur Onder Water BVHAAST 052
Solar Moth 1750 Arch Records S 1795

JAMES BROWN

Solid Gold Polydor 2679 044

DAVE BRUBECK

The Fantasy Years (RI) Atlantic 2SA 317
1975: The Duets (w/PAUL DESMOND) Horizon 3 SP 703
– See also ANTHONY BRAXTON (B) 1974

JOHN CAGE

HPSCHD Nonesuch H 71224
Etudes Australes Tomato Tom 2 1101

ORNETTE COLEMAN

The Shape of Jazz to Come Atlantic SD 1317
Free Jazz Atlantic 1364
Town Hall, 1962 ESP 1006
The Great London Concert Arista/Freedom AL 1900
Saints and Soldiers RCA Red Seal LSC 2982/(RI) *The Music of Ornette Coleman*
RCA SF 7944
Skies of America Columbia KC 31562
In All Languages Caravan of Dreams CDP 85008

JOHN COLTRANE

Giant Steps Atlantic SD 1311/(RI) ATL 50 236
Africa/Brass Impulse AS 6
Impressions Impulse AS 42
Crescent Impulse AS 66
A Love Supreme Impulse AS 77
The John Coltrane Quartet Plays Impulse AS 85
Ascension Impulse AS 95
– See also THELONIOUS MONK

ANTHONY DAVIS

Hemispheres Gramavision GR 8303
Middle Passage Gramavision GR 8401
– See also GERRY HEMINGWAY (B) 1987

MILES DAVIS

Round About Midnight Columbia 949

PAUL DESMOND

East of the Sun Warner Bros 1356/(RI) Discovery DS 840
Two of a Mind (w/GERRY MULLIGAN) (RI) RCA FXLI 7311
Easy Living (RI) RCA PL 42112
Bossa Antigua (RI) RCA PL 45691
The Only Recorded Performance (w/THE MODERN JAZZ QUARTET) Finesse
FINLP 6050
The Paul Desmond Quartet Live Horizon 10 SP 850
Paul Desmond Artists House AH 9402
– See also DAVE BRUBECK

BILL DIXON

"Intents and Purposes" (RI) RCA FXLI 7331
Considerations 1972–1976, 1&2 Fore Three/Fore Five
Bill Dixon in Italy, Vols 1&2 Soul Note SN 1008/SN 1011

ERIC DOLPHY

Out There New Jazz 8252/(RI) OJC 023
Out to Lunch Blue Note BST 84163
Other Aspects Blue Note BT 85131

DUKE ELLINGTON

Black, Brown and Beige (w/MAHALIA JACKSON) Columbia CSP JCL 8015

ETHNIC HERITAGE ENSEMBLE

Three Gentlemen from Chikago Moers Music 01076
Impressions Red UPA 156
Welcome Leo (Finland) LEO 014

VON FREEMAN

Have No Fear Nessa N6

MARVIN GAYE

What's Going On Tamla Motown STML 11190

JIMMY GIUFFRE

The Clarinet Album Atlantic 1238/(RI) 90144
Trio Live in Europe 1961 Raretone S018 FC
Thesis Verve V 8402
Quasar Soul Note SN 1108
– See also LEE KONITZ and THE MODERN JAZZ QUARTET

JOE HARRIOTT

Abstract EMI 33SX 1477
Movement EMI 33SX 1627

JIMI HENDRIX

Electric Ladyland Polydor 2657 012

MILT JACKSON

The Jazz Skyline Savoy MG 12070/(RI) WL 70821

JOSEPH JARMAN

Song For Delmark DS 410
As if It were the Seasons Delmark DS 417
Sunbound AECO 002
Egwu-Anwu (w/FAMOUDOU DON MOYE) India Navigation 1033
— See also ANTHONY BRAXTON (B) 1971

LEROY JENKINS

Solo Concert India Navigation IN 1028
Lifelong Ambitions (w/MUHAL RICHARD ABRAMS) Black Saint BSR 0033
The Legend of Ai Glatson Black Saint BSR 0022
Mixed Quintet Black Saint BSR 0060
— See also ANTHONY BRAXTON (B) 1975

LEE KONITZ

With Warne Marsh Atlantic 1217/(RI) 90050
Meets Jimmy Giuffre Verve 2304 381
— See also WARNE MARSH and LENNIE TRISTANO

STEVE LACY

Reflections New Jazz 8206/(RI) OJC 063
Company 4 (w/DEREK BAILEY) Incus 26
Threads (featuring ALVIN CURRAN, FREDERIC RZEWSKI) Horo HZ 05
The Way hat Hut 2R03/(RI) hat ART 2029
Prospectus hat ART 2001
Hocus-Pocus Les Disques du Crepuscule TWI 683
Only Monk Soul Note SN 1160

GEORGE LEWIS

The George Lewis Solo Trombone Album Sackville 3012
Chicago Slow Dance Lovely Music/Vital Records VR 1101
Shadowgraph Black Saint BSR 0016

George Lewis/Douglas Ewart Black Saint BSR 0026
Homage to Charles Parker Black Saint BSR 0029
– See also ANTHONY BRAXTON (A) 1976; and EVAN PARKER

ALVIN LUCIER

Music on a Long Thin Wire Lovely Music/Vital Records VR 1011/12

FRANKIE LYMON

Why Do Fools Fall in Love? Pye NSPL 28251

WARNE MARSH

Music for Prancing Mode MOD LP 125/(RI) VSOP 8
Warne Marsh Atlantic SD 1291
Jazz Exchange, Vols 1–3 (w/LEE KONITZ) Storyville SLP 1017/SLP 4020/SLP 4096
Warne Out Interplay IP 77 09/(RI) Flyright FLY 211
How Deep, How High (w/SAL MOSCA) Interplay IP 77 25/(RI) Flyright FLY 216
Hot House (w/RED MITCHELL) Storyville SLP 4092
Warne Marsh in Norway: Sax of a Kind Hot Club Records HCR 7
– See also CHET BAKER, LEE KONITZ and LENNIE TRISTANO

KALAPARUSH MAURICE MCINTYRE

Humility in the Light of the Creator Delmark DS 419
Forces and Feelings Delmark DS 425
Peace and Blessings Black Saint BSR 0037
Ram's Run Cadence CJR 1009

JACKIE MCLEAN

A Long Drink of the Blues New Jazz 8253/(RI) OJC 253
Let Freedom Ring Blue Note BST 84106
It's Time Blue Note BST 84179

CHARLES MINGUS

Pithecanthropus Erectus Atlantic 1237/(RI) SD 8809
Mingus Ah Um Columbia CS 8171/(RI) CBS 21071
Presents Charles Mingus Candid CJM 8005/(RI) CS 9005
The Great Concert of Charles Mingus America AM 003/4/5
Let My Children Hear Music Columbia 31039

ROSCOE MITCHELL

Sound Delmark DS 408
Congliptious Nessa N2
– See also ANTHONY BRAXTON (B) 1976, 1977, 1978, 1979, 1980.

THE MODERN JAZZ QUARTET

At Music Inn: Guest Artist – Jimmy Giuffre Atlantic 1247/(RI) 90049
– See also PAUL DESMOND

THELONIOUS MONK

Genius of Modern Music, Vols 1&2 Blue Note (RI) BST 81510/11
With John Coltrane Jazzland 946/(RI) OJC 039

SAL MOSCA

Sal Mosca Music Interplay IP 77 12
For You Choice CRS 1022
– See also WARNE MARSH

JAMES NEWTON

The Mystery School India Navigation IN 1046
Echo Canyon Celestial Harmonies CEL 012
– See also MARK DRESSER (B) 1977

CHARLIE PARKER

Bird on 52nd Street Fantasy/Debut 6011/(RI) Prestige 24009
The Savoy Recordings (Master Takes) Savoy 2201
On Dial, Vols 1–6 (RI) Spotlite 101/2/3/4/5/6

EVAN PARKER

Saxophone Solos Incus 19
From Saxophones and Trombone (w/GEORGE LEWIS) Incus 35
The Snake Decides Incus 49
– See also ANTHONY BRAXTON (B) 1976; and DEREK BAILEY

HARRY PARTCH

From the Music of Harry Partch CRI SD 193
And on the Seventh Day Petals Fell in Petaluma CRI SD 213

The Bewitched CRI SD 304
Harry Partch/John Cage New World NW 214
The World of Harry Partch Columbia MS 7207
Delusion of the Fury Columbia MS 30576

PINSKI ZOO

Introduce Me to the Doctor Despatch Records PATCH 0001
The City Can't Have It Back Dug-Out Records PINS 003
Speak Dug-Out Records PINS 005

SUN RA

Sun Song Transition J10/(RI) Delmark DS 411
Pictures of Infinity Black Lion BL 106
Nuits de la Fondation Maeght (RI) Recommended Records RR 11
Astro-Black Impulse AS 9255
Sleeping Beauty Saturn 79
Sunrise in Different Dimensions hat Hut 2R17/(RI) hat ART 2017
A Fireside Chat with Lucifer Saturn 1984SG-9

FREDERIC RZEWSKI

Attica/Coming Together/Les Moutons de Panurge Opus One 20
Four Pieces (1977) Vanguard VA 25001
– See also ANTHONY BRAXTON (B) 1976; and STEVE LACY

ARNOLD SCHOENBERG

Das Klavierwerk: the Piano Music Deutsche Grammophon 2530 531

ALEXANDER SCRIABIN

The Poem of Ecstasy/Prometheus, the Poem of Fire RCA Red Seal SB 6854

RUTH CRAWFORD SEEGER

String Quartet Nonesuch H 71280
Piano Works (w/DANE RUDHYAR) CRI SD 247

LEO SMITH

Creative Music 1 Kabell 1
Reflectativity (w/NEW DALTA AHKRI) Kabell K2
Song of Humanity (w/NEW DALTA AHKRI) Kabell K3
Divine Love ECM 1143

Spirit Catcher Nessa N 19
Solo Music: Ahkreanvention Kabell K4
Human Rights Kabell/Gramm 24
– See also ANTHONY BRAXTON (B) 1979

JOHN PHILIP SOUSA

Favourite Marches EMI ASD 1651461

KARLHEINZ STOCKHAUSEN

Zyklus für Einen Schlagzeuger/Klavierstück X Wergo WER 60010
Gruppen/Carré Deutsche Grammophon 137 002
Stimmung Hyperion A66115
Sternklang Deutsche Grammophon 2707 123
"Am Himmel wandre Ich . . ." Deutsche Grammophon 2530 876
Musik im Bauch/Tierkreis Deutsche Grammophon 2530 913
Sirius Deutsche Grammophon 2707 122
– See also ANTHONY BRAXTON (B) Schroeder 1982

HORACE TAPSCOTT

Flight 17 (w/THE PAN-AFRIKAN PEOPLES ARKESTRA) Nimbus 135
The Call (w/THE PAN-AFRIKAN PEOPLES ARKESTRA) Nimbus 246
Live at I.U.C.C. (w/THE PAN-AFRIKAN PEOPLES ARKESTRA) Nimbus
357
The Tapscott Sessions, Vols 1–4 Nimbus NS 1581/1692/1703/1814

CECIL TAYLOR

Unit Structures Blue Note BNS 40023
Spring of Two Blue-J's Unit Core Records 30551
Air Above Mountains (buildings within) Enja 3005
Live in the Black Forest MPS 5C 064-62612
Fly! Fly! Fly! Fly! Fly! MPS 0068 263
Garden hat ART 1993/4
Winged Serpent (Sliding Quadrants) Soul Note SN 1089

RICHARD TEITELBAUM

Blends & the Digital Pianos Lumina Records L005
– See also ANTHONY BRAXTON (A) 1982 and (B) 1976

LUCKY THOMPSON

Lucky Strikes Prestige 7365/(RI) OJC 194

LENNIE TRISTANO

Requiem (RI) Atlantic SD 2 – 7003
Live in Toronto 1952 (featuring WARNE MARSH and LEE KONITZ) Jazz
Records JR 5
Continuity Jazz Records JR 6

EDGARD VARÈSE

Ecuatorial/Deserts/Integrales CBS IM 39053
– NB: This LP also includes *Density 21.5*
Arcana/Ionisation/Ameriques CBS 76520

FATS WALLER

Piano Solos (1929–1941) (RI) RCA PM 43270

BIBLIOGRAPHY

This is a general bibliography of books and articles referred to in the text and footnotes, plus a little additional background reading. A complete bibliography of Braxton reviews, interviews, articles etc (up to 1982) can be found in Wachtmeister; I've listed below only Braxton's own major writings plus a brief selection of interviews which he still endorses. There is also a chapter on Braxton in Ullman, and sections on Braxton and other AACM musicians in Litweiler and Wilmer.

Margaret Alic: *Hypatia's Heritage: a History of Women in Science from Antiquity to the Late Nineteenth Century* (London: The Women's Press, 1986)

Lynn V. Andrews: *Medicine Woman* (New York: Harper & Row, 1983)

Kenneth Ansell: 'Anthony Braxton', interview and reviews, *Impetus* 6, 1977

Roland Baggenaes: 'Warne Marsh: Interview', *Coda* (issue 152), December 1976

Derek Bailey: *Improvisation: Its Nature and Practice in Music* (Ashbourne, Derbyshire: Moorland Publishing, 1980)

Roland Barthes: *Mythologies* (St Albans: Paladin, 1973)

Francis Bebey: *African Music: a People's Art* (London: Harrap, 1975)

Martin Bernal: *Black Athena: the Afroasiatic Roots of Classical Civilization, Volume 1 – The Fabrication of Ancient Greece, 1785–1985* (London: Free Association Books, 1987)

Faubion Bowers: *The New Scriabin* (Newton Abbot, Devon: David & Charles, 1974)

Anthony Braxton: untitled composition notes to *Composition 76, For Trio* LP (New York: Arista Records, 1978)

untitled composition notes to *Composition 82, For Four Orchestras* LP (New York: Arista Records, 1978)

'Language Music (1967)' plus composition notes, *Alto Saxophone Improvisations 1979* LP (New York: Arista Records, 1979)

'Co-ordinant Music' plus composition notes, *Performance 9/1/79* LP (Therwil, Switzerland: hat Hut Records, 1981)

NB: These writings have been omitted from the reissue of this record.

'Composition 98', *Composition 98* LP (Therwil, Switzerland: hat ART Records, 1981)

untitled composition notes, *Six Compositions: Quartet* LP (New York: Antilles Records, 1982)

'What We Have Here are Intentions', sleevenotes to Muhal Richard Abrams's

Rejoicing with the Light LP (Milan: Black Saint Records, 1983)
'Composition 113', *Composition 113* LP (Backnang, West Germany: sound aspects, 1984)
untitled notes, *Seven Standards 1985, Volume 1* LP (Stanford, California: Magenta Records, 1985)
Triaxium Writings, Volumes 1–3 (Synthesis Music, 1985)
'8KN – (B–12)', notes to *Composition 17, Anthony Braxton/Robert Schumann*
$$R^{10}$$
Quartet LP (Backnang, West Germany: sound aspects, 1986)
untitled notes, *Five Compositions (Quartet) 1986* LP (Milan: Black Saint Records, 1987)
Composition Notes, Volumes A–E Synthesis Music (publication pending)
NB: For interviews and reviews, see Ansell, Carey, Lock, Bill Smith; for sleevenotes, see Leo Smith.
E.A. Wallis Budge (ed): *The Book of the Dead* (London: Arkana, 1985)
Meinrad Buholzer: 'Cecil Taylor: Interview', *Cadence* (vol. 10, no. 12), December 1984
Fritjof Capra: *The Tao of Physics* (revised edition) (London: Flamingo, 1983)
Joe Carey: 'Anthony Braxton: Interview', *Cadence* (vol. 10, no. 3), March 1984
Catherine Caufield: *In the Rainforest* (London: Picador, 1986)
Richard Cavendish: *The Magical Arts* (London: Arkana, 1984)
Susan Cavin: 'Missing Women: on the Voodoo Trail to Jazz', *Journal of Jazz Studies*, vol. 3, no. 1, Autumn 1975
Bill Cole: *John Coltrane* (New York: Schirmer Books, 1978)
Jonathan Cott: *Stockhausen: Conversations with the Composer* (London: Picador, 1974)
Marilyn Crispell: 'Some Information on My Compositions', part of untitled manuscript (Woodstock: Crispell Publishing, 1986)
Chris Cutler: *File under Popular: Theoretical and Critical Writings on Music* (London: November Books, 1985)
Linda Dahl: *Stormy Weather: the Music and Lives of a Century of Jazzwomen* (London: Quartet Books, 1984)
Cheikh Anta Diop: *The African Origin of Civilization: Myth or Reality* (condensed edition) (Westport: Lawrence Hill & Co, 1974)
Bill Dixon: untitled sleevenotes, *Considerations 2* LP (Milan: Fore, 1981)
NB: For interviews, see Leonardi, Lombardi.
W.E.B. DuBois: *W.E.B. DuBois Speaks: Speeches and Addresses, 1920–1963* (New York: Pathfinder, 1970)
The World and Africa (new enlarged edition) (New York: International Publishers, 1983)
Alan Durant: *Conditions of Music* (London: Macmillan Press, 1984)
Gisela Ecker (ed): *Feminist Aesthetics* (London: The Women's Press, 1985)
Ralph Ellison: *Shadow and Act* (New York: Vintage Books, 1972)
W.Y. Evans-Wentz (ed): *The Tibetan Book of the Dead* (Oxford: Oxford University Press, 1960)
Julio Finn: *The Bluesman: the Musical Heritage of Black Men and Women in the Americas* (London: Quartet Books, 1986)
Ralph J. Gleason: *Celebrating the Duke and Louis, Bessie, Billie, Bird, Carmen,*

Miles, Dizzy and Other Heroes (New York: Delta, 1975)

Peter Gorman: *Pythagoras: a Life* (London: Routledge & Kegan Paul, 1979)

Barbara L. Grant: 'An Interview with the Sybil of the Rhine: Hildegard von Bingen (1098–1179)', *Heresies 10: Women and Music* (vol. 3, no. 2), 1980

Paul Griffiths: *Modern Music: a Concise History from Debussy to Boulez* (London: Thames & Hudson, 1978)

Peter Michael Hamel: *Through Music to the Self* (Shaftesbury, Dorset: Element Books, 1978)

Mike Hames: 'The Death of Albert Ayler', *Wire*, issue 6, Spring 1984

George G.M. James: *Stolen Legacy: the Greeks were not the Authors of Greek Philosophy, but the People of North Africa, Commonly Called the Egyptians* (New York: Philosophical Library, 1954; reprinted San Francisco: Julian Richardson Associates, 1976)

Barbara Jepson: 'Ruth Crawford Seeger: a Study in Mixed Accents', *Heresies 10: Women and Music* (vol. 3, no. 2), 1980

Yosef A.A. ben-Jochannan: *Black Man of the Nile and His Family* (revised and enlarged edition) (New York: Alkebu-lan Books and Education Materials Association, 1981)

LeRoi Jones: *Black Music* (London: MacGibbon & Kee, 1969)

C.G. Jung: *Alchemical Studies* (London: Routledge & Kegan Paul, 1983)

Wassily Kandinsky: *Concerning the Spiritual in Art* (New York: Dover Publications, 1977)

Frank Kofsky: *Black Nationalism and the Revolution in Music* (New York: Pathfinder, 1970)

Lucie Lamy: *Egyptian Mysteries: New Light on Ancient Knowledge* (London: Thames & Hudson, 1981)

Jolyon Laycock (ed): *A Noise in Your Eye: an International Exhibition of Sound Sculpture* (exhibition catalogue) Bristol: Arnolfini, 1985

Laura Lederer (ed): *Take Back the Night: Women on Pornography* (New York: William Morrow, 1980)

Angelo Leonardi: 'Bill Dixon: Interview', *Bill Dixon in Italy, Volume One* LP (Milan: Soul Note Records, 1980)

John Litweiler: *The Freedom Principle: Jazz after 1958* (Poole, Dorset: Blandford Press, 1985)

Graham Lock: 'The Five Colours Blind You, the Five Notes Deafen You', interview with Steve Lacy, *New Musical Express*, 5 March 1983

'Out to Lunch', interview with Cecil Taylor, *New Musical Express*, 18 June, 1983

'Waltzing with Fire', interview with Mal Waldron, *New Musical Express*, 17 December 1983

'Along Came Ra', interview with Sun Ra, *Wire*, issue 6, Spring 1984

'In Struggle, in Grace', interview with Abdullah Ibrahim, *Wire*, issue 8, October 1984

'Windy City Warriors', interview with the Art Ensemble of Chicago, *Wire*, issue 9, November 1984

'Let 100 Orchestras Blow', interview with Anthony Braxton, *Wire*, issue 16, June 1985

'The Indestructible Roach', interview with Max Roach, *New Musical Express*, 31 August 1985

review of Anthony Braxton's *Five Compositions (Quartet) 1986* LP, *Wire*, issue 38, April 1987

Angelo Lombardi: 'Bill Dixon: Interview', *Bill Dixon in Italy, Volume Two* LP (Milan: Soul Note Records, 1980)

Robin Maconie: *The Works of Stockhausen* (London: Marion Boyars, 1981)

Wilfred Mellers: *Music in a New Found Land* (New York: Knopf, 1965)

Carolyn Merchant: *The Death of Nature: Women, Ecology and the Scientific Revolution* (London: Wildwood House, 1982)

John Michell: *The View over Atlantis* (new edition) (London: Abacus, 1975)

Robin Morgan: *The Anatomy of Freedom: Feminism, Physics, and Global Politics* (Oxford: Martin Robertson, 1983)

Paul Oliver: *Savannah Syncopators: African Retentions in the Blues* (London: Studio Vista, 1970)

Fernand Ouellette: *Edgard Varèse* (London: Calder & Boyars, 1973)

Harry Partch: *Genesis of a Music* (second edition) (New York: Da Capo, 1974)

Sally Placksin: *Jazzwomen, 1900 to the Present: Their Words, Lives and Music* (London: Pluto Press, 1985)

Plato: *The Republic* (Harmondsworth, Middlesex: Penguin Books, 1955)

Roy Preiswerk and Dominique Perrot: *Ethnocentrism and History: Africa, Asia and Indian America in Western Textbooks* (New York: NOK Publishers, 1978)

Jill Purce: *The Mystic Spiral: Journey of the Soul* (London: Thames & Hudson, 1974)

'Sound in Mind and Body', *Resurgence*, issue 115, March/April 1986

Sun Ra: 'Astro Black' and 'Darkness Light', poems on the sleeve of *Astro Black* LP (New York: Impulse Records, 1973)

Robert Reisner: *Bird: the Legend of Charlie Parker* (London: Quartet Books, 1974)

Pauline Rivelli and Robert Levin (eds): *Giants of Black Music* (New York: Da Capo, 1979)

J.A. Rogers: *Sex and Race, Volumes 1–3* (St Petersburg, Florida: Helga M. Rogers, 1967–72)

100 Amazing Facts about the Negro (St Petersburg, Florida: Helga M. Rogers)

Dane Rudhyar: *The Magic of Tone and the Art of Music* (Boulder: Shambhala, 1982)

Ross Russell: *Bird Lives! The High Life and Hard Times of Charlie 'Yardbird' Parker* (London: Quartet Books, 1976)

Victor Schonfield: untitled sleevenotes to Sun Ra's *Pictures of Infinity* LP (New York: Black Lion Records, 1968)

Cyril Scott: *Music – Its Secret Influence throughout the Ages* (revised edition) (Wellingborough, Northants: The Aquarian Press, 1976)

Ivan Van Sertima (ed): *Blacks in Science: Ancient and Modern* (New Brunswick: Transaction Books, 1985)

John Shepherd, Phil Virden, Graham Vulliamy, Trevor Wishart: *Whose Music? a Sociology of Musical Languages* (New Brunswick: Transaction Books, 1977)

C.O. Simpkins: *Coltrane: a Biography* (Philadelphia: Herndon House, 1975)

Bill Smith: 'The Anthony Braxton Interview', *Coda* (vol. 11, no. 8), April 1974

'Unit Structures: Cecil Taylor in Conversation', *Coda* (vol. 12, no. 4), March 1975

'Roscoe Mitchell Interview', *Coda*, issue 141, September 1975

'Leo Smith Interview', *Coda*, issue 143, November 1975

'George Lewis: a Conversation', *Coda*, issue 155, May/June 1977

'Leo Smith: Rastafari', *Coda*, issue 192, October 1983

Leo Smith: *notes (8 pieces)/source a new/world/music: creative music* (Leo Smith, 1973)

'Notes on the Creative Artistry of Anthony Braxton', sleevenotes to *The Complete Braxton 1971* LP (New York: Arista Records, 1977)

NB: These notes do not appear on the original Freedom issue of this record

NB: See also Bill Smith, Thompson.

O.G. Sonneck (ed): *Beethoven: Impressions by His Contemporaries* (New York: Dover, 1967)

Eileen Southern: *The Music of Black Americans: a History* (second edition) (London: Norton, 1983)

David Spanier: *Total Chess* (London: Abacus, 1986)

A.B. Spellman: *Four Lives in the Bebop Business* (New York: Limelight, 1985)

George Steiner: *After Babel: Aspects of Language and Translation* (London: Oxford University Press, 1976)

Arthur Taylor: *Notes and Tones: Musician-to-Musician Interviews* (London: Quartet Books, 1983)

Cecil Taylor: 'Sound Structure of Subculture Becoming Major Breath/Naked Fire Gesture', sleevenotes to *Unit Structures* LP (New York: Blue Note Records, 1966)

'Aqoueh R-Oyo', poem on sleeve of *Air Above Mountains (buildings within)* LP (Munich: Enja Records, 1976)

NB: See also Buholzer, Lock and Bill Smith.

Robert Terlizzi: 'The Steve Lacy Interview', *Coda*, issue 153, January/February 1977

Alexander Wheelock Thayer: *The Life of Ludwig van Beethoven* (London: Centaur Press, 1960)

Robert Farris Thompson: 'Mambo Minkisi: the Mind and Music of Leo Smith', review of *notes (8 pieces)* etc, *Coda*, issue 143, November 1975

Michael Ullman: *Jazz Lives* (New York: Perigree Books, 1982)

Hans Wachtmeister: *A Discography and Bibliography of Anthony Braxton* (Stocksund, Sweden: Blue Anchor, 1982)

Alice Walker: *In Search of Our Mothers' Gardens: Womanist Prose* (London: The Women's Press, 1984)

Marina Warner: *Monuments and Maidens: the Allegory of the Female Form* (London: Picador, 1987)

Valerie Wilmer: *As Serious as Your Life: the Story of the New Jazz* (London: Quartet Books, 1977)

Frances A. Yates: *Giordano Bruno and the Hermetic Tradition* (London: Routledge & Kegan Paul, 1978)

The Rosicrucian Enlightenment (London: Ark, 1986)

Copies of the 'Catalogue of Works' (in colour or black-and-white), individual scores, *Tri-axium Writings, 1–3* and, it is to be hoped, *Composition Notes, A–E* can be ordered from Anthony Braxton, c/o Music Department, Mills College, 5000 MacArthur Boulevard, Oakland, CA 94613, USA.

Copies of the untitled manuscript containing 'Some Notes on My Compositions' can be ordered from Marilyn Crispell, P.O. Box 499, Woodstock, NY 12498, USA; copies of her LPs on the Leo label can be ordered from Leo Records, 35 Cascade Avenue, London N10 3PT.

Copies of the *Bass Excursions* cassette can be ordered from Mark Dresser, 23–54 24th Street, L.I.C., NY 11106, USA.

Copies of LPs on the Auricle label can be ordered from Gerry Hemingway, 5–16 47th Road#3L, L.I.C., NY 11101, USA.

Copies of Sun Ra's writings and his LPs on the Saturn label can be ordered from Ra-Legion, P.O. Box 8167, Philadelphia, Pennsylvania 19101, USA; Saturn records are distributed in the UK by Recommended Records, 387 Wandsworth Road, London SW8 2JL.

Copies of Leo Smith's *notes (8 pieces)/source a new/world/music: creative music* and his LPs on the Kabell label can be ordered from Kabell Records, 161 Hightop Circle, Hamden, CT 06514, USA.

INDEX

In cross-references, the members of the quartet are referred to by their initials: AB, MC, MD, GH.

402

Other titles of interest

**BIRD: The Legend
of Charlie Parker**
Edited by Robert Reisner
256 pp., 50 photos
80069-1 $13.95

**CHASIN' THE TRANE
The Music and Mystique
of John Coltrane**
J. C. Thomas
256 pp., 16 pp. of photos
80043-8 $12.95

**ERIC DOLPHY
A Musical Biography and
Discography
Revised Edition**
Vladimir Simosko and
Barry Tepperman
156 pp., 17 photos
80524-3 $11.95

**MINGUS
A Critical Biography**
Brian Priestley
320 pp., 25 photos
80217-1 $13.95

**A CENTURY OF JAZZ
From Blues to Bop, Swing to
Hip-Hop: A Hundred Years
of Music, Musicians,
Singers and Styles**
Roy Carr
256 pp., $9^5/8 \times 11^1/2$
350 illus., 200 in color
80778-5 $28.95

**ASCENSION
John Coltrane and His Quest**
Eric Nisenson
298 pp.
80644-4 $13.95

**BIRD LIVES!
The High Life and Hard Times
of Charlie (Yardbird) Parker**
Ross Russell
431 pp., 32 photos
80679-7 $15.95

**DEXTER GORDON
A Musical Biography**
Stan Britt
192 pp., 32 photos
80361-5 $13.95

FREE JAZZ
Ekkehard Jost
214 pp., 70 musical examples
80556-1 $13.95

**THE FREEDOM PRINCIPLE
Jazz After 1958**
John Litweiler
324 pp., 11 photos
80377-1 $13.95

**IMPROVISATION
Its Nature and Practice in Music**
Derek Bailey
172 pp., 12 photos
80528-6 $13.95

JOHN COLTRANE
Bill Cole
278 pp., 25 photos
80530-8 $14.95